Law and Ethics in Children's Nursing

For Josie, Eve, Martin and Dan, with love (and the NHS which promised and has delivered so much).

Law and Ethics in Children's Nursing

Judith Hendrick, BA, LLM
Solicitor and Senior Lecturer in Law
Oxford Brookes University
UK

⟨W⟩WILEY-BLACKWELL

A John Wiley & Sons, Ltd., Publication

Blackwell Publishing was acquired by John Wiley & Sons in February 2007. Blackwell's publishing programme has been merged with Wiley's global Scientific, Technical, and Medical business to form Wiley-Blackwell.

Registered office
John Wiley & Sons Ltd, The Atrium, Southern Gate, Chichester, West Sussex, PO19 8SQ, United Kingdom

Editorial offices
9600 Garsington Road, Oxford, OX4 2DQ, United Kingdom
2121 State Avenue, Ames, Iowa 50014-8300, USA

For details of our global editorial offices, for customer services and for information about how to apply for permission to reuse the copyright material in this book please see our website at www.wiley.com/wiley-blackwell.

Library of Congress Cataloging-in-Publication Data

Hendrick, Judith.
    Law and ethics in children's nursing / Judith Hendrick.
       p. cm.
    Includes bibliographical references and index.
    ISBN 978-1-4051-6106-0 (pbk. : alk. paper)
    1. Pediatric nursing–Law and legislation–England.   2. Pediatric nursing–Ethics–Great Britain.
I. Title.
    [DNLM: 1. Pediatric Nursing–legislation and jurisprudence–Great Britain.   2. Pediatric
Nursing–ethics–Great Britain. WY 33 FA1 H498L 2010]
    KD2968.N8H46 2010
    174.2′9892–dc22

                                                                              2009040324

A catalogue record for this book is available from the British Library.

Set in 10/11.5 pt Sabon by Aptara® Inc., New Delhi, India
Printed and bound in Malaysia by Vivar Printing Sdn Bhd

1   2010

Contents

CHAPTER 1
An Introduction to Law and Ethics

Learning outcomes

By the end of this chapter you should be able to:

- Recognise the key ethical and legal concepts and principles that underpin health care policy and practice;
- Describe the role of law in developing health care policy and practice;
- Understand how ethical problems occur and the basis on which ethical decisions can be made;
- Critically evaluate the relationship between law and ethics, in particular their interaction in resolving problems that arise in practice.

Introduction

If nurses are to understand the key role played by the law in regulating the relationship between health professionals and children, they need to know how it sets and maintains standards of care and how it ensures that children have access to adequate medical assistance and health care. They need to know, in short, what this introductory chapter sets out to do, i.e. describe the nature of law and explain where it comes from and how it develops. That nurses should study ethics has also been so widely accepted that its inclusion in nurse education is now commonplace. This chapter therefore also attempts to introduce nurses to what we mean when we talk about 'ethics' in health care. However, after a brief analysis of key terms, it focuses on the skills that are required to 'think ethically', i.e. to recognise moral problems and dilemmas in everyday practice and make decisions that can be morally justified.

1.1 What is Law?

Almost every introductory text about the law begins with the obvious question: what is law? Typically, however, no answer is immediately given or even attempted. Instead, the reader is swiftly reminded of the pervasiveness of the law and its ever-increasing control of our professional and social lives. Soon too, there will be an acknowledgement that there are probably as many definitions of law as there are theorists seeking to identify its essential nature – the conclusion being that it is therefore impossible to agree on what it 'is'. That this should be so is then justified by explaining that there are many different ways of thinking about the law. For example, some legal theorists focus on legal structures and processes and therefore claim that law is what legislators, judges and lawyers 'do'. Others, by contrast, prefer to study how law operates 'in context', i.e. how law is inextricably linked to other social phenomenon such as economic, moral and political interests (and the extent to which these contexts shape and are informed by the law). Another common approach is to analyse the law in terms of the functions it performs (e.g. to maintain public order and facilitate cooperative action). Evaluating the law in an attempt to establish criteria for what constitutes 'good' or 'bad' law is another approach in which the relationship between law and morality is the central issue. With so many different perspectives – all asking equally valid questions about the nature of law – it is not surprising that debates about the subject remain as fervent as they were when the ancient Greeks first sought answers to man's place in the social order and the nature of human society some 2500 years ago (see further McLeod, 2009).

1.1.1 Law as a system of rules

The approach taken here to the question, 'What is law?' is a much less ambitious one. It examines basically the extent to which law is a system of **rules**. This approach is a useful starting point not only because it is the most practical way of unravelling the complex range of rules that shape and define professional practice but also because most people have a basic idea of what a rule is, i.e. a statement of accepted standards of behaviour, guiding conduct or action in particular circumstances or situations. Most people, too, can instinctively recognise what many legal rules (or rules of law) seek to achieve; for example, that the criminal law prohibits certain types of behaviour, family law regulates various aspects of marriage and cohabitation, and health care law (or medical law) governs professional practice. That law is in some way different from the web of moral and social 'rules' by which people run their lives is also widely recognised. The difference between legal rules and the wide variety of other formal and informal professional and institutional rules, guidance and policies and practices which regulate nursing practice may, however, be less well understood (see below).

1.1.2 The nature of legal rules

At this stage the distinctive feature of all legal rules that should be grasped is that they must be:

1. Reasonably definite, consistent and understandable,
2. Known in advance, and
3. Recognised and enforced by the courts.

Rules become law when they are recognised by the majority of people in society and are given official backing to enforce them; i.e. they are recognised and applied by the state. A more complex analysis of law which has focused on the role of rules in providing the foundation of a legal system is provided by H.L.A. Hart (1907–1992). In his hugely influential book, *The Concept of Law*, Hart (1994) distinguished between two different types of legal rules (which he categorised as either **primary** or **secondary** rules). Each of these sets of rules interacts with each other in a hierarchical way and when combined, constitute what we commonly understand by the term 'a legal system'. According to Hart, the content of these two sets of rules is determined by five basic features (or *truisms*) of human society.

These are that human beings are:

1. Vulnerable,
2. Approximately equal in power,
3. Capable only of limited altruism (i.e. are generally selfish),
4. Have limited understanding and strength of will, and
5. Live in societies with limited resources.

Given these five generalisations about the human condition, Hart argues that primary legal rules are essential for every society's survival and protect people and their property and ensure that promises are kept. As such, these rules will prohibit violence, theft and deception and will also include how people relate to each other, for example, making contracts and wills. Primary rules can be described as **duty-imposing** because they specify what people can (or cannot do). They therefore create obligations with which members of the society must comply.

In complex and developed societies, primary rules alone need to be supplemented by secondary legal rules to resolve three problems:

1. Uncertainty, e.g. it may not be clear whether a certain rule is a rule of law or some other type of rule.
2. Laws may need adapting or new ones may need to be created as society develops and changes.
3. Inefficiency, i.e. without a mechanism to resolve disputes, primary rules would be ineffective.

To remedy these defects, the secondary rules (which are mostly **power conferring**) must consist of the following: (a) *rules of adjudication*, conferring authority on officials (such as judges) to resolve disputes; (b) *rules of change*, these change legal obligations (whether in the public or private sphere), i.e. they enable people to alter their legal relationships and also facilitate legislative or judicial changes which may be necessary to modernise outdated law; and (c) *rules of recognition*, which establish criteria for validating legal rules, i.e. deciding which ones have legal force. Note that rules of recognition are the most important secondary rules since they provide the definitive test of whether a particular rule qualifies as a rule of a legal system (Adams and Brownsword, 1996, p. 5).

Hart insists that it is the union of primary (which apply to all members of society) and secondary rules (which confer authority on officials) that is at the heart of a legal system. Both must coexist before any society can be said to have a legal system.

As was noted earlier, Hart's approach to law is only one of several possible alternatives. Mindful, too, that this brief and simplified account does little justice to wider aspects of his analysis (on which see Doherty, 2005, Chapter 10), nor to the many other ways legal theorists have distinguished various types of legal rules, it has nevertheless been credited with 'charting the precincts of modern legal theory' (Wacks, 2006, p. 26).

Key point

Rules become law when they are recognised and applied by the state.

1.2 How the Law is Made – the Sources of Law

In this section, we look at how legal rules are made, i.e. the principal sources from which English law is derived.

1.2.1 Legislation

There are two types of legislation – primary and secondary (note that the terms primary and secondary are concerned with the law-making process and should not be confused with Hart's two categories of legal rules).

Primary legislation

Primary legislation (also called statute law) is the most important source of law for several reasons. Firstly, it is enacted by Parliament, the principal law-making body in the UK. Parliament passes about 50 statutes (also called Acts) a year. Secondly, Parliament has the right to pass any law it wishes, although it is subject to European law (see below). Thirdly, Parliament has the authority to delegate law-making powers to other bodies, such as government departments. All statutes have to pass through various stages (as bills) during which they are debated in both houses of Parliament before they reach the statute book.

Whatever its origins, a bill only becomes law when it receives the Royal Assent. Even then the Act may not be immediately implemented, i.e. be brought into force straightaway. Another complicating factor is that not all sections of an Act may come into force at the same time (and some may never be implemented). Much of the structure, organisation and administrative framework of the health service is governed by legislation, some of the most important being the National Health Service (NHS) Act 2006, the Health Act 2006, and the Health and Social Care Act 2008 (note that all statutes passed since 1988 are on the internet and can therefore be easily accessed at http://www.direct.gov.uk).

Activity

Read the Explanatory Note of the Health Act 2006. Does it explain the background to the Act and its main aims clearly?

Secondary legislation

Secondary legislation (also called delegated or subordinate legislation) is the other major source of law. Parliament has the power to delegate to other bodies or persons such as government departments and local authorities. It typically exercises this power when much more detailed rules are needed to flesh out a particular Act. Delegated legislation consists of **Statutory Instruments** or **Orders in Council** in the form of rules, regulations and by-laws. Approximately 3000 such items are produced each year. Secondary legislation is clearly, therefore, a very important source of law. Yet, despite having the same legal force as primary legislation, it is not subject to the same rigorous parliamentary scrutiny (although it can be challenged in the courts). Secondary legislation plays an important role in regulating health care provision (e.g. the Abortion Regulations 1991 and the Medicines for Human Use (Clinical Trial) Regulations 2004.

1.2.2 Statutory interpretation

Once a statute has come into force, the courts may be involved in applying and interpreting it. Thus, although legal language is supposed to be precise, clear and unambiguous, all too often words, phrases or even whole paragraphs may be vague and confusing. Also, many modern statutes deal with very complex subjects. They can therefore be very long and complicated, and errors are almost inevitable – the NHS Act 2006, for example, has 278 sections and 22 schedules. Cases may therefore come to court in which judges have to decide whether a statute applies to the particular facts in question.

So how do judges interpret the words of a statute or find the 'intention' of Parliament as the process of statutory interpretation is often called? Over the years, the courts have developed a variety of techniques, presumptions and aids to interpretation – the so-called rules of interpretation. These rules are not, however, applied by judges in a rigid scientific way. Instead, they give judges a wide discretion to select the approach they think is the most appropriate. This raises a further important question, namely, how 'creative' should judges be in cases where there appears to be no 'right' answer. Given that there may be several different ways of interpreting a particular word or paragraph, all of which could be correct, this is not an uncommon scenario. And if, as it is generally now conceded, judges do have a far more creative role in 'difficult' cases than was previously acknowledged, what limits should be imposed on them to ensure that they do not frustrate the intention of Parliament? Clearly, there are no simple answers to these questions. But what is self-evident is that the process of statutory interpretation owes much to the outlook and influence of those who have the authority to apply the law (see further Elliott and Quinn, 2009, Part 1).

Activity

Read Hendrick (2004, p. 16), *Law and Ethics: Foundations in Nursing and Health Care*. Follow the guidance on how to read a statute.

Key points

- There are two types of legislation: (1) statute law and (2) secondary legislation.
- Statutory interpretation refers to the judicial process of interpreting confusing or ambiguous legislation.

1.2.3 Common law

Common law consists of a system of legal rules that has evolved through court cases over the past 800 years. It is also known as case law or judge-made law. Much of the law regulating the relationship between health care practitioners and patients has developed through case law (in particular, consent and negligence law). When a case comes before a judge, there are two tasks for the court. Firstly, it must decide what facts are relevant, i.e. it must establish what actually happened, and secondly, how existing law applies to the facts. Case law develops from this second task. So how do judges carry out it?

System of precedent

The basic rule is that judges are legally obliged to follow any previous decision that has been made in a higher court. Known as **judicial precedent**, this process essentially requires courts to interpret similar cases – i.e. cases raising similar legal principles and involving similar facts and circumstances – in a similar manner. The system of binding precedent is based on the hierarchy of the courts – i.e. in general, the lower courts are bound to follow the higher courts even though appeals are sometimes possible.

Precedent in practice

Although simple to describe, precedent is much harder to apply in practice. Firstly, it depends on clear and accurate written records being kept of the arguments used in important cases and the legal principles on which the decision is made. This has developed into a system of law reporting of which the two most widely used are the All England Law Reports (All ER) and the Weekly Law Reports (WLR). In addition to paper reporting, there are several legal electronic databases (and the internet can similarly be used to access up-to-date information). Secondly, despite the system of law reporting, it is not always easy to decide what the precedent is – perhaps because two decisions in the law reports are inconsistent. Problems can occur, too, if the legal principles are expressed too narrowly or too widely for them to be useful in later cases (see further McLeod, 2009, Chapter 7).

In the same way that statutory interpretation raises questions about the creative role of judges, so has the system of precedent provoked much debate about the precise role of the judiciary in developing common law. Are they just neutral decision-makers who simply 'discover' the law and then declare it – i.e. they find previous binding decisions and then apply them to the facts of the particular case in question – or do they actually make new law and so have a powerful law-making function? Few now take seriously the claim that judges do no more than find and apply existing legal principles. Indeed, the system itself gives judges wide choices – not just because they can make creative selections from the mass of relevant precedents but also, when faced with an 'inconvenient' precedent, they can resort to various techniques to avoid following it (e.g. by 'distinguishing' cases, see further McLeod, 2009, Part 2, especially Chapter 14).

That judges make new law is also apparent when a novel set of circumstances comes before the court. This happened in the landmark case of *Airedale NHS Trust v Bland* [1993] AC 789, in which the courts had to decide whether the withdrawal of artificial hydration and nutrition from a 21-year-old patient in a persistent vegetative state was lawful. There was neither a precedent to which the courts could refer nor any relevant legislation. So the Law Lords, albeit reluctant to make such a momentous 'wholly new moral and social decision', nevertheless had to decide on the legality of stopping medical treatment (see further Chapter 12).

Activity

Read Hendrick (2004, p. 18). Follow the guidance on how to read a law report.

Key points

- Precedent is the system whereby decisions by judges create laws for later judges to follow.
- Precedent is based on the idea that it is fair and just that 'like cases are treated the same way'.

1.2.4 European law

European Union law

As a member of the European Union (EU), the UK is subject to European law (EU law). Because EU law takes precedence over national law, it can override both UK legislation and the common law. Although the fundamental purpose of the EU is to create a free market for the provision of good and services, EU law has had a significant impact on various aspects of health care law. These include the marketing and manufacture of pharmaceuticals (in particular the quality, safety and efficacy of 'novel' health care products) and the regulation of medical research. EU Directives also now regulate the collection, testing, processing and storage of blood and blood components. Note that it was also as a result of EU law that UK nationals can receive health care services outside national boundaries in certain circumstances (*Watts v Bedford PCT* [2003]). The impact of EU law on public health has similarly been significant, covering, for example, food safety and health promotion (for a detailed discussion of EU legislation, see Hervey and McHale, 2004).

Human rights law

A different source of law – that also originated in Europe – is the European Convention on Human Rights (ECHR). Now that the Convention has been incorporated into English law by the Human Rights Act 1998, it is no longer necessary for individuals to go directly to the Court of Human Rights in Strasbourg (the special court set up to hear breaches of the ECHR), although they still can. The impact of the Human Rights Act 1998 is that, since October 2000, individuals taking a case to the court in England can allege a breach of their human rights, and in reaching their decision, judges must interpret English law in a way which is compatible with the ECHR.

Public bodies, including the health service, must also comply with the Convention. This has led to the courts being much less likely than in the past to routinely, for example, sanction sterilisations on girls and women. Consent law has been the subject of several important human right-based claims (likewise mental health law, access to health services and confidentiality).

1.2.5 Non-legal sources of law

In this section, the impact of what is commonly known as 'soft law' (or quasi-law) will be briefly discussed. This category includes types of rules which, although not law in the strict sense, i.e. they are not usually legally binding, nonetheless play a very important role in regulating professional practice – by, for example, setting the standards by which practitioners will be judged in any legal action. As such, they clearly do have some legal force. The primary source of this type of 'law' derives from communications from the Department of Health (DoH). These typically take the form of health service circulars. Described by the DoH as quasi-legislative, these explain aspects of health care and regulation more fully. They can cover a variety of matters and can be linked to a particular statute or case. The *Gillick* case, for example (*Gillick v West Norfolk and Wisbech AHA* [1986] AC 112), which famously established the legal principle that 'mature minors' could give consent to medical treatment and advice without their parents' knowledge or permission, was swiftly followed by guidance from the DoH, explaining the implications of the case and identifying good practice in providing contraceptive treatment and advice to young people under 16.

National Service Frameworks also have a significant impact on practice. Targeted on key patient groups, the one for children was published in 2004 (see Chapter 6). Other influential guidance may originate from the National Institute of Clinical Excellence (NICE). NICE's primary function is to advise on the most useful and cost-effective treatments. Although the precise legal effect of NICE guidance is uncertain, it is clear that health professionals would need to justify their failure to follow it if 'anything went wrong' (Mason and Laurie, 2006, p. 424).

Another major type of 'soft law' worth noting here is the code of practice. Codes supplement legislation (e.g. the Mental Capacity Act 2005 and the Human Tissue Act 2004) by providing detailed practical guidance on how to make decisions under the Act in question. They are not a definitive guide to the law and most of them do not have the force of law. Nevertheless, they are so influential as to be almost directive, i.e. practitioners are expected to follow them. Hence, failure to do so will not in itself be unlawful but any breach may be used in evidence in any subsequent legal proceedings. Finally, the role of the Nursing and Midwifery Council (NMC) needs to be briefly explained. As a statutory body, one of its key functions is to set standards and guidelines for nursing, midwifery and health visiting. It also publishes a code of professional conduct. Both the code and other guidelines issued by the NMC will be taken into account in disciplinary and complaint proceedings.

> **Activity**
>
> Access the NMC website (http://www.nmc.uk.org). Critically evaluate its key functions, in particular how it regulates the profession.

1.3 Divisions within the Law

Law can be classified in several ways. Some common divisions are the following.

1.3.1 Civil law

Civil law deals with private disputes between individuals and other bodies – such as health authorities and NHS Trusts – claiming or enforcing a legal right. The main aims of civil law are to establish what rights and duties people have towards each other and to provide a system of remedies to resolve disputes. Civil law includes many different areas. Those that are most likely to involve practitioners working with children and young people are as follows.

Tort law

A tort arises from a breach of a general duty imposed by law; i.e. it does not depend on any prior agreement between the parties involved. The main aim of tort law is to compensate the victim (i.e. someone who has been harmed by another's unlawful act). Tort law covers several different areas, but in health care settings negligence and consent-related claims are the most common.

Family law

Family law regulates relationships within the family and so includes disputes about the care and upbringing of children. Child-centred disputes which are most likely to involve nurses will typically relate to controversial medical treatment, disputes about treatment and child abuse and neglect.

Contract law

Contract law is about agreements and promises that are legally enforceable. Employment disputes are contract based, as are those that involve private patients. Contract law can also be used by a victim of a drug-induced injury.

Administrative law

Administrative law governs how public bodies such as local authorities, the courts and other public institutions operate. It therefore includes the law relating to the provision of health services and how health authorities and NHS Trusts exercise their powers and duties. Patients are most likely to use administrative law to, for example, try and force a health service body to provide a drug they have been denied.

1.3.2 Criminal law

The least likely branch of the law to concern nurses in their everyday dealings with patients is criminal law. Put very simply, the basic aim of criminal law is to protect society by prohibiting and controlling behaviour the state considers harmful and disruptive as well as punishing offenders. So, for example, a nurse whose gross negligence led to a patient's death could be criminally liable.

1.3.3 Public law

This comprises criminal law and constitutional and administrative rules governing how public bodies – e.g. local authorities, the courts, civil service and other public institutions – operate. It thus includes law enabling citizens to question how public agencies such as health authorities and NHS Trusts exercise their powers and statutory duties.

1.3.4 Private law

Private law deals with the legal relationship between private individuals and organisations. It has several functions. These include regulating the provision of health care and providing a system of compensation for the victims of malpractice. It also creates rights and duties and other liabilities arising from 'private' arrangements such as property and commercial transactions.

1.4 What is Ethics?

The question, 'What is ethics?' may seem unimportant not least because most health care professionals will be aware – at least on a very general level – that ethics is about what is 'right' and 'wrong', 'good' and 'bad' in human actions. They are likely to be aware too that their professional code of practice sets outs 'ethical' standards which they are expected to follow and that many of their judgements and actions have a 'moral' dimension. Most will also know that the duty to promote the interests and dignity of patients is an ethical obligation arising from the unequal professional–patient relationship – in which patients will almost always have a more vulnerable and dependent role.

But an instinctive awareness of the ethical nature of health care and the moral content of decision-making may be of little use when a 'new' situation arises. It may be new to the individual practitioner or new because no health professional has had to face the kind of issue before. Either way, the intuitive techniques that have been relied on in the past may fail to provide an adequate moral framework for working out how to make the 'right' decision.

It is at this point that the importance of the question, **what is ethics**, becomes more apparent. This is not because it can necessarily be fully answered, but rather that in asking the very question we begin to realise that 'thinking ethically', i.e. understanding and examining how best to live a 'moral life' (Beauchamp and Childress, 2009), may require more than intuition. Instead, we may need an 'ethical toolkit' that can be systematically used to help practitioners identify the most ethically important problems and dilemmas and provide a step-by-step process to resolve them.

The ethical toolkit outlined below (which is based on various decision-making models commonly found in the nursing literature) is not designed to provide a comprehensive and detailed account of every ethical concept or approach to problem solving. Nor will it provide a magic formula for analysing and resolving all ethical questions that will always guarantee that the 'right' solution is reached. Its purpose is rather less ambitious, namely, to provide practical step-by-step guidance to thinking ethically and making moral judgements about what to do in real-life situations and how to justify those actions and decisions within some kind of philosophical framework.

First, however, the convention (adopted in this book) of using the terms 'ethics' and 'morals' (and 'morality') more or less interchangeably must be explained. Although the two terms derive from different roots – ethics coming from ancient Greek and morals from its Latin equivalent – it is common in philosophic literature to assert that there is no real difference between them, in the sense that an 'ethical' action is one that is morally acceptable. Nevertheless, distinctions can be drawn between them. Thus when we use the word 'moral', we are usually describing the standards by which an individual runs his or her own life. Similarly, to describe something as 'immoral' implies that it contravenes the morality of a particular society (in a general sense). In contrast, 'ethics' tends to refer to the science or study of morals, which is a much more theoretical and academic approach.

1.5 Ethical Toolkit

1.5.1 Step 1: Distinguish between facts and values

The first step in deciding what is ethically the right thing to do it is to distinguish between factual information about a patient and value statements. Facts about a patient come from several sources, such as the health care record, diagnostic tests, nursing assessment and the patient's history (provided by the patient and/or his family or carers). But that information alone will not lead to an ethical decision unless the nurse considers the 'facts' within a framework or context of values – from a personal, communal, professional and patient's perspective (Fry and Johnstone, 2008).

So what are values? Values are ideals, beliefs, customs and characteristics that an individual or social group considers valuable and worthwhile. Moral values are those which generally reflect a belief about the value of, for example, human life, self-determination, truth-telling and well-being. Values influence behaviour and help us make choices and decisions because they provide a frame of reference to help us understand new experiences. A person's value system is influenced by many factors including cultural, ethnic, educational, religious and environmental experiences. Some values will remain consistent throughout a person's life, while others may change. The relative importance of particular values may also change over time, and although people will have values in common, there will also be differences.

Facts and values are inextricably linked and can exert considerable influence on each other and our conceptions of them. As a consequence, the more an issue – particularly one with ethical implications – is worked out, the more what counts as a factual consideration is likely to change. In other words, some 'facts' may be initially ignored only to emerge later as the most significant while others that are considered important at the outset are soon forgotten.

Key point

Moral values are concerned with ethical issues and dilemmas such as human life and self-determination.

Activity

Think of an ideal or value that you cherish. Work out when you become aware of its importance.

1.5.2 Step 2: Recognise the moral issues

The second step in moral decision-making is to recognise the moral dimension in a particular situation. Some health care situations will be instantly recognisable as morally significant, e.g. abortion, euthanasia and organ donation. But the moral considerations in deciding, for example, how much information to give a 15-year-old (so that his or her consent can be 'informed') or whether to tell a young person the truth about his or her prognosis may be much less obvious. And some routine aspects of everyday practice such as moving patients or deciding which of several patients in pain to treat first may even appear (wrongly) to be morally neutral. What is ethically important in all these situations, however – and so what gives them their moral dimension – is that they are concerned with the promotion and protection of patients' well-being and welfare. Or to put it another way, the question of 'harm' or 'benefit' to patients is a central issue, likewise the 'duties', 'responsibilities' and 'obligations' health professionals owe to them. Other terms and concepts typically used to denote a situation with a moral element are 'rights' best interests, guilt and shame. Often, too, there will be reference to the rightness or wrongness of a decision or to whether an action is good or bad (or whether something should or should not have been done).

1.5.3 Step 3: Classify the moral problem

Once it has been established that the situation has a moral dimension, it is then necessary to decide whether a **problem** exists and, if so, which type it is. A moral problem can be defined as anything – matter, person, issue, etc. – that is difficult to deal with or hard to understand and requires a moral solution. According to Johnstone (2004), there are at least ten different types of moral problems. Outlined here are some of the most common.

Moral unpreparedness

The problem of moral unpreparedness arises when a nurse lacks the moral knowledge to recognise the moral dimension in a problem situation. She therefore fails to deal with it either appropriately or effectively. Nurses working in a paediatric intensive care unit should, for example, be aware of the moral issues (e.g. the sanctity of life doctrine) surrounding the care and treatment of premature or terminally ill newborn infants so that they can support parents facing very difficult choices, such as whether to withdraw life-sustaining treatment.

Moral indifference

A morally indifferent nurse is one who is not interested in working out what is the right thing to do even though she is well aware that there is a moral problem which should be resolved. Put crudely, she has a 'don't care' attitude. An example would include a nurse who fails to make sure that the wishes of a 15-year-old patient – who does not want surgery – are made known to the relevant person. A nurse who could not be bothered to relieve a patient's pain is another example.

Immoralism

An immoral nurse is one who knowingly and wilfully does something (or fails to do something) that violates a widely accepted ethical standard of professional or general behaviour. Knowing a patient does not want to be included in a research study, for example, but including them anyway would be an example of a deliberate disregard for both national and international codes of practice on ethical research. Note that such conduct would be unethical even if the patient did not suffer any harm.

Moral disagreements

One of the most difficult moral problems to resolve in practice is the moral disagreement. Such disagreements may arise because of different views as to the moral relevance of certain 'facts' or the interpretation and application of various moral standards or concepts. In the abortion debate, for example, although two people may agree that killing an innocent human being is wrong, they may fundamentally disagree about the morality of abortion because of their different views about the moral status of the fetus. Thus, for the person who does not regard the fetus as a human being, abortion will not be morally wrong. On the other hand, the person who claims that the fetus is a human being will consider abortion morally wrong because it involves killing an innocent human being. Moral disagreements can also arise because health professionals may interpret or evaluate moral concepts differently. They may both accept, for example, that the autonomy of mature young people should be respected but disagree about when it should be qualified – particularly perhaps when a young patient is refusing life-saving surgery. Truth-telling and confidentiality may also both be regarded as important moral duties, but again health professionals may disagree about the circumstances when these should be breached.

Moral dilemmas

Basically, a moral dilemma occurs when two or more mutually exclusive moral claims (e.g. a moral principle or duty) clearly apply and both seem to have equal weight, i.e. a difficult problem that seems to have no satisfactory solution because whichever claim is prioritised or chosen results in the other, equally valid moral claim, being violated. A nurse for whom the sanctity of life is a sacred doctrine, for example, will have a difficult moral choice to make when caring for a terminally ill patient in great pain. To alleviate the patient's suffering, she may be required to administer large (and potentially lethal) doses of pain-relieving drugs. The dilemma here is that the sanctity of life principle conflicts with her duty to do 'good' and minimise harm to patients. One of the options the nurse can choose – to resolve the dilemma – is to select one principle over the other. Or she could choose another principle altogether, such as respect for autonomy.

Activity

Read the chapter on 'Making Decisions that are Ethical' in Hawley (2007), *Ethics in Clinical Practice*. Critically consider how she describes an ethical problem.

1.5.4 Step 4: Refer to an overarching ethical theory

Step 4 involves considering two 'parent' competing theoretical perspectives that have dominated Western moral philosophy, namely, consequentialism and deontology. Although these moral theories may provide little practical guidance to resolving concrete ethical problems, they provide an overarching justification for pursuing one course over another.

Consequentialism

According to consequentialist theories, the rightness or wrongness of actions depends on their consequences. Put simply, this means that when a nurse is faced with two (or more) possible courses of action, she should choose the one that has the best overall consequences. The right (or moral) thing to do is that which produces the best possible outcome. In health care contexts, this would include the prevention, elimination or control of disease, relief from pain and suffering, the prolongation of life, and so on. More specifically, the best outcome will depend on the goal chosen by the particular consequentialist theory in question.

The principal example of consequentialist ethics is **utilitarianism** (Grayling, 2009, p. 89). This famous theory comes in many forms, but in essence a utilitarian does not regard actions as inherently good or bad. Rather they are valuable only in so far as they maximise benefits and minimise harms. The theory of utilitarianism is most closely associated with John Stuart Mill (1806–1873) whose famous slogan, 'the greatest good for the greatest number', sums up the central concern of the theory, namely, the welfare of society as a whole, rather than individuals. As a utilitarian therefore, a nurse would make a decision about, for example, truth-telling, by asking this question: what would be the consequences of telling the truth? The morally right approach would be then to act in the way that leads to the desired consequences, i.e. the net balance of pleasure, happiness (i.e. what is good) over pain, unhappiness, suffering, etc. (i.e. harms). Although very popular – not least because it reduces all moral judgements, however complex, to a seemingly straightforward calculation – there are significant weaknesses in Mill's utilitarianism. These include the following:

- Because utilitarians treat human beings as means rather than ends in themselves, the theory can lead to injustice, with individual rights being sacrificed for the sake of the greater quantity of happiness for the collective.
- The theory assumes that concepts such as pleasure, happiness and pain can be accurately measured and estimated (Thompson et al., 2006).
- The theory also assumes (wrongly) that the consequences of actions can always be reliably predicted.

In an attempt to respond to some of these criticisms, different versions of utilitarianism have been developed (for a summary, see Pattinson, 2006). Yet the theory has significant strengths. Firstly, it seems to provide a 'scientific' clear answer to the question about what to do in certain situations. Secondly, it seems to treat individual persons equally because everyone's happiness (and unhappiness) counts. Thirdly, even though concepts such as happiness and pain are not straightforward, they are considered very important features in our lives (Hope et al., 2008).

Key point

Utilitarianism is a moral theory that does not regard actions as inherently good or bad – they are valuable only in so far as they maximise benefits or minimise harms.

Deontology – duty-based theories and rights-based theories

Like utilitarianism, deontology is committed to promoting 'good' outcomes but, unlike its rival, deontology places the individual at the centre. Because rights-based theories and duty-based theories both hold that certain sorts of acts are right or wrong in themselves because of the sort of act they are rather than what effect they have (or may have), they are both commonly referred to as deontological.

Duty-based theories are sometimes described as Kantian because of their association with Immanuel Kant (1724–1804). Kant believed that morality was about complying with a set of compulsory fundamental principles and rules that must be followed whatever the consequences. So, for example, the basic question a nurse should ask in deciding whether to tell the truth would be: what kinds of duty or obligation do I owe? According to Kant, it was wrong to tell a lie no matter how beneficial the consequences. Other Kantian duties include promise keeping, not lying, not betraying, and so forth (the list consists mainly of prohibitions). The key to Kant's version of deontology is the maxim that to act morally you should always treat other human beings as 'ends in themselves' and never merely as 'means'. In other words, it is always wrong to treat people as objects, i.e. mere tools to be used to further your own or others' ends.

Duty-based theories are concerned with the moral quality of a person's acts because they suppose that it is wrong for an individual to fail to meet certain standards of behaviour. At the centre of such theories is the person who must follow the rules (or be punished or corrupted if she does not). **Rights-based** theories also make use of moral rules (and codes of conduct), but they do so in an instrumental way, i.e. to protect the rights of others. As such, these moral rules have no essential moral worth in themselves. At the centre of rights-based theories is the person who has the right to make demands on others (and can thus benefit from others' compliance with those rules). Rights-based theories seek to protect interests or activities that are generally considered of great importance to us, such as the right to be respected and treated as an equal and rational person capable of making his or her own decisions, the right to the truth, the right to privacy and the right not to be injured. There are several types of rights, for example, absolute rights which cannot be infringed and conditional ones which can be qualified in certain circumstances.

Although deontology is regarded as an important response to consequentialism, there are problems with the approach. These include the following:

- It imposes rules that are too absolute and rigid and so cannot take account of differences between cases or accommodate any exceptions to the compulsory rules it prescribes.
- It provides no guidance on how choices should be made when duties or rights conflict (e.g. between telling the truth and lying to protect someone). What should a nurse do, for example, if she is asked by a terminally ill child patient not to tell his parents the truth that he knows he is dying? Keeping that promise may mean that she has to lie to the child's parents.

Finally, it should be noted that the distinction between consequentialism and deontology is not as clear-cut as first seems apparent. Hence, deontologists often accept that where there is no absolute principle to apply, it is appropriate to assess the morality of an action by the consequences it produces. Consequentialists too may borrow from deontology in certain circumstances. For example, they may respect the principle of the sanctity of life – even though killing a patient would produce more good than harm (for that patient). They would do so because the impact on society as whole, over a period, of not respecting the sanctity of life, would be a detriment to that society (Herring, 2008, p. 14).

Key point

Deontology is a moral theory that asserts that, if you wish to act morally, you should never treat others solely as a means but always as an end: it is therefore wrong to treat people as objects.

1.5.5 Step 5: Consider nurse-oriented ethical theories

Two ethical theories that are particularly apposite for decision-making by nurses are **virtue ethics** and **nursing ethics**. Both theories approach ethics from a similar perspective, namely, nurses' experience, i.e. the 'actual business of caring for people' (Campbell et al., 2005). Both theories, too, are often linked together because they adopt a broadly 'feminist' approach to ethical thinking, in other words, the view that women use different strategies (from men) in making ethical decisions. This means they focus on relationships – how they can be nurtured and positively maintained – rather than abstract principles and rules (McHale and Fox, 2007, p. 10).

Virtue ethics
Virtue ethics – first developed by Aristotle in the fourth century – has as its central concern the character and virtuous traits of a person rather than his or her actions. A virtue is a trait of character that is intrinsically valuable or linked to human *flourishing* (Pattinson, 2006). Although the concept of flourishing is problematic – it is, for example, hard to analyse – it is nevertheless generally understood to mean a kind of deep happiness

(Hope et al., 2008). Applied to health care contexts, virtue ethics focuses on the virtues needed to be a 'good' nurse, midwife, physiotherapist, and so on; in other words, the kind of practitioner someone ought to *be* and not just what they ought to *do* in a particular role. According to Beauchamp and Childress (2009, pp. 38–45), the cardinal virtues for health professionals are compassion, trustworthiness, discernment, integrity and conscientiousness. For Johnstone (2004), 'virtuous caring' is integral to moral nursing practice and so would include empathy, genuineness, warmth, kindness, gentleness, nurturance and enablement (amongst others).

It is perhaps not surprising that there has been a resurgence of interest in virtue ethics. As Herring (2008, p. 28) notes, in the heat of the moment, health professionals faced with an appalling ethical dilemma, may not be confident of choosing the 'right' course of action. They are, however, far more likely to be confident that their decision was a compassionate and kind one. Another strength of virtue theory is that it tends to be pluralistic – expressing a number of aspects that are widely considered morally relevant. Note that there is an indeterminate number of specific virtue theories (Hope et al., 2008, p. 28, see further Crisp and Slote, 1997).

Yet, notwithstanding the appeal of virtue ethics, the theories have been criticised on several counts, for example:

- To have any practical application, they need to tell us (but rarely do) how to recognise virtuous persons and virtuous traits.
- They fail to explain adequately their force as a moral action guide (that is compared with, say, other duty-based theories that can rely on moral principles and maxims to justify moral action).
- They impose too high expectations on people to be 'good'; i.e. while many nurses can claim to be, for example, trustworthy and compassionate, few can claim to be 'exemplary' (Pellegrino, 1995, pp. 262–263).

Activity

To find out more about ethical theory and other approaches to ethics, read Appendix 1 in Fry and Johnstone (2008), *Ethics in Nursing Practice*. Identify two advantages and disadvantages to each approach.

Nursing ethics of care

Nursing ethics, which may be taken as a generic term covering the concerns of all those professions allied to medicine, can be simply defined as what nurses do that doctors (and others) do not characteristically do (Hunt, 1998). This means that moral issues should be approached from a nursing perspective, i.e. one that regards caring, rather than cure, as fundamental. It is further claimed that because caring (i.e. the assessment, planning, implementation and evaluation of care) is a different kind of activity from curing (with its emphasis on diagnosis, treatment and prognosis), a distinctive approach to ethical thinking is also required, namely, one that focuses on the relationship between the 'carer' and the 'cared for' (McHale and Fox, 2007).

In brief, nursing theorists – influenced by notions of 'care' first formulated by Gilligan (1982) and Noddings (1984) – assert that given the intimate and ongoing nature of the nursing process, nurses are more likely to identify the ethical issues in everyday, routine practice in contrast to doctors whose medical interventions are more transitory. They are also more likely to see the human, personal, cultural and social aspects of care such as patient's self-esteem and privacy, pain alleviation and comfort (Johnstone, 2004).

But like all other ethical theories, the ethics of care approach has been criticised. A common criticism is that the notion of care is too vague. If it is to form a sound basis for ethical decision-making, a much clearer idea of what 'good' care involves is needed (Allmark, 1995). And some feminists are critical of the approach because they believe it glorifies caring and dependency – both aspects of women's lives, which they claim is harmful to women because it leads to their oppression and subordination (Herring, 2008, p. 28).

1.5.6 Step 6: Use ethical principlism

Principlism is one of the most influential approaches to moral decision-making. It is based on a set of principles, i.e. general standards of conduct that can be applied to any ethical problem. The four principles are **respect for autonomy, justice, beneficence** and **non-maleficence**. The approach was developed by two Americans, Beauchamp and Childress, in the mid-1980s. It was designed to provide a basic analytic framework and a basic moral language, which health professionals could use as an ethical checklist when faced with contentious moral problems. Principlism can be described as a compromise position in so far as it draws on elements from several other theories. These are, in particular, deontology – because it propounds four distinct ethical duties, and consequentialism – because using the four principles should maximise good outcomes (McHale and Fox, 2007, p. 108).

The four principles are briefly outlined here as they will be explored in detail in later chapters.

Respect for autonomy
Autonomy refers to an individual's ability to come to his or her own decisions, i.e. basically how we decide to live our lives. In health care contexts, respect for autonomy means consulting patients and obtaining their informed consent to care and treatment. Respect for autonomy also means protecting those who are incapable of making their own choices because of illness, injury, mental disorder or age.

Justice
In simple terms, justice requires equal treatment of equal cases and the equitable distribution of benefits – in other words, no discrimination on the basis of sex, race, religion, age, and so on. For health professionals, justice is mainly concerned with the fair distribution of scarce health resources (such as money, medicines and beds).

Beneficence
The principle of beneficence stresses the moral importance of 'doing good'. In practice, this means health professionals have an obligation to act for the benefit of their patients, i.e. promote and safeguard their health and welfare. As such, it can require positive action, for example, becoming an advocate for a patient who is vulnerable – because of their age perhaps (see Chapter 4).

Non-maleficence
Non-maleficence is sometimes considered alongside the duty of beneficence but also sometimes distinguished. The principle imposes a duty to do no harm (or to minimise harm). Less onerous generally than beneficence in the sense that it generates fewer obligations to take positive actions, non-maleficence nonetheless requires health professionals to refrain from doing anything that could be detrimental to others, i.e. violating or 'setting back' a person's significant welfare interests. As we see in Chapter 3, beneficence and non-maleficence will normally have to be considered together. In other words, the

benefits and harms of any proposed action will need to be balanced. From this balancing exercise, it will be possible to establish what actions cause the least harm and the most good.

The appeal of principlism lies in its relative simplicity and accessibility – it is much easier to apply to most of the moral problems health professionals face than abstract theories (such as consequentialism). It is also claimed that as the four principles are culturally neutral, they can be respected within all societies, i.e. they can be applied worldwide. Moreover, by applying them in all situations, a degree of consistency can be achieved, i.e. ensuring that all cases will be approached and considered in the same way.

Despite its popularity, the approach has several weaknesses. These include the following:

- Because each principle can be interpreted in many different ways the approach is liable to be applied in an inconsistent way.
- How to decide correctly what relative weight to give each principle and how they should be balanced when they clash. Should autonomy, as Gillon (1994), a leading supporter in the UK of principlism, has suggested, be the 'first among equals'?
- Relying on the four principles leads to a very narrow approach, i.e. making sure that the four principles fit every ethical problem results in decision-making becoming sterile, uniform and boring (Harris, 2003). More seriously, it is likely to result in other relevant issues and arguments being ignored.

Key point

Principlism asserts that there are basic and obvious moral truths that guide deliberation and action.

1.5.7 Step 7: Make a decision

After having considered and evaluated all the options outlined in the six previous steps, the penultimate step is to make a decision. It is important to realise, however, that there is rarely a single correct answer to an ethical problem. So take five nurses using the above step-by-step toolkit. Three may, for example, select consequentialism, and two, deontology (in Step 4) or the principle of autonomy rather than justice (in Step 6). Furthermore, even those choosing the same theory, e.g. consequentialism or the same principle (i.e. autonomy), may interpret them differently and so reach different conclusions. Why? Because moral judgements inevitably reflect an individual's value system. But importantly, this does not reduce the whole decision-making process to mere opinion and 'intuition' (i.e. the idea that something just feels right or wrong even though we cannot explain why), for each choice made must be morally justified, i.e. supported by more objective reasoning.

1.5.8 Step 8: Justify the decision

Justifying a moral decision involves providing the strongest moral reasons behind it. In other words, being able to explain objectively why the decision is the 'right' one. This is a crucial step because clearly not all reasons are 'good' reasons. They may, for example, be mistaken, misguided or misinformed. And even if they are 'good', they may nevertheless be irrelevant or insufficient (Beauchamp and Childress, 2009). So, how can you be sure that a particular decision is morally justified?

Very briefly, we can say that a decision is morally justified if, at the very least:

- **It is based on an accurate assessment of the facts:** An assessment that a 15-year-old is not capable of giving consent must be based on convincing evidence, for example, that her cognitive and emotional ability is limited in some way.
- **The reasoning is valid:** Valid reasoning is an argument that is logical. An argument is a set of reasons supporting a conclusion. A logical argument should contain a series of statements (called premises) that lead logically to a conclusion. For example:

  a. **Premise 1**: All life is sacred.
     Premise 2: I have a life.
     Conclusion: My life is sacred.
     Any other conclusion, for example, 'my life does not matter' is therefore invalid (i.e. nonsensical). It is invalid because it has been shown that all life, including of course my own, is sacred. In other words, an invalid argument is where the premises do not lead logically to the conclusion. For example:

  b. **Premise 1**: No life is sacred.
     Premise 2: I have a life.
     Conclusion: My life is sacred

- **Ethical theories, principles, etc., are applied consistently**: The underlying principle of consistency means that if people conclude that they should make different decisions (or do different things) in two similar situations, then they must be able to point to a morally relevant difference between the two situations that accounts for the different decisions. Otherwise, they are being inconsistent (Hope et al., 2008).

Activity

Work through the case studies in the chapter 'Making Decisions that are Ethical' in Hawley (2007), *Ethics in Clinical Practice*.

Key point

Steps in the ethical toolkit are as follows:

- Distinguish between facts and values.
- Recognise the moral issues.
- Classify the moral problem.
- Refer to overarching theory.
- Consider nurse-oriented ethical theories.
- Use ethical principlism.
- Make a decision.
- Justify the decision.

1.6 The Relationship between Law and Ethics

In this final section, we compare the role of ethics and law in health care. That there is a close relationship between the two was recognised over a century ago by Lord Chief Justice Coleridge when he asserted that 'It would not be correct to say that every moral obligation involves a legal duty; but every legal duty is founded on a moral obligation'

(*R v Instan* [1893] 1 QB at 453). More recently, it has been observed that 'it is pointless to attempt to disengage the moral discourse from the legal dispute – when we talk about legal rules, we are inevitably drawn into a discussion of moral rules' (Mason and Laurie, 2006, p. 2). As we see below, however, although law and ethics are inextricably linked, there are fundamental differences between them too.

1.6.1 Similarities between law and ethics

- Both are usually normative; i.e. they tell us how we ought to behave. Both, therefore, are concerned with what a particular society views as right or wrong, good and bad. As such, they can be described as forms of social control, using rules, principles and standards to prescribe behaviour and so determine what kinds of actions are prohibited, permitted or required (McLeod, 2009).
- Both share a common vocabulary – in which terms such as rights, duties, responsibilities and obligations dominate, as do concepts such as fairness, justice and equality – and have common roots that can be traced back to custom and also Judaeo-Christian religious traditions.
- Both influence the formulations of codes of practice (e.g. *The Code: Standards of Conduct, Performance and Ethics for Nurses and Midwives*, NMC, 2008) as well as circulars and guidelines regulating health care practice.
- Issues that are typically ethically controversial such as abortion, reproductive technologies, the care and treatment of the terminally ill, embryonic stem cell research and the fair distribution of scarce health resources are usually also legally problematic. It is therefore not surprising that ethical principles and theories influence new legislation (such as the Mental Capacity Act 2005, which seeks to protect the autonomy interests of people over 16 who lack capacity). Judges too adopt philosophical arguments to justify their decisions, especially when they are required to develop the law to meet new situations – although they rarely use them explicitly. An exception was *R v Cambridge HA ex. parte B* [1995] 2 All ER 129. The case involved a 10-year-old girl with leukaemia who unsuccessfully challenged the health authority's decision not to fund further experimental treatment. In refusing to overturn the health authority's decision, one of the judges expressly applied utilitarian considerations, namely, the need to reach a decision that led to the maximum advantage of the maximum number of patients (Hendrick, 2000, p. 25).
- Both ethics and law reflect and respond to changes in society's value system – although the law can be changed at any time by human action, whereas something cannot just be decreed good or bad and automatically become so.

1.6.2 Differences between law and ethics

- Breach of a moral rule does not necessarily involve a formal or official sanction, but breach of legal rule will nearly always ultimately result in a sanction of some sort.
- The law is enforceable in court; morality does not necessarily attract legal sanctions (unless it also involves a breach of the law).
- Although what is ethical will usually be legal and vice versa, this is not always so. Thus, some ethical principles are too vague to be translated into law or the law may not be a suitable instrument to enforce a moral idea. Telling lies, for example, is widely condemned as immoral yet there are very few laws against it. Or the law may not be an appropriate tool for enforcing a moral idea – English law does not force people to be Good Samaritans, for example.

- Moral values are personal to the individual and are not always shared; legal rules affect everybody (or a particular group without exception).
- Ethical standards – as set out in the NMC Code (2008) – are designed to encourage optimum standards (i.e. the best you can do). In contrast, the law is concerned with setting minimum standards below which practitioners must not fall. As such, it accepts much lower thresholds of behaviour. Accordingly, the questions asked when legal decisions have to be made are likely to include, for example, 'What can I get away with?' 'Will I be sued if I pursue this course of action?'

From the brief comparison between law and ethics (and the outline of the law in the first section of this chapter), it is self-evident that the law provides a framework within which professional practice can develop. Whether health care decisions should always be subject to legal scrutiny and control is, of course, another question altogether. What is beyond doubt – as we shall see in subsequent chapters – is that the courts are increasingly likely to be involved in making decisions that are essentially matters of ethics.

References

Adams, J.J. and Brownsword, R. (1996) *Understanding Law*. London: Sweet & Maxwell.

Allmark, P. (1995) Can there be an ethics of care? *Journal of Medical Ethics* 21:19.

Beauchamp, T.L. and Childress, J.F. (2009) *Principles of Biomedical Ethics*, 6th edn. Oxford: Oxford University Press.

Campbell, A., Gillett, G. and Jones, G. (2005) *Medical Ethics*, 4th edn. Oxford: Oxford University Press.

Crisp, R. and Slote, M. (1997) *Virtue Ethics*. Oxford: Oxford University Press.

Doherty, M. (2005) *Jurisprudence: The Philosophy of Law*, 4th edn. London: Old Bailey Press.

Elliott, C. and Quinn, F. (2009) *English Legal System*, 10th edn. Harlow: Pearson Education.

Fry, S.T. and Johnstone, M.J. (2008) *Ethics in Nursing Practice: A Guide to Ethical Decision-Making*. Oxford: Blackwell.

Gilligan, C. (1982) *In a Different Voice: Psychological Theory and Women's Development*. Cambridge, MA: Harvard University Press.

Gillon, R. (1994) Medical ethics: four principles plus attention to scope. *British Medical Journal* 309:184.

Grayling, A.C. (2009) *Ideas That Matter: A Personal Guide for the 21st Century*. London: Weidenfeld and Nicolson.

Harris, J. (2003) In praise of unprincipled ethics. *Journal of Medical Ethics* 29:303.

Hart, H.L.A. (1994) *The Concept of Law*. Oxford: Oxford University Press.

Hawley, G. (ed.) (2007) *Ethics in Clinical Practice: An Interprofessional Approach*. Harlow: Pearson Education.

Hendrick, J. (2000) *Law and Ethics in Nursing and Healthcare*. Cheltenham: Stanley Thornes.

Hendrick, J. (2004) *Law and Ethics: Foundations in Nursing and Health Care*. Cheltenham: Nelson Thornes.

Herring, J. (2008) *Medical Law and Ethics*, 2nd edn. Oxford: Oxford University Press.

Hervey, T. and McHale, J. (2004) *Health Law and the European Union*. Cambridge: Cambridge University Press.

Hope, T., Savulescu, J. and Hendrick, J. (2008) *Medical Ethics and Law: The Core Curriculum*, 2nd edn. Edinburgh: Elsevier.

Hunt, G. (1998) Nursing ethics. In Craig, E. (ed.) *Routledge Encyclopaedia of Philosophy*. London: Routledge.

Johnstone, M.J. (2004) *Bioethics: A Nursing Perspective*, 4th edn. Edinburgh: Churchill Livingstone/Elsevier.

Mason, J.K. and Laurie, G.T. (2006) *Mason and McCall Smith's Medical Law and Ethics*, 7th edn. Oxford: Oxford University Press.

McHale, J. and Fox, M. (2007) *Health Care Law: Text and Materials*. London: Sweet & Maxwell.

McLeod, I. (2009) *Legal Method*, 7th edn. Basingstoke: Palgrave Macmillan.

NMC (2008) *The Code: Standards of Conduct, Performance and Ethics for Nurses and Midwives*. London: NMC.

Noddings, N. (1984) *Caring: A Feminine Approach to Ethical and Moral Education.* Berkeley, CA: University of California Press.

Pattinson, S.D. (2006) *Medical Law and Ethics.* London: Sweet & Maxwell.

Pellegrino, E. (1995) Towards a virtue based normative ethics for the health professions. *Kennedy Institute of Ethics Journal* 5(3):253.

Thompson, I.E., Melia, K.M., Boyd, K.M. and Horsburgh, D. (2006) *Nursing Ethics*, 6th edn. Edinburgh: Elsevier.

Wacks, R. (2006) *Philosophy of Law: A Very Short Introduction.* Oxford: Oxford University Press.

CHAPTER 2

Childhood, Children's Rights and Welfare

Learning outcomes

By the end of this chapter you should be able to:

- Explain what is meant by the notion of 'childhood';
- Discuss the law's role in shaping contemporary knowledge about childhood;
- Differentiate between a moral right and a legal right;
- Compare and contrast the different approaches to the notion of children's rights;
- Describe how the welfare principle works.

Introduction

This chapter begins by asking what may seem to be relatively simple questions, such as who is a child in law, when does childhood begin and end in law and how does the law regulate children's lives in the intervening years? The next section focuses on the relationship between law and childhood and briefly explores how the law reflects prevailing ideas about childhood. The chapter then examines the concept of childhood from a historical perspective, demonstrating how perceptions of childhood have changed over time. The remaining sections include an analysis of the concept of 'rights', in particular, theories of children' rights and how they can be classified. The final section introduces the welfare principle.

2.1 Legal Definitions of the Child and Childhood

2.1.1 Who is a child in law?

In legal terms, a 'child' is normally a person under the age of majority – now 18. This is the position both at common law and usually (unless stated otherwise) in legislation as well as in international treaties. What this legal definition of a child fails to tell us, however, is when does childhood begin in law?

2.1.2 When does childhood begin in law?

It is a well-established principle of English law that the fetus or unborn child is not recognised as a legal person in its own right until birth. Accordingly, it is only once a baby is born alive and has a separate existence from its mother that any legal action can be brought on its behalf (*Re F* [1988] 2 All ER 193). But despite its lack of legal status, the fetus does have some legal protection before birth. Thus, in criminal law, if the fetus is harmed in utero as a result of a crime committed against its mother then, in certain circumstances, the perpetrator can face criminal charges. In tort law, too, a fetus can sue for certain pre-birth injuries.

2.1.3 The intervening years – birth to 18

Between birth and the age of majority (at 18), children and young people clearly become increasingly able to make decisions for themselves. This developing maturity is recognised by both statute and common law.

Statute law
According to statute law, once a particular age is attained, a 'child' is legally entitled to carry out a particular activity (or make a decision) irrespective of her actual maturity and understanding. However, there is little consistency in the huge number of statutory provisions regulating young people's lives (such as their leisure activities, employment and housing). Thus, even though some statutes broadly correlate with research material about children's cognitive abilities, many do not. This is particularly noticeable in relation to the older teenagers (between 16–18) – a majority of whom have the developmental skills for relatively sophisticated decision-making – but who are nevertheless subject to severe legal restrictions when seeking employment and financial independence (Fortin, 2003, p. 92). As a consequence, many, especially those who want to leave home, are forced to 'exist in a legal "twilight zone" between minority and adulthood' (Bainham, 1988, p. 63).

Statutes governing the activities of young people under 16 similarly seem to set arbitrary and inflexible age limits below which children are regarded as incompetent and above which they are given the freedom to carry out the activity in question. Again, therefore, it seems that some statutes fail to acknowledge subtle differences between how, for example, a 12-year-old thinks and feels compared to, say, a 15-year-old (Coleman and Hendry, 1999).

Below is a sample of age-based legislation governing various activities.

At 5, children:
• Can drink alcohol in private (Children and Young Person's Act 1933), and
• Become of compulsory school age (Education Act 1996).

At 10, children:
• Have full criminal responsibility (Crime and Disorder Act 1998),
• Can be detained by the police,
• Can have their fingerprints taken (Police and Criminal Evidence Act 1984), and
• Can have an antisocial behaviour order made against them (Crime and Disorder Act 1998).

At 12, children:
• Can be trained to participate in dangerous performances (Children and Young Person's Act 1933), and
• Can buy a pet (Pet Animals Act 1951).

At 14, children:
• Can get a 'light-work' job part-time (Children and Young Person's Act 1933), and
• Can ride on a horse on a road without protective headgear (Protective Headgear for Young Riders Act 1990).

At 16, children:
- Can leave school (Education Act 1996),
- Can marry with parental consent (Marriage Act 1949),
- Can leave home (Children Act 1989),
- Can consent to all sexual activities (heterosexual and homosexual) (Sexual Offences Act 2003),
- Can work full-time (but not in a betting shop or bar during opening times) if they have left school (Education Act 1996), and
- Can get a National Insurance number.

At 17, children:
- Can join the armed forces,
- Can hold a licence to drive a car (Road Traffic Act 1988), and
- Can buy or hire firearms or ammunition (Firearms Act 1968).

At 18, children:
- Can do most things that adults can do such as vote, gamble, serve on a jury, buy cigarettes, tobacco and cigarette paper.

At 21, children:
- Can adopt a child (Adoption and Children Act 2002).

The above list is just a sample of the wide variety of statutes governing children's lives (for a comprehensive account of the legal rights and responsibilities of children, see Bainham, 2005, Chapters 9, 14 and 15).

Activity

Consider critically the age restrictions imposed by statute outlined above. Do you think any should be changed? If so, why?

Common law

At common law, all activities not covered by legislation are governed by the maturity test famously established by the House of Lords in the 1986 *Gillick* case. Briefly, the case established the legal principle that 'mature minors' could, in certain circumstances, make their own decisions, i.e. when they had sufficient understanding and intelligence to be capable of making up their own minds. According to Lord Scarman, this was a more realistic way of determining legal competence than fixing an artificial age limit as it allowed the law to be sensitive to human development and social change and reflect what 'nature knows', i.e. that 'growing-up is a continuous process' ([1986] AC 112 at 186). As we see (in Chapter 4), the *Gillick* maturity test has been restrictively applied in subsequent case law. It has thus not turned out to be the landmark for children's rights that many anticipated (Lowe and Douglas, 2006, p. 364).

2.1.4 When does childhood end in law?

Childhood – at least in legal terms – normally ends at 18, the current age of majority. This is the age when those with parental responsibility (usually a child's legal parents, see further Chapter 8) cease to have the legal duty to, for example, maintain their children, and provide them with essential health care, food and shelter. But this is not always so. Consider, for example, the legal liability to support a child over 18 in advanced education (Bainham, 2005, p. 87). Parental responsibility in relation to a disabled child may also extend into adulthood in certain circumstances (see further Corker and Davis,

2000). Note that generally throughout this book reference to children usually means younger children who lack maturity and understanding to make important decisions for themselves. Older children who are able to do so are referred to as young people.

Key points

- A fetus in not recognised as a legal person until birth but can sue for injuries suffered in utero.
- At common law, all activities are governed by the maturity test established in the *Gillick* case (1986).

2.2 The Relationship between Law and Childhood

It is widely agreed that both statute and common law reflect 'a sense of deep confusion' regarding the point at which children are regarded as competent to take responsibility for their activities and decisions (Fortin, 2003, p. 93). But according to some legal scholars (e.g. King and Piper, 1995; Monk, 2004), it is not surprising that the law fails to provide a consistent and coherent 'rule book' specifying accurately what children can do (and when). This is because the law is not simply a value-free neutral system of rules. Rather, age-based statutes (and common law decisions determining legal capacity) reflect contemporary ideas about what constitutes a 'proper' childhood (and what is expected of 'good' parents). As there is 'no uniform, coherent image of children but, rather many different and sometimes conflicting images', the law will therefore inevitably reflect the 'many different stories of childhood' (Monk, 2004, p. 161).

That the law enshrines several different versions of children simultaneously is perhaps not surprising. This is because the law does more than just simply regulate what children can do at particular ages and how adults (parents, professionals and 'the state') should behave towards them. In short, it reinforces prevailing knowledge and understanding about what it is to be a child. However, as we shall see from the historical outline below, that knowledge is constantly evolving and therefore not only changes over time but also (at any one time) can reflect conflicting images of the position of children in society. To understand how our ideas about childhood are influenced and shaped, we therefore need to understand how childhood has been perceived during different historical periods.

Activity

Critically consider the contradictory images of childhood sexuality that Monk identifies in the chapter 'Childhood and the law: in whose best interests?', *An Introduction to Childhood Studies* (ed. M.J. Kehily).

2.3 The Nature of Childhood

The term 'childhood' can be simply defined as a distinct, separate and fundamentally different social group or category (Gittins, 2004, p. 27). Typically, this transitory stage (or state of incompetence relative to adulthood) is characterised by dependency and powerlessness (Archard, 1993, p. 30). Of course, much of our understanding of childhood is derived from our own experiences and memories (Gittins, 2004, p. 26). And although we may therefore all recognise that others experience their childhoods differently, there is nevertheless a common assumption that childhood has somehow always 'been there'. Yet, as we see below, the notion of childhood is a contested subject.

2.3.1 Historical perspective

The debate about the nature of childhood can be broadly divided into two main groups of writings: (1) medieval and early modern historians, whose main concern was to establish whether the concept of childhood existed at all prior to the seventeenth century; i.e. whether children were regarded as a separate and different social group from adults; (2) nineteenth- and twentieth-century historians, who have proposed a *developing* concept of childhood (Hendrick, 1992, p. 1).

Medieval and early modern period

Any discussion of the nature of childhood must begin with Philippe Aries's ground-breaking claim that in Western Europe the concept of childhood is a relatively modern one. His book, *Centuries of Childhood*, was the first general historical study of childhood. In essence, Aries argued that 'the idea of childhood did not exist in medieval society' (Aries, 1962, p. 125). By this he did not mean that adults were indifferent to the physical vulnerability of young children but rather that in the Middle Ages children (from about the age of seven) were regarded as 'miniature adults' (or adults in the making). However, from the fifteenth century onwards, according to Aries, perceptions of childhood began to change in that a more sophisticated idea of what is involved in being a child began to develop. Thus, in the sixteenth century, adults were beginning to see children as a 'source of amusement and relaxation' even though it was not until the seventeenth century that the difference between the two ages (under and over seven) began to be appreciated. By the mid-eighteenth century, a new concept of children had emerged that paved the way to the modern idea of childhood, that is, as a distinct social/age group occupying a central place in the family.

Aries based much of his theory on how children were represented in medieval art (particularly religious art), but he also used evidence derived from literary texts, manuals and styles of dress. His theory has had an enormous influence on the study of childhood not only because he drew attention to the significance of children within the family but also because he gave an impetus to historical research on the changing ideas about, and meaning of, childhood (Gittins, 2004, p. 38; Prout, 2005, p. 9).

However, later historians (e.g. Cunningham, 1991; Pollock, 1983) have criticised Aries' basic theory and methodology and some of his conclusions. Briefly, the main criticisms are the following: (1) his data are unreliable, inconsistent or unrepresentative; (2) he takes evidence out of context and uses atypical examples; and (3) he places too much emphasis on the writings of moralists and educationalists but largely ignores economic and political factors.

Perhaps the most damning criticism is Archard's claim that because Aries draws no distinction between the *concept* of childhood and the *conception* of childhood, his basic thesis is fundamentally flawed (Archard, 1993, pp. 21–24). In brief, Archard's argument is this: to have a *concept* of childhood is to recognise that there is a difference between children and adults. But to have a *conception* of childhood is to have an idea of (i.e. to specify) what those differences are. According to Archard, all societies have (at all times) a *concept* of childhood but there are many different *conceptions*. These conceptions, he continues, have made different claims about how long childhood lasts; its nature (i.e. precisely what qualities distinguish it from adulthood); and its significance (how important those differences are). Archard therefore concludes that by making an 'ill-judged leap' from *concept* to *conception*, Aries may 'be wrong to think that it is only modern society which has a concept of childhood' (Archard, 1993, p. 29). This conclusion – i.e. that although prior to the seventeenth century, children were viewed differently from today, a perception of their distinctiveness nevertheless existed – is now widely accepted (Hendrick, 1992).

Nineteenth and early twentieth centuries

Historians of the nineteenth and twentieth centuries propose not so much the sudden and dramatic emergence of the concept of childhood, as the continuing transformation or reconstruction of competing and often class-based perceptions (Hendrick, 1992, p. 1). This *developing* concept of childhood, that is, the idea that childhood is *evolutionary* and is therefore continually transformed and reconstructed, is attributed by scholars (e.g. Cunningham, 1991; Hendrick, 1997; Steedman, 1990) to a number of factors, in particular:

- Labour and factory reform legislation in the 1830s – reducing working hours and limiting child labour.
- The introduction of compulsory mass schooling in the 1870s and 1880s.
- The Child Study Movement (which began in the 1890s) and the 'scientific' interest in children it triggered – using techniques of natural history in the study of child development.
- Rising standards of living due to regular and less physically debilitating jobs, increased wage rates, improved housing, garden space, domestic technology, varied leisure facilities and paid holidays (Burnett, 1982; Hopkins, 1994).

While all the above-mentioned factors have undoubtedly influenced (and altered) perceptions of childhood, there is broad consensus (Hopkins, 1994; Wardle, 1974) that it was the introduction of compulsory schooling (in the late nineteenth century) that most transformed attitudes to children. The substitution of 'schooling' for 'work' had a profound impact on how childhood was perceived because it (a) lengthened the years of 'childhood', (b) reinforced notions of the characteristics that were said to constitute a 'proper' childhood, namely, ignorance, innocence and dependence, and (c) popularised the idea that children were different from adults in development, behaviour, knowledge, skills and in their dependence on adults (Hendrick, 1997).

As the twentieth century progressed (particularly from 1920s), and notwithstanding class differences, there is broad agreement that attitudes towards children became more liberal and humane (Hendrick, 1997, p. 34). The rise in more progressive childrearing can be largely attributed to the following:

- A decline in family size (down from an average of six children in the 1860s to three in the 1900s and two in 1920). Fewer children meant that the home was less overcrowded, easier to clean; there was more time for individual affection and less pressure to impose strict discipline (Thompson, 1977).
- Increasingly influential discipline of psychology – which broadened the concept of welfare by emphasising that children's psychological and emotional well-being was as important as their physical well-being (Douglas, 2004, p. 79).
- The impact of World War II which led to a more democratic approach in social thinking, in particular by emphasising reciprocity in the parent–child relationship and the inculcation of child discipline through guidance and understanding (Beekman, 1977).

Late twentieth century and contemporary images of childhood

It is widely agreed that the most profound transformations in the meaning of childhood and in the experiences of children have occurred since the 1960s. These transformations have been largely attributed to two conflicting assessments of the position in children in society. Thus on the one hand, is the claim that childhood is *disappearing*, that is, that children are treated like adults at an earlier and earlier stage. Features of this trend are said to include, in particular, the sexualisation and commercialisation of childhood – by, for example, the use of child models to advertise adult products and the tendency of children's clothes to resemble adult fashions (Humphries et al., 1988). The influence of television and increasing violence of juvenile crime has also been blamed for rushing children through what should be an innocent and stress-free time of life (Postman, 1983).

However, an alternative idea about children's place in society also emerged in the latter part of the twentieth century. Influenced in particular by the children's rights movement – which broadly speaking developed in the 1970s and 1980s – the claim was that there was no justification for denying children the rights (e.g. political, economic and social) enjoyed by adults. As we see below, there is a wide spectrum of opinion about the scope and nature of the concept of children's rights. Importantly, however, the idea that children should be perceived as rights bearers rather than passive 'objects of concern' (Butler-Sloss, 1989) shifted the focus of concern about children. No longer just the victims of adult authority, children began to be increasingly seen as active participants in family life entitled to make decisions for themselves and to challenge adult perceptions of what was best for them (James and Prout, 1997; Smart et al., 2001).

As Axford notes, this changing perspective has contributed to a greater interest in studying children per se (Axford, 2008, p. 5). Yet the nature of childhood evidently continues to be hotly contested – hence the conflicting contemporary images of modern young people. Thus concern about the disappearance of childhood continues alongside fears that the boundary between childhood and adulthood is steadily being reinforced more than ever as children are increasingly excluded from public spaces (through fear for their safety or because of concerns about their behaviour (Mayall, 2002; Valentine, 2004). We are all now familiar, too, with the starkly contrasting images of children that are routinely presented in the media, that is, of children who are weak, feral, threatened and threatening. As Herring (2009, p. 399) asks: 'are [children] little angels or little devils?' Unsurprisingly, these multiple versions of childhood both define and complicate the debate about the nature of contemporary childhood.

In conclusion, what therefore emerges from this historical overview is that there is no objectively true definition of childhood (Fionda, 2001; Stainton-Rogers, 2001). In other words, childhood is a *social construction* (Bainham, 2005; Herring, 2009). Put very simply, the term 'social construction' refers to the idea that childhood must be understood as a historical, social and cultural phenomenon. According to this view, although biological immaturity may be natural and universal, what particular societies make of such immaturity differs through time and between different cultures (see further Prout, 2005, pp. 83–111).

Activity

How would you describe an 'ideal childhood'?

Key points

- All societies (at all times) have a concept of childhood.
- Attitudes towards children are shaped by class and culture.
- Various constructions of childhood have been identified during different historical periods.
- The values and beliefs that inform legal decisions and legislation reflect contemporary knowledge about childhood.
- Competing and conflicting constructions of childhood may coexist simultaneously.

2.4 Rights

Rights talk is commonplace in contemporary society. Few governments can now escape pressure to safeguard or promote the rights of a huge variety of groups, individuals and organisations (Wacks, 2006). In the UK, the importance of rights is reinforced by the Human Rights Act (HRA) 1998, which entitles citizens to a wide range of 'fundamental' rights and freedoms, e.g. to a fair trial, respect for private and family life, freedom of thought and religion. The language of rights is also common in health care contexts. We talk, for example, of the right to autonomy, to die with dignity, to confidentiality, and so on. That rights play an important role in the discussion of contentious moral issues such as abortion, euthanasia and embryo research is also indisputable.

But claiming a right can mean different things in different contexts. We need, in other words, to distinguish between those rights that we think should be recognised by the law and other rights. Hence, we may believe that we ought, for example, to have a right to work and a right to health care. Yet we may nevertheless also recognise that claiming these kinds of rights is problematic – not least because of the public expenditure they entail. Furthermore, if rights are to have moral significance, we need to be careful about their content (i.e. the particular action that the right holder is demanding). Otherwise, we run the risk that by demanding an escalating variety of rights – to almost anything (e.g. the right to a slug-free garden) – the value of rights as 'the ubiquitous, global currency of moral argument' will be undermined (Sumner, 2000).

Activity

Before you read the next section, make a list of the five most important rights you believe you have.

2.4.1 How rights work

The starting point for any analysis of rights is the work of the American jurist, Wesley Hohfeld (1879–1917). Although his analysis – set out in 'Some fundamental legal conceptions as applied to judicial reasoning' (Hohfeld, 1913) – refers specifically to legal rights, it can be applied to other rights. Hohfeld proposed that the phrase **X has a right to do R** could basically mean one of four things, namely:

1. A **claims** right means that Y (or anyone else) is under a *duty* to allow X to do R; i.e. Y therefore owes X a duty, or to put it another way, X has a *claim* against Y. An example of a claims right is a patient's right to a certain level of health care (arising, for example, from a nurse's duty of care).
2. A **liberty/privilege** arises when Y owes no duty. Rather X is free to do (or not do) something (i.e. whatever R represents). An example would be X's right to private health insurance.
3. A **power** exists when X can alter/create legal relations with other persons. An example would be X's power to give away her property.
4. An **immunity** describes a situation where X is not subject to Y's (or anyone's) power to change her legal position. In essence, this is therefore a right that protects X from interference by another person. An example would be X's immunity from being sacked for belonging to a trade union.

According to Hohfeld, these basic 'rights' are the lowest common denominator in all legal relationships, and any other rights that a person may claim to have can ultimately be reduced to a category of one of these four.

Hohfeld's scheme has not been as widely used as he advocated. Yet despite its limitations (on which see Doherty, 2005; Sumner, 2000; Wacks, 2006), his analysis has been very influential. Its appeal is easy to explain. First, it is relatively simple and easy to apply. Second, it is universal in the sense that the scheme of analysis can be applied effectively to the investigation of moral rights. Third, by reminding us to use the term 'right' in a very strict sense (rather than indiscriminately), we are alerted to the subtle differences between claims, liberties, powers and immunities (and the relationships between them).

2.4.2 Types of rights

In this section, we distinguish briefly between various types of rights. However, it is important to remember that, essentially, claiming a right is a rule-governed activity. As Beauchamp and Childress explain, 'whether the rules are legal, moral or institutional all rights exist or fail because the relevant rules either allow or disallow the claim in question' (Beauchamp and Childress, 2009, p. 357).

Moral rights

Moral rights, i.e. rights that are justifiable by moral principles and rules, have the following characteristics:

1. *Natural*: Exist by virtue of humanity.
2. *Universal*: Everyone has them regardless of where they live or what sort of society exists.
3. *Equal*: Apply to everyone regardless of age/gender/ethnicity/physical or mental capacity.
4. *Inalienable*: Cannot be given or taken away.

As Bridgeman notes, claims to moral rights are politically important because they establish minimal entitlements. They also give individuals the means to redress wrongs and resolve conflict (Bridgeman, 2007, p. 17). In any given society, many moral rights are converted into legal rights. For example, the moral right that young children have to health care is given legal effect by the Children and Young Person's Act 1933 and the Children Act 1989.

Activity

Think of a moral right you do not think should be converted into a legal right. Explain why.

Legal rights

Legal rights, i.e. rights that are justifiable by legal principles and rules, have the following characteristics:

1. *Artificial*: Created by the government.
2. *Particular*: Apply to a particular group or certain individuals.
3. *Not universal*: Not everyone in society has them.
4. *Alienable*: Can be given up and/or modified.

Legal rights are often also moral rights, but not always. Many legal rights, for example, are simply matters of technical qualification and so have no moral content at all (Almond, 1993, p. 261). Furthermore, some legal rights allow us to do things that are 'bad' for us. This means that exercising a legal right is not necessarily to our advantage.

Activity

Give an example of a legal right that allows you to do something that is 'bad' for your health. Give reasons why the law should not prohibit such behaviour.

Human rights

In modern societies, the phrase 'human rights' refers to a set of basic civil liberties that should be available to everyone in a democratic country. Different legal systems may recognise different rights, but generally they will include rights to say, think and believe what you like; to form groups; to protest peacefully; not to be imprisoned (or otherwise punished) without a free trial; not to be tortured and so on. Although the justification for human rights is essentially ethical, they are almost always also aspired to as legal rights (Almond, 1993, p. 261).

The notion of human rights has evolved over several generations (Wacks, 2006). The first generation of rights were civil and political and were developed in the seventeenth and eighteenth centuries by English political philosophers such as Locke (1632–1704) who claimed the rights to life, liberty and property. These rights are negative in the sense that they prohibit interference with rights holders' freedom. The second generation of human rights consisted mainly of social, economic and cultural rights. They are positive rights entitling the rights holder to, for example, education, medical care and food. The third generation of human rights – contained in the Universal Declaration of Human Rights and Fundamental Freedoms (the Declaration) – was adopted by the United Nations in 1948.

The Declaration was followed by the European Convention for the Protection of Human Rights and Fundamental Freedoms (hereafter the 'Convention'), which was signed in 1950. The UK was the first country to ratify the Convention (in 1951). In establishing for the first time a system of international law that made states accountable to their citizens, the Convention was indeed radical. However, it was not until 1998 that the Convention was finally incorporated into English law (by the HRA 1998).

Human Rights Act 1998

Prior to incorporation, UK citizens wishing to pursue a claim for breach of their human rights had to apply directly to the European Court of Human Rights in Strasbourg. This was invariably a lengthy and expensive process. It still remains an option of last resort but is rarely now taken as the Convention is now applicable directly in the UK courts. The Act strengthens the protection of individual rights by UK courts and provides improved remedies where these are violated. Thus, for example, since October 2000, individual judges must 'take into account' any relevant Strasbourg jurisprudence; the courts must 'so far as possible' interpret legislation in a way which is compatible with Convention rights, and public authorities (including the health service, local authorities and the police) must comply with the Convention.

The Act's implementation was hailed as 'the point at which children came of age, in terms of rights enforcement' (Fortin, 2003, p. 53). This was because it gave children in the UK (just like adults) the right to complain in UK courts about any alleged breach of a Convention right by any public authority, such as a hospital trust or local education authority. Yet many commentators were more sceptical about the Act's potential for promoting children's rights (see, e.g. Bainham, 2002; Herring, 1999). They claimed that although the Convention rights were available to all human beings, they had an adult focus (indeed, children are rarely specifically mentioned, either in the Convention or its Protocols).

Almost 20 years after the Act was implemented, there is evidence to support both viewpoints. Thus, in a growing list of cases concerning children, judicial readiness to cite Convention rights (and the United Nations Convention on the Rights of the Child, UNCRC, 1989, see below) in support of domestic provisions is certainly evident (see, e.g. *Re S* [2001] EWHC Admin 334; *Re T*; (*Abduction: Child's Objection to Return*) [2000] 2 FLR 192; Re C (HIV Test) [1999] 2 FLR 1004; see further Williams, 2007, pp. 261–262). When children make their own applications – particularly in certain areas such as education, youth crime and child protection – there is also no doubt that children's demands for full protection of the Convention have usually been met (Fortin, 2006, p. 304).

On the other hand, in private law, disputes between parents' (e.g. about residence or contact arrangements) and children's rights seem less well developed. Several commentators ascribe this apparent reluctance to embrace the human rights ethos to the attachment of the courts to the welfare principle (Bainham, 2002; Choudhry and Fenwick, 2005). But even in cases where children are separately represented – and thus more likely to be treated as independent 'rights holders' – their potential rights may 'disappear under a welter of experts' assertions regarding various aspects of their future care' (Fortin, 2006, p. 303).

Activity

Which rights in the HRA 1998 are most relevant to health care?

Absolute versus conditional rights

An absolute right is one that cannot be infringed in any circumstances. The problem for anyone asserting that a right is absolute is the potential conflict between two (or more) absolute rights. In other words, it may be impossible to respect one absolute right without infringing another. For example, an (absolute) right to freedom of expression may conflict with another's (absolute) right not be offended. The potential conflict between absolute rights explains why very few are recognised in the HRA 1998, notably Article 3 (the absolute right not to suffer torture). Other rights safeguarded in the Act are conditional (i.e. qualified) in the sense that they can be interfered with in certain circumstances. Even the right to life in Article 2 may need to be balanced against another's (or several others').

Positive and negative rights

Positive rights require people to act in certain ways, whereas negative rights prohibit actions or behaviour. Herring (2008, p. 18) illustrates the difference as follows: although the negative right not to have treatment given to you (that you object to) is a strongly protected negative right, the positive right to receive treatment which you want is far less strongly protected, if at all (see further Beauchamp and Childress, 2009, pp. 352–353). Note that according to Brykczynska (1993), negative rights are not easy for children to achieve, e.g. it is difficult for a child to avoid corporal punishment.

Key points

- Rights can be classified in a number of ways, i.e. as moral, legal and human rights.
- Rights can be absolute or conditional (i.e. qualified in some way).
- All the rights in the HRA 1998 (except Article 3) are qualified.
- The HRA 1998 entitles UK citizens to invoke Convention rights directly in UK courts.

2.5 Children's Rights

Several decades ago the concept of children's rights was famously described by Rodham (1973) as 'a slogan in search of a definition'. Although the concept has been much debated since then and is better understood and more widely accepted, it remains elusive. This is partly because, as with all rights talk, distinctions are not always made between the various different types of rights that can be claimed on behalf of children (e.g. moral, human and/or legal rights). Nor is it always apparent whether the rights claimed are against the state or are concerned with children's relationship with their parents (and/or other individuals). There are uncertainties too about the precise scope of some of the rights that are commonly claimed. For example, few would deny that children have rights to adequate food, medical care and education. But the content of these rights may be very uncertain. Thus, agreement on what constitutes adequate care and nourishment for a newborn baby may be far easier to reach than on what constitutes an adequate education for an older child (Bainham, 2005, p. 102). Another complicating factor is that there are several different theories of children's rights that offer different explanations of whether children can be rights holders at all. The most influential are summarised below.

2.5.1 Theories of children's rights

There are broadly two main competing theories of children's rights.

The will theory

Put simply, the will theory of rights assumes that the right holder can decide when (and whether) to exercise the right in question (Feinberg, 1980; Hart, 1984). In other words, she has a choice about whether to enforce the right or waive it. Crucially, therefore, the will theory is founded on the capacity of the right holder to act autonomously. For some theorists (e.g. Campbell, 1992; MacCormick, 1982), this essential feature is the fatal flaw in the theory's ability to accommodate the concept of children's rights. How they ask, can a child – who lacks the physical and mental capacity to enforce or relieve others from their duties towards her – be described as having any rights at all? In other words, if children lack the ability to make choices, they cannot claim to be rights holders. An alternative approach must therefore be sought if incompetent children are to be realistically regarded as rights holders – one that does not depend on the ability to make choices.

The interest theory

For theorists (such as Campbell, 1992; MacCormick, 1982; Raz 1984), someone has a right if they have an *interest* which is sufficiently important to impose on others a duty to protect it. Thus, the interest theory of rights does not depend on children having adult capacities. Rather, it is based on the idea that children have certain interests which require protection. So, for example, when we speak of a child having a right to education, what we mean is that because the child has an interest in being educated, others are under an enforceable duty to provide her with appropriate education.

Because the interest theory does not deny children rights merely because some of them are insufficiently mature to make informed choices, it may seem attractively straightforward. But inevitably the theory creates its own uncertainties. Not least is the problem of (a) reaching agreement on a core list of children's interests, (b) deciding *who* should have the duty to protect those interests and (c) identifying *which* interests should be transformed into moral or legal rights (Buck, 2005, p. 14).

A popular version of the interest theory of rights that attempts to answer some of these criticisms is Eekelaar's thesis (1986). Eekelaar proposed three separate kinds of children's interests which could form the foundation of rights claims, namely:

1. *Basic interests*: These interests – which parents have a duty to protect – include children's need for physical, emotional and intellectual care. In cases of abuse or neglect, the state has an obligation to intervene.
2. *Developmental interests*: This group of interests should provide 'all children an equal opportunity to maximise the resources available to them during their childhood so as to minimise the degree to which they enter adult life affected by avoidable prejudices incurred during childhood' (Eekelaar, 1986, p. 173). Development interests are a broader, more ill-defined set of interests than basic interests. Accordingly, Eekelaar concedes that apart from education, they would be difficult to transform from moral rights into legal rights.
3. *Autonomy interests*: This category largely consists of the freedom for children to choose their own lifestyles and enter into social relationships of their choosing, irrespective of the adult world's wishes.

Eekelaar regarded autonomy interests as subordinate to both children's basic and developmental interests. So, for example, a child's autonomous decision to binge drink should be overridden – because otherwise her basic and developmental interests would be prejudiced. Eeklaar's interest in children's right to autonomy reflects his concerns that the adult world is too often reluctant to recognise a child's voice where it does not conform to the 'welfare principle'.

There are several advantages to Eekelaar's approach. Firstly, it illustrates the potential conflicts, not only between the three separate interests (or rights) which children can claim but also the relationship between those rights and those of parents (and others) in the adult world (Bainham, 2005). Secondly, it demonstrates how theories about the concept of children's rights can be applied in more practical contexts (Fortin, 2003). Thirdly, it explains why children cannot have all the rights of adults, yet at the same time shows how children can make certain decisions for themselves (Herring, 2009).

Activity

Compare and contrast the interest theory of rights and the will theory of rights.

Key points

- There are two main theories of children's rights: the will theory and the interest theory.
- The interest theory of rights does not depend on children having adult capacities.
- Eekelaar's version of the interest theory proposes that children have three separate interests: basic, developmental and autonomy interests.

2.6 Classification of Children's Rights

In this section, some of the most common ways in which children's rights have been classified are outlined. In his seminal book, *The Rights and Wrongs of Children*, Freeman

(1983) proposed four categories of rights, namely:

1. **Welfare rights:** Described as human rights (and based on the United Nations Declaration of the Rights of the Child 1959 (see below), the rights claimed, for example, to adequate nutrition, housing and medical care, are similar to Eekelaar's basic interests. They are typically vague and are essentially rights which children *ought* to have against everyone.
2. **Protective rights:** These generally consist of rights to protection from, for example, negative behaviour and activities such as inadequate care and abuse and environmental pollution. Protective rights seek to set a minimum standard of acceptable behaviour enforced mainly through the criminal law.
3. **Right to be treated like an adult:** This category includes the rights and liberties enjoyed by adults which, it is claimed, should be extended to children (unless there is a good reason for not doing so). Suspicious that some age-based restrictions were not based on any objective test of rationality, Freeman advocated that legal capacity should be determined on a case-by-case basis.
4. **Rights against parents:** Concerned with self-determination and autonomy, the rights asserted – which could range from the trivial (i.e. choice of hairstyle, clothes, etc.) to the more serious (e.g. consent to medical treatment) – aim to give children more independence in family life.

Freeman (who is generally described as a 'liberal paternalist') has long argued that society must take 'children's rights more seriously' if their lives are to be improved through recognition of their 'humanity, integrity, individuality and personality' (Freeman, 1997, p. 21). But although he recognises the fundamental idea of children having 'rights', he nevertheless reminds us that the passing of laws is only the beginning since 'the true recognition of children's rights requires implementation in practice' (Freeman, 1997. p. 101).

According to an alternative scheme proposed by Bevan (1989), children's rights consist of two broad categories.

1. **Protective rights:** Included in this category are children's rights to nurture, love, care, and so on, as well as protection from abuse and neglect. These protective rights derive from children's innate dependence and vulnerability and their need for nurture, love and care (Fortin, 2003, p. 17).
2. **Assertive rights:** Echoing some of the claims of the so-called child liberationists (who generally argue for children to be given all the rights that adults enjoy), the assertion here is that children are confined to 'childishness' because they are denied adult human rights such as the right to self-determination and other decision-making rights.

Note finally that while thinking about children in terms of protecting and promoting their individual rights may reflect the current approach of law and policy, there is a contrary view. O'Neill, for example, argues that the concept of children's rights is very different from other rights and as such parallels cannot be drawn (O'Neill, 1992, pp. 24–42).

Key points

- There are several different ways of conceptualising children's rights.
- Two broad approaches to children's rights categorise rights as either (a) protective (or welfare) rights or (b) assertive rights.

> **Activity**
>
> Consider the role of the Children's Commissioner for England in advancing children's health rights (http://www.childrenscommissioner.org.uk).

2.7 Common Themes

As the above outline demonstrates, there are several different theoretical approaches to children's rights (likewise how children's rights can be classified). Yet, although it is therefore self-evident that 'children's rights' is not a unitary concept, some common themes can be discerned – whether they are expressly stated or implied. In brief, these are as follows:

- **The importance of rights:** Rights are important because those who lack rights are like slaves, i.e. the means to the ends of others. The strength of a rights-based approach is its recognition of humans as individuals whose dignity, integrity and personality are worth protecting.
- **Need for protection:** Despite the vocabulary of rights, a strong paternalistic or welfarist element is evident. It seems, therefore, that a concern and interest in rights is consistent with the recognition that vulnerable and dependent children need protection from harm – whether from themselves or others.
- **Autonomy:** Because children have the potential to develop their abilities, that is, the potential to develop the rationality and reason to exercise choice and make decisions, their capacity for self-determination should be acknowledged (and encouraged) as they mature.
- **Duty:** The imposition of a duty on someone is a necessary corollary of any right asserted on behalf of children. The duty can be imposed on a primary carer (such as a parent) or other entity, for example the state.
- **Concept of childhood:** Rights that are claimed on behalf of children inevitably reflect potentially conflicting constructions of childhood in which children may be perceived as simultaneously innocent and vulnerable and as threatening and 'dangerous'.

2.8 Children and International Law

This section briefly considers some of the most important international treaties and conventions that are relevant to children (note that treaties are often referred to by different names, such as Declarations, Pacts, Charters, Covenants, Protocols and Conventions).

2.8.1 Historical outline

Declaration of Geneva in 1924

Concern for the huge number of children orphaned and displaced by World War I prompted the League of Nations to set up a Committee for the Protection of Children in 1919. This led to the adoption of the Declaration of Geneva in 1924 – a milestone in international law as it was the first declaration of human rights by any intergovernmental organisation. The Declaration's five brief principles emphasised children's welfare and represented 'the means requisite for the child's normal development'. Overall, the Declaration adopted a paternalistic stance; i.e. children were very much seen as passive objects of concern rather than as active subjects (Buck, 2005, p. 12).

United Nations Declaration of the Rights of the Child 1959

The 1959 Declaration contained ten principles. These were based on those in the 1924 Declaration but were broader and more detailed. Despite adopting a more rights-based vocabulary, the ethos of the Declaration was essentially protectionist. The underlying theme was therefore to safeguard children's welfare, not to promote their autonomy (Freeman, 1997, p. 50).

United Nations Convention on the Rights of the Child 1989

The 1989 Convention (UNCRC) represents a commonly agreed world standard for the treatment of children (McGlynn, 2006, p. 68). The Convention covers a wide spectrum of 'rights', namely, civil and political, social, economic, cultural, recreational and humanitarian. The general aims of the UNCRC – which has 54 Articles and applies to children under 18 – have been referred to as the '4 Ps' – *prevention*, *protection*, *provision*, and *participation* (Van Bueren, 1995). The most significant health-related articles are the welfare principle (Article 3.1), right to life (Article 6), expression of child's views (Article 12) and health (Article 24). The UK ratified the UNCRC in 1991, but, unlike the ECHR, it does not form part of English law. This means that children cannot take legal action in English courts (or elsewhere) alleging a breach of their Convention rights. It is therefore unsurprising that neither moral nor legal rights claimed in the UNCRC have been directly engaged to resolve issues concerning children's health (Bridgeman, 2007, p. 17)

Activity

In the light of Article 24, critically consider UNICEF's latest report on the health of children in the UK (http://www.unicef.org/crc).

The Charter of Fundamental Rights of the European Union 2000

This Charter is significant in so far as it represents the first recognition of children as independent subjects of Union law and policy, i.e. with needs and interests that are separate from those of their families (McGlynn, 2006, pp. 67; see further, pp. 42–77).

2.9 The Welfare Principle

The welfare principle (which is also commonly referred to as the 'best interests' or paramountcy principle) has been a cardinal feature of child law since the early twentieth century. Yet it was not until the Children Act 1989 that any statutory attempt was made to clarify the nature and scope of the concept, or even to indicate the kinds of factors courts should consider when making a decision about a child's upbringing.

Section 1(1) of the Children Act 1989 now clearly states that whenever a court determines any question with respect to a child's upbringing (or the administration of their property), the child's welfare shall be the court's paramount consideration. According to a seminal case in 1970 (*J v C* [1970] AC 668), the word 'paramount' means that the child's welfare is the sole consideration.

2.9.1 What does welfare mean?

The Act does not define 'welfare'. Instead, it lists the factors judges must consider in most contested cases. These are listed in s.1(3):

a. The ascertainable wishes and feelings of the child concerned (considered in the light of his age and understanding).
b. His physical, emotional and educational needs.
c. The likely effect on him of any change in his circumstances.

d. His age, sex, background and any characteristics of his which the court considers relevant.
e. Any harm which he has suffered or is at risk of suffering.
f. How capable each of his parents, and any other person in relation to whom the court considers the question to be relevant, is of meeting his needs.
g. The range of powers available to the court under this Act in the proceedings in question.

How these various factors are interpreted in practice will depend on the facts of each case. In other words, the welfare test applies a particularist, not a universal assessment (Bridgeman, 2007, p. 102). Furthermore, it is clear (as we shall see in subsequent chapters) that opinions may differ widely over the evidence needed to establish each factor and the weight that it should be given (Elliston, 2007, p. 13).

2.9.2 When does the welfare principle apply?

The principle applies whenever a court makes a decision about children's upbringing (or the administration of their property). The term 'upbringing' has been defined expansively in case law as 'the bringing up, care for, treatment, education, and instruction of the child by its parents or by those who are substitute parents' (*Re X (A Child)*[2001] 1 FCR 541). In health care contexts, the welfare principle thus applies to applications (under s.8 of the Act) to determine what medical treatment a child should receive. It also applies where the court is exercising its inherent jurisdiction (see, e.g. *Re T (A Minor) (Wardship: Medical Treatment)* [1997] 1 FLR 502). So, regardless of the route taken to bring the issue of a child's medical treatment before the courts, the decision will be governed by the welfare principle (unless a particular statute provides otherwise).

2.9.3 Criticisms of the welfare principle

For some scholars, the welfare principle is a 'guiding standard', which enables identification of the relevant factors and a helpful checklist to achieve the best possible outcome in each instance (Harington, 2003). It has also been applauded for its great flexibility (Douglas, 2004) because it can legitimately result in different conclusions, depending on such factors as the weight accorded to medical evidence and the values and beliefs of the decision-maker (Bridgeman, 2007, p. 103).

But others are more critical of the principle. Some of the main criticisms are as follows:

- *'Welfare' is interpreted too narrowly*: It is argued that the law adopts too narrow an interpretation of 'welfare'. Thus, it focuses only those aspects of welfare that judges, social workers or adult parties can influence. This means that other equally important factors – such as financial, environmental and educational factors – all of which can significantly affect a child's welfare, are neglected, if not ignored altogether (King and Piper, 1995).
- *Uncertainty*: It is claimed that the welfare principle is inconsistent and unpredictable. The uncertainty arises from the many 'unknowns' concerning welfare – for example, there may be conflicting evidence about the 'relevant facts' (Herring, 2005; Moonkin, 1985).
- *Value-laden*: In allowing adults to make decisions from their perspectives – drawing upon their ideals of what it is to be a child and their memories of their own childhood reinterpreted from their position as adults – it acts as a smoke screen for bias, paternalism and capricious decision-making (Parker, 1994).
- *Inappropriate prioritisation*: By prioritising the best interest(s) of the child, the legitimate interests of others may be ignored or underestimated (Eekelaar, 2002; Reece, 1996).

Key points

- The welfare principle applies whenever a court makes a decision about a child's upbringing.
- The welfare principle makes the child's welfare the paramount consideration for the court.
- Section 1(3) of the Children Act 1989 (the welfare checklist) sets out the factors courts must consider when applying the welfare principle.

References

Almond, B. (1993) Rights. In Singer, P. (ed.) *A Companion Guide to Ethics*. Oxford: Blackwell.

Archard, D.W. (1993) *Children: Rights and Childhood*. London: Routledge.

Aries, P. (1962) *Centuries of Childhood*. Harmondsworth: Penguin.

Axford, N. (2008) *Exploring Concepts of Children's Well-Being*. Bristol: Policy Press.

Bainham, A. (1988) *Children, Parents and the State*. London: Sweet & Maxwell.

Bainham, A. (2002) Can we protect children and protect their rights? *Family Law* 32:239.

Bainham, A. (2005) *Children: The Modern Law*. Bristol: Jordan Publishing.

Beauchamp, T.L. and Childress, J.F. (2009) *Principles of Biomedical Ethics*, 6th edn. Oxford: Oxford University Press.

Beekman, D. (1977) *The Mechanical Baby: A Popular History of the Theory and Practice of Child-Rearing*. Westport, CT: Hill.

Bevan, H. (1989) *Child Law*. London: Butterworths.

Bridgeman, J. (2007) *Parental Responsibility: Young Children and Health Care*. Cambridge: Cambridge University Press.

Brykczynska, G. (1993) Ethical issues in paediatric nursing. In Glasper, E.A. and Tucker, A. (eds) *Advances in Child Health Nursing*. London: Scutari.

Buck, T. (2005) *International Child Law*. London: Cavendish.

Burnett, J. (ed.) (1982) *Destiny Obscure: Autobiographies of Childhood, Education and Family from the 1820s to the 1920s*. London: Routledge.

Butler-Sloss, E. (1988) *Report of the Inquiry into Child Abuse in Cleveland 1987*. London: HMSO.

Campbell, T. (1992) The rights of the minor. In Alston, P., Parker, S. and Seymour, J. (eds) *Children, Rights and the Law*. Oxford: Clarendon Press.

Choudhry, S. and Fenwick, H. (2005) Taking the rights of parents and children seriously: confronting the welfare principle under the Human Rights Act. *Oxford Journal of Legal Studies* 25:453.

Coleman, J. and Hendry, L. (1999) *The Nature of Adolescence*. London: Routledge.

Corker, M. and Davis, J. (2000) Disabled children: invisible under the law. In Cooper, J. and Vernon, S. (eds) *Disability and the Law*. London: Jessica Kingsley.

Cunningham, H. (1991) *The Children of the Poor: Representations of Childhood since the Seventeenth Century*. Oxford: Blackwell.

Doherty, M. (2005) *Jurisprudence: The Philosophy of Law*, 4th edn. London: Old Bailey Press.

Douglas, G. (2004) *An Introduction to Family Law*, 2nd edn. Oxford: Oxford University Press.

Eekelaar, J. (1986) The emergence of children's rights. *Oxford Journal of Legal Studies* 6:161.

Eekelaar, J. (2002) Beyond the welfare principle. *Child and Family Law Quarterly* 14:237.

Elliston, S. (2007) *The Best Interests of the Child in Healthcare*. London: Routledge-Cavendish.

Feinberg, J. (1980) *Rights, Justice and the Bounds of Liberty*. Princeton: Princeton University Press.

Fionda, J. (2001) Legal concepts of childhood: an introduction. In Fionda, J. (ed.) *Legal Concepts of Childhood*. Oxford: Hart.

Fortin, J. (2003) *Children's Rights and the Developing Law*, 2nd edn. London: Butterworths.

Fortin, J. (2006) Accommodating children's rights in a post human rights era. *Modern Law Review* 69:299.

Freeman, M. (1983) *The Rights and Wrongs of Children*. London: Francis Pinter.

Freeman, M. (1997) *The Moral Status of Children*. The Hague: Martinus Nijhoff.

Gittins, D. (2004) The historical construction of childhood. In Kehily, M.J. (ed.) *An Introduction to Childhood Studies*. Buckingham: Open University Press.

Harington, J.A. (2003) Deciding best interests: medical progress, clinical judgement and the 'good family'. *Web JCLI* 3:52.

Hart, H.L.A. (1984) Are there any natural rights? In Waldron, J. (ed.) *Theories of Rights*. Oxford: Oxford University Press.

Hendrick, H. (1992) Recent findings of research in economic and social history of children and childhood. *Refresh* 15.

Hendrick, H. (1997) *Children, Childhood and English Society*. Cambridge: Cambridge University Press.

Herring, J. (1999) The welfare principle and the rights of parents. In Bainham, A., Day-Sclater, S. and Richards, M. (eds) *What is a Parent?* Oxford: Hart.

Herring, J. (2005) Farewell welfare. *Journal of Social Welfare and Family Law* 27:159.

Herring, J. (2008) *Medical Law and Ethics*, 2nd edn. Oxford: Oxford University Press.

Herring, J. (2009) *Family Law*, 4th edn. Harlow: Pearson.

Hohfeld, W. (1913) Some fundamental legal conceptions as applied to judicial reasoning. *Yale Law Journal* 23:16.

Hopkins, E. (1994) *Childhood Transformed*. Manchester: Macmillan.

Humphries, S., Mack, J. and Perks, R. (1988) *A Century of Childhood*. London: Sidgwick & Jackson.

James, A. and Prout, A. (eds) (1997) *Constructing and Reconstructing Childhood*. London: Falmer Press.

King, M. and Piper, C. (1995) *How the Law Thinks about Children*. Aldershot: Arena.

Lowe, N.V. and Douglas, G. (2006) *Bromley's Family Law*, 10th edn. Oxford: Oxford University Press.

MacCormick, N. (1982) *Legal Right and Social Democracy: Essays in Legal and Political Philosophy*. Oxford: Clarendon Press.

Mayall, B. (2002) *Towards a Sociology of Childhood*. Buckingham, PA: Open University Press.

McGlynn, C. (2006) *Families and the European Union: Law, Politics and Pluralism*. Cambridge: Cambridge University Press.

Monk, D. (2004) Childhood and the law: in whose best interests? In Kehily, M.J. (ed.) *An Introduction to Childhood Studies*. Maidenhead: Open University Press.

Moonkin, R. (1985) *In the Interests of Children*. New York: W.H. Freeman.

O'Neill, O. (1992) Children's rights and children's lives. *International Journal of Law and the Family* 6:24.

Parker, S. (1994) The best interest of the child: principles and problems. In Alston, P. (ed.) *The Best Interests of the Child: Reconciling Culture and Human Rights*. Oxford: Clarendon Press.

Pollock, L. (1983) *Forgotten Children: Parent–Child Relations from 1500–1900*. Cambridge: Cambridge University Press.

Postman, N. (1983) *The Disappearance of Childhood*. London: W.H. Allen.

Prout, A. (2005) *The Future of Childhood*. London: Routledge Falmer.

Raz, J. (1984) Legal rights. *Oxford Journal of Legal Studies* 4:1.

Reece, H. (1996) The paramountcy principle: consensus or construct? *Current Legal Problems* 49:267.

Rodham, H. (1973) Children under the law. *Harvard Educational Review* 43:487.

Smart, C., Neale, B. and Wade, A. (2001) *The Changing Experience of Childhood*. Cambridge: Polity Press.

Stainton-Rogers, W. (2001) Constructing childhood, constructing child concern. In Foley, P., Roche, J. and Tucker, S. (eds) *Children in Society*. Buckingham: Open University Press.

Steedman, C. (1990) *Childhood, Culture and Class in Britain: Margaret McMillan 1860–1931*. London: Virago.

Sumner, L.W. (2000) Rights. In La Follette, H. (ed.) *The Blackwell Guide to Ethical Theory*. Oxford: Oxford University Press.

Thompson, P. (1997) *The Edwardians: The Remaking of British Society*. London: Weidenfeld and Nicholson.

Valentine, G. (2004) *Public Space and Culture of Childhood*. Aldershot: Ashgate.

Van Beuren, G. (1995) *The International Law on the Rights of the Child*. The Hague: Martinus Nijhoff.

Wacks, R. (2006) *Philosophy of Law: A Very Short Introduction*. Oxford: Oxford University Press.

Wardle, D. (1974) *The Rise of the Schooled Society*. London: Routledge and Kegan Paul.

Williams, J. (2007) Incorporating children's rights: the divergence in law and policy. *Legal Studies* 27:261.

CHAPTER 3
Responsibility, Accountability and Negligence

Learning outcomes

By the end of this chapter you should be able to:

- Understand (and distinguish between) the legal and ethical concepts of accountability and responsibility;
- Discuss the principles of beneficence and non-maleficence and explain their interrelationship;
- Identify those situations which involve morally culpable conduct;
- Describe the ethical objectives of the law of negligence;
- Explain how the law of negligence works.

Introduction

This chapter explores why accusing, condemning and avenging has become part of daily life. Why, in other words, when care or treatment 'goes wrong' our usual response is to apportion blame, demand retribution and seek compensation. Undoubtedly, the media bear some of the responsibility for the bad press that health care receives. Its selective reporting of clinical negligence – which typically focuses on sensational claims or those which generate the highest awards – can distort the overall status of claims and errors (Runciman et al., 2007). Yet, as Harpwood (2007) points out, there is a core of truth in the media coverage and genuine public concern about the level of claims. However, it is perhaps our inability to distinguish between culpable acts and situations in which no culpability should be attributed that has most contributed to the 'epidemic of blame' in health care (Mason and Laurie, 2006, p. 295).

To understand our current blaming culture, the moral considerations that underpin tort law need to be analysed, in particular the connection between moral culpability (i.e. fault or blame) and liability in negligence law. This involves analysing the concepts of responsibility and accountability – in both their moral and legal versions – and the ethical objectives of the law of negligence. But first, two key ethical principles, notably beneficence and non-maleficence – that provide the moral foundations for the various obligations in the Nursing and Midwifery Council's (NMC's) *Code: Standards of Conduct, Performance and Ethics* (NMC, 2008) – must be outlined.

3.1 Beneficence: 'Doing Good'

Put simply, the principle of beneficence means that nurses must act in ways that benefit others. The principle of beneficence is widely understood to entail a protective duty of responsible care for others, in particular the 'weak and vulnerable' (Thompson et al., 2006), or doing 'what is best for patients' (Hope et al., 2008, p. 15).

In essence, the principle of beneficence refers to the moral importance of 'doing good' both in actions and in attitudes. It also includes values of caring such as compassion, competence, conscience, commitment, empathy and sympathy, and altruism (Hendrick, 2004, p. 72). The fundamental obligation to act positively for the benefit of others underpins the NMC Code (2008). It begins by stating: 'The people in your care must be able to trust you with their health and well-being.' Justifying that trust includes 'working with others to protect and promote the health and well-being of those in your care, their families and carers, and the wider community'.

Expressed in such broad terms, it would seem that the duty to benefit others is an ethical duty of care, which could potentially impose a very heavy moral burden on nurses – perhaps even to put the interests of patients above their own interests (Lesser, 2007, p. 109). Others, however, reject the idea that health professionals acting in a beneficent manner towards their patients are necessarily showing morally good or indeed altruistic qualities. Downie and Macnaughton (2007, p. 40), for example, maintain that the moral duty of beneficence is simply a job description. In other words, beneficence is just part of what a health professional does for a living. As such, if it is a moral duty at all, it is no different from what is expected in most jobs.

3.1.1 Defining 'benefit'?

Generally, terms such as 'well-being', 'best interests' and 'health' are used to explain the 'benefits' that nurses are expected to promote. Such words cover both physical and psychological benefits, i.e. something of positive value such as the prevention of illness, injury and disease; the restoration of health; the alleviation of suffering and the prolongation of life (Fry and Johnstone, 2008). Yet most of these terms are inherently subjective. In other words, how they are interpreted in practice will depend on an individual's particular beliefs and values. To ensure that nurses do not impose their own views of what is 'good' for a patient, another principle, namely, respect for patients' autonomy, will need to be followed (see Chapter 4). Note that the 'benefits' that nurses are expected to bestow are primarily owed to their own patients and clients. Yet they may also owe a duty of beneficence, albeit a weaker one, towards others, such as a patient's family, informal carers and also other health and social care professionals.

Activity

Think about how you must act to 'benefit' your colleagues and people in the community.

3.2 Non-Maleficence: Avoiding Harm and Risk

3.2.1 Defining harm

In broad terms, the principle of non-maleficence means that nurses have a duty not to harm patients. Normally, the principle of non-maleficence only requires *intentionally refraining from actions* that cause harm (Beauchamp and Childress, 2009, p. 151). It can therefore be described as a less morally demanding principle than beneficence, which requires positive action.

More specifically, the term 'harm' can refer to physical as well as psychological harm. As such, it could embrace almost every condition – ranging from the severe to the relatively trivial – that might cause pain, discomfort, humiliation, offence or even annoyance. In addition, delays and inconveniences can also be seen as a form of harm since they may have a significant impact on a patient's well-being (Runciman et al., 2007, p. 37). A more contested issue is whether 'harm' should be defined only by patients themselves, i.e. subjectively, or be given the meaning the patient would give it only if his wishes reflect accepted norms in society (Herring, 2008, p. 23).

3.2.2 Defining 'risk'

Because ethics is concerned with the moral duty of nurses to act in their patients' best interests, it is perhaps not surprising that the key concept in the NMC Code (2008) is *risk* rather than *harm*. Thus, for example, the section concerned with managing risk (which is supplemented by guidance on the environment of care) advises practitioners how to anticipate, avoid and reduce risk. The Code's focus on risk (rather than harm) can be partly attributed to the higher profile given to risk management in the training and work environment (Torgesen, 2008). The concept of risk also reflects the ethical notion that nurses may be morally to blame if they have exposed patients to serious or unnecessary risk even if no harm has been caused. As Lesser (2007, p. 106) explains, a health professional who has subjected a patient to unnecessary risk but without harm (i.e. there is no danger of legal action) ought nevertheless to have a 'bad conscience'. In short, ethics requires nurses not just to do no harm but also not to risk doing harm.

But as Quick notes, the term 'risk' is a much theorised and multifaceted concept that operates at a number of different and overlapping levels in the medical setting. It covers both *medical* risk, i.e. risk to patients and *professional* risk, i.e. risks of complaints and litigation (Quick, 2006, p. 33; see further pp. 22–43). Here, we use the term very simply to describe a clinical situation where 'something has gone wrong'. Note that the term 'risk' can refer to either the probability of a negative outcome or its magnitude (Beauchamp and Childress, 2009, p. 221). Either way, the perception and assessment of risk differ markedly from person to person.

3.2.3 Balancing risks and harms

The issue here is this: almost all care and treatment involves some degree of harm or risk. In short, pain, discomfort and so on, may be unavoidable. This means that if avoiding or minimising risk is prioritised it may not be possible to treat patients at all. But not do so, i.e. not to care for patients, would also cause them some harm. Deciding what cause of action most benefits patients therefore inevitably involves weighing up potential benefits and harms (and their probabilities) (Hope et al., 2008, p. 15). In some cases – for example, when the likelihood of a cure is high and side effects of treatment are minor – the balancing exercise may be straightforward. But in others, it may be by no means clear how to balance risks and possible benefits, especially if each available course of action has different types of risks (Runciman et al., 2007, p. 33).

Key points

- The duty to act beneficently applies to patients, their carers and families and the wider community.
- Non-maleficence means acting in such a way as to avoid causing harm or risk of harm.
- Balancing benefit and harm means making sure that benefits always outweigh harm.

3.3 Moral Responsibility and Accountability

The principles of beneficence and non-maleficence provide the moral foundations for the various professional obligations in the NMC Code (2008). Yet they provide little practical guidance about how nurses should act ethically in discharging their duty of care in specific situations. For such guidance the concepts of responsibility and accountability need to be understood.

3.3.1 Defining responsibility

Ordinarily, the term 'responsibility' is used to describe an action or decision for which a person can be held morally responsible. In other words, a moral judgement is made about the consequences of their behaviour; that is, we blame (or praise) them for the result or outcome of their actions etc. Put this way, moral responsibility is clearly a prerequisite for guilt and punishment or credit and reward (Young, 1991). But if blame or praise is to be 'fairly' attributed, various conditions must normally be satisfied. In particular, most people would agree that someone is only responsible for something that is 'within [their] control' (Duff, 2001). To describe a nurse as responsible in this sense is to say that she has a genuine choice about how to act; i.e.:

- She knows what she is doing (Thompson et al., 2006).
- She has acted 'freely' – that is, that she could have acted differently or made a different decision (Young, 1991).
- She has acted voluntarily – i.e. there was no coercion.
- She has the capacity to guide her actions and decisions through moral principles and ideals.
- She can distinguish between right and wrong.
- She either intended or should have foreseen the consequences of her actions (Lucas, 1993).

All the above-mentioned conditions can, of course, be satisfied to a greater or lesser extent. And in some cases too, one or several conditions might not be satisfied at all. For example, a nurse might lack the power, skill or authority to act or may be under threat or duress. According to Thompson et al. (2006, p. 84), these are (amongst others) 'excusing conditions' which should be taken into account in determining the degree of guilt that should be attributed to someone for the action etc. in question.

3.3.2 Who is a 'responsible' person?

A concept that is closely related to that of responsibility is the idea of a 'responsible person' (not least because it is the failure to act as a responsible person that makes a nurse *accountable* for her behaviour). Broadly, a 'responsible person' is someone who can be left in charge, i.e. be relied on to 'do her job'. Used in this way the word 'responsible' is an adjective, denoting a quality of character (Lucas, 1993, p. 11). For Thompson et al. (2006, p. 84), a responsible nurse is:

- Capable of acting as an independent moral agent,
- Competent to perform the task in hand,
- Has proved that she is reliable and trustworthy, and
- Acknowledges a legal or moral obligation.

Nurses work in a wide variety of health care settings. The specific competencies and skills required of a 'responsible nurse' may therefore vary considerably. Yet as NMC guidance on working with children and young people makes clear, practitioners must 'ensure that they remain competent to perform the range of nursing interventions required for the children and young people in your care'. Furthermore, they are reminded to 'use reflective practice, supervision, work-place and other forms of learning to maintain and enhance their skills and knowledge, particularly those deemed of higher risk such as the administration of medicines and invasive interventions' (NMC, 2008).

But irrespective of the specific 'job' of an individual nurse, to be responsible for something is to be accountable for it (Duff, 2001; Lucas, 1995). This perhaps explains why responsibility and accountability are widely viewed as virtually synonymous (Savage and Moore, 2004). Yet although responsibility can be inclusive of accountability, the two concepts can be differentiated in the sense that responsibility is self-reflexive (i.e. relating to oneself as a moral agent) whereas accountability relates to one's relationship with other agents.

Activity

Would you describe yourself as a responsible person? Think about times when you have not 'acted responsibly'. Why not?

3.3.3 Defining accountability

Put very simply, accountability means being answerable to someone, i.e. being able to explain yourself (Runciman et al., 2007, p. 98). In this general sense, accountability is therefore a commonplace concept – i.e. we all understand the idea that we are accountable to 'significant others', i.e. parents, children, neighbours and so on. Put another way, we sometimes have to answer the question: 'Why did you do it?' Reference to a nurse's accountability essentially begs the same question, albeit with certain moral expectations. These are that the patient and others have a moral right to an explanation of why something happened, and that the nurse has a moral duty to provide one.

Moral accountability basically means that a nurse must:

- Acknowledge the moral requirement to be answerable to patients and clients as well as groups of people such as employers, colleagues and professional regulators (such as the NMC) and society as a whole;
- Be willing and ready to accept responsibility for errors, misjudgements and negligence;
- Be prepared to change in the light of improved understanding gained from others (Hunt, 1994);
- Be committed to ensuring that the same thing does not happen again.

A practitioner's personal accountability is emphasised very forcibly in the NMC Code (2008) which states: 'as a professional you are personally accountable for actions and omissions in your practice and must always be able to justify your actions'.

3.3.4 What is a nurse accountable for?

But *what* precisely must a nurse explain? In brief, a nurse's accountability means she must justify her judgements, decisions, actions, omissions and intentions. Crucially too, she must explain the 'moral baggage' from which these 'technical or cognitive competencies' arise (Thompson et al., 2006, p. 103). The term 'moral baggage' refers to a nurse's personal attitudes, beliefs and values as well as unexamined moral assumptions. The argument is that nurses' moral baggage affects the way they relate to people. In particular, it may cause them to be uneasy or judgemental about patients' lifestyles or choices. However, because nurses have a moral duty to ensure that their own value judgements do not adversely affect the way they care for their patients, they must critically appraise their personal attitudes throughout their practice. In this inclusive sense, moral accountability is therefore a much more 'holistic' concept – one which embraces actions, omissions, etc., and the traits of 'morally competent or virtuous individuals' (Thompson et al., 2006, p. 104). Finally, it is important to point out that although accountability is something that all practitioners must accept, it should not be confused with culpability. In other words, to say that you are accountable is not to say that you are also culpable (i.e. blameworthy). This raises questions about what we mean by the concept of blame.

Key points

- Moral responsibility means accepting and carrying the burden of judgement and decisions in matters of right and wrong.
- Moral accountability means answering for one's actions, i.e. explaining why something was (or was not) done.

Activity

Think of a situation in which you could justify your action 'professionally' but not morally.

3.4 Blame

This chapter began by asking why a blaming culture has become our dominant re- sponse to treatment that has 'gone wrong'. Why, in other words, do we *assume* that if there has been a harmful outcome then it must be someone's fault? Of course, it is a truism to say that blame has a legitimate place in improving health care. Yet, if we ascribe blame inappropriately, there is a danger that the moral significance of the concept may be eroded, lost altogether or, worse still, lead to cover-ups, rather than to addressing inherent problems in health care systems (Bagian, 2002; Marx, 2001; Reason, 1997).

3.4.1 Defining blame

How, then, can moral significance be restored to the concept of blame? Or to put it an- other way, how can we learn how to properly distinguish morally relevant wrongdoing (i.e. conduct that is truly culpable) from 'accidents' for which no one is morally respon- sible? A useful starting point is to acknowledge that blame is a multilayered term; that is, it can be categorised into a number of levels. Merry and McCall Smith (2001) iden- tify five such levels (what follows is a summary of their approach (with some examples adapted)).

First-level blaming

Example 3.1

A nurse who trips and breaks a patient's radio can be 'blamed' in the sense that she has caused the radio to break.

Blame for the broken radio in this example is used to signify causal responsibility; i.e. we are simply saying that a person, by his or her actions, omissions, etc., has caused something to happen. But concluding that the person is responsible for an event – which is essentially a factual matter – implies no moral culpability or fault on his or her behalf. A person may therefore be identified as the physical cause of an event, but to have done nothing wrong in moral terms.

Second-level blaming

> **Example 3.2**
>
> In an emergency, a nurse independent prescriber wished to administer a drug to a patient. Unbeknown to her, another person had incorrectly substituted one drug for another in the appropriate section of the drug drawer. Under the distracting influence of the emergency and under acute pressure to act, the nurse drew up and administered the incorrect drug. The patient died. The nurse only discovered she had given the patient the incorrect drug when she discovered the empty ampoule. No other aspect of the nurse's treatment was deficient.

The second-level blaming is attributed for an action which falls short of a certain *absolute* standard of care. The standard is absolute in the sense that it is the one prescribed in the textbooks; that is, it sets out what *ought* to be done in the circumstances. In the above-mentioned example, because it is *not reasonable* (in an objective sense) to give the wrong drug, the nurse would probably be held liable in negligence. Yet it is claimed that she is morally blameless because this absolute standard fails to take into account the subjective state of the nurse's mind. In other words, it ignores the fact that there are empirical and theoretical data to suggest that all practitioners make mistakes in administering drugs at some time even when trying their best to avoid errors (Merry and McCall Smith, 2001, p. 134).

According to Merry and McCall Smith, the nurse's action in the above-mentioned example is not morally culpable if it is caused because she either:

a. Read the label *incorrectly* due a problem of 'mindset' (i.e. she interpreted the label as saying what she expected it to say); or
b. *Unintentionally* failed to read the label altogether (possible because of pressure of time or a momentary lapse of attention).

The reason why these are morally blameless actions is because they can be described as skill-based 'errors'. Although the term 'error' is a contested concept (Quick, 2006, p. 24), the term is used here to describe those errors that typically occur because of inattention, distraction and multitasking (for details of how various different errors are described, see Espin et al., 2006; Reason, 1990). Most importantly, although foreseeable in a general sense (that such errors will be made from time to time), such skill-based errors are essentially unavoidable even by 'competent' practitioners (Merry and McCall Smith, 2001, p. 107). As such, practitioners should not be blamed (in moral terms) although they are nevertheless likely to be found liable in negligence for such errors (Harpwood, 2007).

> **Activity**
>
> Read the report by the National Patient Safety Agency (2009) on hospital drug errors affecting children. How many children does it suggest suffer from medical errors every year? (http://www.npsa.nhs.uk)

Third-level blaming

The third-level blaming is attributed for actions that have fallen short of the standard that a *reasonable* person can be expected to reach, i.e. the way that things *are* done by reasonably competent practitioners. The assumption here is that a person has chosen to deviate from this reasonable standard (even though a safer option was available). So even allowing for the human limitations of reasonable people and even though there is no intent to cause harm, it is appropriate to attribute some degree of moral culpability – because a choice was possible. Of course, this means that a person who could not have acted otherwise – in the sense that they could not reasonably have avoided doing the act in question – remains blameless.

Using the above-mentioned example, the nurse is responsible for the third-level blame if she intentionally does not read the label – presumably because she thought it was acceptable not to given the emergency circumstances. Nevertheless, her failure is morally culpable – even if she did not appreciate the implications of her omission. Why? Because other 'genuinely reasonable nurses would read the label' (Merry and McCall Smith, 2001, p. 245).

Fourth-level blaming

The fourth-level blame attaches to actions taken by someone who knows they are 'risky' but who takes them nevertheless. Such behaviour is normally described as 'reckless'. Recklessness can be either objective or subjective. Objective recklessness asks: might a reasonable person foresee a risk of some harm occurring? Subjective recklessness requires the risk-taker herself to have some knowledge or appreciation of the relevant risk (Jefferson, 2006). Normally, subjective recklessness is essential if moral culpability is to be attributed for a harmful health care outcome.

Using the drug administration example, a nurse would be morally culpable for the fourth-level blame if she realised the risk of not reading the label but failed to read it anyway. In other words, she is subjectively reckless.

Fifth-level blaming

The last level of blame applies to those actions which are taken by someone who un-ambiguously intended to cause harm. In short, they deliberately attempt to cause harm. Clearly, behaviour in this category is undoubtedly morally culpable.

In summary, according to Merry and McCall Smith, moral culpability should only be attached to actions within levels three, four and five – i.e. the levels which depend on a person making a free choice about how to act. Yet in practice, negligence claims are typically made for actions that fall within the second-level of blame (i.e. in respect of actions that were unavoidable). The effect of this undue emphasis on blame is to promote an adversarial response, which in turns feeds upon blame. As they conclude:

> Blame is a powerful weapon. When used appropriately, and according to morally defensible be-haviour, it has an indispensable role in human affairs. Its inappropriate use, however, distorts tolerant and constructive relations between people. ... The law sometimes understands this and attributes liability appropriately. In many other cases, however, crude legal notions of negligence fail to achieve a distinction between unavoidable and inevitable mishaps (which are frequently true accidents) and faulty or culpable behaviour. Injustice is the result. (Merry and McCall, 2001, p. 248)

Key points

- Blame can be categorised into five different levels.
- Fault (in law) is not necessarily coterminous with moral culpability.

> **Activity**
>
> 1. Read Quick (2006, pp. 22–43). Do you agree with his conclusion? Explain your answer.
> 2. Think about an 'accident' at your work place. Was it unavoidable? If so, why? If not, who was to blame?

3.5 Ethical Objectives of the Law of Negligence

When things 'go wrong' in health care, redress is often sought through the legal system, usually by way of a claim for negligence. As we see below, liability in law depends on a finding of fault (which meets the legal definition of negligence). Because the law of negligence is therefore clearly linked to the apportioning of blame, it has been described as a complex set of ethical precepts about how people may, ought and ought not to behave in their dealings with others (Cane, 2006).

The main ethical objectives of the law of negligence are described in the following section.

3.5.1 Compensation – paying for the harm done

Essentially, compensation (also called 'needs provision') seeks to restore the victim to the position she would have been in had she not been injured (Stauch et al., 2006, p. 326). The compensatory principle recognises that although money cannot compensate for the loss of a loved one (or serious permanent injury), it can perhaps compensate for the loss of earning potential, higher living expenses, the cost of long-term care and so on.

The main benefits of compensation are the following: the threat of litigation may operate as a deterrent for negligent behaviour; it encourages initiatives to reduce risk and therefore enhances safety; and it leads to the establishment of guidelines by which standards of care can be measured. But obtaining compensation through the tort system is slow, traumatic and expensive (Lunney and Oliphant, 2008). Furthermore, it is not self-evident why the needs of victims of medical blunders should be favoured over the needs of victims of naturally occurring events (Pattinson, 2006, p. 91). Relevant, too, is the argument that it is unjust to prioritise compensation for the victims of medical negligence given that the money to fund compensation comes from the same limited pot of health care resources that funds the National Health Service (NHS) (Harris, 1997).

3.5.2 Deterrence – preventing future harm

The deterrent principle (or 'risk reduction') is simple: the possibility of civil sanction will cause the defendant to behave differently in the future. Deterrence theory assumes that fearing the consequences of liability – both financially and in terms of professional reputation – practitioners will reflect on their errors and take greater care to avoid inflicting harm in the future (Harpwood, 2007). Risk-management practices will also be encouraged. As an ethical objective, deterrence has limited application in health care contexts for several reasons: individual practitioners rarely pay compensation (under the doctrine of vicarious liability, it is shifted to their employers); and because in practice medical accidents are always unintended (i.e. caused inadvertently), it is difficult to see how making practitioners 'pay' can alter their behaviour (Murphy, 2007).

3.5.3 Retribution – punishing wrongdoing

Simply put, retribution (also called 'corrective justice') is about punishing wrongdoing; that is, a person who has knowingly done wrong deserves to be punished. In other words, the wrongdoer gets his 'just deserts'. Retribution is a backward-looking theory focusing on a past wrong that needs to be redressed. Many commentators now consider that criminal law and/or professional and disciplinary procedures are a more appropriate way of punishing wrongdoing in health care (Mason and Laurie, 2006; Pattinson, 2006).

Other limitations of the retributivist approach are that medical negligence is not necessarily coterminous with moral culpability and can be established even if the defendant acted 'blamelessly'; practitioners rarely pay damages themselves – the real 'defendants', i.e. those who pay compensation, are NHS employers and their insurers.

Key points

- The law of negligence is a system of ethical rules and principles of personal responsibility for conduct.
- Several competing ethical objectives underpin the law of negligence, namely, compensation, deterrence and retribution.

3.6 Legal Responsibility and Accountability

This section outlines the circumstances in which nurses can be held legally accountable for their conduct. It therefore focuses on the tort system, i.e. negligence law – the most common action in health care contexts for NHS patients seeking compensation. Because of limited space, only the substantive law will be outlined (for a more detailed analysis, see Cameron and Gumbel, 2007). Limited space also prevents a discussion of NHS complaint procedures (see McHale and Tingle, 2007, Chapter 3).

3.7 The Law of Negligence

To succeed in a negligence claim, patients must prove the following three elements:

1. A duty of care was owed to the claimant (the name for the person suing for compensation).
2. The defendant breached that duty, i.e. failed to reach the standard of practice required by the law.
3. Damage (that the law recognises) ensued, i.e. the injuries suffered were caused by that failure.

3.8 Duty of Care

3.8.1 Nurse's personal liability

Here we focus on the personal responsibility of nurses to their patients and how the law decides in what circumstances they may owe a duty of care to a wider group of people (whether they are using the health service or not). The duty of care arises in health care contexts whenever a practitioner has assumed responsibility for a patient or client. In most professional contexts, this is fairly easy to establish (Lewis, 2006). Thus, children's nurses clearly owe a duty of care to all their existing child patients in whatever setting they practise – i.e. within a child's own home, hospital, school or the community.

Less straightforward is whether a duty of care is owed in other circumstances. Does a nurse owe a duty to assist accident victims she comes across while off-duty, for example (the so-called Good Samaritan scenario)? And what duty does she owe to a patient's relatives or carers? In such situations (and others where the existence or scope of the duty is unclear), the existence of a duty of care will be determined according to guidance provided by the House of Lords in *Caparo Industries v Dickman* [1990] 2 AC 205.

According to *Caparo*, a duty of care arises when there is:

a. Foreseeability of damage,
b. Sufficient proximity between the parties, and
c. It was just and reasonable to impose a duty.

As the three limbs of the *Caparo* test are deliberately vague, it has been possible to develop the concept of a duty of care incrementally, i.e. on a case-by-case basis. In other words, by limiting the duty of care, the courts have ensured that 'socially useful activities' have not been curtailed. This policy-driven approach is usually referred to as the 'floodgates argument', i.e. the risk that recognising a duty of care might lead to a flood of negligence claims (Lunney and Oliphant, 2008, p. 144).

3.8.2 Primary liability

Also called direct liability, this type of liability refers to the responsibility of health care organisations (rather than individual practitioners) to provide a 'reasonable regime of care'. This means they must engage competent staff and provide proper and safe equipment and premises – of a standard that could properly be expected of a hospital of the size and type in question (Lewis, 2006, p. 67). Primary liability therefore enables hospitals and health authorities to be held legally responsible for organisational failures, such as defective equipment, too few suitably qualified staff, and inadequate supervision and training (see Newdick, 2005, Chapter 7).

The problem of a 'systems failure' was highlighted by the Bristol Inquiry into the standards of care given to young children (DoH, 2001). The Inquiry found that the shortcomings found at Bristol (which included paediatric care being provided on split-sites and no systematic way of monitoring clinical standards) had caused the deaths of between 30 and 35 more children under 1 year of age than might have been expected in other paediatric units (Bridgeman, 2007). *Robertson v Nottingham Health Authority* [1997] 8 Med LR 1 is another example. Here, a hospital was found liable for failing to ensure that there was a reliable communication system between doctors and nurses. As a consequence, a baby (with prenatal distress) suffered brain damage because her delivery was postponed for 6 hours.

The concept of primary liability has the potential to be widely applied and may be particularly useful as more and more tasks are devolved to nurses (that were previously performed by doctors) because of pressure on resources (Lee, 2007, p. 160). How far it will be developed by the courts is, however, difficult to predict with any certainty.

3.8.3 Vicarious liability

Although nurses are individually responsible for their own negligence, it is rare that they will have to bear the cost of any claim personally. The reason is that under the doctrine of vicarious liability their employers are sued instead. In other words, employers in the health service, e.g. NHS Trusts, or GP practices employing their own staff, are indirectly responsible for the negligent acts and omissions (clinical and non-clinical) of their employees (providing the negligence occurred in the course of employment). This means that it is crucial not just to identify a practitioner's employer but also to establish whether the act (or omission) in question was being carried out for the benefit of her employer (see further Dimond, 2008, Chapter 4, pp. 67–72).

Key points

- A duty of care is owed by nurses to their existing patients.
- Whether a duty is owed to others is determined by (a) foreseeability of damage, (b) proximity between the parties and (c) whether it is just and reasonable to impose a duty.
- Hospitals (and other provider units) can be directly liable for failing to provide a 'reasonable regime of care'.

Activity

You are shopping in a supermarket. A young child has an accident and is bleeding profusely. What would you do? What does the NMC Code say you should do? Does the law oblige you to help?

3.9 Breach of Duty

3.9.1 Setting the standard – the *Bolam/Bolitho* test

Once a duty of care has been established, a claimant has to prove that the duty of care was breached. Basically, this means proving that nurses (likewise other practitioners) have failed to reach the legal standard of care. The crucial question is therefore: what standard of care does the law require? A very general initial answer is that the law expects nurses to exercise *reasonable care and skill* in all the tasks they undertake.

The *Bolam* test
The phrase 'reasonable care and skill' was defined – in the famous case of *Bolam v Friern Hospital Management Committee* [1957] 2 All ER 118 – as that which accords with 'accepted practice', i.e. a responsible body of medical opinion. Or to put it another way, nurses will not be negligent if they have reached the 'ordinary skill of an ordinary competent nurse' doing the same kind of work. So, for example, a practice nurse working in a general practice surgery or in the community is judged by the standards of other practice nurses working in the same settings. Although *Bolam* was widely applied, it has generated much criticism (for a summary of criticisms, see Herring, 2008, pp. 96–102). In particular, it seemed to allow health professionals to set their own standard of care (without external scrutiny) and to escape liability simply by getting another practitioner to confirm that she or he would have acted as the defendant did (Pattinson, 2006, p. 74).

The *Bolitho* modification
Although this analysis of *Bolam* is perhaps a caricature (Foster, 2007, p. 94), the *Bolam* test was widely regarded as impregnable until it was challenged by the House of Lords in *Bolitho v City and Hackney Health Authority* [1997] AC 23. Put simply, *Bolitho* emphasised that courts had a proactive role and so could scrutinise 'accepted practice' (i.e. professional opinion) to ensure that it was indeed 'reasonable, had a logical basis … and that the experts had weighed up the risks and reached a defensible conclusion'.

Despite the 'new' more interventionist approach that *Bolitho* signified, it is evident from the subsequent case law that it is only very rarely that medical opinion has been dismissed as negligent (Herring, 2008; Jackson, 2006; Mason and Laurie, 2006; Newdick, 2005; see also *Smith v Southampton University Hospital NHS Trust* [2007] EWCA Civ 387).

The combined effect of *Bolam* and *Bolitho* means that:

- The standard of care applies to treatment, diagnosis and disclosure of information (Pattinson, 2006, p. 72).
- The standard of care is objective, i.e. which practitioners *ought* to reach. As such, it takes no account of 'human failings' such as a single lapse in an otherwise trouble-free career (Lee, 2007, p. 153).
- The standard of care requires those with a specialist training, e.g. nurse practitioners in neonatal care, accident and emergency nursing, and clinical nurse and theatre nurse specialists (likewise those who have consultant nurse roles), are judged according to the standards of other reasonably competent practitioners who have the same specialist training. So, for example, a nurse who prescribes drugs will be expected to comply with guidance issued by the DoH (2006) and will be judged by the standard of the experienced nurse undertaking such a role. In other words, enhanced prescribing powers not only expand responsibility but also the risk of expansion of liability (McHale and Tingle, 2007, p. 94).
- The law does not expect nurses to reach the highest level of skills but rather those of an ordinary competent practitioner.

3.9.2 Applying *Bolam/Bolitho*

Although the *Bolam* case established the legal standard of care, subsequent case law has set guidelines about how the standard should be applied in various health care contexts. The most important issues relevant to nurses are the following.

Differences of opinion

Sometimes a particular treatment or procedure can be carried out in several different ways – how then should the law decide which one is 'accepted practice'? The courts have repeatedly emphasised that they will not choose between competing views and practices to decide which one is 'best' (*Maynard v West Midlands RHA* [1985] 1 All ER 635). So the fact that a nurse does something differently from her peers is not in itself evidence of negligence (providing she can show that at least some other reasonably competent practitioners would have acted in a similar way). Because of *Bolitho*, however, she must demonstrate that her approach was one that could stand up to logical analysis.

Prevailing circumstances and conditions

It is clear that the standard of care is not fixed (even though it is objective). This means that what is considered 'reasonable care' will be affected by prevailing circumstances (Jackson, 2006). Accordingly, the standard nurses are expected to reach in an emergency – such as when a hospital is coping with a major disaster or when caring for a victim at the scene of an accident – will not be the same as that which would normally be expected (in a well-equipped intensive care unit, for example). That said, practitioners trained to deal with emergencies will be expected to reach the 'reasonable' standard of someone with such expertise. Note, too, that the law does not expect practitioners to have the benefit of hindsight – they are therefore judged according to the knowledge available at the time of the incident rather than later (*Roe v Minister of Health* [1954] 2 QB 66).

Inexperience

The law does not accept a defence of inexperience, lack of ability or lack of knowledge. The leading case on this is *Wilsher v Essex AHA* [1988] 2 WLR 557 (see below) in which several general principles about the liability of student or inexperienced staff were laid down (see also *Dejmal v Bexley HA* [1995] 6 Med LR 269), namely:

- Trainees 'learning on the job' satisfy the required standard of care if they seek help and guidance of a more experienced colleague (i.e. they are appropriately supervised).
- The standard of care must be set according to the 'post' occupied rather than the rank or status of the actual postholder and his/her personal ability. This means that a person acting in a particular capacity must exercise the skill of a reasonably competent person occupying such a post.
- Nurses who take on delegated tasks they are not qualified to carry out remain personally liable.

Scarce resources

The question of whether the standard of care can be modified to reflect available resources is clearly a timely one. Should the law, in other words, take into account staff shortages and so on? The answer is clear: the law does expect that a certain minimum level and fixed standard of care should be met despite financial constraints (Jackson, 2006, p. 134). In *Bull v Devon AHA* [1993] AC 1074, for example, there was a delay of 68 minutes before a suitably qualified doctor could deal with an emergency as a result of which a baby suffered brain damage. The health authority claimed that given available resources it had organised its maternity services as best it could. This 'defence' was rejected by the Court of Appeal – a precedent that suggests that nursing staff who fail to reach a *Bolam* standard can no more plead lack of resources than tiredness or inexperience in their defence (Lee, 2007, p. 159; see also *Ball v Wirral HA* [2003] Lloyds Rep Med 165).

Key points

- The *Bolam/Bolitho* test sets the legal standard of care.
- A nurse will normally reach the legal standard of care if she follows 'accepted practice'.
- 'Accepted practice' must be 'logical and defensible'.

Activity

How up to date does the law expect practitioners to be? (See *Crawford v Board of Governors of Charing Cross Hospital* 1953), *The Times*, 8 December 1953).

3.9.3 Guidelines/clinical governance

Guidance is commonly issued by a wide range of professional bodies, such as the Royal Colleges, General Medical Council and Nursing and Midwifery Council. Sometimes such guidance is explicitly referred to by courts (as in, for example, *Sutton v Population Services Family Planning Ltd* (1981), *The Times*, 7 November; *Re C (A Minor)* (1997) 40 BMLR 31; *Airedale NHS Trust v Bland* [1993] AC 789). Other guidance that is relevant in this context includes clinical guidelines, protocols and practice parameters – all of which are now widely disseminated throughout the NHS (usually within a clinical governance framework). The term 'clinical governance' is basically shorthand for all the processes and activities needed to guarantee 'best practice' (McSherry and Pearce, 2002). It incorporates clinical risk management and CNST (Clinical Negligence Scheme for Trusts) compliance (McHale and Tingle, 2007, p. 81). Note, finally, the role of NICE (National Institute for Health and Clinical Excellence). One of its aims is to issue guidelines in key areas of health care. Although such guidance cannot be binding on particular health care professionals, if a patient is refused treatment that has been recommended by NICE, then the practitioner could face legal action unless she can justify her actions (Herring, 2008, p. 66, and see *West Bromwich Albion v El-Safty* [2006] EWCA 1299 and http://www.nice.org.uk).

Activity

Access the National Patient Safety Agency website (http://www.npsa.nhs.uk). Which patient safety initiatives are currently most relevant to your practice?

3.9.4 The legal significance of guidelines

Although clinical guidelines and other guidance discussed above lack direct legal force, they can nevertheless have significant legal significance via the law of negligence – not least because they represent evidence of what is considered 'accepted' practice (Pattinson, 2006, p. 78). In other words, 'if something goes wrong', departing from conventional practice – which includes current guidelines – will need to be justified, bearing in mind that situations change and guidelines may not fit the current clinical setting. Put another way, the *Bolam/Bolitho* framework will apply to the creation and use of guidelines (Samanta et al., 2006; McHale and Tingle, 2007, p. 83). Whether this approach is appropriate, is, of course, another matter. Thus not all commentators are convinced by the emerging reliance on guidelines. Teff (2000, pp. 67–80), for example, suggests that they may represent a new kind of medical paternalism and may therefore divert attention from what constitutes 'health' for a particular patient. Similarly, Hurwitz (2004, pp. 1024–1028) warns against using guidelines that are, by definition, meant to have general application, and thus might not take account of the patient's particular circumstances.

Key points

- Clinical guidelines may impact on the operation of the *Bolam/Bolitho* test.
- Clinical guidelines are not a substitute for professional judgement.
- Courts will not automatically accept clinical guidelines as 'accepted practice'.
- Clinical guidelines that are based on evidence-based evaluations are likely to be considered 'accepted practice'.

3.9.5 The Compensation Act 2006

One of the ways the government hoped to deal with the so-called compensation culture was to introduce a statutory approach to the standard of care (Harpwood, 2007, p. 205). The Act did not create new law but aimed to remind judges that when they assess the standard of care they should not set it too high – otherwise they might deter socially useful activities. In a clinical context, the intention was to make sure that, for example, Good Samaritan health professionals would not be put off giving assistance for fear of being sued or because of a risk-obsessed culture (Tingle, 2007, p. 71).

3.10 Causation

3.10.1 Factual causation

The third element in a negligence claim is the causation one. There are two types of causation: *factual causation* and *legal causation*. Factual causation requires the claimant to show a historical connection between the defendant's negligence and her injuries (Lunney and Oliphant, 2008, p. 211). In theory, proving that the defendant's breach of duty caused (or materially contributed to) the claimant's injuries should be relatively easy to establish since the standard of proof is the civil one, namely, the balance of probabilities, i.e. that it was more likely than not or at least a 51% chance that the negligent conduct caused the injury (Lewis, 2006, p. 254). Yet case law on causation has consistently shown how this element is, in practice, the most difficult hurdle for claimants to overcome.

Lewis (2006, pp. 321–342) explains why:

- The aetiology of medical conditions is notoriously complex and obscure;
- The position may be complicated by the presence of an underlying illness or pre-existing vulnerabilities;
- The problem of ascertaining exactly what was done in the course of treatment;
- The difficulty of securing expert evidence;
- The 'sad fact of life' that, as is not uncommon, vital records go 'missing'.

It is perhaps not surprising that the law reports are full of cases where the defendant has succeeded on some causation argument or other (Lewis, 2006, p. 229). That said, in some cases the so-called 'but for' test works to favour the claimant.

The 'but for' test

The 'but for' test is the usual starting point for establishing negligence. According to this test, claimants simply need to show that 'but for' the defendant's conduct they would not have been injured. For example, in *Edler v Greenwich and Deptford Hospital Management Committee* (1953), *The Times*, 7 March, an 11-year-old girl became ill with abdominal pains and vomiting. Her father took her to hospital where she was examined by a casualty doctor who found nothing wrong and sent her home. The following day she returned, when she was found to have a ruptured and gangrenous appendix. She died. The casualty doctor was found liable for failing to diagnose appendicitis – a misdiagnosis which led to the girl's death. The test clearly therefore works well in straightforward cases but not in the following types of cases.

Challenges to the 'but for' test

- **The injury would have been caused anyway:** In *Barnett v Chelsea and Kensington HMC* [1968] 1 All ER 1068, a night watchman had gone to hospital with abdominal pains after drinking tea. The casualty doctor told him to go home (without examining him). He later died. His wife sued, but even though the court held the doctor had breached his duty of care, the claim failed. Why? The negligence did not cause the death, which was due to arsenic poisoning. In other words, even if the doctor had examined him, there was nothing he could have done to save his life (see also *Kay v Ayrshire & Arran HB* [1987] 2 All ER 417, where scientific evidence was unable to show that the deafness suffered by a 2-year-old boy was caused by a massive overdose of penicillin, 300 000 units instead of 10 000, that he had been given).
- **Several possible causes:** Here the problem is that there is no definitive answer to the question whether the injury would have been caused 'but for' the defendant's conduct – i.e. the reply is 'we don't know' or 'we don't know for certain'. In short, the claimant's injuries could have been caused by several factors unrelated to and irrespective of the defendant's negligence.

This was the problem facing Martin Wilsher (*Wilsher v Essex AHA* [1998] AC 1074). In that case it was clear that a doctor had negligently administered excess oxygen – inserted into a vein rather than an artery. However, even though it was well known that this could cause blindness, there were several other possible causes of blindness in premature babies. With so many potential competing causes, the scientific evidence linking the negligence with the harm was at best ambivalent and at worst inconclusive. Martin, therefore, lost his case – he was unable to prove the negligence caused (or materially contributed to) his blindness.

- **Loss of a chance:** The claim in 'loss of chance' cases is that the defendant's failure to treat has denied the patient a chance of recovery or at the very least a better medical result. These so-called lost opportunity cases are especially problematic for claimants because they cover cases where a cure is uncertain despite proper treatment. Yet as Lewis notes, not only are such claims very common but the case law is exceptionally complex (Lewis, 2006, p. 255, and see *Hotson v East Berkshire HA* [1987] AC 750; *Gregg v Scott* [2005] UKHL 2).

  In brief, a claimant will only succeed if she can show that it is more likely than not that her injuries would have been avoided if the defendant had not been negligent.

3.10.2 Legal causation

The final hurdle in a negligence claim is legal causation. Briefly, this requires the claimant to show that her injuries were 'reasonably foreseeable', i.e. that they were not too remote. In the vast majority of claims, the foreseeability test is easy to establish. Yet sometimes a consequence may be considered too remote (and so not the responsibility of the defendant) because the chain of causation has been broken by some intervening event. The courts may also – for financial or policy reasons – refuse to recognise a certain type of injury. This explains why so-called secondary victims, i.e. those who 'witnessed' exceptionally horrifying negligent conduct, have only relatively recently been able to obtain compensation for psychiatric disorders (commonly referred to as 'nervous shock'). Such claims are now recognised – although strict criteria have to be met, i.e. the claimant must be suffering a psychiatric injury going beyond the normal ambit of grief, fear or distress (see e.g. *Tredget and Tredget v Bexley HA* [1994] 5 Med LR 178, and see Khoury, 2006, for a detailed analysis of causation in medical claims).

Finally, a brief note about what a claimant may be compensated for – the overall aim of compensation being that it should be 'fair and reasonable' given the injury suffered. Damages may be awarded for:

- Pain and suffering (i.e. from the injury itself or consequential treatment),
- Loss of amenity (i.e. the loss of faculty or function),
- Expenses incurred as a result of the injuries,
- Loss of earnings, and
- Future losses.

Note also that compensation can be reduced if the claimants are partly at fault – this is called contributory negligence (see further McGregor, 2009).

Key points

- Factual causation means that claimants must prove, on the balance of probabilities, that the breach of duty caused (or materially contributed to) their injuries.
- Legal causation means that claimants can be compensated for injuries that are 'reasonably foreseeable'.

3.11 Reform

The major criticisms of the current system were clearly identified in a comprehensive study by the Chief Medical Officer (DoH, 2003). In particular, the law was said to be complex, unfair, slow and costly. It also discouraged the reporting of errors. It is therefore no surprise that the vast majority of claims never come to trial but are settled out of court (Lewis, 2006). Several options were considered by the Chief Medical Officer, e.g. a no-fault system (as exists in New Zealand). However, it was the proposals for a redress scheme which were eventually adopted (NHS Redress Act 2006). Briefly, the Act covers NHS liability to compensate patients up to £20 000. Redress may include compensation, an explanation, an apology and a report on how to prevent similar cases arising in the future (for an overview of the Act and other possible options, see Harpwood, 2007, Chapter 6).

Case study

Amy is a theatre nurse. One day, when there is a shortage of appropriately qualified nurses available, she is asked to perform a procedure that she has seen many times, but never carried out herself. Normally, she would not have been asked to do so, but given staffing levels and her fear of being thought incompetent, she goes ahead.

Regrettably, things go badly wrong and the patient, Betty (aged 10), suffers not just more pain that would normally be the case but also long-term harm.

Is Amy to blame for the harm Betty suffers and is she likely to be found liable for negligence?

3.11.1 Inexperience

Moral and professional responsibility

In failing to acknowledge that she was not competent to carry out the procedure, Amy has clearly broken the ethical principles of non-maleficence and beneficence. Together they impose (a) a duty to safeguard and promote Betty's well-being and cause her no harm, and (b) a duty not to undertake tasks that she is not qualified to carry out.

Amy should therefore have either (a) refused to perform the procedure or (b) made sure that she asked an appropriately qualified person to check that she had done it correctly.

So, is Amy to blame? There is little doubt that Amy has not acted as a 'responsible person' in performing an expanded or advanced role. It would seem therefore that she is morally culpable for the 'third-level' blame. In other words, she has made a decision to deviate from the standard that a 'reasonable' practitioner can be expected to reach. Thus, even if she did not intend to cause Betty harm, she is nevertheless morally responsible – at least to some degree – for the consequences of her actions.

Note that Amy has also breached the NMC Code (2008). It states that practitioners must 'recognise and work within the limits of their competence'. They must also 'have the knowledge and skills for safe and effective practice when working without direct supervision'.

The final issue to address is the responsibility of the health professional who delegated the task to Amy. Assuming she was an appropriately qualified nurse, she has both a moral and a professional responsibility to 'delegate effectively' (NMC, 2008). What this means is that she must 'establish that anyone she delegates to is able to carry out her instructions' and that they are 'supervised and supported'. Any failure to do so means that she remains personally accountable and could have her fitness to practise brought into question (NMC, 2008).

Legal responsibility

Applying the three elements in negligence law, we need to consider the following:

a. *Does Amy have a duty of care?*
Amy clearly has a duty of care to Betty, an existing patient.

b. *Has Amy breached the duty of care?*
Amy clearly cannot claim her inexperience as a defence. Betty is entitled to receive a reasonable standard of care. If Amy was in any doubt about her competence, she should at the very least have called for assistance – in which case the fact that she had called for help would mean that she reached the *Bolam/Bolitho* standard. Accordingly, she would not be personally liable as the law allows inexperienced staff to 'learn on the job' – but only if they rely on supervision when carrying out new or unfamiliar tasks (see the *Wilsher* case).
   Note that the person who delegated the task to Amy could be legally responsible if she knew (or ought to have known) that she was not competent to perform it.

c. *Has Amy caused (or materially contributed to) the harm Betty has suffered?*
There is no doubt that Amy has caused (both factually and legally) the harm Betty has suffered; i.e. her injuries are 'reasonably foreseeable'.

3.11.2 Staff shortages

Moral and professional responsibility

If lack of resources jeopardises the provision of safe and appropriate care, then again the principles of beneficence and non-maleficence come into play. At the very least they require Amy to follow the NMC Code on managing risk as well as guidance on the environment of care (NMC, 2008). Both of these identify procedures that must be followed – in particular, the obligation to inform someone in authority – if a patient's care is at risk. There is no evidence that Amy did this or even asked for help. Accordingly, she would have to justify the failure to follow required procedures.

3.11.3 Legal liability

The factors that would be considered in deciding whether Amy is personally liable include (a) whether she had informed her manager that because of pressure of work (caused by staff shortages) she could not provide a reasonable standard of care; (b) whether someone should have supervised her; (c) whether the procedure could have been postponed; and (d) whether the incident was reasonably foreseeable.

   Depending on the answers to the above, it is possible that instead of Amy being personally liable, her employers are directly liable – for failing to provide a safe working environment by, e.g. not monitoring work levels regularly and not ensuring that there were enough qualified staff to provide a reasonable standard of care.

3.12 The Relationship between Law and Ethics

In this last section, the legal and ethical concepts of responsibility and accountability are briefly compared.

3.12.1 Similarities between law and ethics

- **Common vocabulary:** The concept of fault which suggests that moral culpability (i.e. blameworthy conduct) underpins terms such as duty of care and reasonableness. Other common concepts are personal responsibility and accountability.

- **Common functions:** These include prescribing and defining 'acceptable behaviour' and setting standards of care. The ethical objectives of the law of negligence, i.e. deterrence, are also reflected in professional codes of ethics.
- **Similar outcomes:** Practitioners who fail to reach acceptable standards can be sued and/or face disciplinary action.
- **Blame:** In attributing blame, both law and ethics seek to distinguish conduct that should attract legal or professional sanction and conduct that is 'unavoidable' and therefore blameless.

3.12.2 Differences between law and ethics

- **Duty of care:** The ethical duty of care is wider than the legal duty. Health professionals may, for example, have a moral duty to act as 'Good Samaritans' but legally have no responsibility to do so.
- **Standard of care:** The legal standard of care, which aims to set a minimum level of competence which practitioners must not fall below, is lower than the ethical standard, which aims for the best possible level of care.
- **Harm:**
  - If causation (factual and legal) is not proved, there is no legal liability even if a practitioner has breached his/her duty of care. But a practitioner may be morally and professionally accountable even if a patient is not harmed.
  - Only certain types of harm can be compensated for in law, i.e. those that are reasonably foreseeable. But both morally and professionally, practitioners are accountable for all the harm they cause.

References

Bagian, J.P. (2002) *VHA National Patient Safety Improvement Handbook*. Washington, DC: Department of Veterans Affairs, Veterans Health Administration.

Beauchamp, T.L. and Childress, J.F. (2009) *Principles of Biomedical Ethics*, 6th edn. Oxford: Oxford University Press.

Bridgeman, J. (2007) *Parental Responsibility, Young Children and Healthcare Law*. Cambridge: Cambridge University Press.

Cameron, C. and Gumbel, E.A. (2007) *Clinical Negligence: A Practitioner's Handbook*. Oxford: Oxford University Press.

Cane, P. (2006) *Atiyah's Accidents, Compensation and the Law*, 7th edn. Cambridge: Cambridge University Press.

Dimond, B. (2008) *Legal Aspects of Nursing*, 5th edn. Harlow: Pearson.

DoH (2001) *Bristol Royal Infirmary Enquiry: Learning from Bristol*. London: DoH.

DoH (2003) *Making Amends: A Consultation Paper Setting out Proposals for Reforming the Approach to Clinical Negligence in the NHS*. London: DoH.

DoH (2006) *Improving Patients' Access to Medicine: A Guide to Implementing Nurse and Pharmacist Independent Prescribing within the NHS*. London: DoH.

Downie, R.S. and Macnaughton, J. (2007) *Bioethics and the Humanities*. New York: Routledge-Cavendish.

Duff, R.A. (2001) *Punishment, Communication and Community*. New York: Oxford University Press.

Epsin, S., Levinson, W. and Regehr, G. (2006) Error or act of God: a study of patients' and operating room team members' perceptions of error definition, reporting and disclosure. *Surgery* 139(1):6.

Foster, C. (2007) Negligence: the legal perspective. In Tingle, J. and Cribb, A. (eds) *Nursing Law and Ethics*, 3rd edn. Oxford: Blackwell.

Fry, S.T. and Johnstone, M.J. (2008) *Ethics in Nursing Practice: A Guide to Ethical Decision Making*. Oxford: Blackwell.

Harpwood, V. (2007) *Medicine, Malpractice and Misapprehension*. Abingdon: Routledge-Cavendish.

Harris, J. (1997) The injustice of compensation for victims of medical accidents. *BMJ* 314:1821.

Hendrick, J. (2004) *Law and Ethics: Foundations in Nursing and Health Care*. Cheltenham: Nelson Thornes.

Herring, J. (2008) *Medical Law and Ethics*, 2nd edn. Oxford: Oxford University Press.

Hope, T., Savulescu, J. and Hendrick, J. (2008) *Medical Ethics and Law: The Core Curriculum*, 2nd edn. Edinburgh: Elsevier.

Hunt, G. (1994) *Ethical Issues in Nursing*. London: Routledge.

Hurwitz, B. (2004) How does evidence based guidance influence the determination of medical negligence? *BMJ* 329:1024.

Khoury, L. (2006) *Uncertain Causation in Medical Liability*. Oxford: Hart.

Jackson, E. (2006) *Medical Law: Text, Cases and Materials*. Oxford: Oxford University Press.

Jefferson, M. (2006) *Criminal Law*. Harlow: Pearson.

Lee, R. (2007) Responsibility, liability and scarce resources. In Tingle, J. and Cribb, A. (eds) *Nursing Law and Ethics*, 3rd edn. Oxford: Blackwell.

Lesser, H. (2007) An ethical perspective: negligence and moral obligations. In Tingle, J. and Cribb, A. (eds) *Nursing Law and Ethics*, 3rd edn. Oxford: Blackwell.

Lewis, C. (2006) *Clinical Negligence*. London: Tottel.

Lucas, J.R. (1995) *Responsibility*. Oxford: Clarendon Press.

Lunney, M. and Oliphant, K. (2008) *Tort Law: Text and Materials*, 3rd edn. Oxford: Oxford University Press.

Marx, D. (2001) *Patient Safety and the 'Just Culture': A Primer for Health Care Executives*. New York: Columbia University.

Mason, J.K. and Laurie, G.T. (2006) *Mason and McCall Smith's Medical Law and Ethics*, 7th edn. Oxford: Oxford University Press.

McGregor, H. (2009) *McGregor on Damages*, 18th edn. London: Sweet & Maxwell.

McHale, J. and Tingle, J. (2007) *Law and Nursing*, 3rd edn. London: Butterworth Heinemann.

McSherry, R. and Pearce, P. (2002) *Clinical Governance: A Guide to Implementation for Healthcare Professionals*. Oxford: Blackwell Science.

Merry, A.F. and McCall Smith, A. (2001) *Errors, Medicine and the Law*. Cambridge: Cambridge University Press.

Murphy, J. (2007) *Street on Torts*, 12th edn. Oxford: Oxford University Press.

Newdick, C. (2005) *Who Should We Treat?* 2nd edn. Oxford: Oxford University Press.

NMC (2008) *The Code: Standards of Conduct, Performance and Ethics for Nurses and Midwives*. London: NMC.

Pattinson, S.D. (2006) *Medical Law and Ethics*. London: Sweet & Maxwell.

Quick, O. (2006) Outing medical errors: questions of trust and responsibility. *Medical Law Review* 14(1):22.

Reason, J. (1990) *Human Error*. New York: Cambridge University Press.

Reason, J. (1997) *Managing the Risks of Organisational Accidents*. Aldershot: Ashgate.

Runciman, B., Merry, A. and Walton, M. (2007) *Safety and Ethics in Healthcare: A Guide to Getting It Right*. Aldershot: Ashgate.

Samanta, J., Mello, M., Foster, C. and Tingle, J. (2006) The role of clinical guidelines in medical litigation. *Medical Law Review* 14(3):321.

Savage, J. and Moore, L. (2004) *Interpreting Accountability: An Ethnographic Study of Practice Nurses, Accountability and Multidisciplinary Team Decision Making in the Context of Clinical Governance*. London: Royal College of Nurses.

Stauch, M., Wheat, K. and Tingle, J. (2006) *Text, Cases and Materials on Medical Law*, 3rd edn. Abingdon: Routledge-Cavendish.

Teff, H. (2000) Clinical guidelines and medical practice. In Freeman, M. (ed.) *Law and Medicine*. Oxford: Oxford University Press.

Thompson, I.E., Melia, K.M., Boyd, K.M. and Horsburgh, D. (2006). *Nursing Ethics*, 5th edn. Edinburgh: Elsevier.

Tingle, J. (2007) The policy dimension: the legal environment of the new NHS. In McHale, J. and Tingle, J. (eds) *Law and Nursing*, 3rd edn. Edinburgh: Elsevier.

Torgesen, I. (2008) Risk management. *Nursing Times* 104:17.

Young, R. (1991) The implications of determinism. In Singer, P. (ed.) *A Companion Guide to Ethics*. Oxford: Blackwell.

CHAPTER 4
Autonomy and Consent

Learning outcomes

By the end of this chapter you should be able to:

- Discuss the principle of autonomy and its practical implications;
- Demonstrate an understanding of how to respect patients' autonomy;
- Consider the role of paternalism;
- Critically reflect on the pre-eminence of autonomy;
- Describe the legal principles that underpin the law of consent.

Introduction

The principle of autonomy is now so widely accepted as ethically important that it barely needs an introduction. Similarly, the claim that 'informed' consent is the legal expression of patients' human right to have their autonomy respected is so endlessly repeated that it has been described as the most hackneyed theme in health care (Manson and O'Neill, 2007, p. 183). Yet it is only in the last few decades that autonomy and informed consent have become such dominant concepts. So what does it mean to be an autonomous person? And how can patients' autonomy be respected in practice? In addition to these fundamental questions, this chapter considers whether the 'triumph' of autonomy has encouraged such elaborate consent requirements and impossibly high legal standards that they are routinely ignored in practice. Is it time, in short, to rethink the concept of informed consent or at the very least to question its pre-eminence?

Of course, these kinds of questions have important ethical and legal implications for all patients. Yet in relation to children and young people, they are perhaps even more contentious – prompting us to reconsider the nature and scope of parental decision-making. Current thinking about when adolescents should be able to make their own decisions – to give consent, and, more controversially, to refuse it – may also need to be reassessed. Not surprisingly, it is these aspects of autonomy that have been the most challenging for the courts.

4.1 Autonomy

4.1.1 What is autonomy?

The word 'autonomy' comes from the Greek: *autos* (self) and *nomos* (rule or law). It is commonly defined very broadly as self-determination, i.e. the idea that we should have the right to decide how to run our own lives and make our own critical life decisions (Faden and Beauchamp, 1986, p. 54). But despite the concept's high profile in contempor-ary health care, a more precise definition of its precise nature and scope remains elusive (Beauchamp and Childress, 2009, p. 99). Thus, according to Dworkin (1988, p. 6), the concept has been equated with liberty, dignity, integrity, individuality, self-knowledge and critical reflection. Other writers have associated autonomy with 'privacy', voluntariness, choosing one's own moral position and accepting responsibility for one's choices (Faden and Beauchamp, 1986). What emerges from these various definitions is nevertheless the idea that, whether autonomy is valued intrinsically or instrumentally, it is valued because it protects individual choice and with it individual independence (see Manson and O'Neill, 2007, p. 19; and Beauchamp and Childress, 2009, Chapter 4 for a detailed analysis of autonomy).

4.1.2 The concept of children's autonomy

Although the general importance of autonomy has long been recognised, the claim that children, as human beings, should, like adults, have the right to lead their own lives according to their own conception of a 'worthwhile' life is much more recent (Lindley, 1989, p. 75). The overriding importance of children's right to autonomy was asserted by the early child liberationists writing in the 1970s (e.g. Foster and Freed, 1972; Holt, 1974). But it was Farson who expressed this idea most forcibly: 'the issue of self-determination is at the heart of children's liberation...in fact the acceptance of the child's right to self-determination is fundamental to all rights to which children are entitled' (Farson, 1974, p. 27).

This 'extreme' version of child liberation is little supported today – not least because it seems to ignore the realities of younger children's physical dependence on their parents (Fox Harding, 1997). Nevertheless, although few commentators now claim complete personal autonomy for *all* children, there is near unanimity amongst writers that as children mature they should have more extensive rights to self-determination (Fortin, 2003, p. 19). Certainly, the idea that children who are able to form their own views and express them freely should have a right 'to be heard' is now widely acknowledged. Indeed, such a right is recognised by Article 12 of the UN Convention on the Rights of the Child (CRC) 1989 (see Chapter 2). Allowing a child's wishes to be determinative is, however, another matter altogether.

It seems then that the concept of children's autonomy needs to be clarified. Does it mean that children should have greater rights to participate in decision-making, i.e. to be consulted and have their wishes 'taken seriously'? Or does it mean that their autonomous decisions should always be respected, i.e. that their choices must be accepted by health professionals whatever the outcome? These questions are addressed below when we consider the role of paternalism.

Activity

Compare the Nursing and Midwifery Council's (NMC) approach to children's autonomy. See *Advice for Nurses Working with Children and Young People*; NMC, 2008 (http://www.nmc-uk.org/), with the General Medical Council's (GMC), *0–18 Years: Guidance for All Doctors*; GMC, 2007 (http://www.gmc.uk.org).

4.1.3 Respect for autonomy

In health care ethics, it is the principle of respect for autonomy to which writers most often refer (e.g. Hope et al., 2008). Respect for autonomy means treating patients as persons with rights and not as objects of care. This involves discussing proposed treatment with them in an open and honest way and 'taking their autonomous choices seriously and by not overriding or ignoring them' (Cribb, 2007, p. 23). As the NMC Code (2008) makes clear, 'Treat people as individuals and respect their dignity' and later, 'You must uphold people's right to be fully involved in decisions about their care.' The Code also reminds practitioners that they must 'respect and support people's rights to accept or decline treatment'. Such a right can, however, only be exercised by patients who can act autonomously. And as we see below, even if young people are capable of acting autonomously, their right to decide what treatment to accept or refuse may be overridden.

4.1.4 What is an autonomous person?

The following conditions are usually regarded as essential for people's actions and decisions to be autonomous, i.e. genuinely their own.

Liberty

The term 'liberty' means that a person makes decisions 'voluntarily', i.e. free from unwanted interference and controlling influences. This means that patients should not be coerced or manipulated into accepting treatment they do not want. Yet as Elliston (2007, p. 71) reminds us, our thought processes, behaviour and actions are inevitably subject to various external and internal influences. In other words, in so far as we are all the product of our genetic and biological make-up and our environment, our ability to be free of 'controlling influences' can never be absolute. Hence, what we really mean – when we describe ourselves as autonomous – is that we have a 'substantial degree of liberty' so that we can behave in a self-governing way.

Capacity (or competence)

The capacity to make decisions essentially means the ability to make evaluations about what kind of life we want and what we think is best for us (Hope et al., 2008, p. 40). Where children are concerned, one of the most ethically contentious questions is when children have capacity, i.e. develop the cognitive and evaluative skills to make choices that others should respect (providing they are rational, see below). There is a vast literature on the subject of children's capacity and ability to understand information about diagnoses, procedures, risks and so on. Only a summary can be provided here (see further Alderson and Montgomery, 1996, Chapter 3; Fortin, 2003, 2006). There is nevertheless some common ground:

- Children's abilities to make medical decisions are routinely underestimated (Alderson and Montgomery, 1996).
- Children mature at different rates. Furthermore, competence depends not only on maturity and social circumstances of the person making the decision but also on the content and context of the decision in question (Fortin, 2003, p. 74).
- The ability to think objectively and understand other viewpoints (likewise to cope with abstract concepts) develops with age (Coleman and Hendry, 1999).
- Autonomy for children must be 'developmentally appropriate'; i.e. for a preschool child it means being able to express choices (e.g. about food); for adolescents it encompasses much wider 'freedoms', such as to pursue chosen social interests (Axford, 2008, p. 21).
- Whereas the concept of moral relativism is not available for the 12-year-old, by the age of 14 or 15, the adolescent is able to think critically and pragmatically (Coleman and Hendry, 1999).

Rational evaluation

As we have noted above, the ability to make evaluations is an essential element in capacity. Demanding that those evaluations are rational simply means that they are consistent with a person's 'life plans'. As Hope et al. (2008, p. 41) explain, there are three components of rational evaluation, namely, (1) it is based on correct understanding of the relevant facts, (2) the information (in particular various options available) is evaluated without making a relevant error of logic and (3) the person has been able to imagine situations and feelings and to relate all these to the making of the decision.

Key points

- The principle of autonomy implies that people have the freedom to decide how to run their lives.
- The concept of children's autonomy can be understood in several ways, e.g. a right to decide whether to accept or refuse treatment, or a right to participate in decision-making, i.e. be consulted.
- Autonomy for children refers to their evolving capacity to make informed choices.

4.2 Respecting and Enhancing Children's Autonomy

This section focuses on aspects of the consent process that are relevant to all child patients. In other words, it covers not just older children and adolescents who have the capacity to act autonomously but also those who lack such capacity but who nevertheless have a right to participate in decision-making.

4.2.1 Communication

The word 'communication' is a blanket term that covers a diverse range of actions and behaviours. Widely recognised as a complex two-way collaborative process, the focus is now on how to ensure that communication is 'effective' (Godfrey, 2008). It has also been claimed to be the single most important way of securing a patient's cooperation and willingness to participate in treatment (Thompson et al., 2006). Noting the importance of being attentive to the particular needs of children and young people (and their parents), NMC guidance advises that effective communication involves finding out what they want and need to know, what issues are important to them, and what opinions and fears they have about their health. As such, practitioners must get to know their child patients as individuals and communicate with them *directly*. They must also be prepared to be flexible and patient and to use play or other means of communication if appropriate (see also GMC, 2007, paras 14–21, guidance on communication with young people).

Much of the recent guidance on communication with children and young people builds on research that has shown that when children acquire knowledge about their condition, treatment and prognosis, they are more willing to cooperate with treatment, they understand better when and why to take drugs, they endure painful treatments more patiently and recover better (Alderson, 2000; Tates and Meeuwesen, 2001). Research has also highlighted how health professionals need to identify ways in which they can facilitate communication by, for example, acknowledging children's need for privacy and reassurance that their confidentiality will be respected (Moules and Ramsay, 1998, pp. 278–280). For others, however, the key to effective communication is a 'listening and attentive culture' where children can be listened to at any time and where listening is 'focused', i.e. involves eye contact, not interrupting, and reflecting (by summarising the speaker's thoughts to clarify meaning, Butts and Rich, 2005, p. 241).

4.2.2 Giving information

Without accurate and accessible information, patients cannot make meaningful and rational choices. But recognising the ethical importance of providing information and agreeing precisely what should be disclosed are quite another matter. Much of the debate on information disclosure focuses on deciding *what* information should be made available (particularly side effects and risks). And while practitioners are not expected to inform their patients about *everything* which they could inform them, the moral requirement to provide 'sufficient' or 'adequate' information is now rarely questioned (Manson and O'Neill, 2007, p. 29). That children too have a right to information is acknowledged by Article 13 of the United Nations Convention on the Rights of the Child 1989. It grants children the right to express, seek and receive information in any medium they wish.

The concept of 'adequate' information in relation to children and young people means that practitioners should explain what needs to be done and why, and whether there are any choices to be made (NMC, 2008). In other words, this includes information (that is easy to understand and appropriate to the child's age and maturity) about the child's:

- Condition,
- The purpose of investigations and treatments (and what they involve, i.e. pain and stays in hospital),
- Chances of success,
- Who is responsible for (and involved in) their care, and
- Their right to change their mind or to ask for a second opinion (GMC, 2007).

Most importantly, guidance from both the NMC and GMC emphasises that whatever information is provided, it must be explained honestly. In addition, practitioners must check that the information is understood.

4.2.3 Facilitating children's participation in decision-making

Even though children may lack the capacity to act autonomously, their right to participate in decision-making is underpinned by Article 12 of the CRC. The word 'participation' is necessarily a multilayered concept, involving many different processes (see, e.g. Sinclair, 2004). According to Alderson and Montgomery (1996), there are four levels at which children can participate. These include being informed, expressing a view, influencing the decision and being the decider. But here we focus briefly on the ways in which children's participation can, in practice, be facilitated – the aim ultimately being to 'empower them' (NMC, 2008). The most effective mechanisms for enhancing and encouraging participation include the following (Franklin and Sloper, 2005):

- **Clarity and shared understanding:** Tokenism and misunderstandings are likely unless the purpose, objectives, parameters and possible outcomes of participation are made clear (Sinclair, 2004).
- **Staff training and skills development:** The importance of changing attitudes about childhood and adolescence – particularly concerning consent, competence, and the idea of partnership between health professionals and their patients – has been highlighted in several studies (Alderson and Montgomery, 1996; Beresford and Sloper, 1999).
- **Organisational culture, systems and structures:** Acknowledging that the culture and structure of an organisation can impact on children's ability to participate may require a fundamental reappraisal of attitudes, procedures and styles of work across all levels.

Activity

Consider how you apply the values that have been identified in the 'Values for Integrated Working with Children and Young People', 2007 (available from Children's Working Network: http://www.childrensworkforce.org.uk).

Key points

Respecting children's autonomy requires:

- Effective communication,
- Providing 'adequate' information in an honest way, and
- Facilitating children's participation in decision-making.

4.3 Challenging the Pre-Eminence of Autonomy

The principle of respect for autonomy has fundamentally changed attitudes towards the health professional–patient relationship over the past few decades – not least by making it more equal and patient-centred (Hope et al., 2008, p. 40). Notwithstanding the significance of these developments and the undisputed importance of autonomy, some commentators now question whether it should be the sole or primary ethical principle (for a summary, see Herring, 2008, pp. 173–175; see also Foster, 2009).

Here are a few of the challenges to the 'triumph' of autonomy.

4.3.1 Not all autonomous choices are 'worthwhile'

The word 'worthwhile' is used here to reflect claims made by some critics that autonomous choices do not automatically deserve respect. Keown, for example, considers that autonomy merits respect only if it is exercised in accordance with a framework of 'sound moral values'. He asks, therefore, why choices that are 'patently immoral' or are clearly 'inconsistent with well-being and human flourishing merit respect' (Keown, 2002). The difficulty with this argument is, of course, that concepts such as 'well-being' and 'flourishing' can be defined in many different ways (see, e.g. Hope et al., 2008, Chapter 3). Who then should decide what is the 'correct' definition?

4.3.2 Other ethical principles are equally important

Another challenge claims that the excessively individualistic emphasis on autonomy has resulted in other equally important ethical principles, such as justice and beneficence, being overlooked (Jackson, 2006, p. 187). Most importantly, however, it is suggested that it has led to a far more fundamental value, notably *trust* between health professionals and their patients, being eroded (O'Neill, 2002). That trust is the cornerstone to better patient care is clearly acknowledged in the revised NMC Code (2008), which begins by reminding nurses and midwives that 'the people in your care must be able to trust you with their health and well-being'. There is a danger, too, that because of the pre-eminence of autonomy the pursuit of community goals may be ignored. For example, allowing parents to refuse to have their children vaccinated (without medical reason) may increase the risk to other children in the community. In other words, public health policies can be undermined if their implementation depends on individual consent (O'Neill, 2003, p. 5; see also Quick, 2006).

4.3.3 Autonomous decision-making – ritual or reality?

Briefly, the argument here is that unless health professionals are sure that patients – whether adults or children – fully understand all the important issues surrounding treatment, 'consent giving' may be a 'meaningless charade'. As Herring notes, following a diagnosis and suggestion of treatment, very few patients will disagree with the proposal. They may feel, for example, that they have no real choice or are weaker, less articulate, more malleable and so may have their autonomy 'used against them' (Herring, 2008, p. 177).

A similar point is forcibly made by Manson and O'Neill (2007). Their arguments are complex and what follows is a very brief summary. In tracing the development of the concept of informed consent, they acknowledge that in the name of respecting autonomy there has been a huge expansion of consent requirements in the last few decades – i.e. standards of disclosure are more exacting; demands for more explicit and more specific consent are more widely endorsed; and finally, ever more elaborate consent forms are increasingly devised and required. Yet many of developments have focused rather narrowly on what is presumed to be ethically important, namely, 'information transfer' – i.e. health professionals disclosing information about certain things, such as risks and benefits of treatment.

However, Manson and O'Neill claim that this model of communication (which focuses on *what is said*) is much more likely to baffle, mislead and manipulate patients. Why? Put simply, it is because this approach ignores some of the most basic essential elements of 'successful communication', i.e. those aimed at sharing information intelligibly, feasibly and relevantly with the patient to build up trust. They propose, therefore, that we need to focus less on adopting ever more elaborate and prescriptive approaches to the way consent is sought, given and refused and more on *how* we can communicate more successfully (see further Chapters 3 and 4).

Activity

Do you think the emphasis on patients' autonomy has gone too far in relation to children and young people?

4.4 Paternalism

This section focuses on what happens when autonomy is limited or for some reason or other parents wish to override their child's decision and thus override their autonomy. In other words, we are concerned here with the concept of parental paternalism.

4.4.1 Defining paternalism

Paternalism is a complex concept and can be understood in several ways, e.g. in language, attitudes and treatment decisions. Put simply, it basically involves making a decision on someone else's behalf – in the belief that 'it is for their own good', i.e. in their best interests. Paternalistic practice was once common in health care (Mason and Laurie, 2006), but it is now much more difficult to justify – at least in relation to adults (Farsides, 2007, p. 144). However, the right of parents to make decisions on behalf of their children continues to be largely unchallenged. Indeed, it has been described as 'essential to the relationship between the parent and child', which, if relinquished, would amount to a 'failure in nurturing' (Gaylin, 1982).

4.4.2 Justifying parental paternalism

The idea that parental paternalism is 'good' for children can be explained by the widely held belief that it is 'natural' that parents should be responsible for and have rights over their children (Herring, 2009, p. 403). It is also widely assumed that parents are their children's best advocates. This is not only because they are expected to know more about them than anyone else but also because it is presumed that most parents will do their utmost to safeguard their children's interests (Elliston, 2007, p. 29). It is therefore not surprising that parents have a very wide discretion to make decisions on their children's behalf (by virtue of the concept of 'parental responsibility', see below). Yet that discretion is not unlimited, as we see below.

Incompetent children

Newborn babies and young children who lack the abilities required to make autonomous decisions can be described as having limited autonomy. Their involvement in decision-making is thus likely to be minimal (if it exists at all). It is not therefore surprising that parents have the moral and legal right (and the responsibility) to make decisions on their behalf. However, even though parents have a very wide discretion in how they raise their children, their decisions can be challenged if they fall below certain minimum standards. These standards are set out in legislation (i.e. the Children and Young Person's Act 1933) and the common law (see Chapter 2) but are determined by agencies such as social workers, police and the courts.

As Elliston (2007, p. 34) explains, however, in practice, parents' wishes (including refusal of treatment) will normally be respected unless they will have a seriously detrimental impact on their children, i.e. expose them to unacceptable risk of harm. In deciding whether such harm is likely, she proposes a 'reasonableness' test. Broadly, this allows parents to take into account the rights of other family members and their own rights to determine the values that are important to them in raising their children (provided these do not fall below societal standards for child welfare; Elliston, 2007, p. 37). A similar approach, i.e. one that prioritises parental autonomy (providing it meets acceptable standards of child welfare) is also advocated by Diekema (2004).

Mature teenagers

Overriding the autonomous choices of older children and teenagers who are able to act autonomously is more ethically controversial than making decisions for younger, incompetent children. Debates about the merits of paternalistic interventions by parents most commonly arise when 'mature' young people choose to refuse life-saving treatment, i.e. only rarely are concerns raised about a mature child's consent to treatment. To many, this seems illogical (e.g. Bainham, 1992; Brazier, 2003). In other words, to recognise a mature child's moral right to consent to treatment (under the *Gillick* test, see below), but not to refuse treatment, implies that a child's right to have her autonomy respected only applies if she gives the 'right' answer (Herring, 2009, p. 185).

Essentially, there are two competing approaches to the issue of decision-making by mature adolescents:

1. *Child liberation*: Once children have the capacity to make their own decisions, there is no justification for paternalistic intervention; i.e. their wishes must be respected whatever the outcome. In other words, age-based constraints are unjustifiably discriminatory (Elliston, 2007, p. 45). Lindley similarly finds it difficult to justify paternalistic restrictions on all adolescents under 18 simply because of their minor status. He therefore proposes a more sophisticated approach to children's liberation, which recognises that by the time children are 13, they have sufficient competence to make a life plan (Lindley, 1989, pp. 88–92).

2. *So-called liberal paternalism*: A more gradualist approach that acknowledges that as children mature – particularly when they approach adulthood – they should be increasingly entitled to make their own decisions (Eekelaar, 1994; Freeman, 2007; Lowe and Juss, 1993). Nevertheless, they should be protected from making those that are self-destructive, i.e. threaten death or serious physical or mental harm.

According to Fortin, it is the second approach which is now the most widely supported, i.e. the view that decision-making cannot be delegated to *all* children whatever their age, but that paternalism should nevertheless be kept to a minimum (and must be carefully justified, particularly when adults override children's own choices). But as she concludes, 'the difficulty is to find a formula that protects children and adolescents from making life-threatening mistakes, but restrains autocratic and arbitrary adult restrictions on their potential for autonomy' (Fortin, 2003, p. 26).

> **Key points**
>
> - Paternalism means making decisions on someone else's behalf.
> - Paternalistic intervention by parents is justifiable when their children are too young or immature to make their own decisions.
> - Parental paternalism is harder to justify in relation to 'mature' children and adolescents who can act autonomously.

4.5 The Law of Consent

The legal principles that underpin the law of consent were first recognised in the English case of *Slater v Baker and Stapleton* (95 Eng Rep 860 (KB 1767)) in 1767. Since then, the courts have repeatedly confirmed that the law regards the right to bodily integrity as an inviolable principle. This means that it is unlawful to touch patients without their prior consent.

As regards children and young people, the conventional approach to consent was uncontroversial, at least in the past. Thus, the law recognised parental consent as simply part of the normal care of children whatever their age (Elliston, 2007, p. 49). In the last few decades, however, this paternalistic approach has been harder to justify. Yet as we see, even though the courts now recognise the right of 'mature' children and young people to make more of their own health care decisions than in the past, they have nevertheless retained the power to overrule their autonomous decisions in certain circumstances.

4.5.1 The concept of 'informed consent'

Despite the widespread reference in medico-legal texts to the concept of informed consent, no such concept is recognised in English law (Mazur, 2008, p. 255; McHale, 2007, p. 109). It was first used in a 1957 Californian case (*Salgo v Leland Stanford Junior University Board of Trustees*) and was soon adopted throughout the US. Yet as Mason and Laurie (2006, p. 396) note, the concept is essentially no more than a broad expression of principle, which tells us nothing about what counts as informed consent or how we can tell that the circumstances surrounding a given event satisfy the requirements. A more important question is, therefore, how English courts have developed the concept of consent (for an analysis of how consent is used in medical law, see Beyleveld and Brownswood, 2007).

4.5.2 Nurses' role in the consent process

A nurse's role in the consent process ultimately depends on her particular role – as primary carer or advocate.

Primary carer

A nurse will be the primary carer if she is the person directly responsible for providing treatment, such as giving an injection, taking a blood sample or if she is washing or dressing a patient. If so, she will be responsible for obtaining consent. In certain circumstances, however, the nurse may seek consent on behalf of colleagues – especially if she has been specially trained to do so (NMC, 2008).

Advocate

A nurse's advocacy role involves supporting and counselling patients who may be confused or uncertain about an aspect of the consent process (McHale, 2007, p. 114). As the NMC (2008) guidance on consent notes, a nurse is often best placed to know and to judge what information a person requires in order to make a decision.

Whether a nurse is the primary carer or an advocate, she should ensure that an accurate record of all discussions and decisions is made (see further NMC guidance on record keeping; NMC, 2008).

4.5.3 Forms of consent

Only exceptionally – such as in mental health settings, abortion, infertility and organ and tissue donation – does the law lay down rules about what form consent should take. In all other cases the law is silent. This means that consent can be either express/explicit (either written or oral) or implied. All are equally valid.

Express/explicit

It is standard practice in the National Health Service (NHS) to use model forms covering most forms of treatment or other invasive procedures; once signed by a patient (or a person with parental responsibility, see below), these forms provide the best evidence that consent was actually given (unless it is clear, for example, that the patient did not understand what she was signing or had not been given adequate information). In other words, a patient's signature on a consent form does not necessarily make it legally valid.

Oral consent is typically given for routine, less risky or less lengthy procedures. Widely used in everyday practice, it is nevertheless less reliable as a form of consent, being harder to prove later on.

Implied

Consent is implied when no words are used and no forms are signed, but by her actions or behaviour – for example a patient nods her head, rolls up her sleeve or opens her mouth – consent is demonstrated. This form of consent is the weakest.

Activity

Download consent forms from the Department of Health (DoH) website (http://www.dh.gov.uk/consent) relating to children under 18 and compare them with those of adults (i.e. those of 18 and over).

4.5.4 Failure to obtain consent – battery/negligence

It is theoretically possible that a nurse could face criminal charges if she intentionally or recklessly touches a patient without consent. But liability in tort law for *battery* or *negligence* is much more likely. Battery actions are very rare in health care contexts largely because they only apply when there was no 'real' consent – i.e. it was obtained against the patient's will by fraud or because the wrong operation is performed on the wrong patient.

A more likely claim is for negligence – the allegation being that although consent was given it was inherently flawed. The 'flaw' is typically that crucial information was withheld. As we see below, what this means is that to avoid liability in negligence practitioners must provide patients with '*adequate*' information. However, even if a patient can prove she was not adequately informed, she must still satisfy the *causation* element in a negligence claim. Essentially, the patient is therefore saying: if the health professional had given me information, e.g. about a particular risk, I would not have consented to treatment. But I did consent (because I was not told of the risk) and as a result I have suffered harm – *caused* by the health professional's negligent failure to disclose.

4.6 Essential Requirements for Consent to be Legally Valid

Whatever form consent takes, it is only legally valid (i.e. 'real') if three essential criteria are met. These are that the patient (or her proxy, i.e. anyone with 'parental responsibility') makes her decision voluntarily, has adequate information, and has capacity.

4.6.1 Voluntariness

Simply put, consent is voluntary (i.e. free or real) when it is given without coercion, force, manipulation or undue influence. In practice, whether undue influence has been exerted depends on several factors, including the effect of tiredness, pain and drugs. The fact that patients may be particularly vulnerable to advice from health professionals who may use their expertise to press their own ethical views must also be taken into account (likewise the relationship of the 'persuader' to the patient, especially if she is a parent; see *Re T* [1992] 4 All ER 649).

4.6.2 Adequate information – the legal standard of disclosure

The question, how much information does the law require health professionals to disclose, may seem a relatively simple one. Yet the answer is far from clear. Why? Firstly, because there are two possible approaches, namely, the 'patient' standard and the 'professional' standard. Secondly, whatever approach is taken, a decision of some court or other can be found to endorse the preferred approach (Mason and Laurie, 2006, p. 399). Briefly, the two approaches are the following.

'Patient' standard
This approach requires health professionals to disclose broadly what an average 'reasonable' or 'prudent' patient (with that particular illness or condition) would want to know. Basically, apart from irrelevant material, this approach means that patients must be as fully informed as possible.

'Professional' standard

According to this approach, health professionals set their own standards of disclosure – although in deciding what to disclose they do have to follow accepted (i.e. responsible) practice. In short, the *Bolam/Bolitho* test applies to information disclosure (see Chapter 3).

4.6.3 Current approach taken by the courts

The seminal case of *Sideway v Bethlem RHG* [1985] 1 All ER 653 is the usual starting point for any discussion of the legal standard of disclosure. What follows is a summary of the key points that can be derived from the case (and subsequent cases, particularly *Pearce v United Bristol Healthcare NHS Trust* [1999] 48 BMLR 118; *Smith v Tunbridge Wells HA* [1994] 5 Med LR 334; *Chester v Afshar* [2004] UKHL 41) and current guidance from the DoH (2001a, b):

- Patients must be given enough information to make a balanced judgement, that is, be told in broad terms the nature and purpose of the procedure, its likely risks, in particular those that are 'significant' or 'material' (i.e. those that would affect the judgement of a 'reasonable' patient), any alternatives to the proposed treatment and their likely risks, any uncertainties, and the risks incurred by doing nothing.
- Whether a risk is 'significant' will be determined by reference to the possible benefits of the procedure, and depend on both the severity and the likelihood of possible harm (Pattinson, 2006, p. 112).
- In applying the *Bolam/Bolitho* test to information disclosure, the medical opinion justifying non-disclosure has to be both *reasonable* and *responsible*.
- The process of informing the patient and obtaining consent should be regarded as a process and not a one-off event.
- Information provided should be tailored to the needs, circumstances and wishes of the individual.
- Patients who ask direct questions should be answered fully.
- Under the doctrine of 'therapeutic privilege', health professionals can withhold information – providing they can justify doing so, i.e. because the patients are so 'fragile' that full disclosure would harm them.

Summarising the above, it seems that the legal standard of disclosure does not require all risks to be disclosed. Nevertheless, the law has certainly become more pro-claimant and patient-centred than in the past (Mason and Laurie, 2006; McHale, 2007; Pattinson, 2006). As such, it is likely to become increasingly difficult to justify withholding information.

Activity

Do you think 'therapeutic' privilege is more likely to be relied on in respect of child patients? If so, is it justified? Can you think of examples in your practice?

Key points

- To give valid consent, patients need to be provided with enough information to make a balanced judgement.
- Patients who ask direct questions should be answered truthfully.

4.6.4 Capacity – competent 16- and 17-year-olds

Giving consent

It was noted above that for consent to be legally valid, three criteria must be satisfied, namely, voluntariness, adequate information and capacity. Here we focus on capacity, the third element (note that the terms 'capacity' and 'competence' are commonly used interchangeably). Children generally achieve adult status at 18, but in relation to medical treatment young people reach maturity at a younger age by virtue of the Family Law Reform Act (FLA) 1969 (s.8). The Act gives competent 16- and 17-year-olds the same right to consent to medical treatment as adults; i.e. they can give consent irrespective of their parents' wishes.

According to the Mental Capacity Act (MCA) 2005, young people are competent if they can:

1. Understand and retain information relevant to the decision,
2. Use and weigh up the information as part of the process of making the decision, and
3. Communicate the decision by any means (MCA 2005, s.3(1)).

The main points to note about the combined effect of the MCA 2005, FLA 1969, Children Act 1989 and the common law (all of which overlap) are as follows:

- The MCA defines competence in negative terms; i.e. it sets out requirements for lack of decision-making, caused by an impairment of, or a disturbance in the functioning of, the mind or brain (s.2(1)).
- Young people over 16 are (like adults) presumed to be competent unless there is evidence to the contrary.
- The 'treatment' (under the FLA 1969) includes surgical, medical and dental treatment as well as nursing and other care. A young person's consent to treatment not covered by the Act (e.g. cosmetic surgery) would be valid only if she satisfied the *Gillick* competency test (see below).
- Capacity is 'function' specific, i.e. assessed by reference to a particular decision and presupposes the capacity for rational thought (Pattinson, 2006, p. 132).
- Lack of capacity cannot be established merely by reference to a young person's age or appearance; i.e. capacity must not be assessed in a prejudicial way (see further MCA sections 1–4).
- A young person's valid consent can be overruled by a court, but not by anyone else (Elliston, 2007, p. 89).

Refusing consent

Competent 16- and 17-year-olds were once thought to have the same legal right to refuse treatment as adults; i.e. it is unlawful for health professionals to touch competent patients who have made it clear that they do not wish to receive treatment (*R (Burke) v GMC* [2005] EWCA Civ 1003 CA). But in *Re W* [1992] 4 All ER 627, the courts made it clear that even though a refusal by a competent 16- or 17-year-old was a very important factor for health professionals to consider, it could nevertheless be overruled by a court or anyone with *parental responsibility* (see Elliston, 2007, Chapter 3 for a critique of the law's approach).

Who has parental responsibility?

Only those with parental responsibility (apart from the court) can override a competent 16- or 17-year-old's refusal. The combined effect of the Children Act 1989, Children Act 2002 and the Civil Partnership Act 2004 is that the following have parental responsibility:

- Both parents, if they are married.
- The mother, even if she is not married to the father.

- The father who has made a parental responsibility agreement, or has been granted a parental responsibility order or a residence order.
- The father who has registered the birth of the child jointly with the mother (in England and Wales). Note that this only applies to children born since 1 December 2003.
- A step-parent – defined to include civil partners (by agreement or court order).
- Adoptive parents.
- 'Special' and ordinary guardians.
- Other people who have parental responsibility because of a court order, e.g. a residence order granted to grandparents or a care order or emergency protection order granted to a local authority.

Two final points about parental responsibility must be noted. First, health professionals can usually rely on the consent of any person with parental responsibility; i.e. a person with parental responsibility can act alone without consulting or agreeing with the other parent (s.2(7) Children Act 1989, see below for exceptions). Secondly, the consent of the persons with parental responsibility (which is being relied on to override a competent young person's refusal) is only legally valid if they themselves are competent, have adequate information and make their decision voluntarily (see above).

Key points

The Family Law Reform Act 1969 means that competent 16- and 17-year-olds can:

- Give valid legal consent without regard to their parents' wishes,
- Have their consent overridden by a court, and
- Have their refusal of treatment overridden by a court or by anyone with parental responsibility.

4.6.5 Capacity – *'Gillick* competent' under 16-year-olds

Giving consent

Although post-*Gillick* case law has disappointed child liberationists, the decision (*Gillick v West Norfolk and Wisbech AHA* [1986] AC 112) was nevertheless a landmark one. This was because in acknowledging, for the first time, young people's independent legal right to consent to treatment (i.e. without their parents' knowledge or consent), it appeared to usher in new era of respect for children's right to autonomy. It was therefore perhaps not surprising that the phrase '*Gillick* competence' soon became one of the most commonly used (if not always well understood) legal concepts.

Yet despite its pervasive use, the concept suffered from an inherent weakness, notably uncertainty. Much of the debate about the precise meaning of the concept stemmed from the subtle differences in the speeches of Lords Fraser and Scarman. However, it was not until *R (on the application of Axon) v Secretary of State for Health and the Family Planning Association* [2006] EWHC 37, that the courts explicitly revisited the meaning of *Gillick* competency. Mrs Axon challenged 2004 DoH advice on the provision of contraceptive services and on sexually transmitted diseases to girls under 16. The judge dismissed her application on the basis that he was bound by the *Gillick* precedent. In so doing he made it clear that although *Gillick* competence should be assessed using Lord Fraser's five guidelines, Lord Scarman's comments must be read into them. Accordingly, it now seems that to satisfy the '*Gillick* competency' test children must be able to:

- Understand the *medical* issues: that is the nature of their condition, the proposed treatment, side effects and consequences of agreeing to or refusing treatment.

- Have *sufficient maturity* to understand what is involved: that understanding applies to all relevant matters and is not limited to *family* and *moral* aspects. As such, it includes *social* and *emotional* aspects of the decision as well.

The following additional factors should be noted:

- Children under 16 are presumed to be incompetent; i.e. they must prove they are competent (unlike 16- and 17–year-olds who are presumed to be legally competent).
- The degree of understanding and maturity required will vary according to the complexity of the treatment and the associated risks. In other words, serious treatment requires a higher degree of maturity and understanding than routine procedures with few side effects. Note that it is unclear whether the complexity of the decision itself (rather than the gravity of the treatment, or its outcome) is also a relevant factor.
- Children should be encouraged to involve their parents in decision-making (see further Elliston, 2007, pp. 77–84).

Refusing consent
As to the rights of *Gillick* competent children under 16 to refuse treatment, there is no doubt that just like competent 16- and 17-year-olds, their refusal can be overridden, both by a court or anyone with parental responsibility. Indeed, in no reported English case has a child's refusal of consent been upheld – either because the courts have required greater levels of decision-making ability than for giving consent or because their interpretation of the child's best interests has taken priority (see further *Re E* [1993] 1 FLR 386; *Re M* [1999] 2 FLR 1097; *Re L* [1998] 2 FLR 810; Chapter 3). Not surprisingly, debates prompted by these cases mirror those made in relation to 16- and 17-year-olds.

Key points

'*Gillick* competent' under 16-year-olds can:

- Give valid legal consent without their parents' knowledge or consent,
- Have their consent overridden by a court, and
- Have their refusal overridden by a court or anyone with parental responsibility.

4.6.6 Incompetent under 18-year-olds proxy decision-making

Children and young people under 18 who are incompetent cannot give valid legal consent. Permission for treatment therefore has to come from someone else, namely, a proxy. As we saw above, this will usually be a parent (or other person with parental responsibility). Consent by proxies is only legally valid if they are competent, have adequate information and act voluntarily (see above). But what if a mother with parental responsibility is herself under 18? Although it is common in practice to obtain her consent (as well as that of one of her parents), such 'dual' consent is legally unnecessary; i.e. health professionals can rely on the consent of any person with parental responsibility (even if she/he is under 18; Dimond, 2008, p. 335). For proxy consent to be lawful, treatment must be in the child's best interests. So what does this concept mean?

4.6.7 Best interests

The MCA 2005 defines the concept of 'best interests' in some detail (see s.4). But here we focus instead on how the concept is defined according to the Children Act 1989 (and case law). This is because it is anticipated that 16- and 17-year-olds (whose capacity is determined by the MCA 2005) will fail the test because they are 'overwhelmed by the implications of the decision'. As such, the MCA will not apply (i.e. they are not incompetent according to the Act, Code of Practice, 2007, para 12.13). Furthermore, case law has repeatedly shown that in relation to disputed medical treatment (i.e. involving refusal of consent by mature young people) the issue of competence is rarely explored as the courts simply apply the best interests test (Elliston, 2007, p. 127).

Defining 'best interests'

As we saw in Chapter 2, the Children Act 1989 sets out the factors that are relevant to the assessment of a child's welfare (the terms 'welfare' and 'best interests' are used interchangeably). In the vast majority of cases, decisions by proxies will be followed without any legal challenge. But in disputed cases, resort to the courts will be necessary (see below). According to case law (see, e.g. *Re A, Male Sterilisation* [2000], 1 FLR 549; *Wyatt v Portsmouth Hospital NHS Trust* [2005] EWCA Civ 1181) and guidance from GMC (2007), NMC (2008) and DoH (2001a, b), the concept of best interests should be interpreted as follows:

- Generally, proxies have a wide discretion to determine treatment.
- Certain procedures are unquestionably within its scope, such as any treatment which is therapeutic, i.e. intended to benefit the child. This would cover routine treatment for a specific condition such as a physical illness (or psychiatric disorder) as well as major surgery – providing it involves conventional treatment.
- Diagnostic procedures and preventive measures such as vaccinations will similarly normally be considered in a child's best interests.
- Best interests are not limited to 'medical interests' but encompass medical, emotional and all welfare issues, including whether proposed treatment is 'to the emotional, psychological and social benefit of the child'.
- In assessing best interests, a *balance sheet* should be drawn up. This involves weighing up actual benefits against disbenefits, possible benefits and disadvantages (with an estimate of their probability) so as to arrive at a sum of certain and possible benefits against certain and possible disadvantages.
- When best interests are being assessed in cases where proxies are refusing consent to treatment, the courts almost always prioritise medical expertise and evidence of what is 'best' above any other consideration (Elliston, 2007, p. 143).
- The views of the child or young person (including their cultural, religious or other beliefs) should be considered. Those of parents, those close to the child and other health care professionals should similarly be considered.
- Unjustified assumptions about a child's best interests should not be made on irrelevant or discriminatory factors such as their behaviour, appearance or disability.

Limits to proxy decision-making

Although the law gives proxies a wide discretion to determine treatment, it does impose limits, i.e. decisions that are not in the child's best interest. Consider, for example, treatment to lengthen limbs or cosmetic surgery for children with Down's syndrome. According to Savulescu (2007, p. 32), these (and other) controversial choices by parents should meet higher standards before they are respected, in particular they must be *safe* enough, compared to other interventions children are exposed to; the parent's choice must be based on a plausible conception of well-being and a better life for the child and not on some idiosyncratic, unjustifiable conception of the good life and the choice must be consistent with the development of autonomy and a reasonable range of future life plans for the child. Finally, it is important to note that some procedures require the court's prior authorisation. These include non-therapeutic sterilisations, abortion, and donation of non-regenerative tissues.

> **Key points**
>
> - Proxy consent or refusal of treatment will only be valid if it is in the child's best interests.
> - The best interest principle is defined by the Children Act and interpreted by case law, professional guidance and guidance from DoH.

4.7 Disagreements – the Court's Role

Consent-related disputes are only very rarely taken to court, but there have been several examples where the court's supervisory and protective roles have been invoked, notably in the following types of disputes (note that the reference to parents below refers to those with parental responsibility).

4.7.1 Parents and children

Typically, these types of disagreements will involve a competent young person who, for example, consents to treatment which a person with parental responsibility opposes. Or she may refuse treatment but a parent consents (see, e.g. *Northamptonshire HA v Official Solicitor and Governors of St Andrew's Hospital* [1994] 1 FLR 162).

4.7.2 Parents and health professionals

The few cases that have reached the courts have usually been prompted by parents seeking treatment, which doctors do not consider to be in the child's best interests (see *Wyatt v Portsmouth NHS Trust* [2005] EWCA Civ 1181 and *Glass v UK* [2004] ECHR 102). Other litigated cases typically involve parents with strong religious beliefs rejecting treatment proposed by doctors (see, e.g. *Re S* [1993] 1 FLR 376; *Re O* [1993] 2 FLR 149; see further Chapter 12).

4.7.3 Parents and parents

As was noted above, health professionals can usually provide treatment as long as they have the consent of a person with parental responsibility. A few procedures, however, are considered so important that they can only be carried out if those with parental responsibility agree (or a court order is obtained). These include immunisation, male circumcision and probably non-therapeutic cosmetic surgery (see, e.g. *A and D v B and E* [2003] EWHC 1376; *Re J* [1999] 2 FLR 678).

The disputes noted above are the most likely to reach the courts, but the courts may also be involved when there is doubt about, for example, a young person's competence. But irrespective of the reason for the court's involvement, it has a very wide discretion to make any order – provided it is in the child's best interests. This means that it can overrule parents, competent children and young people and health professionals. No court, however, will require health professionals to provide treatment against their clinical judgement.

4.8 Emergencies

The final aspects of the law relevant to children's nursing are prompted by 'emergency' situations when it may not be possible to get valid legal consent from the child (or a proxy).

4.8.1 Necessity

Supposing a child is rushed to hospital following an accident. Given the urgency of her situation, can she be treated without a proxy's consent (or a court order)? Under the doctrine of necessity, health professionals could lawfully provide treatment to save the life (or prevent serious deterioration in the health) of a child or young person, without consent (*Re O* [1993] 2 FLR 149). However, as the scope of the doctrine of necessity is uncertain, treatment should be limited to that which is necessary to meet the emergency. Note, however, that despite the absence of clear legal authority, it is assumed that the doctrine of necessity would also apply to routine emergency minor treatment (Lavery, 1990).

4.8.2 Temporary carers

A situation might arise when a child's temporary carer – for example, childminder – is the only person available to give consent to treatment. According to the Children Act 1989 (s.3(5)), a person with care of a child may do what is reasonable in all the circumstances to promote and safeguard the child's welfare. This provision would cover minor treatment but not major irreversible surgery or treatment to which a parent objects (Herring, 2008).

Case study

Derek is 17. Seriously ill with leukaemia, he urgently needs a blood transfusion. But Derek is a Jehovah's Witness (a belief his mother, Shirley, but not his father, Marc, shares). Derek's doctor wants him to have the transfusion but is relying on his father's (Mark's) consent. Heather, a nurse who has cared for Derek for some time, is convinced that Derek has not been given enough information, in particular about alternative treatment or consequences of different types of treatment. Consider the following issues:

1. The nurse's role as a patient advocate.
2. Whether Derek's wishes should be respected.
3. What legal options are available in the light of Derek's and his mother's refusal.
4. What difference it would make if Derek were 15.

4.8.3 Advocacy role

Ethical approach

As the NMC Code (2008) (and supplementary guidance, 2008) make clear, the nurse 'must act as an advocate for those in her care, helping them to access relevant health care, information and support'. What does this mean in relation to Derek? To answer this question, the nurse has to resolve several questions, notably:

- Is Derek sufficiently autonomous to make his own health care decisions, i.e. to determine his own personal goal, understand available options, decide on a life plan and act on his choices?
- Has communication with him been 'effective'?
- Has 'adequate' information been provided?
- Has Derek's right to participate in decision-making been facilitated?
- Can paternalism, i.e. withholding information, be justified?

Once these questions are addressed, Heather will be better placed to decide what her professional and ethical responsibilities are. There is no doubt that, at the very least, she should tell the doctor of her concerns. If this fails to remedy the situation, she should consider providing the information herself – providing, of course, she is fully informed herself of the relevant issues. Yet if she adopts this course of action, she runs the risk that her assessment of the amount of information Derek requires is wrong, and he may, for example, be unable to cope with it (McHale, 2007).

Legal position
There is no express recognition in English law of the role of patient advocate. That said, Heather has a legal duty to tell the doctor of her concerns. If her concerns are ignored, the legal position is less clear. Should she decide to provide the information herself, in effect, refuse to follow doctor's orders, she may face disciplinary action. But, given that there is now greater recognition of young people's right to autonomy, this outcome is unlikely. Ultimately, Heather's legal responsibility would turn on what other professionals working in the same field would have done (i.e. the *Bolam/Bolitho* test would apply).

4.8.4 Refusal of consent

Ethical approach
For Derek's refusal of treatment to be respected, it must be a decision he is capable of reaching of his own free will. In short, he must be sufficiently autonomous to make the decision. His capacity to do so is therefore a central issue. Yet even supposing Derek has the required capacity to make rational evaluations (for which, of course, he must have been provided with adequate information), paternalistic intervention could arguably be justified on the basis that Derek should be protected from making a life-threatening 'mistake'. On the other hand, it could be argued that age-based constraints are morally indefensible, and Derek's autonomy should be respected, whatever the outcome.

Legal position
As Derek is 17, the assumption is that he has capacity. If this is in doubt, his capacity will be assessed according to the MCA 2005. But to give valid legal consent (or a refusal), Derek must also act voluntarily and have been given enough information to make a balanced judgement. This last element seems not to have been satisfied. Yet even if Derek could give valid consent, his refusal of consent may not be determinative, especially as he is refusing life-saving treatment. This is because anyone with parental responsibility, i.e. Mark, could authorise treatment – assuming it was in Derek's best interests (*Re W* [1993]). A court could also override Derek's (and Shirley's) refusal. Indeed, given the seriousness of the dispute, court intervention is the best option.

If Derek were 15, his capacity would be assessed according to the *Gillick* competency test. But his refusal could be vetoed by anyone with parental responsibility or a court.

4.9 The Relationship between Law and Ethics

4.9.1 Similarities between law and ethics

- **Principle of autonomy:** Both law and ethics seek to protect a patient's rights – to make autonomous choices, to self-determination and bodily integrity.
- **Free consent:** Both law and ethics are committed to preventing coercion, manipulation and undue pressure.
- **Basic elements:** The same basic elements – capacity, voluntariness and sufficient information – are essential for a patient to be able to give valid legal consent and be considered sufficiently autonomous to make a decision.

- **Paternalism:** Both law and ethics have mechanisms for making decisions on behalf of competent young people; i.e. paternalistic intervention can be justified in moral terms to protect a young person from making a self-destructive decision; the corresponding principle justifying paternalistic intervention in law is the best interest principle.

4.9.2 Differences between law and ethics

- **Advocacy:** The moral concept is more developed than its legal counterpart; i.e. there is no recognition in law, as regards children and young people, of the role of the advocate (the exception being under the MCA 2005).
- **Information disclosure:** Despite the law's recognition of enhanced disclosure, the ethical standard of disclosure is more patient-oriented in so far as it requires more detailed and fuller disclosure than is normally required by the *Bolam/Bolitho* standard.
- **Truth-telling:** The moral and professional obligation to tell the truth to children and young people is stronger than the legal one where the doctrine of therapeutic privilege may be more readily invoked to justify withholding information.

References

Alderson, P. (2000) *Young Children's Rights: Exploring Beliefs, Principles and Practice*. London: Jessica Kingsley.

Alderson, P. and Montgomery, J. (1996) *Health Care Choices: Making Decisions with Children*. London: Institute for Public Policy Research.

Axford, N. (2008) *Exploring Concepts of Children's Well-Being*. Bristol: Policy Press.

Bainham, A. (1992) The judge and the competent minor. *Law Quarterly Review* 108:194.

Beauchamp, T.L. and Childress, J.F. (2009) *Principles of Biomedical Ethics*, 6th edn. Oxford: Oxford University Press.

Beresford, B. and Sloper, P. (1999) *The Information Needs of Chronically Ill or Physically Disabled Children and Adolescents*. York: York Social Policy Research Unit.

Beyleveld, D. and Brownswood, R. (2007) *Consent in Law*. Oxford: Hart.

Brazier, M. (2003) *Medicine, Patients and the Law*, 3rd edn. London: Penguin.

Butts, J.B. and Rich, K.L. (2005) *Nursing Ethics: Across the Curriculum into Practice*. Boston, MA: Jones & Bartlett.

Coleman, J. and Hendry, L. (1999) *The Nature of Adolescence*. London: Routledge.

Cribb, A. (2007) The ethical dimension: nursing practice, nursing philosophy and nursing ethics. In Tingle, J. and Cribb, A. (eds) *Nursing Law and Ethics*. Oxford: Blackwell.

Diekema, D.S. (2004) Parental refusals of medical treatment: the harm principle as threshold for state intervention. *Theoretical Medicine and Bioethics* 25(4):243.

Dimond, B. (2008) *Legal Aspects of Nursing*, 5th edn. Harlow: Pearson Education.

DoH (2001a) *Guide to Consent to Treatment*. London: DoH.

DoH (2001b) *Seeking Consent: Working with Children*. London: DoH.

Dworkin, G. (1988) *The Theory and Practice of Autonomy*. Cambridge: Cambridge University Press.

Eekelaar, J. (1994) The interests of the child and the child's wishes: the role of dynamic self-determination. *International Journal of Law and the Family* 8:42.

Elliston, S. (2007) *The Best Interest of Children in Healthcare*. London: Routledge-Cavendish.

Faden, R. and Beauchamp, T.L. (1986) *A History and Theory of Informed Consent*. New York: Oxford University Press.

Farsides, B. (2007) An ethical perspective – consent and patient autonomy. In Tingle, J. and Cribb, A. (eds) *Nursing Law and Ethics*, 3rd edn. Oxford: Blackwell.

Farson, R. (1974) *Birthrights*. London: Collier Macmillan.

Fortin, J. (2003) *Children's Rights and the Developing Law*. London: Reed Elsevier.

Fortin, J. (2006) Accommodating children's rights in a post Human Rights Act era. *Modern law Review* 69:299.

Foster, C. (2009) *Choosing Life, Choosing Death: The Tyranny of Autonomy in Medical Law and Ethics*. Oxford: Hart.

Foster, H. and Freed, D. (1972) A bill of rights for children. *Family Law Quarterly* 6:343.

Fox Harding, L. (1997) *Perspectives in Child Care Policy*. London: Longman.

Franklin, A. and Sloper, P. (2005) Listening and responding? Children's participation in healthcare within England. *International Journal of Children's Rights* 13(112):11.

Freeman, M. (2007) *Understanding Family Law*. London: Thompson (Sweet & Maxwell).

Gaylin, W. (1982) Who speaks for the child? In Gaylin, W. and Macklin, R. (eds) *Who Speaks for the Child?* New York: Plenum Press.

GMC (2007) *0–18 Guidance for All Doctors*. London: GMC.

Godfrey, K. (2008) Values for integrated work with children: supplement to the NMC code of standards. *Nursing Times* 104:17.

Herring, J. (2008) *Medical Law and Ethics*, 2nd edn. Oxford: Oxford University Press.

Herring, J. (2009) *Family Law*, 3rd edn. Harlow: Pearson Education.

Holt, J. (1974) *Escape from Childhood: The Needs and Rights of Childhood*. New York: E.P Dutton.

Hope, T., Savulescu, J. and Hendrick, J. (2008) *Medical Ethics and Law: The Core Curriculum*, 2nd edn. Edinburgh: Elsevier.

Jackson, E. (2006) *Medical Law: Text, Cases and Materials*. Oxford: Oxford University Press.

Keown, J. (2002) *Euthanasia, Ethics and Public Policy: An Argument Against Legislation*. Cambridge: Cambridge University Press.

Lavery, R. (1990) Routine medical treatment of children. *Journal of Social Welfare and Family Law* 375:386.

Lindley, R. (1989) Teenagers and other children. In Scarre, G. (ed.) *Children, Parents and Politics*. Cambridge: Cambridge University Press.

Lowe, N. and Juss, S. (1993) Medical treatment, pragmatism and the search for principle. *Modern Law Review* 56(6):865–872.

Manson, N.C. and O'Neill, O. (2007) *Rethinking Informed Consent in Bioethics*. Cambridge: Cambridge University Press.

Mason, J.K. and Laurie, G.T. (2006) *Mason and McCall Smith's Law and Medical Ethics*, 7th edn. Oxford: Oxford University Press.

Mazur, D.J. (2008) Consent and informed consent: their ongoing evolution in clinical care and research on humans. *Sociology Compass* 2/1:253.

McHale, J. (2007) Consent to treatment: children and the mentally ill. In McHale, J. and Tingle, J. (eds) *Law and Nursing*, 3rd edn. Edinburgh: Elsevier.

Moules, T. and Ramsay, J. (1998) *The Textbook of Children's Nursing*. Cheltenham: Stanley Thornes.

NMC (2008) *Advice for Nurses Working with Children and Young People*. London: NMC.

O'Neill, O. (2002) *Autonomy and Trust in Bioethics*. Cambridge: Cambridge University Press.

O'Neill, O. (2003) Some limits to informed consent. *Journal of Medical Ethics* 29:4.

Pattinson, S.D. (2006) *Medical Law and Ethics*. London: Sweet & Maxwell.

Quick, O. (2006) Outing medical errors: questions of trust and responsibility. *Medical Law Review* 14(1):22.

Savulescu, J. (2007) Autonomy, the good life and controversial choices. In Rhodes, R., Francis, L.P. and Silvers, A. (eds) *The Blackwell Guide to Medical Ethics*. Oxford: Blackwell.

Sinclair, R. (2004) Participation in practice: making it meaningful, effective and sustainable. *Children and Society* 18(2):106.

Tates, K. and Meeuwesen, L. (2001) Doctor–parent–child communication: a (re)view of the literature. *Social Science and Medicine* 56:839.

Thompson, I.E., Melia, K.M., Boyd, K.M. and Horsburgh, D. (2006) *Nursing Ethics*, 5th edn. Edinburgh: Elsevier.

CHAPTER 5

Confidentiality, Medical Records and Data Protection

Learning outcomes

By the end of this chapter you should be able to:

- Describe the legal duty of confidentiality;
- Understand the relationship between confidentiality, autonomy, privacy and trust;
- Critically consider why confidentiality is ethically important;
- Identify the situations when confidentiality can be breached.

Introduction

The importance of maintaining confidentiality in health care has been recognised continuously over the last two and half millennia. Medical confidentiality has also been consistently upheld as a core value throughout Europe (EU, 2005). That nurses are therefore expected to rigorously comply with the increasingly stringent ethical and legal controls that aim to protect patients' confidentiality is self-evident (NMC, 2008b).

Whilst few would challenge the idea that adult patients have a legitimate expectation that the information they give nurses will be kept secret, this 'culture of confidentiality' is not always extended to children and young people. Certainly, research has shown that young people, especially adolescents, are significantly worried about the confidentiality of their health information (Carlisle et al., 2006). Research has also highlighted how confidentiality for younger children has almost always focused on parents' perceptions with little attention being given to the child's point of view (Campbell and Ross, 2003). A further complicating factor is that many different agencies may be involved in a child's care – making uniform standards of confidentiality difficult to maintain (Tan et al., 2007).

Yet guidance from the NMC (2008a), GMC (2007) and DoH (2003) makes it clear that although disclosure of information to parents is an integral part of the care of the very young, as children develop the capacity to act autonomously they should enjoy the same rights to confidentiality as do adults. However, as seen below, the duty of confidentiality is not absolute. It can be breached – for example, where child abuse or neglect is suspected. But as McHale (2007) notes, the increasing sophistication and complexity of health care means that the boundaries of confidentiality are less easy to define than they were in the past. As a consequence, deciding when breaches of confidentiality are justified (morally and legally) can be a very difficult judgement call.

This chapter considers the factors that should be taken into account in deciding whether to breach a child or young person's confidentiality. It also explores how the duty of confidentiality can be supported on moral and legal grounds and the criteria that must be satisfied before children can access their medical records. But the chapter begins by defining what is meant by the term 'confidential' and other related concepts such as privacy and trust.

5.1 Explaining Confidentiality

5.1.1 What is 'confidential' information?

There is surprisingly little clear guidance on precisely what information that is gained in a professional–patient (or client) relationship should be considered confidential (Smukler and Holloway, 2001, p. 61). The NMC Code, for example, simply refers to 'private and personal information' or 'sensitive' information (NMC, 2008b). In contrast, GMC guidance to doctors (0–18 years, GMC, 2007) implies that *any* information about child patients is confidential, although earlier GMC guidance refers to 'personal' information (GMC, 2004).

In the absence of clear authority, it is nevertheless widely assumed that the term 'confidential' is generally understood to apply to personal details about the physical and mental health of patients (Cain, 2001; McHale, 2007). This would include any symptoms they have, even though the sensitivity of these can vary enormously from, say, a cold (which few patients would worry about disclosing) to sexual anxieties (which most patients would wish to keep secret; Hendrick, 2000, p. 92). On the other hand, information which is normally described as part of 'social chit-chat' or the things that are in the public domain (i.e. widely known about people such as how many siblings they have) is usually not considered confidential. Nonetheless, given that people's perceptions of what they consider confidential are essentially subjective, it is arguable that all personal information (however trivial or even non-medical) should be assumed to be confidential.

5.1.2 Forms of confidential information

Confidential information may be contained in a variety of forms, such as medical illustrations, videos, X-rays, photographs, fax communications and tissue samples. Typically, the most important source of information about patients will be their health records (both electronic and manual). These will include details of their medical histories, medical observations, provide evidence of the care that is planned, decisions made, test results, reports from consultants and nurses' notes (see further DoH, 2003). Although a patient's records are the most obvious repository of information, nurses can acquire much information in other ways – for example, from telephone consultations or when working in the community (Cain, 2001). Take the following situation: a health visitor visits a house to check up on a young child who has missed several vaccinations. Whilst there, she notices small burn marks on the child, who seems very undernourished. Clearly, the health visitor will need to take appropriate action if she suspects abuse (Dimond, 2008, p. 184; see further Chapter 11). Thus, even though she has not been specifically entrusted with confidential information (i.e. in a formal context), she has nevertheless acquired crucial information about the child's welfare.

5.2 Children and Confidentiality

As we see below, a legal duty of confidentiality is owed to children and young people who are able to form a relationship of confidence, i.e. understand what it means to trust someone with secret information. By way of introduction, we note here how this relationship develops over time as children mature, i.e. how children learn the ability to manage the responsibility of confidentiality as they grow up – a process usually referred to as *relative confidentiality* (Bailey, 2001, p. 72). According to Tan et al., young people cannot develop the ability to handle confidential information without practice. They thus propose a step-by-step process whereby initially information which is not critical is kept secret, but that gradually the scope and importance of information is increased (Tan et al., 2007, p. 203).

This approach can be described as an incremental one. Certainly, it is one which is both expected and encouraged in guidance from the NMC (2008c) and GMC (2007). Note too that given the changing attitudes of society to the concept of children's autonomy, nurses need to satisfy themselves that when young people are involved in making difficult choices involving confidential information they must try and ensure that these choices are as autonomous as possible. As Bailey (2001, p. 77) explains, part of this process means being open with them about the 'absolute' boundaries of confidentiality, in particular informing them that in some circumstances confidences may have to be broken.

Activity

Read the NMC advice (2008c) on confidentiality (http://www.nmc-uk.org). Does it make any special reference to children?

5.3 Ethical Justifications for the Duty of Confidentiality

Confidentiality is one of the oldest codified moral commitments in health care (Gillon, 2001, p. 425). It is therefore not surprising that all the major moral theories emphasise its importance. This section examines the most common ethical justifications for maintaining confidentiality. But we begin by outlining the notion of trust – a concept which underpins virtually all ethical justifications for the obligation of confidentiality.

5.3.1 Trust

That medical care and treatment depends on trust is now widely acknowledged. Indeed, as McLean and Mason (2003, p. 30) assert (in describing the doctor–patient relationship): 'there can be few relationships where the *need* for trust in confidence is so obvious that the parties to that relationship expect their confidences to be respected'. A similar relationship of trust exists between nurses and their patients because their relationship is also a 'fiduciary' one, i.e. 'special' in the sense that it establishes duties and obligations that go beyond the scope of ordinary social intercourse (Beauchamp and Childress, 2009, pp. 311–317).

Indeed, as NMC advice makes clear: 'safe, effective and appropriate children's nursing involves more than just the application of theory to practice; it involves building trusting relationships with children and young people and with their parents' (NMC, 2008a). Similarly, the first sentence of the NMC Code proclaims: 'the people in your care must be able to *trust* you with their health and well-being' (NMC, 2008b). Yet, although the importance of trust is widely acknowledged, the concept remains an elusive and slippery one. Essentially, however, as Quick (2006, p. 35) explains, trust in professionals is based on technical competence, specialised knowledge, skill and dedication to act responsibly in the patient's interests. But although trust is necessary in asymmetrical relationships, it is now recognised that trust is a *mutual* process, reflecting a relationship in which care and treatment are discussed and agreed, rather than a model whereby the health professional identifies the problem, and proposes the solution – which the patient simply accepts or rejects (Herring, 2008, p. 232). Similarly, for Murphy (1998, p. 168), the importance of fostering trust is that it 'foregrounds core virtues like intimacy, commitment and risk', i.e. virtues which encourage 'talk' between the patient and health professionals.

5.3.2 Consequentialist arguments

Many consider the primary justification for maintaining confidentiality to be that it produces better medical consequences (e.g. Beauchamp and Childress, 2009; McHale, 1993). This and similar arguments are described as consequentialist because they focus on the future beneficial consequences (to patients and society) that arise from confidentiality. One such argument is this: if patients cannot trust health professionals to keep their secrets, they will feel betrayed and thus more likely to withhold potentially significant (but embarrassing) details, or worse still, may not seek care or treatment at all. As a consequence, the care they receive (if any) may be compromised, not least because without full and frank disclosure of symptoms and so forth, accurate diagnoses and prognoses may not be possible. Nor may recommended treatment be the best available if patients have not been honest for fear that sensitive information may become widely known. A teenager, for example, who wants contraceptive treatment is unlikely to seek advice from health professionals if she thinks her parents will be told, against her wishes.

As to the effect on society as a whole, the claim is that patients with, for example, transmissible diseases (especially sexually transmissible ones) will continue to seek treatment only so long as they trust health professionals to keep their confidences. Accordingly, there will be more opportunities for patients to be 'educated and influenced' in ways that may reduce the chances of the disease being passed on to others (Gillon, 2001, p. 427). Secondly, supposing a nurse decides to breach a patient's confidentiality, as this becomes more widely known, other patients may also begin to lose trust in that specific nurse and so fail to disclose 'embarrassing' symptoms. More seriously, a lack of trust could then 'spread' – leading to a belief that nurses as a group are generally untrustworthy. The consequence of this could ultimately be poorer health care for a larger number of people (see further Hope et al., 2008, pp. 96–97).

5.3.3 Respect for autonomy

Another common moral perspective for maintaining confidentiality is respect for autonomy. According to Vedder (1999, p. 142), there are two sides to autonomy in the context of confidentiality. First, it has to do with considering individuals to be 'masters' of their own 'well-being' – a term which can mean different things to children and young people than to adults (Axford, 2008). But crucially, we now take for granted the idea that running our own lives includes controlling what happens to our personal information – much of which may consist of the most intimate and sensitive aspects of ourselves – in other words, deciding what 'private' information should be disclosed (if any), what should be kept secret (or revealed only to the few) and who should have access to that information.

The second aspect of autonomy can be viewed as an expression of esteem for the dignity of individual persons, because in doing so they are regarded seriously, in other words as beings who are capable of making choices and acting in the morally right way (Vedder, 1999, p. 145). Now that there is growing awareness of how children's cognitive capacities develop, in particular how their thinking becomes more abstract, multidimensional, self-reflective and self-aware as they mature, so there is increasing recognition that they should have greater autonomy to make their own decisions (including what happens to their personal information; Bailey, 2001, p. 76).

5.3.4 Privacy

A closely related moral justification for the duty of confidentiality is sometimes grounded in another concern – to protect a person's privacy. The term 'privacy' has been described as a sweeping phrase, which is as comprehensive as it is vague (Wacks, 1980). Certainly, it is an amorphous concept whose meaning is difficult to pin down. But according to Stone (2008, p. 465), most discussions of the concept begin by equating privacy with the 'right to be let alone'. But in health contexts, privacy is more concerned with the control of personal information and with preventing access to that information by others – i.e. what is described as 'informational privacy' (Mason and Laurie, 2006, p. 224). Privacy in this sense recognises the importance attached in contemporary society to the idea that individuals have the right to their own 'space'. Indeed, perhaps the easiest way to understand the concept of privacy is to think of it as a collection of spaces. The most intimate space (which only the person himself/herself has access to) contains the person's most secret thoughts, feelings, hopes, fears, etc. Other wider, less private spaces hold information to which a person's family, friends and so forth, have access. And the widest space of all is the public domain to which the whole world has access (Brown et al., 1992, pp. 96–97).

However it is defined, a right to privacy is now increasingly seen as a basic human need and a necessary condition of self-hood, hence its protection (or rather, of a right to a 'private life') in the Human Rights Act 1998 (Article 8).

Activities

Compare and contrast the justifications for confidentiality. Which do you find the most convincing? Explain why.

Key points

- The moral duty of confidentiality means that secret or private information must not be disclosed.
- Ethical justifications for confidentiality include consequentialism, respect for autonomy, trust and privacy.

5.4 The Moral Case for Breaching Confidentiality

Almost all moral theories acknowledge that health professionals owe their patients a duty of confidentiality (Pattinson, 2006, p. 174). The importance of maintaining confidentiality is similarly emphasised in professional codes of ethics (likewise the NHS Confidentiality Code (DoH, 2003) which binds everyone working in the NHS). Yet without exception they also all recognise that the duty of confidentiality is not absolute. In other words, in some circumstances a patient's confidentiality can (or should) be breached (see, e.g. GMC, 2007; ICN, 2005; NMC, 2008b). However, guidance in the codes about these 'circumstances' is typically very vague and thus of little practical use in individual cases. Whilst this is understandable – there can be no hard and fast rules given the variables in each case – it does mean that practitioners may have to undertake a complex ethical balancing exercise to decide whether the duty of confidentiality should be overridden by other more compelling moral considerations.

The 'confidentiality' dilemmas that children's nurses are most likely to face are those which allow disclosure with the patient's consent, in the patient's best interests, in the public interest and those which are required by law (all of which overlap). These are discussed in detail although other permissible disclosures are also briefly mentioned.

5.4.1 Consent

The least morally controversial and the most straightforward exception to the duty of confidentiality is when patients consent to information being passed on. Their consent must, however, be given freely, i.e. free from undue pressure or influence. Establishing that consent is truly free can, of course, be quite another matter. As Mason and Laurie point out, 'What patient at a teaching hospital outpatient department is likely to refuse when the consultant asks: You don't mind these young doctors being present, do you?' In these kinds of situations, few patients – especially a young person – would be able to resist such pressure (Mason and Laurie, 2006, p. 258).

There are two types of consent: explicit and implied.

Explicit consent

The NHS Confidentiality Code (DoH, 2003) provides detailed guidance about obtaining explicit consent to disclose information. Although not focused on children and young people, the approach it requires clearly applies to those to whom a duty of confidentiality is owed. When nurses are relying on consent, the Code makes it clear that they must provide:

- Honest, clear, objective information about information uses and their choices;
- An opportunity for patients to talk to someone they can trust and of whom they can ask questions;
- Reasonable time (and privacy) to reach decisions;
- Support and explanations about any form they may be required to sign;
- Evidence that consent has been given.

In addition, the information provided must cover:

- A basic explanation of what information is recorded and why, and what further uses may be made of it;
- A description of the benefits that may result from the proposed use or disclosure of the information;
- How the information will be protected;
- Any outcomes, implications or risks if consent is withheld;
- An explanation that consent can be withdrawn (see further DoH, 2003, Annex B, 16–21).

Implied consent

In practice, explicit consent to disclosure is rare. Much more typical – and more complicated – is when patients are said to have given implied consent to disclosure. Implied consent is based on the widely held assumption that because patients realise that confidential information has to be passed back and forth between their health care 'team' (and between different organisations involved in health care provision) they implicitly give consent to its disclosure. Indeed, to suggest otherwise, i.e. that specific consent must be obtained *every* time one member of a health team wanted to discuss a patient's care with another member would be arguably absurd (McLean and Mason, 2003, p. 34). Yet it has been suggested that the whole notion of implied consent is a fiction, particularly when the disclosure of information is not directly related to a patient's treatment, i.e. it relates to clinical audit, monitoring public health and research and so on (Herring, 2008, p. 209).

Because of these concerns the combined effect (in brief) of professional guidance (e.g. GMC, 2004; NMC, 2008b and c), DoH (2003, 2006) now makes it clear that practitioners can only rely on implied consent provided several conditions are complied with. These include the following:

- Patients must be made aware about how and why information is shared by all those who will be providing their care.
- Information must only be given to those who genuinely 'need to know'.
- Patients must be made aware that their information may be used to support clinical audit and other work to monitor the quality of care (see further DoH, 2003, Annex C).
- It cannot be assumed that patients impliedly consent to information being disclosed for purposes not directly concerned with their health care; additional efforts to gain consent are required.
- Patients generally have the right to object to the use and disclosure of information (but see below).

5.4.2 Public interest

The concept of public interest is probably the most important exception to the duty of confidentiality, but it is also the most troublesome, largely because no single definition of what it amounts to exists. Given the absence of any clear boundaries and its potentially very broad scope, it is perhaps not surprising that this exception poses the most dilemmas in practice. Most commentators, nevertheless, agree that, very broadly, public interest covers matters thought to be '*for the good of society*'. Slightly more specific guidance about the scope of public interest is provided in professional codes. According to the NMC Code (2008b), for example, nurses are told that confidentiality can be breached if they 'believe someone may be at risk of harm' (supplemental advice further defines public interest as: 'protecting individuals, groups or society as a whole from the risk of significant harm, such as child abuse, crime or drug trafficking', NMC Code, 2008c; see also DoH, 2003, Annex B, paras 27–34). In summary, it seems that information that identifies a child or young person *can* be disclosed (without consent) in the following situations.

Child protection
When there is reasonable suspicion that a child is suffering (or is likely to suffer) 'significant harm' (see further Chapter 11).

Preventing serious harm to others
Disclosures that are intended to prevent serious harm are widely supported – not just by practitioners but also by the public (Jones, 2003). More controversial is how serious the harm (or its risk) must be to justify breaching confidentiality. Guidance from the NHS cites examples of behaviour that warrant breach of confidentiality, notably child abuse or neglect (including the impact on siblings who know of the abuse), assault, traffic accident or the spread of infectious diseases. Also identified as potentially harmful is serious fraud or theft involving NHS resources (such as prescription frauds), which would also be likely to harm individuals waiting for treatment (DoH, 2003, p. 35).

In practice, the key factors nurses should take into account in reaching their decision and assessing the risk to 'others' include not just the probability that the predicted harm will materialise but also the magnitude of the harm. So the less serious the potential harm, the greater the moral obligation not to breach confidentiality. Other factors that may also have to be taken into account include the extent to which there are ways (other than breaching confidentiality) in which the potential harm can be prevented or minimised. Note finally the importance of recording reasons for the decision that was ultimately made, i.e. why it was decided to disclose information (or not).

Preventing or detecting 'serious' crime

Disclosures that are intended to prevent and support the detection, investigation and punishment of serious crime (usually against the person) are also widely accepted. But again there is no clear definition of what amounts to 'serious' crime. According to DoH (2003), it would include murder, manslaughter, rape, treason, kidnapping, child abuse or other cases where individuals have suffered *serious harm*. Serious harm to the security of the state or to public order would also fall into the category. In contrast, theft, fraud or damage to property, where loss is less substantial, would generally not warrant breach of confidence (DoH, 2003, p. 35).

As with preventing harm to others, each case must be decided on its merits. In cases where decisions are finely balanced, it may be necessary to seek legal advice (DoH, 2003, p. 34).

5.4.3 In the child's or young person's best interests

There may be times when the sharing of information (that may be of the most personal and private kind) will be necessary in order to protect the best interests of children and young people. Those most at risk of having intimate details of their lives revealed are likely to suffer from a wide range of 'problems' such as anorexia nervosa, depression, severe anxiety, self-harming, drug addiction or 'antisocial' behaviours which may include violence, arson and sexual offences (see further Bailey, 2001, pp. 72–73). In most of these cases – especially in cases of serious mental disorders – information will need to be shared with (or requested from) parents (and other family members) who may be participants in treatment, but also various health and welfare agencies (such as social services, schools and child health services).

The degree to which information needs to be shared (and the nature of that information) depends on a range of factors, such as the following:

- The child or young person's current vulnerability and capacity (which can change over time);
- Closeness of the relationship between the child or young person and her parents;
- Degree of involvement of the parents in their child's care and treatment;
- Emotional maturity of the child;
- Severity of the mental disorder or distress and its impact on decision-making;
- Degree of care and protection required (see further Tan et al., 2007, pp. 202–205).

Whatever the specific mental health issue, however, Tan et al. stress the importance of gaining trust: 'Wherever possible, consensus and prior agreement should be obtained concerning the extent and degree of information sharing with families and other professionals and agencies ... and even when confidentiality must be overridden, the principle of respect for privacy, autonomy and respect for family life should be maintained as far as possible' (Tan et al., 2007, p. 205).

5.4.4 Disclosures to parents

In some circumstances, confidential information will have to be shared with a child or young person's parents (or other person with parental responsibility) or their carer simply because they are too young and immature to understand what it means to trust another person with 'secret' information. Few would disagree that discussing a 5-year-old's need for a tonsillectomy with her parents is in her interests. Similarly, a child may be too ill and thus lack the capacity to make her own treatment decisions. In such cases, disclosures to parents will almost always be in the child's interests (Dimond, 2008; GMC, 2007; Hendrick, 1997; McLean and Mason, 2003).

More controversial are cases where a competent young person is, for example, refusing treatment for a life-threatening condition. According to the DoH (2003, Annex B, para 9), in this kind of situation it would be justifiable to breach confidentiality to the extent of informing those with parental responsibility – who may then be able to provide the necessary consent.

> ### Activity
>
> Read Disclosure Model B.1 of the NHS Code of Confidentiality (DoH, 2003) (http://www.dh.gov). Consider whether you comply with its recommendations in practice.

> ### Key points
>
> - The moral duty of confidentiality is not absolute.
> - Confidentiality may be breached in the following circumstances: consent, public interest, in a child's best interests.

5.5 The Law of Confidentiality

This section outlines the law of confidentiality as it affects nurses. It focuses in particular on the legal exceptions to the duty of confidentiality but begins by examining how the concept is defined and its legal sources.

5.5.1 The legal definition of confidentiality

Despite the long-recognised legal right to confidentiality – in *Wood v Wyatt* (unreported but cited in *Prince Albert v Strange* [1849] 41 ER 1171), publication of the diaries of George III's doctor was restrained (McHale, 1993) – the law on breach of confidence has developed in a piecemeal way. That explains why there is no single authoritative legal definition of 'confidential information'. Case law (e.g. *AG v Guardian Newspapers (No 2)* [1990] 1 AC 101; *Ashworth Hospital Authority v MGN* [2002] UKHL 29) has nonetheless established that the courts will generally enforce a duty of confidentiality in certain conditions if the information:

- Is of a *private* or *intimate* nature, i.e. not a matter of public knowledge;
- Is not useless or trivial in nature (note that it is up to the patient to decide what is trivial);
- Must have been given in a situation where there is an obligation not to disclose it, i.e. a fiduciary (trusting) relationship exists.

Whether there is also a need to show that someone will suffer as a result of the release of information is unclear. What is self-evident, however, is that these conditions are vague and question-begging. Nonetheless, there is little doubt that medical information will generally be considered confidential (Brazier and Cave, 2007; Jackson, 2006; Pattenden, 2003).

5.5.2 Legal sources of confidentiality

There are several legal sources of the duty of confidentiality. These include the following.

Contract law

Nurses' contracts of employment with their employers normally contain an implied or express contractual term that they will respect patients' confidentiality.

Negligence

Patients basing their right to confidentiality in the law of negligence would need to establish that the duty of care incorporates an assurance that their private affairs will be kept secret. Even if successful, a patient is only likely to be awarded limited damages (Herring, 2008, p. 194).

Equity

Equity developed hundreds of years ago to provide 'real' justice, i.e. rights and remedies not available under more rigid common law principles. In this context, equity will generally enforce an obligation to respect patients' confidences once a fiduciary relationship has arisen (such as exists between nurses and their patients).

Statutory obligations

Here we focus on the Data Protection Act (DPA) 1998, which is one of the most important statutes governing confidentiality apart from Article 8 of the Human Rights Act 1998, which itself establishes a right to 'respect for private and family life, home and correspondence' (*Campbell v MGN* [2004] UKHL 22 and Wacks, 2008).

The DPA 1998 – which is notoriously complex and lengthy – provides a framework governing the 'processing' of 'personal data'. The term 'processing' is very widely defined. Essentially, therefore, *any* activity in relation to an individual's 'personal data' (which includes a patient's 'health record', whether manual or electronic) will constitute 'processing' (see section on access to records for a detailed definition of 'health record'). The Act imposes constraints on the processing of personal data in relation to living individuals. Basically, it identifies eight principles that set out standards for handling such data; i.e. its processing must be 'fair' and lawful; the data must be accurate, kept up to date, adequate, relevant and so on.

But because 'health records' are classified as 'sensitive personal data', they are protected by additional safeguards. These basically prevent the information being processed unless special conditions are met; i.e. information about a patient's health can be used where it is necessary (a) to protect the vital interests of a patient (who cannot consent); (b) in connection with the administration of justice; or (c) for medical purposes (where the information is being used by a health professional). Note that this list is not exhaustive (see further Schedule 3).

Activity

1. Access the NHS confidentiality code of practice (http://www.doh.gov.uk/). Do you find its advice about children and confidentiality helpful?

Key points

-   The courts will recognise a legal duty of confidentiality if the information is private, it is not trivial in nature and there is a fiduciary relationship.
-   The DPA 1998 is the main statute protecting patients' confidentiality.

5.6 Children's Legal Right to Confidentiality

Whether or not a duty of confidentiality is owed to children and young people turns on the age and the maturity of the child in question.

5.6.1 The 16- and 17-year-olds

Adolescents in this age group have the same legal rights as adults in relation to consent to treatment. As such, they have a corresponding right to confidentiality (Herring, 2008). But the duty only arises if they are competent (see Chapter 4). If not, then just as with incompetent adult patients, the duty to act in the patient's best interests (see below) may mean that confidential information can be disclosed to relatives (normally their parents).

5.6.2 *Gillick* competent children under 16

As great a legal duty of confidentiality is owed to *Gillick* competent minors as competent 16- and 17-year-olds, i.e. they should be treated as adults. This is because it can be assumed that if they are mature enough to consent to treatment then they also have sufficient understanding and intelligence to enter into a confidential relationship (Brazier and Cave, 2007, p. 406; *R (on the application of Axon) v Secretary of State for Health* [2006] EWHC 37). As such, they are entitled to make decisions about the use and disclosure of information they have provided in confidence; e.g. they may be receiving treatment or counselling about which they do not want their parents to know (DoH, 2003).

5.6.3 Incompetent under 16-year-olds

The question whether a child who fails to pass the *Gillick* competency test (and is therefore not competent to consent to treatment) may nevertheless have a right to confidentiality has been the subject of much debate (for a summary, see Montgomery, 2003, pp. 308–311). Briefly, there are two different approaches. One view is that even though children may lack the capacity to consent, they may nevertheless have sufficient maturity to form a relationship of confidence, i.e. to understand what it means to trust someone with 'secret' information (and thus have an expectation that the information will not be disclosed without their consent). If so, then they are owed a duty of confidentiality (see *Re C (A Minor) (Wardship: Medical Treatment)* [1990] Fam 39; *Venables v NGN* [2001] Fam 430; Herring, 2008; Kennedy and Grubb, 2000; Loughrey, 2003; Montgomery, 2003).

Briefly, the alternative approach rejects the notion that incompetent children are owed a duty of confidentiality. As Kennedy (1991) asserts, the obligation of confidence is about enabling autonomous decision-making. If the child is not able to make a decision then autonomy is not an issue.

Note finally that most commentators agree (despite the absence of clear authority) that very young children, who are neither *Gillick* competent nor capable of forming a relationship of confidence, are not owed a duty of confidentiality – the effect of which is that confidential information should normally be disclosed to their parents (or others with parental responsibility); only exceptionally – such as when child abuse is suspected – should this not be the case.

> **Key points**
>
> - Young people aged 16 and 17 have the same legal right to confidentiality as adults.
> - *Gillick* competent children under 16 have a legal right to confidentiality.
> - Incompetent children under 16 have a right to confidentiality if they can form a relationship of confidence.

5.7 Legal Exceptions to the Duty of Confidentiality

We noted above that all professional codes of ethics recognise that the duty of confidentiality is not absolute. Not surprisingly, the law adopts a similar approach. Accordingly, this section focuses on the legal exceptions that are most relevant to children's nursing (other exceptions are outlined briefly).

5.7.1 Consent

This exception mirrors the moral case for breaching confidentiality (see above).

5.7.2 Public interest

The scope of the common law public interest exception – which gives nurses the option of breaching confidentiality but does not oblige them to do so – is as uncertain as the professional exception. It is similarly the most contentious because there is no authoritative legal definition of the phrase 'public interest'. Instead, it seems that breaches are lawful 'whenever the public interest in maintaining confidentiality is outweighed by the public interest in disclosure' (per Lord Goff in *AG v Guardian* [1990] 1 AC 109, 281). What this means is that the interest of those claiming confidentiality has to be considered alongside the interests of others – the public generally or identifiable individuals (or an individual) who may be harmed unless confidentiality is breached. There is little doubt, however, that it will normally be lawful to breach confidentiality to prevent or detect serious crime or harm to others.

Preventing harm to others

Some guidance on the circumstances that may justify disclosure on the basis of a threat of serious harm to others can be derived from the leading case of *W v Edgell* [1990] 1 All ER 835. W was a psychiatric patient who was being detained indefinitely in a secure hospital following his conviction for killing five people 10 years previously. He applied to be discharged, and a report of his mental health was prepared by Dr Edgell. Edgell strongly opposed W's transfer to a regional secure unit – the first step towards his eventual release – because of his long-standing and continuing interest in home-made bombs. In short, Edgell claimed that W remained very dangerous. In fact, he was so concerned that even though W withdrew his application, Edgell sent a copy of the report to the medical director of the hospital and the Home Office. W sued Edgell for breach of confidence. W was unsuccessful. The court held that the duty of confidentiality owed to W was outweighed by the overriding interest in public safety.

The combined effect of *W v Edgell* (and subsequent cases, e.g. *R v Kennedy* [1999] 1 Cr App R 54; *Woolgar v Chief Constable of the Sussex Police* [1999] 3 All ER 604) about the scope of the 'public interest' in law can be summarised as follows:

- Before disclosure can be justified, there must be a real, serious and significant risk of danger to the public.

- The risk to the public must arguably be to their physical safety, i.e. danger of physical harm or disease.
- The risk must be a serious possibility (and an ongoing one).
- Disclosure must be limited to those with a legitimate interest in receiving the information.
- Only such information as is strictly necessary should be revealed.

From the above, there is no doubt that it would be lawful to disclose confidential information (to the relevant authorities) about the threat posed by a mentally ill patient who poses a potential threat to the public (or a specified person). In *Re L (Care Proceedings: Disclosure to a Third Party)* [2000] 1 FLR 913, for example, a paediatric nurse, who suffered from a severe personality disorder, tried to prevent information about her mental health problems being given to the United Kingdom Combined Council (UKCC) (following care proceedings). The court decided that she posed a risk to children in her care. Accordingly, it authorised disclosure of expert medical reports to the UKCC – on the basis that the public interest outweighed her right to confidentiality.

Preventing or detecting serious crime
As we saw above, professional guidance (e.g. GMC, 2004; NMC, 2008b and c) and NHS guidance (DoH, 2003) state clearly that breaching confidentiality can be justified to prevent, investigate or detect serious crime (such as murder, manslaughter and child abuse). Whilst the law also recognises this exception to the duty of confidentiality, it should be noted that this exception is not synonymous with the exception based on preventing harm to others (although there is considerable overlap between the two). Thus, there is a public interest in the detection of crime even when there is no risk of reoffending and even though the crime did not involve physical injury (Jackson, 2006, p. 347).

In the absence of any definitive legal guidance on what amounts to 'serious crime', the case of *Woolgar v Chief Constable of Sussex Police* [1999] 3 All ER 604 is instructive. W, a registered nurse, and the matron of a nursing home were interviewed by the police following the death of a patient. No charges were brought but the matter was referred to the UKCC. The UKCC asked the police to disclose any relevant information. In such situations, it is normal police procedure to ask permission from those who had given statements. W refused to give consent and sought an injunction to prevent the police disclosing a tape of her interview. The High Court refused to grant the injunction. W's appeal to the Court of Appeal failed because the court held that disclosure was justified 'for the protection of health or morals, or for the protection of the rights and freedoms of others'.

Child protection
It is similarly widely accepted that it would be lawful (under the public interest exception) to disclose information – to, e.g. social services or the police – that a patient is abusing a child (likewise if a child patient is a victim of abuse or neglect; *Re M* [1990] 1 All ER 205, see further Chapter 11).

5.7.3 In the child's best interests

The legal position mirrors the moral case for breaching confidentiality noted above.

5.7.4 Disclosures to parents

Again, the legal position mirrors the moral case (see above). This is because there is no doubt that the 'right' of very young children (or incompetent older children) to confidentiality does not involve keeping treatment information from their parents. Indeed, only if parents are properly informed can they exercise parental responsibility and so make treatment decisions that are in their children's best interests. Effectively, then, we can say that a nurse's duty of confidentiality is owed to the family unit of parent(s) and child rather than the child alone (Jackson, 2006, p. 333). As Thorpe LJ said in *Re C (A Minor) (Wardship: Medical Treatment)* [1990] Fam 39, 'the parents undoubtedly owe C a duty of confidentiality, save in so far as C's welfare otherwise requires'.

5.7.5 Disclosures to the police

A nurse can become involved in police investigations in a variety of situations. She may, for example, be treating a patient who she suspects has committed a criminal offence or the police may ask her when a patient can be questioned. And what should she do if she discovers a crime whilst working in the community? As Dimond explains, the nurse's legal position in all these (and similar) situations is clear: there is no general legal duty to report crime to the police. This means that nurses do not have to volunteer information to them that a young person has committed a crime (Dimond, 2008, p. 185). Nevertheless, nurses must not obstruct police investigations (e.g. by giving false or misleading information). Note that refusing to answer police questions with a 'lawful excuse' is not obstruction – the lawful excuse being the duty of confidentiality (*Rice v Connolly* [1966] 2 All ER 649; see also sections 9, 12 and 14 of the Police and Criminal Evidence Act 1984), which requires the police to seek the court's permission should they want access to medical records and diagnostic samples of humans (see further McHale, 2007, pp. 151–152).

5.7.6 Statutory obligations

Several statutes impose obligations on health professionals to breach confidentiality. These include legislation to combat terrorism, notify authorities of births, deaths and notifiable diseases – e.g. smallpox and typhus, some forms of venereal disease and food poisoning – and provide information about abortions, namely, the patient's NHS number, date of birth, and full postcode (see further Hope et al., 2008, pp. 101–104).

5.7.7 Civil proceedings and court orders

Sometimes health records may be relevant in civil proceedings, particularly in negligence claims and child protection cases. Unless these are volunteered, a court order (called a subpoena) may be issued requiring any relevant evidence (including confidential information) or witnesses in the interests of justice. Failure to comply with such an order can result in contempt of court (for which the nurse may be imprisoned). A case which illustrates the court's approach is *Re C* [1991] FLR 478. It concerned the proposed adoption of a 1-year-old baby. A day before the adoption hearing, the mother withdrew her consent to the adoption. The adopting parents' solicitor then produced a document, sworn voluntarily by the mother's general practitioner (GP), containing evidence of her mental state and fitness to bring up a child. The mother objected to this evidence being admitted, claiming it was a breach of her confidentiality. She lost her action as the court held that the GP's evidence was highly relevant. In short, the baby's welfare – and the need for the court to have all the relevant information – outweighed the legal duty of confidentiality owed to the mother.

5.7.8 Research, teaching and audit

Without access to information about patients and their diseases, much vital research could not be carried out. Similarly, patient information may be necessary to train health professionals, carry out audits of patient care and compile health statistics. Ideally, patients' consent should be sought but this is not always feasible – for example, in research involving a large number of patients. In such cases anonymised data (i.e. non-identifying) may be used (see *R v Department of Health, ex parte Source Informatics Ltd* [2001] QB 424). Note too section 251 of the NHS Act 2006, which is a major exception to the duty of confidentiality in so far as it *permits* disclosure of medical information without a patient's consent 'in the interest of improving patient care' or in the public interest provided there is no reasonably practicable alternative (see further http:// www.dh.gov.uk/ipu/confiden/protect/).

> **Key points**
>
> - Confidentiality is not an absolute legal principle.
> - Legal obligations to breach confidentiality include notifiable diseases, terrorism, births, deaths, court orders and termination of pregnancy.
> - Legally permissible breaches include public interest, in the best interests of the child, to parents and consent.

5.8 Access to Records

5.8.1 Data Protection Act 1998

The main statute regulating patients' access to their records is the DPA (although Article 8 of the Human Rights Act 1998 also protects patients' right of access to medical records, as does the Access to Medical Records Act 1990, which applies to deceased patients). The DPA gives every living person the right to apply for access to their health records (but note that the Act as a whole refers to 'personal data', a term which includes health records but is much broader, see above). Certain key terms are defined as follows:

- *Health record*: It is a record consisting of information about the physical or mental health or condition of an identifiable individual made by or on behalf of a *health professional* in connection with the care of that individual.
- *Types of health records*: A health record can be recorded in a computerised or in a manual form (or a mixture of both). It can include such things as handwritten notes, letters to and from other health professionals, laboratory reports, radiographs and other imaging records, e.g. X-rays and not just X-ray reports, printouts from monitoring equipment, photographs, videos and tape recordings of telephone conversations.
- *Private/NHS*: The Act applies not just to NHS records but also to the private health sector.
- *Health professional*: This term is defined expansively and so includes doctors, dentists, nurses, midwives, health visitors, occupational therapists and most kinds of other 'conventional' health professionals (as well as some complementary medicine practitioners such as osteopaths and chiropractors; see further s.69).

5.8.2 Access to a child's record

There is no specific provision in the DPA about access by child patients. However, most commentators assume that section 7 accords children and young people a right to access their health records if they are competent enough to request access, i.e. able to understand the nature of and likely consequence of such a request (see, e.g. Kennedy and Grubb, 2000, p. 1028; Pattinson, 2006, p. 205).

Those with parental responsibility can request access to their child's health record. But this will not be granted unless the young person consents or they are incapable of understanding the nature of the request and the granting of access is in their best interests.

5.8.3 Withholding information

Access to health records is qualified; i.e. it can be denied in certain circumstances. For example, the child may not be considered sufficiently competent to understand the nature of an application for access. Several other exemptions also apply (see s.33). In brief, the most important qualification to access by children and young people (although it applies to *all* applicants) is that information may be denied or limited:

- Where disclosure 'would be likely to cause serious harm to the physical or mental health or condition of the patient or any other person' (which may include a health professional), or
- Where giving access would disclose information relating to or provided by a third person who has not consented to the disclosure (unless it is reasonable to comply with the access request without that consent; see further Data Protection (Subject Access Modifications) (Health) Order 2000).

5.8.4 Inspecting health records

The Act gives patients the right, among other things, to be:

1. Informed whether personal data are being 'processed';
2. Given a description of the data held, the purposes for which it is held and to whom the data may be disclosed;
3. Given a copy of the data in an 'intelligible form';
4. Given information on the source of the data (see further s.7).

The Act also contains detailed provisions about the procedure to be followed to gain access to records (including time limits and costs). Most importantly, once they have seen their records, patients are entitled to have the record rectified if it is inaccurate (see further s.14).

Key points

- The main statute governing children's access to their health records is the DPA 1998.
- Children and young people can access their records if they are competent i.e. understand the nature of requesting access.
- Children's legal right to see their records is not absolute.

> **Case study**
>
> Carol, a sexually active 15-year-old who has been in and out of care for the past few years, has recently been diagnosed as HIV positive. She refuses to let her partner Jeff be told about her HIV status even though she knows he may become infected. Indeed, she explicitly tells Barack, the doctor, that she only came for a check-up because she knew that if she were HIV positive he could not tell anyone unless she consented. Carol agrees that the practice nurse, Penelope, can be told (providing she too keeps the diagnosis secret).
>
> Barack thinks that Carol's confidentiality should be respected. However, the practice nurse, Penelope, thinks that Jeff has a right to know.
>
> Must Carol's confidentiality be respected or can Penelope inform Jeff of Carol's HIV status?

5.8.5 Ethical considerations

There is little doubt that Penelope owes Carol a duty of confidentiality. By expressly telling Barack that she expects him to keep her diagnosis a secret (except in relation to Penelope), she clearly understands the nature of a trusting relationship.

As regards Penelope's moral obligation to maintain confidentiality, there are several approaches she could take. One is to regard confidentiality as an absolute principle that should not be breached for any reason. Another is to treat it as a qualified principle, which would mean that confidentiality could be breached in certain circumstances – e.g. if another person could otherwise be seriously harmed. A third approach, which falls somewhere between the two, is for Penelope to do all she can to protect Jeff but at the same time to maintain Carol's confidentiality. She could, for example, use every effort she can to persuade Carol to take precautions.

Assuming Carol fails to be persuaded (e.g. to take precautions) and assuming Penelope decides to breach Carol's confidentiality, could she justify her actions? Given the 'serious' and very real 'risk' – i.e. that Jeff will be infected, and disclosure is the only practical way of protecting him – there is little doubt that her breach could be justified on 'public interest' grounds. Certainly, conventional wisdom in medical ethics is that disclosure is ethically permissible. Some commentators, however, are not persuaded that in HIV situations the duty of confidentiality can be breached. In short, they argue for an unqualified duty (see e.g. Kipnis, 2006)

5.8.6 Legal position

In legal terms, the first question is again whether Carol is owed a duty of confidentiality. The answer is yes. Carol clearly understands the nature of a confidential relationship and so is owed the same duty of confidentiality as an adult.

The second issue is whether Penelope could justify informing Jeff of Carol's HIV status. There has been no case directly on this issue or any other authoritative legal guidelines. Nonetheless, legal commentators generally agree that passing on information to a patient's partner without consent is legally permissible (under the 'public interest' exception) – assuming that (a) every effort is made to persuade the patient to do so, and (b) the partner faces a 'real' risk of 'serious harm' (Dimond, 2008; Herring, 2008; Montgomery, 2003; Pattinson, 2006). It should also be noted here that it is a serious criminal offence for someone who knows she/he is HIV positive to infect a partner (without telling him/her of the risk, see *R v Dica* [2004] EWCA Crim 1231 and see further Michalowski, 2004).

Note finally that whether a court would endorse the breach of confidentiality would ultimately depend on the specific facts of each case and guidance from cases like *W v Edgell* [1990].

5.9 Relationship between Law and Ethics

5.9.1 Similarities between law and ethics

- **Justification:** The ethical and legal duty of confidentiality can be justified on both consequentialist and deontological grounds (i.e. on the basis of respect for autonomy and privacy).
- **Breaching confidentiality:** In neither law nor ethics is confidentiality regarded as an absolute principle; rather it is qualified. That means there may be good reasons to breach patient's confidentiality.
- **Exceptions to the duty of confidentiality:** The legal and ethical grounds for breaching confidentiality are broadly similar and include consent, public interest and disclosures required by statute or court order.

5.9.2 Differences between law and ethics

- **Origins:** The moral duty to protect patients' confidentiality goes back to the fifth century BC. The legal sources are much more recent.
- **Clarity:** Professional codes and guidelines about the scope, nature and exceptions to the duty of confidentiality are usually much clearer than the law.

References

Axford, N. (2008) *Exploring Concepts of Children's Well-Being*. Bristol: Policy Press.
Bailey, S. (2001) Confidentiality and young people. In Cordess, C. (ed.) *Confidentiality and Mental Health*. London: Jessica Kingsley.
Beauchamp, T.L. and Childress, J.F. (2009) *Principles of Biomedical Ethics*, 6th edn. Oxford: Oxford University Press.
Brazier, M. and Cave, E. (2007) *Medicine, Patients and the Law*. London: Penguin.
Brown, J.M., Kitson, A.L. and McKnight, T.J. (1992) *Challenges in Caring*. London: Chapman & Hall.
Cain, P. (2001) The limits of confidentiality in healthcare. In Cordess, C. (ed.) *Confidentiality and Mental Health*. London: Jessica Kingsley.
Campbell, E. and Ross, L.F. (2003) Professional and personal attitudes about access and confidentiality in the genetic testing of children: a pilot study. *Genetic Testing* 2:123.
Carlisle, J., Shickle, D., Cork, M. and McDonagh, A. (2006) Concerns over confidentiality may deter adolescents from consulting their doctors: a qualitative exploration. *Journal of Medical Ethics* 32(3):133.
Dimond, B. (2008) *Legal Aspects of Nursing*, 5th edn. Harlow: Pearson Education.
DoH (2003) *Confidentiality: NHS Code of Practice*. London: DoH.
DoH (2006) *The Protection and Use of Patient Information*. London: DoH.
European Union (2005) *European Standards on Confidentiality and Privacy in Healthcare (EuroSO-CAP)*.
Gillon, R. (2001) Confidentiality. In Kuhse, H. and Singer, P. (eds) *A Companion Guide to Bioethics*. Oxford: Blackwell.
GMC (2004) *Confidentiality: Protecting and Providing Information*. London: GMC.
GMC (2007) *0–18 Guidance for All Doctors*. London: GMC.
Hendrick, J. (1997) *Legal Aspects of Child Care Law*. London: Chapman & Hall.
Hendrick, J. (2000) *Law and Ethics in Nursing and Health Care*. Cheltenham: Stanley Thornes.
Herring, J. (2008) *Medical Law and Ethics*, 2nd edn. Oxford: Oxford University Press.
Hope, T., Savulescu, J. and Hendrick, J. (2008) *Medical Ethics and Law: The Core Curriculum*. Edinburgh: Elsevier.
ICN (2005) *Code of Ethics for Nurses*. Geneva: ICN.
Jackson, E. (2006) *Medical Law: Text, Cases and Materials*. Oxford: Oxford University Press.
Jones, C. (2003) The utilitarian argument for medical confidentiality: a pilot study of parents' views. *Journal of Medical Ethics* 29:348.

Kennedy, I. (1991) *Treat Me Right: Essays in Medical Law and Ethics*. Oxford: Oxford University Press.

Kennedy, I. and Grubb, A. (2000) *Medical Law: Text and Materials*, 3rd edn. London: Butterworths.

Kipnis, K. (2006) A defense of unqualified medical confidentiality. *American Journal of Bioethics* 6(2):7.

Loughrey, J. (2003) Medical information, confidentiality and a child's right to privacy. *Legal Studies* 23(3):510.

Mason, J.K. and Laurie, G.T. (2006) *Mason and McCall Smith's Medical Law and Ethics*. Oxford: Oxford University Press.

McHale, J. (1993) *Medical Confidentiality and Legal Privilege*. London: Routledge.

McHale, J. (2007) Privacy, confidentiality and access to health-care records. In McHale, J. and Tingle, J. (eds) *Law and Nursing*, 3rd edn. Edinburgh: Churchill Livingstone/Elsevier.

McLean, A.M. and Mason, J.K. (2003) *Legal and Ethical Aspects of Healthcare*. Cambridge: Cambridge University Press.

Michalowski, S. (2004) *Medical Confidentiality and Crime*. Oxford: Oxford University Press.

Montgomery, J. (2003) *Health Care Law*. Oxford: Oxford University Press.

Murphy, T. (1998) Health confidentiality in the age of talk. In Sheldon, S. and Thomson, M. (eds) *Feminist Perspectives on Health Care Law*. London: Cavendish.

NMC (2008a) *Advice for Nurses Working with Children and Young People*. London: NMC.

NMC (2008b) *The Code: Standards of Conduct, Performance and Ethics for Nurses*. London: NMC.

NMC (2008c) *Confidentiality*. London: NMC.

Pattenden, A. (2003) *The Law of Professional Client Confidentiality: Regulating the Disclosure of Confidential Information*. Oxford: Oxford University Press.

Pattinson, S.D. (2006) *Medical Law and Ethics*. London: Sweet & Maxwell.

Quick, O. (2006) Outing medical errors: questions of trust and responsibility. *Medical Law Review* 14(1):22.

Smukler, G. and Holloway, F. (2001) Confidentiality in community psychiatry. In Cordess, C. (ed.) *Confidentiality and Mental Health*. London: Jessica Kingsley.

Stone, R. (2008) *Textbook on Civil Liberties of Human Rights*, 7th edn. Oxford: Oxford University Press.

Tan, J.O.A., Passerini, G.E. and Stewart, A. (2007) Consent and confidentiality in clinical work with young people. *Clinical Child Psychology and Psychiatry* 12(2):191.

Vedder, A. (1999) HIV/AIDs and the point and scope of medical confidentiality. In Bennet, R. and Erin, C.A. (eds) *HIV and AIDS: Testing, Screening and Confidentiality*. Oxford: Oxford University Press.

Wacks, R. (1980) *The Protection of Privacy*. London: Sweet & Maxwell.

Wacks, R. (2008) *Law: A Very Short Introduction*. Oxford: Oxford University Press.

CHAPTER 6

Justice and Access to Health Care

Learning outcomes

By the end of this chapter you should be able to:

- Understand what is meant by the phrase 'the fair distribution of health resources';
- Describe the various mechanisms for rationing health care;
- Debate the different moral perspectives on the problem of scarce health resources;
- Assess the role of law in challenging rationing decisions.

Introduction

The National Health Service (NHS) has been described as Britain's greatest institution (Hutton, 2000) and one of the best health services in the world (DoH, 2007). Created in 1948, the NHS was founded by a Labour government deeply committed to 'socialised medicine', i.e. comprehensive free medical care for the entire population. Yet, notwithstanding its continuing popularity (and national mandate), the NHS has been blighted by underfunding and in almost 'perpetual crisis' since its inception (Hutton, 2000; Webster, 2002). Thus long waiting lists, cancelled operations, staffing shortages, mismanagement, lack of accountability and spiralling costs are still a cause for concern, much as they have been for the last 60 years. 'Tragic' stories that reflect the wide geographical variations in access to treatment – the so-called postcode lottery – are also now standard media fare fuelling the perception that desperately sick patients have no option but to take legal action to secure their 'right' to treatment.

As the demand for health services continues to outstrip supply, it is inevitable that the NHS will be increasingly forced to make controversial decisions about how to allocate scarce resources 'fairly'. Of course, questions about how priorities should be set have long been at the centre of health care. But now that 'rationing' is more visible and openly debated than in the past, the ways in which decisions are made are more likely to be contested and challenged. This chapter looks at the ethical implications of allocating scarce resources and how various competing theories of justice offer different guidance about how to allocate scarce resources fairly. Legal analysis will focus on the law's role in guaranteeing access to health care. But the chapter begins by briefly describing the standing of children's health care services, outlining the standards which are currently being implemented (through the National Service Framework for Children and Young People 2004) and defining some key terms, e.g. the meanings of 'health' and 'well-being'.

6.1 Children's Health Care Services

Children born in the UK at the beginning of the twenty-first century have a longer life expectancy and generally enjoy better overall health than any previous generation (Bridgeman, 2007, pp. 47–51). Nevertheless, they make significant use of health care services – from routine health promotion and treatment for minor illnesses or unexpected injury to more serious long-term and life-threatening illnesses. Consider the following statistics (DoH, 2003; 2007):

- One in ten children will experience a diagnosable mental health condition.
- Well over half a million currently alive will live with a disability.
- Over 800 000 children and young people a year will be admitted to hospital for urgent care.
- In a typical year, the average preschool child will see their general practitioners (GPs) six times while a child of school age will go two or three times.
- Serious illness requiring intensive care will affect 1 in 1000 children.
- One in ten babies born each year will require admission to a neonatal unit, of whom about 2% will need intensive care.

It has, of course, long been recognised that the health of children depends on a variety of factors of which health care is only one (World Health Organization (WHO), 2008). Poverty, in particular, has lasting consequences for children and young people, causing health inequalities, which persist throughout life (National Audit Office, 2004). Health inequalities do not, however, fully explain the state of children's health services that the Kennedy Report (2001) described. The Report followed the public inquiry into the care of children undergoing cardiac surgery at Bristol Royal Infirmary between 1984 and 1995. Of its many key findings, it noted that the inadequacy of resources at Bristol PCS was typical of the NHS as a whole (p. 8); how health care services had persistently failed to give greater priority to the specific needs of children, even though this had been recommended by successive independent reports going back at least 40 years (p. 416) and that policy makers had difficulty in fully (and consistently) accepting or acknowledging that the health care needs of children and young people were different from those of adults (p. 419). The Report made 198 recommendations, most of which were in line with government policy and were, with few exceptions, accepted (Klein, 2006, p. 230). Most importantly, one of its key recommendations was that the proposed National Service Framework (NSF) for children should be agreed and implemented as a matter of urgency.

6.1.1 The National Service Framework for Children, Young People and Maternity Services

In England, the NSF for children set out a ten-year programme for improving the health and well-being of children and stimulating sustained improvement in child health services (note that Wales has developed a similar children's NSF, while Scotland has a separate strategy; see further http://www.dh.gov.uk). This was to be achieved by setting national standards of care as part of the government's overall strategy for tackling child poverty and improving the lives of children and families.

The NSF – which defines children and young people as under 19 years – has three parts. Part I sets out five universal national standards (i.e. they apply to all children):

1. *Promoting health and well-being, identifying needs and intervening early*: This is a wide-ranging standard, which includes providing information and support services. It assumes, of course, that there is agreement on what activities and other measures should be considered health promoting (which some question, e.g. Holland, 2007, pp. 101–110).

2. *Supporting parenting:* This second standard aims to ensure that parents and carers have information, support and access to the services that are essential if children are to have 'optimum life changes and are healthy and safe' (DoH, 2004b, p. 14).
3. *Child, young person and family-centred services:* Building on the Kennedy Report, this standard aims to ensure that children receive high-quality services, which are coordinated around their individual and family needs.
4. *Growing up into adulthood:* This standard seeks to ensure that age-appropriate services are available to children as they grow up.
5. *Safeguarding and promoting the welfare of children and young people:* The main focus here is how to safeguard children who are suffering harm or neglect (see further Chapter 11).

Part II of the NSF consists of five standards that apply to specific groups of children, e.g. children who are ill or in hospital, disabled children and those with complex health needs. Other standards cover children's mental health and psychological well-being and medicines for children and young people. Part III applies to maternity services.

Activities

1. Access the NSF website (http://www.dh.gov.uk) and consider how Part II and the Child Health Promotion Programme affect your practice.
2. Access the Health Commission's website (http://www.healthcarecommission.org.uk/). Critically assess its review of the implementation of the NSF to date (DoH, 2004a).
3. What are the essential features of a children's trust?

6.2 Defining Terms

This section briefly considers key terms used in rationing debates.

6.2.1 Health care resources

The term 'health care resources' is typically defined very broadly as anything that can reasonably be expected to have a positive effect on health. It thus includes medical resources such as drugs and treatments but also the many resources used for pollution control, shelter and food required for normal growth and functioning (Buchanon, 1997). Given the wide remit of the Children's NSF, the term also covers health education and promotion, care and treatment of children and young people who are ill, in hospital, are disabled, and so on. That the term 'health resources' should be defined expansively reflects the Every Child Matters agenda (DES, 2004, of which the NSF forms an integral part). This agenda requires health services to be integrated with other key services (such as education and children's social services) to provide 'a seamless web between universal services to promote children's well-being and targeted services for children in need' (Bridgeman, 2007, p. 64; see further DES, 2004, at http://www.everychildmatters.gov.uk).

Note finally that reference to health care resources for children includes the services that are provided at every level of the NHS: primary care, in the community, and in hospitals (accident and emergency, secondary care and specialist tertiary care). It also encompasses all related resources, e.g. personnel (i.e. doctors, nurses, allied health professionals, administrative staff and so on), equipment, research projects and buildings.

> **Key points**
>
> - The NSF sets out a long-term strategy for improving the health and well-being of children and young people.
> - The Every Child Matters agenda sets out a vision of integrated and universal children's services to promote children's well-being and targeted services for children in need.

6.2.2 Health

There is no universal understanding of the term 'health'. In other words, there are widely differing views about the definition of health and how it should (or can) be measured. According to Downie and McNaughton, health lacks a clear identity of its own because there are so few descriptions of 'being healthy' in literature. By contrast, because experiences of disease, illness, bereavement and death are 'intense and have a certain duration', they have become 'objects of attention in their own right'. This explains why they have generated such a 'rich variety of images' (Downie and McNaughton, 2007, p. 75).

The absence of a clear definition of the concept of health perhaps explains the continuing debate about its essential nature (see, e.g. Calnan, 1987; Davey et al., 2001; Helman, 2007, Chapter 5; Holland, 2007). Nonetheless, there is broad consensus on the following, i.e. that health is:

- A multifaceted and multidimensional concept, influenced by a range of factors – emotional, physical, environmental, political and social;
- A value-laden evaluative concept (i.e. specific to time, place and culture) that cannot be pinned down in a single definition;
- A term with several meanings – scientific and medical as well as popular meanings, i.e. something we all value.

That the concept of 'health' is at the very least ambiguous is clearly evident. Nonetheless, broadly speaking, two main views about its meaning are generally accepted, i.e. the negative and positive views (both of which are, of course, value-laden concepts).

Negative view

According to this view, to be healthy is to lack something; i.e. health is the absence of disease or illness. This negative approach can be described as intuitive in so far as it describes how most people think of health (Holland, 2007, p. 91).

Positive view

A positive conception of health is that to be healthy is to have or be something. In other words, this approach does not equate health with the absence of disease or illness, but instead describes a 'healthy person' as someone who enjoys 'well-being' (Holland, 2007, p. 93). According to the WHO, for example, health is a state of complete physical, mental and social well-being and not merely the absence of disease or infirmity (see further http://www.worldhealth.org).

Note finally that because the health care needs of children and young people are different from those of adults, they may experience and see the world differently (Kennedy, 2001, p. 419). As such, how they define and understand the concept of health may similarly differ from an adult's perception.

6.2.3 Well-being

Interest in the concept of well-being has burgeoned in recent years – typically as part of the psychological study of human happiness. As Hope et al. (2008, pp. 35–38) explain, there are three fundamentally different concepts that psychologists use to measure well-being:

1. Happiness as a subjective experience. The idea here is to assess the particular level of happiness (or unhappiness) we experience at a moment in time.
2. Happiness as a judgement we each make about our feelings and life experiences.
3. Happiness as a multidimensional concept encompassing what we consider to be elements of a happy and fulfilled life.

But even though the concept of well-being has entered public policy rhetoric in recent years, it is only recently that it has been systematically applied to children. Yet although concern with children's well-being is a welcome development, the literature reveals that the concept can be understood and defined in several different ways, namely, in terms of need, violated rights, poverty, poor quality of life and social exclusion (all of which are sometimes used interchangeably). As a consequence, we need to be alert not just to the subtle distinctions between these concepts but also to how different professions or disciplines will tend to use one term rather than another – e.g. health professionals are likely to focus on quality-of-life measures and lawyers on rights (Axford, 2008, pp. 1–11).

The point to emphasise here is that if children's health services are to be improved and integrated (as required by the NSF and Every Child Matters agenda) then a common understanding of the various conceptions of children's well-being is a prerequisite. At the very least, children's nurses need to be aware that there are different ways of thinking about children's well-being (see further Axford, 2008, Chapters 3 and 11).

Activity

Reflect on how you define 'being healthy' and well-being. Consider how your understanding of the concepts may differ from one of your young patients.

Key points

- The concept of health is subjective and value-laden (which means that people understand the term in different ways).
- The concept of children's well-being can be defined in terms of needs, violated rights, poverty, poor quality of life and social exclusion.

6.3 Rationing Health Care Resources

The 'tragic choices' involving scarce health resources that always generate the most media coverage inevitably involve 'life-and-death' cases. Denying a child chemotherapy that is 'too expensive' or postponing a baby's life-saving heart surgery because of staff shortages are typical examples. That these kinds of decisions are the most morally agonising is perhaps self-evident. Yet, even though they cannot normally be resolved instinctively (as is the case with routine small-scale resource decision-making), they nonetheless raise the same ethical issues. Before exploring these, however, we need to consider what the term 'rationing' means, whether it is inevitable and what forms it takes. But we begin by distinguishing between the various different contexts in which rationing occurs.

6.3.1 Rationing contexts

The different levels at which allocation decisions can be made are as follows:

- *Macro-level*: These are decisions about how much public money should be allocated to health care (which has to compete with education, housing, defence and so on).
- *Meso-level*: It involves priority setting at regional level – for example a Primary Care Trust (PCT) deciding which services and treatments should be prioritised such as mental health or paediatric care.
- *Micro-level*: Decisions at this 'coal face' level may involve choosing between individual patients, i.e. which patient will be allocated the only bed left in intensive care. These kinds of decisions are sometimes referred to as 'bedside rationing' (defined as the withholding of a medically beneficial service because of that service's cost to someone other than to the patient; Ubel and Goold, 1997, p. 75, and see further Menzel, 2007, p. 306).

Although these different levels of decision-making are widely recognised, albeit with slight variations (see, e.g. Beauchamp and Childress, 2009; Hunter, 1997), they are closely interconnected. Thus, as Klein et al. (1996, p. 10) explain, if the first two levels limit what is on offer (by limiting the scope of services) they inevitably limit, but do not necessarily eliminate, the discretion of those operating (such as nurses) at the third level. The interrelationship between all levels also explains why Thompson et al. (2006, pp. 228–229) suggest that even though nurses will be mostly involved in micro-level decision-making they should nevertheless actively participate in debates about rationing in other contexts too, e.g. as managers or policy makers.

6.3.2 Defining 'rationing'

The word 'rationing' has become an emotionally laden word in common parlance. In other words, depending on the context in which it is used and the kind of rationing that is involved, it is likely to provoke either approval or profound anger (Klein et al., 1996, p. 7). It is therefore particularly important to have a clear idea of what the word means. Regrettably, given the 'tremendous variation in what people mean when they talk about healthcare rationing' (Ubel and Goold, 1998, p. 214), this is no easy task. Thus, as Syrett (2007, p. 16) notes, some definitions of rationing focus upon administrative decisions to limit access to resources in times of national emergencies, such as in wartime Britain. But in other accounts, the word is used to describe the process of decision-making by individual health care practitioners exercising their expert medical judgement (i.e. in deciding who to treat at the micro-level (see further Syrett, 2007, pp. 16–20).

Another complicating factor is that in debates about health care resources the terms 'rationing' and 'priority-setting' are often used interchangeably – the implication being that both processes are synonymous. In so far as the objects of both are essentially the same – to 'identify treatments or services that will receive a favourable distribution of resources and those that will not (and in some case may receive nothing at all)' – then it may not be important to distinguish between them (Baggott, 2004, p. 205). Yet the two terms certainly have different emotional connotations. In brief, these are that the term 'rationing' is the more pejorative and morally loaded term (invoking images of very difficult decisions and tragic consequences for patients unfairly denied life-saving treatment). By contrast, the term 'priority-setting' is much more neutral. In particular, it implies that the process of allocating scarce resources is a positive and rational exercise in which informed choices are made about distributing resources effectively and thereby promoting community welfare (Syrett, 2007, pp. 22–23). That the term 'priority-setting' is the preferred one in official documentation is thus unsurprising (Newdick, 2005).

Notwithstanding the considerable overlap between the two terms (see further Tragakes and Vienonen, 1998), this chapter will use the word 'rationing' to describe the 'fact' that as health care resources cannot be provided to everyone, choices have to be made about (a) *who* should get treatment, (b) *what* treatments they should receive and (c) *how* these decisions should be made. Clearly, of course, this approach assumes that it is only meaningful to talk about rationing where the treatment is beneficial. In other words, rationing does not arise where a patient is not offered treatment because it is not clinically effective (Herring, 2008, p. 52).

Key points

- Rationing is a process or mechanism for allocating scarce health resources.
- Rationing involves deciding (a) *who* should get treatment, (b) *what* treatments should be provided and (c) *how* these decisions are made.
- Rationing can take place at several different levels, namely, macro-level, meso-level and micro-level.
- The terms 'rationing' and 'priority-setting' are often used interchangeably.

6.3.3 Is rationing inevitable?

There is a wide consensus – indeed the conventional wisdom is – that health care rationing is not only inevitable in the NHS but also becoming increasingly necessary (see, e.g. Ham, 2004; Jackson, 2006; Syrett, 2007). In summary, the most common explanations for the inevitability of rationing are as follows:

- *Demographic changes*: As life expectancy has increased markedly since the 1940s, the cost of supporting the ageing population has increased – from the treatment of acute and chronic conditions to providing long-term care.
- *Technological and scientific progress*: New drugs and innovations in surgery and diagnostics have revolutionised medical practice and created possibilities of treatments – to diagnose, cure and keep alive patients with conditions that were untreatable in the past (Klein, 2006, p. 253; see further Rivet, 1998, for a history of the impact of changes in medical practice and technology on the NHS).
- *Changing patient expectation of health services*: The combined effect of the 'marketisation' of the NHS (which transformed patients into 'consumers'), the decline in deference to (and erosion of trust in) the medical profession, and the availability of information technology have all contributed to a more demanding 'health aware' public, increasing the upward pressure on health care costs (Syrett, 2007, p. 44).

Some commentators, however, question whether rationing is either inevitable or necessary. Harris (2001, p. 293), for example, challenges the assumption that resources are finite. Others argue that, at the very least, the need for rationing could be reduced by, e.g. eliminating ineffective treatments (Light, 1997) or managing the NHS more efficiently (Mullen, 1998). The UK could also, of course, just spend more of its GNP on health care (Klein et al., 1996). It will nevertheless be assumed here that the correct approach is this: even though reform of the NHS might reduce rationing, it will not remove it altogether (Pattinson, 2006, p. 44). Indeed, for Syrett (2007, p. 34), it is likely to be increasingly necessary.

6.4 Forms of Rationing – How is Health Care Rationed?

This section describes some of the most common strategies or mechanisms that can be adopted to bridge the gap between supply and demand for health care.

6.4.1 Types of rationing

The following different types of rationing are widely recognised (see, e.g. Harrison and Hunter, 1994; Klein et al., 1996; Newdick, 2005; Syrett, 2007):

1. **Denial:** This is the most visible and brutal strategy. It involves denying beneficial treatment – either to an individual or to a group of patients.
2. **Selection:** A closely related strategy in which treatment is refused on the basis of patients' particular characteristics or lifestyle (e.g. obesity or smoking and drinking) and has the same outcome as denial.
3. **Deflection:** Here, would-be beneficiaries of health care are directed to another service; i.e. a health care problem is redefined as a social service one.
4. **Dilution:** This form of rationing involves spreading a service around more thinly. In other words, no one is denied treatment, rather, they just get 'less' of it. Examples include practitioners spending less time with patients or ordering fewer tests.
5. **Delay:** Various techniques can be used under this strategy, which basically aims to reduce demand. One of the most common forms it takes is the waiting list and arranging appointments weeks (or even months) ahead.
6. **Deterrence:** Rationing by deterrence again attempts to dampen demand – typically by charging patients (dental/prescription charges), or putting services in inconvenient locations, or by 'unhelpful' administrative staff (i.e. dismissive GP receptionists).
7. **Termination:** This strategy involves withdrawing previously available services or treatments from the 'menu' or alternatively discharging patients earlier from hospital than in the past.

It should be noted that the forms of rationing described above have all been practised in the NHS since its inception, (Baggott, 2004, p. 206). That there is a complex interaction between them and that they may not necessarily be either consciously or deliberately used is also widely recognised (Syrett, 2007, p. 49). That they will all be used in different ways – reflecting the specific context of the service or treatment being provided is similarly widely acknowledged (Klein et al., 1996, p. 12).

Another widely recognised distinction is between *implicit* and *explicit* rationing (see, e.g. Locock, 2000; Tragakes and Vienonen, 1998). Briefly, rationing is explicit if a clear attempt is made to distinguish who will receive what; the decisions are understood and agreed by a group of people, not just the individual (such as by the National Institute of Clinical Excellence, NICE; Locock, 2000, p. 93). In contrast, rationing is implicit when the criteria used to allocate resources are not made clear; i.e. the reasoning (e.g. costs of treatment, needs or age of the patient) upon which decisions are made will not be articulated. Examples of implicit rationing include rationing by deterrence, delay, deflection and dilution (Baggott, 2004, p. 205).

Activity

Consider which rationing mechanism is most prevalent in your practice.

6.4.2 National Institute for Health and Clinical Excellence guidance

Set up in 1999, the incongruously named NICE was a key mechanism in the Blair government's attempt to address the so-called postcode lottery. As the then Health Secretary said, 'NICE would help to bring order and rationality to a system that all too often had appeared arbitrary and unfair' (Millburn, 1999). NICE's role is to provide national guidance on the promotion of good health and the prevention and treatment of ill-health (see NICE, 2005, for a detailed description of its functions and geographical coverage). The two areas of guidance that have the most significant resource implications are:

a. Recommendations to practitioners on the use of new and existing medicines and treatments, and interventional procedures, and
b. Clinical guidelines, i.e. recommendations on the appropriate treatment and care of people with specific diseases and conditions.

The criteria on which NICE bases it recommendations include clinical and economic evidence (measuring how well the medicine or treatment works) as well as economic evidence, i.e. how well treatment etc. works in relation to how much it costs. Importantly, its recommendations on the use of medical technologies (but not clinical guidelines) have mandatory funding requirements. As Syrett (2007, pp. 71–72) explains, this means that NICE's decisions will frequently, in practice, pre-empt local choices on priorities. Cookson et al. have also raised concerns about the equity of NICE's decisions. They claim that because of fixed budgets NICE's emphasis on reducing the postcode lottery means that its guidance will be funded by cutting (or by diluting, delaying, deterring or deflecting) other services (Cookson et al., 2001, pp. 743–745).

Activity

Access NICE's website (http://www.nice.org.uk). Consider how effective it has been in eliminating postcode lottery in your practice.

Key points

- Explicit rationing refers to more transparent and visible processes – adopted, for example, by NICE.
- In implicit rationing the reasoning involved is not made clear; it usually refers to rationing decisions made by practitioners at the micro-level.

6.5 Distributing Scarce Resources – How to Make 'Moral' Decisions

It is clearly important to identify the various different rationing techniques. Yet they tell us little about the moral values and principles that guide decision-making, i.e. what ethical considerations should be borne in mind when a nurse has to decide, for example:

- How to prioritise her time and skills,
- Which patient to care for first, and
- Which treatments to give to which particular patients.

These are typical examples of decision-making at the coalface (i.e. the micro-level). Some, of course, may be made instinctively. But others – e.g. deciding which patient should have the last intensive care bed – will be much more morally agonising. Another distinction (not always made clear in the literature) is that scarcity of resources can be either radical or comparative. As Harris explains, it is *radical* when there are not enough resources to treat everyone, with the result that some will not be treated at all (or die before their turn arrives). By contrast, *comparative* scarcity is where patients will be prioritised but will nonetheless all be treated eventually (Harris, 2001, p. 293).

But as we see below, whether scarcity is radical or comparative, rationing decisions have a clinical component as well as an ethical dimension, namely, that resources should be allocated as *fairly* as possible, i.e. in accordance with justice (Stauch et al., 2006, p. 40).

But what does the concept of justice mean in this context? Even though it is a moral value that we all consider desirable – in the sense that everyone claims to want justice and to know how to make the 'right' decision when resources are scarce – few of us understand or interpret the concept in the same way. Commonly, however, justice is thought of in two ways: justice as fairness and justice as appropriate punishment for wrongdoing (Seedhouse, 1988). Because this chapter deals with the allocation of health resources, it focuses on justice as fairness – an aspect of justice that philosophers call *distributive justice*.

6.5.1 Ways of thinking about 'justice'

Very briefly, the following are the most common criteria for distributing scarce resources fairly:

- Treatment should be provided on the basis of 'need'.
- Younger patients should be given priority.
- Patients who are responsible for their own ill-health should bear the cost of their treatment (or be given a lower priority).
- A free market in health care should replace rationing; i.e. patients should be free to purchase health care.
- Patients should be treated 'equally'.
- Priority should be given to patients who have waited the longest.
- Treatment should be given to those who would benefit most.
- Treatments which cost less should be prioritised.
- Priority should be given to treatments that help the greatest number of people.

The two main competing ethical theories that underpin these kinds of debates are utilitarianism and deontology (see Chapter 1). But here we focus on the principles of justice that are most commonly discussed in this context (for a detailed analysis of other ethical approaches, see Beauchamp and Childress, 2009; Butler, 1999).

Activity

Read Daniels (1985), *Just Health Care*, pp. 1–34. Do you agree that health care has special moral importance? If so, why?

Key points

- The two main ethical theories that underpin the rationing debate are utilitarianism and deontology.
- The concept of 'distributive justice' is concerned with allocating scarce resources fairly.

6.5.2 Justice and 'need'

Focusing on the 'individualistic' approach – that resources should be provided to meet an individual's 'need' – is a good starting point as a principle of distributive justice for several reasons: the concept of need corresponds most closely with the founding principles of the NHS (Hendrick, 2004); it is popular – i.e. widely regarded (by the public and the media) as the most morally acceptable way of distributing resources between patients (Syrett, 2007, p. 88); there has been a revival of interest in using measures of need as a precursor to distributing services (not just health but also children's services, housing and social services; Axford, 2008); and, finally, need is a core concept in the Children Act 1989 (see Chapter 11). As a principle of distributive justice, need is nevertheless a problematic concept.

6.5.3 The problematic nature of 'need'

Although we can agree with Butler (1999, p. 88) that no centrally funded health care system openly dismisses the relevance of need in the way resources are rationed, the concept is, in practice, an imperfect criterion for distributing scarce health resources fairly. Consider, for example, the following conceptual problems:

- Health professionals (likewise other professionals and the public) interpret and use the term 'need' differently. It is therefore not surprising that their different sets of values and methodological approaches produce contrasting ideas not only about what 'need' is but also how it can be measured (Axford, 2008, pp. 22–28).
- What a person is considered to need varies with age, physical and mental capacity and outlook. However, despite extensive research on how needs vary over time, it seems that few people have tried to identify the fundamental requirements of a healthy childhood (Axford, 2008, p. 16).
- Little distinction is usually made in everyday speech between the concepts of need and demand – the assumption being that they are synonymous. But although they are closely related, they can be distinguished. As Matthew explains, a 'need' for treatment exists when an individual has an illness or disability for which there is an effective treatment or cure. A demand for care exists when an individual considers he has a need and wishes to receive care (Matthew, 1971, p. 27).

6.5.4 Common themes

It is evident from the above that the concept of need begs more questions than it answers. Nonetheless, there is broad agreement that:

- Need may be defined in relation to 'benefit' (or as some call it 'therapeutic merit'; Wicks, 2007, p. 6). Combining need with benefit – in the sense that patients can plausibly be said only to need treatment if they have the capacity to benefit from it – of course assumes first, that we can predict the outcome of treatment (i.e. the probability of medical success) and second, that we can objectively measure 'success' (which Newdick, 2005, amongst others, doubts). That said, once need is defined in terms of capacity to benefit, information on the effectiveness of treatment (i.e. evidence-based medicine) becomes relevant (Syrett, 2007, p. 87)
- The concept of need can be defined expansively or narrowly – what Axford refers to as a *thick* or *thin* definition. The thick notion is culturally determined. It is thus relative to, for example, an individual's aspirations and ideals and the social, historical and geographical context of their lives. By contrast, the *thin* notion of need is objective and universal – allowing us (in theory) to distinguish between 'basic' needs, i.e. those that are indispensable to life and those that are merely desirable, i.e. life-enhancing (Axford, 2008, pp. 16–20).

- Need, however it is defined, is a culturally variable, elastic and slippery term which is infinitely expandable – whether the concept is consumer led (i.e. defined by patients) or professionally led (i.e. this is no more precise but is defined by 'experts' in the light of the new treatments, services and so on that become available; Baker, 1995).

In conclusion, it is evident that several questions still remain; in particular, it is not clear (a) what should count as a need and (b) how one individual's needs are to be weighed against those of others (Pattinson, 2006, p. 50).

Activity

Consider whether it is feasible to 'rank' needs so that scarce health resources are allocated to patients with the 'greatest' need. What hierarchy of needs would you adopt?

Key points

- The concept of 'need' as a criterion of rationing corresponds closely with the founding principles of the NHS.
- What a person is considered to need varies with age and physical and mental capacity.
- Need can be defined expansively or narrowly.
- Need is a value-laden concept and infinitely expandable.

6.5.5 Age-based rationing

The idea that a patient's age should be a relevant criterion for health care rationing is controversial one. We can set the scene with this scenario: a 15-year-old and her grandmother are both drowning. There is only one lifebelt. There is little doubt that most of us (including grandmothers) would want the girl to be saved (Shaw, 1999, p. 374). But does this intuitive preference for the 15-year-old withstand ethical analysis in the context of health care? Here we consider the main arguments relied on by those who defend 'ageism' (i.e. the explicit preference for younger patients) in rationing scarce health care resources (typically, 'expensive' technology, intensive care and transplants).

General arguments

There are several variants of the age-based criteria to rationing. However, all can be described as egalitarian in so far as they consider the fairest way to distribute resources is to ensure that, as far as possible, individuals receive 'equal shares' (note there are other egalitarian approaches; see Syrett, 2007, pp. 90–91). Broadly, the arguments are as follows:

a. *Economic*: Firstly, it is argued that treating the elderly will cost more than treating younger patients because they may take longer to recover. Treatment is thus less cost-effective (Jackson, 2006, p. 57). Secondly, treatment costs money which the taxpaying working population can provide. In short, it is in the interest of 'the old people of the future' to spend more keeping the young and the working healthy than the retired (Shaw, 1999, p. 375).

b. *Medical*: It is claimed that treating older patients is less likely to be successful because there is greater chance that they will have other illnesses or disorders, which will affect the outcome of treatment (Jackson, 2006, p. 2007). As Beauchamp and Childress explain, age may also be an indicator of the probability of surviving a major operation. A related argument is that because older people have a shorter life expectancy, the benefits (in terms of life years gained from treatment) will be less (Beauchamp and Childress, 2009, pp. 273–274).

c. *Moral*: An influential moral argument is proposed by Callahan (1990). He argues that society should guarantee a fair amount of health care to all individuals throughout their lives. But once they reach their natural lifespan – say, in their late 70s or 80s – death is a relatively acceptable event. In other words, although the 'elderly' have a right to the basic minimum of care, they should forgo expensive life-extending treatment in the interest of younger people (see also Daniels, 1988, 'fair opportunity' approach).

Not surprisingly, all the above age-based arguments have been extensively criticised on several grounds – not least how to define 'young' and 'old'. A major moral objection is that proposals for age-based rationing perpetuate injustice by stereotyping the elderly, treating them as scapegoats in the face of rising health care costs (Beauchamp and Childress, 2009, p. 273). A related objection is that making generalisations about a class of persons ('the elderly') violates the principle of individual autonomy (Syrett, 2007, p. 91). Other critics challenge assumptions that the elderly are less likely to benefit from treatment – e.g. a fit older person can benefit more from treatment than an unfit younger person.

The 'fair-innings' argument

The fair-innings argument is arguably the most explicit age-based criterion. Its essence is captured in the following passage:

> It is a truth that while it is always a *misfortune* to die when one wants to go on living, it is not a *tragedy* to die in old age; but it is, on the other hand, both a tragedy and a misfortune to be cut off prematurely. (Harris, 1985, p. 93)

Notwithstanding the vagueness of concepts such as 'old age' and 'prematurity', the fair-innings argument asserts that there is normal span of years (say, 70) that can reasonably be said to constitute a fair share of life. Anyone who fails to reach this age has been 'short-changed' (in contrast to those on 'borrowed time' who live longer than 70). The young therefore have the 'right' to expect (on grounds of fairness) that they will be given the chance to live those additional years. As a consequence, society should maximise their chances of living those additional years by giving them priority when life-extending treatment is scarce (see further Williams, 1997).

This brief account of the fair-innings approach does not do justice to the complexity of the philosophical arguments on which it is based (on which see, e.g. Daniels, 1988). Nor does it make clear that there are in fact two broad versions – one always favours treating the younger patients but the second would only distinguish between patients on the basis of age if the older patients have had their fair innings (see further Jackson, 2006, pp. 57–59; Lockwood, 1988, for another variant). Finally, it is worth noting the midway position favoured by Harris. Whilst he does not regard age as a general rationing criterion, he nevertheless concedes that in 'hopefully rare cases where a choice has to be made' we should choose to give as many people as possible the chance of a fair innings (Harris, 2005a, p. 372).

Activity

Do you consider age-based arguments persuasive? Justify your answer.

> **Key points**
>
> - Age-based arguments refer to the preference for treating younger patients.
> - Age-based arguments consider age to be one of the most morally significant factors in rationing scarce resources.
> - The fair-innings approach builds on our intuition that everyone is entitled to a normal lifespan.

6.5.6 Justice and maximising welfare (the QALY approach)

The final approach – developed by health economists – is a theory called quality-adjusted life years (QALYs). Widely used as a decision-making criterion (e.g. by NICE), it is probably the most popular way of analysing the cost-effectiveness of treatment (Herring, 2008, p. 69). It is a particularly relevant criterion as far as children and young people are concerned because, as we see below, one of the major criticisms levelled against it is that it is ageist; i.e. it favours younger patients.

How QALYs are worked out

In the words of one of QALY enthusiast, the approach aims to do 'as much good as possible', i.e. improving people's life expectancy and the quality of their lives (Williams, 1998). Basically, the QALY approach aims to ensure that priority should be given to treatments that help the greatest number of people. It asks the following questions:

- How many extra years will a particular treatment provide the patient?
- What will their quality of life be in those extra years?
- How expensive is the treatment (Herring, 2008, p. 70)?

Once these factors have been assessed, QALY 'scores' can be worked out for different treatments. Essentially, these are league tables of the treatments that offer the best value for money. Patients who score 'well' are those who are the cheapest to treat and who will achieve the best quality of life over the longest period (i.e. the cost per QALY is low). In contrast, patients who are expensive to treat or whose life expectancy is short or whose quality of life is not likely to increase significantly score low marks on the scale; i.e. the cost per QALY will be high (Hendrick, 2000, p. 130).

Problems with QALYs

Costs and efficiency are central to the QALY approach. To that extent, therefore, it can be said to introduce a degree of objectivity into the ranking of treatments. Furthermore, by combining effects on life expectancy and effects on quality of life in a single measure, policy makers can compare contrasting treatments for a particular condition. Yet, despite these advantages, the approach has been extensively criticised. Briefly, its critics claim that it is neither as objective nor as accurate as its advocates contend (for a detailed discussion of these arguments, see Herring, 2008, pp. 69–72; Jackson, 2006, pp. 47–57; Newdick, 2005, pp. 21–36). Note too the claim made by Harris – a fierce critic of QALYs – that the approach is unjust because it will place those who have the misfortune of having both a poor quality of life and life expectancy in 'double jeopardy'; i.e. the same disadvantages will be used to give them less priority (Harris, 1987, 1995; for a reply, see Singer et al., 1995, 1996).

But here we focus in particular on the moral objection that QALYs are ageist (i.e. they favour younger people and unjustly discriminate against the elderly).

Age and QALYs

The argument that QALYs are inherently ageist is this: because QALYs are the product of quality and length of life measures, the cost per QALY will rise in inverse proportion to life expectancy. This means that QALYs will tend to disadvantage the elderly because they have a shorter life expectancy in general than do younger people (Hope et al., 2008, p. 205). The discriminatory potential of QALYs is further compounded by the fact that the quality of life of the elderly is likely to be lower (Syrett, 2007, p. 90), and Harris claims that the QALY approach is 'not so nice' because of its inherent ageism (Harris, 2005a, b).

Yet, notwithstanding the above criticism, it can be argued that the QALY approach does not explicitly discriminate against the elderly; i.e. the old are not discriminated against because they are old since a child with a short life expectancy would be treated in the same way as an 'old' person with the same life expectancy, assuming that their quality of life and cost are the same (Hope et al., 2008, p. 205). It is also possible to argue, of course, that even if it is inevitable that however impartially the QALY theory is expressed it will, in practice, discriminate against the old, it is nevertheless morally justifiable to do so, i.e. to favour the young when resources are scarce (see, e.g. Nord's cost-effectiveness analysis, 'saved young life equivalents'; Nord, 1992).

In conclusion, it should be evident from the above that there is no 'right answer' to problems of allocation of scarce resources. In other words, all the rationing criteria are problematic in one way or another. The apparent impossibility of consensus on the principles of distributive justice perhaps explains why aggrieved patients are increasingly likely to take legal action.

Key points

- Costs and efficiency are central to the QALY approach.
- The QALY approach aims to calculate the most efficient use of resources that will improve the quality of people's lives over the longest period.
- QALYs are widely used as a decision-making criterion (e.g. by NICE).

Activity

Consider the impact of the NHS Constitution (2009) on your practice (http://www.dh.gov.uk/en/Healthcare/NHS).

6.6 Rationing and the Law

This section looks at the role of law in guaranteeing access to health care. But it begins by briefly discussing whether the law recognises a 'right' to health care. This is followed by an outline of the main statutes governing the provision of health services.

6.6.1 Is there a legal 'right' to health care?

Since the Human Rights Act 1998 (HRA) came into force in 2000, rights talk has become more commonplace. But the rights culture does not, on its own, explain why needy patients – who in the early years of the NHS regarded access to health care as a privilege – now demand it as a 'right'. Newdick attributes this transformation in patients' perceptions to several factors: patients were more passive and deferential in the past and the medical profession was more paternalistic. Not surprisingly, patients were thus less critical of the way the NHS was managed and run (Newdick, 2006, p. 573). However, the introduction of market forces in the early 1990s (and the resultant focus on the patient as 'consumer'), rising expectations of health care and the more visible role of the government in the rationing debate have encouraged more rights-conscious patients to pursue (or at least threaten to pursue) their claims to health care through the courts.

The main legal options available to aggrieved patients are considered below, but first we focus on the most relevant Articles of the HRA (which incorporates the European Convention on Human Rights).

The Human Rights Act 1998

Article 2: Right to life: Article 2 imposes a positive obligation on states to intervene to protect life (Hoffman and Rowe, 2006, p. 118). However, the European Court of Human Rights has made it clear that countries have a wide discretion to assess their own priorities in allocating health resources (*Osman v UK* [1998] 29 EHRR 245; Brazier and Cave, 2007, p. 34). It is therefore extremely unlikely that patients could successfully use this Article to force health authorities to fund treatment which has been refused either on cost or clinical grounds (Jackson, 2006, p. 92).

Article 3: Protection from torture or inhuman or degrading treatment: It is conceivable (but very unlikely) that a patient denied treatment could succeed under this Article (*R v North West Lancashire HA ex parte A and others* [2000] 1 WLR 977; Pattinson, 2006, p. 49). Nevertheless, there is an argument that the Article does at the very least give patients a right to basic care (Herring, 2008, p. 61).

Article 14: Protection from discrimination: This Article – which prohibits discrimination on the grounds of, for example, sex, race, colour, language and religion (note that this is an illustrative list rather than an exhaustive one) – could be invoked if a patient was denied life-saving treatment on the basis of their age or disability (Sullivan, 1998). As Herring notes, the key issue in such a claim would be whether the decision was 'objectively justifiable'. If it was, the decision could not be challenged (Herring, 2008, p. 61).

In conclusion, most commentators agree that claims under the HRA will only very rarely provide the basis of a right to treatment (Herring, 2008; Jackson, 2006; Pattinson, 2006; Syrett, 2007; Wicks, 2007).

National Health Service Act 2006

The main legal framework governing the provision of health services is now the NHS Act 2006. Amongst other things, it requires the Secretary of State to continue the promotion in England of a comprehensive health service designed to secure improvement:

a. In the physical and mental health of the people of England, and
b. In the prevention, diagnosis and treatment of illness.

It also imposes a further duty on the Secretary of State to provide 'to such extent as he considers necessary to meet all reasonable requirements', services including hospital accommodation, medical, dental, nursing and ambulance services and such other services as are required for the diagnosis and treatment of illness (see further Schedule 1 and Parts 4, 5 and 6). Note that the duties imposed on the Secretary of State can be delegated to, for example, PCTs and NHS Trusts.

In addition to the various duties under the NHS Act 2006, other statutes such as the NHS and Community Care Act 1990 cover a wide range of other health-related services provided by local authorities.

6.7 Using the Law to Gain Access to Treatment

The combined effect of the HRA 1998 and the NHS Act 2006 is that comprehensive legal duties are imposed on the government to provide health services. Since the HRA is unlikely to be useful to patients wanting to challenge a rationing decision, we now consider the other main legal options.

6.7.1 Breach of statutory duty

As was noted above, the NHS Act 2006 seems to impose extensive duties on the Secretary of State to provide a comprehensive health service. However, except for the duty to provide medical examinations and care of state school pupils at regular intervals, almost all are qualified in that they only have to be provided 'to the extent that the Secretary of State considers necessary to meet all reasonable requirements'. As such, those exercising them have considerable discretion to decide how they are implemented (Hendrick, 2000, p. 134). More importantly, as Jackson explains, the Secretary of State's statutory duty does not require him 'to provide comprehensive access to all types of treatment, but rather to promote a comprehensive health service, i.e. to ensure that the NHS provides an adequate service' (Jackson, 2006, p. 99).

What does the above mean for patients hoping to challenge a rationing decision on the basis of a breach of statutory duty under the NHS Act 2006? There have been a few cases on this point, but all were unsuccessful. The unwillingness of the courts to question how the government allocates health resources is well summed up by Lord Denning, who stated, 'The Secretary of State says that he is doing his best he can with the financial resources available to him: and I do not think that he can be faulted in the matter' (in *R v Secretary of State for Social Services ex parte Hinks* (1980) 1 BLMR 93; see also *R v HIV Haemophiliac Litigation* (1990) 41 BLMR 171).

Key points

- A refusal to fund treatment because a child is disabled could be a breach of Article 14.
- Under the NHS Act 2006, the Secretary of State must provide a comprehensive health service.
- Almost all the duties under the Act are qualified, as provision must meet 'reasonable requirements'; claims by patients are therefore unlikely to succeed.

6.7.2 Judicial review

Judicial review actions are rare – even though the extensive media coverage they typically generate may suggest otherwise. Nevertheless, they are potentially a more promising option for patients wishing to challenge rationing decisions (and are expected to increase given the more explicit forms of rationing by, for example, NICE). To succeed, a patient will need to establish any one of the following grounds that:

a. The decision was unlawful (i.e. outside the health authority's statutory powers);
b. The decision was irrational, i.e. unreasonable in the sense that no reasonable health authority would have made the same decision; or
c. There was some procedural impropriety.

However, in first few cases to reach the courts (most of which are based on the 'irrational' ground), the judges seemed as reluctant to question how health authorities distribute scarce resources as they had been in claims alleging breach of statutory duty. Certainly, this was evident in *R v Central Birmingham ex parte Walker* (1987) 3 BLMR

32 and *R v Central Birmingham HA ex parte Collier* (unreported 6 January 1988), in which the judges made it clear that even patients facing death could not expect a court to interfere with a health authority's decision about how it allocated its resources (unless it had acted unreasonably).

Even in the much publicised and poignant case of *R v Cambridge HA ex parte B* [1995] 1 WLR 898 – the case was widely reported as one of the most explicit examples of rationing in the 'new' NHS – the court repeated once again that it had no right to interfere with a health authority's rationing decision (not to fund chemotherapy treatment costing £75 000 for a 10-year-old girl suffering from leukaemia). As such, the judicial approach continued to be one of deference and restraint (Syrett, 2007, p. 133).

But in two later cases – *R v North Derbyshire HA ex parte Fisher* [1997] 8 Med LR 327 and *R v North West Lancashire HA ex parte A and others* [2000] 1 WLR 977, patients seemed to have had more success in challenging rationing decisions. In both cases it was claimed that the health authority has acted 'irrationally'; i.e. there had been a flaw in the authority's decision-making process, namely, that it had failed to provide proper explanations for its decision to refuse treatment. However, as Jackson points out, these kinds of cases may in practice simply be cosmetic exercises. This is because complying with the court's decision may simply require the authority to explain clearly why it had refused treatment. In other words, the outcome of such cases is not necessarily that a patient will actually receive treatment – instead, they may just receive a 'personalised justification' for the refusal (Jackson, 2006, p. 87; see also Foster, 2007; Pattinson, 2006, p. 46).

Two other cases which were similarly treated – at least by the media – as victories for patients were *R (Rogers) v Swindon NHS Primary Care Trust* [2006] EWCA Civ 392 and *R (Otley) v Barking & Dagenham NHS PCT* [2007] EWHC 1927. Yet, notwithstanding that in both cases the courts held that the health authorities had acted irrationally, the patients' 'victory' was more apparent than real. This was because neither of the relevant health authorities had openly acknowledged that they had taken budgetary considerations into account in reaching their decisions not to fund treatment (in fact, in the *Swindon* case, the PCT insisted that cost was irrelevant to its conclusion). In other words, it is widely agreed that the patients' claims would have failed if the authorities had based their decision on scarce resources. As Herring explains, these decisions are not therefore saying that cancer patients have a right to drugs that can benefit them but rather that rationing decisions must be made openly (Herring, 2008, p. 59; see further Foster, 2007; Newdick, 2007; Syrett, 2006).

Of wider relevance, perhaps, is the first judicial review case in which NICE guidance has been challenged: *Eisai Limited v NICE* [2007] EWHC 1941. The case involved technical issues and *Eisai* succeeded only on one ground, that of discrimination. According to Syrett, however, the case is important because it reflects how the courts can ensure that decision-making is 'sufficiently transparent to be comprehensible to those it affects and to the wider public' (Syrett, 2008, p. 140).

Activity

Read Newdick (2007), 'Judicial review: low priority treatment and exceptional case review', *Med LR*, pp. 236–244. Do you agree with his conclusion that 'it is not difficult for a sufficiently motivated court to find *something* amiss with the process [of decision-making]'.

6.7.3 European law

Following *R (on the application of Watts) v Bedford PCT and Secretary of State for Health* [2003] EWHC 2228 and [2004] EWCA 166 and Case C-372/04, it seems that patients can be reimbursed for medical treatment received abroad if waiting lists in a Member State of residence are overlong (i.e. exceed a medically acceptable period given the patient's condition and clinical needs). However, as McHale explains, the decision is not total carte blanche to patients who do not want to wait for treatment (see further McHale, 2007, pp. 90–108).

The conclusion that emerges from this overview of the law is that although there is a debate to be had about the court's 'proper' role in rationing decisions (i.e. should it be more interventionist or not), English courts remain generally reluctant to engage in questions of resource allocation. As Simon Brown LJ explains: 'if there were to be developed a comprehensive framework for healthcare prioritisation, underpinned by an explicit set of ethical and rational values, questions of resource allocation might cease to be purely "political" and, implicitly, would become properly subject to judicial scrutiny' (*Pfizer (No. 2)* [2003] 1 CMLR 19).

Key points

- Judicial review actions by patients denied treatment are unlikely to be successful.
- Patients can be reimbursed for medical treatment received abroad in certain circumstances.

Case study

Jaymee is 10 years old. Suffering from cancer since the age of 5, she has had a bone marrow transplant, two courses of chemotherapy and whole body irradiation. But despite a brief remission, she has relapsed. Doctors have estimated her life expectancy as between 6 and 8 weeks. But a second opinion (from the USA) suggests that, with further treatment – a third course of chemotherapy and a second bone marrow transplant, costing £75 000 – there is an 18% chance of a full recovery. Her doctors think this is optimistic and consider the chance of success to be no higher than 10%. The health authority therefore refused to fund the treatment (on the basis that it is not in her best interests and is too costly (given its chance of success)).

1. Does Jaymee have a moral right to treatment?
2. Could she enforce her 'right' to treatment through the courts?

6.7.4 Jaymee's moral rights

In considering whether Jaymee has a moral right to treatment, there are several competing approaches that can be taken. This chapter has focused on three approaches in particular, namely, need, age and QALYs. As we have noted, all are problematic in one way or other. Thus, for example, in one sense it can certainly be argued that Jaymee needs treatment. But if we define need in terms of benefit, her moral claim is perhaps weaker especially given the chance of the treatment 'succeeding'. Because Jaymee is a child, it could also be argued – adopting the egalitarian fair-innings argument – that she should be given treatment in preference to older patients. But can this be justified on economic and medical grounds? As regards the QALY approach, this too is beset with difficulties, not least the quality of Jaymee's life during further treatment, the uncertainty about for how long treatment could prolong her life, and its cost. In other words, could the money be better spent on treating a greater number of patients?

It is perhaps worth noting here that this case study is based on *R v Cambridge HA ex parte B* [1995] 2 All ER 129. Of particular relevance is the court's explicit reliance on utilitarian arguments as the moral basis for its decision (not to fund treatment). As Sir Thomas Bingham said, 'Difficult and agonising judgements have to be made as to how a limited resource is best allocated to the maximum advantage of the maximum number of patients. That is not a judgement which a court can make.'

6.7.5 Jaymee's legal rights

As far as legal action is concerned, there is little prospect that Jaymee could successfully invoke the HRA 1998 to obtain treatment (whether she based her claim on Articles 2, 3 or 14). Nor is she likely to succeed in an action alleging a breach of statutory duty (under the NHS Act 2006). Finally, there is the possibility of an action for judicial review. However, as case law has repeatedly shown, this too has only a slim chance of success – i.e. it would depend on Jaymee establishing that the health authority's decision not to fund treatment was 'irrational'.

6.8 The Relationship between Law and Ethics

- Justice is a fundamental principle both in law and ethics. This is because achieving justice can be said to be the ultimate goal of the law. Similarly, justice is a core principle in ensuring that limited health care resources are distributed fairly.
- Egalitarian concepts, in particular 'equality', not only are founding principles of the NHS, but are also enshrined in the NHS Act 2006 in so far as it is intended to provide a comprehensive health service, irrespective of age, sex, occupation and so on. As such, it can be said that the principle of equality is given legal force.
- The concept of need is another common fundamental principle underpinning law and ethics that guarantees that rationing takes place within a moral and legal framework.

References

Axford, N. (2008) *Exploring Concepts of Child Well-Being.* Bristol: Policy Press.
Baggott, B. (2004) *Health and Health Care in Britain*, 3rd edn. London: Palgrave Macmillan.
Baker, R. (1995) Rationing, rhetoric, and rationality. In Humber, J.M. and Almeder, R. (eds) *Allocating Health Care Resources.* Totowa, NJ: Humana Press.
Beauchamp, T.L. and Childress, J.F. (2009) *Principles of Biomedical Ethics*, 9th edn. Oxford: Oxford University Press.
Brazier, M. and Cave, E. (2007) *Medicine, Patients and the Law.* London: Penguin.
Bridgeman, J. (2007) *Parental Responsibility, Young Children and Healthcare Law.* Cambridge: Cambridge University Press.
Buchanon, A. (1997) Healthcare delivery and resource allocation. In Veatch, R. (ed.) *Medical Ethics*, 2nd edn. London: Jones and Bartlett.
Butler, J. (1999) *The Ethics of Health Care Rationing: Principles and Practices.* London: Cassell.
Callahan, D. (1990) *What Kind of Life: The Limits of Medical Progress.* New York: Simon & Schuster.
Calnan, M. (1987) *Health and Illness: The Lay Perspective.* London: Tavistock.
Cookson, R., McDaid, D. and Maynard, A. (2001) Wrong SIGN, NICE mess: is guidance distorting the allocation of resources? *British Medical Journal* 323(7315):743.
Daniels, N. (1985) *Just Health Care.* Cambridge: Cambridge University Press.
Daniels, N. (1988) *Am I My Parents' Keeper?* Oxford: Oxford University Press.
Davey, B., Gray, A. and Seale, C. (2001) *Health and Disease: A Reader.* Buckingham: Open University Press.
DES (2004) *Every Child Matters: Change for Children.* London: DES.
DoH (2003) *Getting the Right Start: NSF for Children: Standards for Hospital Services.* London: DoH.
DoH (2004a) *A Review of Progress of the NSF.* London: DoH.
DoH (2004b) *NSF for Children, Young People and Maternity Services.* London: DoH.

DoH (2007) *Children's Health Our Future: A Review of Progress of NSF for Children, Young People and Maternity Services*. London: DoH.

Downie, R.S. and McNaughton, J. (2007) *Bioethics and the Humanities*. New York: Routledge-Cavendish.

Foster, C. (2007) Simple rationality? The law of healthcare resource allocation in England. *Journal of Medical Ethics* 33:404.

Ham, C. (2004) *Health Policy in Britain*, 5th edn. London: Palgrave Macmillan.

Harris, J. (1985) *The Value of Life: An Introduction to Medical Ethics*. London: Routledge.

Harris, J. (1987) QALYfying the value of life. *Journal of Medical Ethics* 3:118.

Harris, J. (1995) Double jeopardy and the veil of ignorance – a reply. *Journal of Medical Ethics* 21:151.

Harris, J. (2001) Micro-allocation: deciding between patients. In Kuhse, H. and Singer, P. (eds) *A Companion Guide to Bioethics*. Oxford: Blackwell.

Harris, J. (2005a) It's not NICE to discriminate. *Journal of Medical Ethics* 31:373.

Harris, J. (2005b) NICE and not so nice. *Journal of Medical Ethics* 31:685.

Harrison, S. and Hunter, D. (1994) *Rationing Healthcare*. London: Institute of Health Policy Research.

Helman, C.G. (2007) *Culture, Health and Illness*, 5th edn. London: Hodder Arnold.

Hendrick, J. (2000) *Law and Ethics in Nursing and Health Care*. Cheltenham: Stanley Thornes.

Hendrick, J. (2004) *Law and Ethics: Foundations in Nursing and Health Care*. Cheltenham: Nelson Thornes.

Herring, J. (2008) *Medical Law and Ethics*, 2nd edn. Oxford: Oxford University Press.

Hoffman, D. and Rowe, J. (2006) *Human Rights in the UK: An Introduction to the Human Rights Act 1998*, 2nd edn. Harlow: Pearson Education.

Holland, J. (2007) *Public Health Ethics*. Cambridge: Polity.

Hope, T., Savulescu, J. and Hendrick, J. (2008) *Medical Ethics and Law: The Core Curriculum*, 2nd edn. Edinburgh: Elsevier.

Hunter, D.J. (1997) *Desperately Seeking Solutions to Rationing in Healthcare*. Harlow: Longman.

Hutton, W. (2000) *New Life for Health: The Commission on the NHS*. London: Vintage.

Jackson, E. (2006) *Medical Law: Text, Cases and Materials*. Oxford: Oxford University Press.

Kennedy, I. (2001) *The Report into the Inquiry into Children's Heart Surgery at the Bristol Royal Infirmary 1984–1995: Learning from Bristol* CM 5207(1). London: DoH.

Klein, R. (2006) *The New Politics of the NHS from Creation to Reinvention*, 5th edn. Abingdon: Radcliffe.

Klein, R., Day, P. and Redmayne, S. (1996) *Managing Scarcity*. Buckingham: Open University.

Light, D. (1997) The real ethics of rationing. *British Medical Journal* 315:112.

Lockwood, M. (1988) Quality of life and resource allocation. In Bell, J. and Mendus, S. (eds) *Philosophy and Medical Welfare*. Cambridge: Cambridge University Press.

Locock, L. (2000) The changing nature of rationing in the NHS. *Public Administration* 78:90.

Matthew, G. (1971) Measuring need and evaluating services. In McLachen, G. (ed.) *Portfolio for Health*. Oxford: Oxford University Press.

McHale, J. (2007) Rights to medical treatment in EU law. *Medical Law Review* 15(1):99.

Menzel, P. (2007) Allocation of scarce resources. In Rhodes, R., Francis, L.P. and Silvers, A. (eds) *The Blackwell Guide to Medical Ethics*. Oxford: Blackwell.

Millburn, A. (1999) *Modern Services, Modern Choices: Tackling the Lottery of Healthcare*. London: DoH.

Mullen, P. (1998) Is it necessary to ration health care? *Public Money and Management* 18:52.

National Audit Office (2004) *Tackling Cancer*. London: TSO.

Newdick, C. (2005) *Who Should We Treat?* 2nd edn. Oxford: Oxford University Press.

Newdick, C. (2006) The positive side of healthcare rights. In McLean, S. (ed.) *Law, Ethics and Healthcare*. Farnham: Ashgate.

Newdick, C. (2007) Judicial review: low priority treatment and exceptional case review. *Medical Law Review* 15(2):236.

NICE (2005) *A Guide to NICE*. London: NICE.

Nord, E. (1992) An alternative to QALYs. *British Medical Journal* 305:875.

Pattinson, S.D. (2006) *Medical Law and Ethics*. London: Sweet & Maxwell.

Rivet, G. (1998) *From Cradle to Grave*. London: King's Fund.

Seedhouse, D. (1988) *Ethics at the Heart of Health Care*. Chichester: John Wiley & Sons.

Shaw, A.B. (1999) In defence of ageism. In Kuhse, H. and Singer, P. (eds) *Bioethics: An Anthology.* Oxford: Blackwell.

Singer, P., McKie, J., Kuhse, H. and Richardson, J. (1995) Double jeopardy and the use of QALYs. *Journal of Medical Ethics* 21:144.

Singer, P., McKie, J., Kuhse, H. and Richardson, T. (1996) Double jeopardy: the equal value of lives and the veil of ignorance – a rejoinder to Harris. *Journal of Medical Ethics* 22(4):195.

Stauch, M., Wheat, K. and Tingle, J. (2006) *Text, Cases and Materials on Medical Law*, 3rd edn. Abingdon: Routledge-Cavendish.

Sullivan, D. (1998) The allocation of scarce resources and the right to life under the European Convention of Human Rights. *Public Law* 389.

Syrett, K. (2007) *Law, Legitimacy and the Rationing of Health Care: A Contextual and Comparative Perspective.* Cambridge: Cambridge University Press.

Syrett, K. (2008) NICE and judicial review: enforcing accountability for reasonableness through the courts. *Medical Law Review* 16(1):127.

Thompson, I.E., Melia, K., Boyd, K. and Horsburgh, D. (2006) *Nursing Ethics*, 5th edn. Edinburgh: Elsevier.

Tragakes, E. and Vienonen, M. (1998) *Key Issues in Rationing and Priority Setting for Healthcare Services.* Copenhagen: WHO.

Ubel, P. and Goold, S. (1997) Recognising bedside rationing: clear cases and tough calls. *Annals of Internal Medicine* 126:74.

Ubel, P. and Goold, S.J. (1998) Rationing health care: not all definitions are created equal. *Archives of Internal Medicine* 158:209.

Webster, C. (2002) *The NHS: A Political History*, 3rd edn. Oxford: Oxford University Press.

WHO (2008) *Inequalities in Young People's Health.* Geneva: WHO.

Wicks, E. (2007) *Human Rights and Healthcare.* Oxford: Hart.

Williams, A. (1997) Intergenerational equity: an exploration of the 'fair-innings' argument. *Health Economics* 6(2):117.

Williams, A. (1998) Economics, QALYs and medical ethics: a health economist's perspective. In Souzy, D. (ed.) *Ethics and Values in Health Care Management.* London: Routledge.

CHAPTER 7

Young People and Sexuality

Learning outcomes

By the end of this chapter you should be able to:

- Discuss the legal regulation of birth control;
- Understand the ethical and legal issues raised by abortion;
- Assess the ethical and legal implications of sterilisation.

Introduction

Ever since the historic 1986 *Gillick* case, famous, among other things, for the immortal words of Lord Templeton ([1985] 3 All ER 402 at 432) that there are many things which a girl under 16 needs to practise, but sex is not one of them, the law's role in regulating adolescent fertility and sexuality has been controversial. And yet the case did not, as is commonly assumed, herald a fundamental change in the provision of contraceptive advice and treatment to underage girls. For well before then – over a decade earlier in fact – guidance from the Department of Health had made it clear that such treatment could be lawfully provided in certain circumstances irrespective of parental consent.

While the legal issues surrounding minors and contraception are now well settled, some aspects of birth control continue to cause controversy, in particular those methods of contraception which destroy a fertilised egg. That is because for those who see fertilisation as the beginning of life any act which has this effect is immoral. The issue of when life begins is, however, usually discussed in the context of abortion. This chapter follows this tradition. As such, it will limit discussion of birth control to the legal issues it raises. It will, however, discuss both law and ethics in relation to abortion and the sterilisation of minors.

7.1 Abortion: Fetal Rights

The arguments for and against abortion are now so well-rehearsed that the chances of there being anything new to say are indeed remote (Harris and Holm, 2005). While this may be true – at least in relation to what has traditionally been the focus of debates around the ethics of abortion, notably the moral status of the fetus – other issues relating to abortion have begun to provoke controversy. These include questions about, for example, using the ovarian tissue of aborted fetuses in fertility treatment, and selective abortion in the case of multiple fetuses. However, as Bennett and Harris (2007) point out, how we answer these questions (which for reasons of space are not discussed in this book) will depend on the central questions of whether a fetus has a right to life. It is therefore this question that we primarily address in this chapter and the related issue of whether a pregnant woman's right to self-determination should trump any right the fetus might be ascribed.

7.1.1 The moral status of the fetus

At the heart of the abortion debate is the question of the moral status of the fetus. This is the key factor in determining the permissibility of abortion because to be in possession of moral status means that an 'entity' has certain rights. Furthermore, as Pattinson explains, the criterion of moral status determines the extent to which our moral obligations to the unborn child's interests can come into conflict with our moral obligations to the pregnant woman (Pattinson, 2006, p. 211). It is therefore unsurprising that several competing (and overlapping) moral theories offer various accounts of what distinguishes the fetus from other species (for a detailed analysis of these, see Beauchamp and Childress, 2009, Chapter 3). The implicit assumption in many of these theories is that the fetus is special in moral terms because it is a 'person' (or has the potential to become one). But according moral status to the fetus on the basis of its claim to personhood necessarily requires us to identify the capacities that are normally associated with personhood, i.e. what it is to be a person. Or, as Harris (1985, p. 14) puts it, identifying what it is that is so different about a person that justifies valuing such a creature above others. This raises two related issues (which for convenience are discussed separately below): firstly, the characteristics an entity must possess before it can be considered a person, and secondly, the moment in time when a human organism becomes a person.

7.1.2 What makes 'something' a person?

One of the most well-known attempts to identify the features that make an individual a person was by the seventeenth century philosopher John Locke. He considered a person to be 'a thinking intelligent being that has reason and reflection' (Locke 1690/1964:188, quoted in Harris and Holm, 2005, p. 115). Since then, of course, the concept has been refined many times with most modern versions listing a cluster of the distinctive properties of personhood (see, e.g. Harris, 1985; Singer, 1993; Tooley, 1983; Warren, 1973, 1997). Yet it nevertheless remains unclear whether *all* these properties are relevant (or a specific combination) or indeed whether *any* of them are sufficient on their own to make something a person. Nonetheless, it is widely accepted that the following mental capacities are 'important' to being a person: rationality (the ability to reason), sentience (i.e. the capacity to feel pain and pleasure), self-consciousness (e.g. being capable of valuing one's own existence, having desires and being able to imagine the future), the ability to form relationships, and moral agency (i.e. the capacity to regulate one's own actions through moral principles). Not surprisingly, each criterion has its supporters and critics. Many are also controversial – as they would exclude not only fetuses but also a significant number of children and incapacitated adults (Jackson, 2006, p. 589). Equally problematic is that they do not provide a clear answer to the question: at what point in time does a fetus become a person.

7.1.3 When does 'personhood' materialise?

Various times have been proposed as the moment when personhood is acquired. The most common are as follows:

- The moment of conception (a related alternative approach is that even if a fetus is not a person at this time, it nevertheless has the potential to become a person; see further Marquis, 2006).

- Fourteen days (when the primitive streak occurs).
- Quickening (when the mother feels the fetus is moving).
- Viability (when the fetus is capable of existing independently of the mother, currently about 22 weeks).
- Sentience (i.e. is capable of sensation).
- Birth.

Again, unsurprisingly, all these 'times' are problematic in one way or other not least because of the difficulty of providing objective criteria for identifying that crucial 'moment' (see Herring, 2008, pp. 283–290, for a summary of the main criticisms). Given the lack of consensus of what the concept of personhood means (and when it materialises), some philosophers have abandoned the idea that there are morally significant characteristics (or moments in time) in favour of the so-called gradualist approach. As such, they do not claim that the fetus should be granted full moral status from the moment of creation. Nor do they hold that the fetus has no moral status, until at least birth. Rather, they consider the fetus to have an intermediate moral status that develops over time; i.e. its moral worth increases with gestational age until it acquires full moral status at birth. According to this approach, the longer the pregnancy, the greater must be the justification for terminating the life of the fetus (Quinn, 1984, pp. 24–54; Scott, 2007, pp. 20–23).

Key points

- So-called pro-life campaigners claim that the fetus has the same right to life as a 'person' and thus the right not to be deliberately killed.
- A 'person' is a human being that has certain identifiable characteristics and capacities.

7.2 Abortion: Maternal Rights

In this section, we focus on a cluster of related rights that are conveniently captured by the slogan 'a woman's right to choose' – a slogan which is normally associated with the rise of the women's liberation movement in the 1970s. The slogan conveys in simple terms the idea that because pregnancy is a uniquely female experience it must be controlled by individual women and not by others. But as Whyte (1997, p. 16) points out, unlike the pro-life lobby, who can usually easily express their message in headline-grapping sound-bites (such as abortion is killing, killing is bad and abortion is bad), pro-choicers have much more complex arguments to get across – not just the right of women to decide but also a 'tangle of moral, personal and social factors'. This is perhaps why it has been suggested that the language of 'choice' should be abandoned because it allows abortion to be depicted as a matter of a woman's convenience and thus obscures the complex moral reasoning process of most women who have abortions (Fox, 1998, p. 98). Those who claim that a woman's right to control her own body is one of the most basic of human rights typically rely on an assortment of related 'rights' to support their approach. These include the following.

7.2.1 Right to self-defence

Briefly, this approach maintains that a woman is entitled to defend herself against an intruder who threatens her in some way, e.g. from the pain and injuries, etc. that pregnant women can experience (McDonagh, 1999). There are many problems with this approach. For example, the self-defence argument may be easy to justify when pregnancy threatens the mother's life or if the pregnancy was non-consensual (if the woman was raped, for example). But it is far harder to justify an abortion on this basis when the risk to the mother's health is less serious (Mason, 1998).

7.2.2 Autonomy

In their most extreme form, autonomy arguments assert that a woman's right to self-determination, liberty and bodily integrity means that she should be able to decide not to continue with the pregnancy at whatever stage (and for whatever reason). But as Warren (1993, p. 306) points out, it is one thing to have a right, and another to be morally justified in exercising that right. This raises the question of whether autonomy-based arguments can ever support abortion on demand, especially if the reasons are 'trivial'.

7.2.3 Ownership

A variant on autonomy and self-defence arguments is based on the notion that women have rights to ownership of their bodies. In a hugely influential article, Thomson (1971) asks you to imagine waking up one morning (having been kidnapped by the Society of Music Lovers) to discover that you are attached – through your circulatory system – to a famous unconscious violinist (with kidney disease). Unless he remains plugged into you for 9 months he will die. Thompson's argument is that most of us would agree that we have the right to unplug ourselves; i.e. we are not morally required to stay connected, even if we concede that the violinist has a right to life. Using this analogy, Thompson hopes to avoid the need to settle the question of the moral status of the fetus. In other words, even if the fetus has the moral status (equivalent to a normal adult), a woman has no moral duty to remain pregnant as she has no moral duty to allow the violinist to use her kidneys for 9 months. Or to put it another way, since a woman 'owns' her body she has the right to reject a fetus as a wrongful trespasser (Harris and Holm, 2005, p. 124).

Thompson's arguments are, of course, much more subtle and complex than this. Moreover, she does not argue that abortion is always permissible but rather for the permissibility of abortion in some cases (for a critique, see Hare, 1975; Herring, 2008, pp. 293–296; Singer, 1993).

Key points

- Pro-choice arguments assert that a woman has the right to decide when (and in what circumstances) not to continue with a pregnancy.
- A pregnant woman can rely on several rights when asserting that she has a 'right to choose', i.e. a right to self-determination, self-defence, autonomy and ownership.

7.3 A Compromise Position

We conclude this section with a very brief outline of Dworkin's so-called compromise position on the abortion debate. It is described as such because of his central premise that even though opinions about abortion may seem polarised, the great majority of people (liberal and conservative) 'believe, at least intuitively that the life of a human organism has intrinsic value' (Dworkin, 2001, p. 158). Additionally, Dworkin argues that both camps share the conviction that at some point a fetus becomes sentient and both agree that a late-term abortion is graver than an early-term one. This leads him to conclude that their different perspectives are not irreconcilable. Rather, they can be explained by the different ways in which both camps interpret the sacredness of human life (i.e. what is required by respect for human life). As Dworkin explains, two 'things' make a life sacred. One is the 'natural investment in human life', i.e. the miracle of human life (Dworkin, 2001, p. 170). The other is the 'human investment', which reflects the creative process of a person 'leading their life' (Dworkin, 2001, p. 171).

And it is the differences of opinion about the relative importance of the 'natural' and 'human' contributions to the inviolability of human life that Dworkin claims are the key to the apparent deep divisions about the morality of abortion. He therefore poses the following question: 'is the frustration of a biological life, which wastes (the 'natural') human life, nevertheless sometimes justified in order to avoid frustrating a human contribution to that life or to other people's lives, which would be a different kind of waste? If so, when and why' (Dworkin, 2001, p. 180). Regrettably, Dworkin fails to provide any easy answers to these fundamental questions.

Activity

Are you persuaded by Dworkin's compromise position? Justify your answer.

7.4 The Law of Abortion

As is well known, the Abortion Act 1967 radically reformed the law of abortion and made it much more widely available. It also clarified the law, thereby removing almost all the uncertainties which had previously existed as to when an abortion was or was not lawful. Before looking at the Act in more detail, the following general points are worth noting:

- The Act assumes that the decision to terminate a pregnancy is a question which requires clinical expertise (but see Sheldon, 1997, who questions whether this is necessarily so).
- It is a mistake to assume that women have a legally enforceable right to abortion. Instead, it gives doctors a gate-keeping role, i.e. the right to decide whether a woman's particular circumstances meet the requirements of the Act.
- The need for medical approval and the inherent vagueness of the statutory grounds strongly suggest that the Act's purpose is to protect medical discretion rather than women's rights (Jackson, 2006, p. 603).
- It is almost impossible to successfully prosecute a doctor for illegally performing an abortion unless it could be proved that she/he acted in bad faith or failed to follow the Act's procedural requirements (Mason and Laurie, 2006, p. 162; see also *R v Smith* [1974] 1 All ER 376).

7.5 When is an Abortion Legal?

Abortions are legal provided they are performed in accordance with the provisions of the Abortion Act 1967 (as amended by the Human Fertilization and Embryology Act 1990), i.e. by a doctor, after two doctors have decided 'in good faith' that one or more of the four grounds specified in the Act apply. These are summarised below:

s.1(a) that the pregnancy has not exceeded its 24th week and the continuation of the pregnancy would involve risk, greater than if the pregnancy were terminated, of injury to the physical or mental health of the pregnant woman or any existing children of her family

- This ground is commonly known as the social ground and accounts for the vast majority of abortions (in 2007, 90% of abortions in England and Wales were carried out under 13 weeks' gestation).
- It can be interpreted narrowly or broadly. So, although there must be some risk in continuing with the pregnancy, it does not have to be a serious one. Note also that the risks of pregnancy are not constant. Hence, the risks associated with pregnancy increase with age, whereas an abortion poses greater risk to younger women.
- The meaning of 'mental health' is unclear. At its most restrictive it could limit abortions to those cases where the pregnant woman would otherwise suffer some form of mental illness. It can, however (and typically is in practice), be interpreted more broadly to include much less severe conditions.
- The ground allows 'actual and foreseeable environment' (i.e. social factors) to be taken into account (see s.1(2)). This would clearly be an important factor to consider in teenage pregnancies, where there was limited family or social support (Herring, 2008, p. 267).
- This ground is the only one with a time limit (up to 24 weeks).

s.1(b) that the termination is necessary to prevent grave permanent injury to the woman's physical or mental health

- The Act gives no guidance on the meaning of 'grave permanent injury', but it is assumed that temporary, easily curable conditions are not included. Accordingly, it is harder to prove.
- As with the first ground, s.1(2) applies, i.e. social factors can be taken into account.

s.1(c) that the continuation of the pregnancy would involve risk to the life of the pregnant woman, greater than if the pregnancy were terminated

- As with the first ground, the risk of continuing the pregnancy must be balanced against that of ending it (albeit risks to life rather than health).

s.1(d) that there is substantial risk that if the child were born it would suffer from such physical or mental abnormalities as to be seriously handicapped

- This ground (which in 2007 accounted for approximately 1% of all abortions; Scott, 2007, p. 119) is usually referred to as the 'fetal disability' ground. It is the most difficult to interpret because the Act fails to define the terms it uses (nor has there been any judicial interpretation of the ground).
- In only one case has a legal attempt been made to question the discretion of doctors. This was *Jepson v the Chief Constable of West Mercia Police Constabulary* [2003] EWHC 3318. Reverend Jepson asked the police to investigate doctors who had authorised an abortion for bilateral cleft lip and palate at 28 weeks. The Crown Prosecution Service decided not to prosecute.
- According to guidance from the BMA (2007), in deciding whether to terminate a pregnancy under this ground, doctors should consider the seriousness of a handicap according to the following criteria: the probability of effective treatment, either in utero or after birth; the child's probable potential for self-awareness and potential ability to communicate with others; and the suffering that would be experienced by the child when born or by the people caring for the child (see further guidance from Royal College of Obstetricians and Gynecologists, RCOG, 2001).
- The fetal abnormality ground is especially controversial not least because it clearly grants far less protection to a 'seriously handicapped' unborn child than a non-handicapped unborn child (for further discussion of the ethical concerns raised by late abortions, see Scott, 2007, pp. 71–137; Wicks et al., 2004, Chapter 4).

Other points to note are the following. Firstly, that in emergencies (i.e. when an abortion is immediately necessary to save the life of or to prevent grave permanent injury to the physical or mental health of the pregnant woman, s.1(4)), it is not necessary either to perform an abortion in an approved place or to seek a second doctor's opinion. Secondly, nursing staff who, for example, administer prostaglandin infusions are acting lawfully providing they are acting under the instructions of a doctor (*Royal College of Nursing v The Department of Health and Social Security* [1981] 1 All ER 545, and see Dimond, 2008, p. 388).

Key points

- An abortion is illegal unless one or more grounds specified in the Act applies.
- The Abortion Act gives health professionals who carry out abortions according to the Act immunity from prosecution – it does not decriminalise abortion in general.

Activity

Read Royal College of Nursing (RCN, 2008, pp. 5–9) guidance on abortion services. Critically consider the role development for nurses that it identifies (http://www.rcn.org.uk).

7.6 Adolescents and the Abortion Act

Although the UK has one of the highest teenage pregnancy rates in Europe, the abortion rate amongst teenagers is relatively low (Fortin, 2003, p. 139). As regards the law, the crucial issue is, of course, the law of consent.

7.6.1 Giving consent

The 16- and 17-year-olds
Competent 16- and 17-year-olds can give a valid consent to an abortion (by virtue of s.8 of the Family Law Reform act 1969) irrespective of their parents' wishes. If they are not competent, but an abortion is in their best interests, then anyone with parental responsibility (or a court) can consent on their behalf. If there is any doubt as to either the minor's capacity or best interests (e.g. lack of unanimity amongst health professionals or where the patient, her immediate family or the fetus' father opposes or expresses views inconsistent with a termination), a declaration should be sought from the court (*D v An NHS Trust* [2003] EWHC 2793).

Under 16-year-olds
Girls under 16 can give valid consent providing they are *Gillick* competent (see Chapter 4). Best practice guidance issued by the Department of Health should also be followed (DoH, 2004). Note in particular that the *Gillick* competence test does not state clearly what degree of maturity adolescents must have reached in order to be considered competent. Fortin (2003, p. 139) maintains, however, that any girl asking for an abortion should be deemed sufficiently competent to consent to such a procedure. The legal position is more problematic when there is a disagreement between an adolescent and her parents. Such cases rarely reach the courts, but there have been two apposite cases. Thus in *Re B* [1991] 2 FLR 426a, 12-year-old wanted an abortion, as did her 16-year-old boyfriend and her grandparents with whom she had lived most of her life. Her mother, however, strongly opposed abortion. The court overruled the mother's wishes and gave permission for the abortion to go ahead. In a similar case – *Re P* [1986] 1 FLR 272 – the

court also authorised an abortion in respect of a 15-year-old girl in local authority care who already had an 11-month-old son.

7.6.2 Refusing consent

The above two cases involved girls who wanted a termination. But what is the legal position if a competent under 18-year-old does not want an abortion? Theoretically, an abortion could be carried out – relying on the consent of a person with parental responsibility or a court (providing it was in the girl's best interests). It is nevertheless very unlikely that a court would authorise an abortion against the wishes of a competent minor (per Balcombe LJ in *Re W* [1992] 4 All ER 627, at 645).

Activity

Read *Re B* and *Re P*. Do you think that the courts made the 'right' decision? If not, why not?

7.7 Other People's Legal Rights

Here we briefly consider the rights of fathers and nurses (or other health professionals) and other interested parties.

7.7.1 A father's rights

Despite several attempts by fathers to prevent their partners having abortions – on the basis that as the unborn child's father they have 'rights' too – their claims have been rejected in the English courts (and by the European Court of Human Rights). Nor does the father have any legal right to be consulted about a proposed abortion so that, even if he cannot prevent it, he can at least have some say in the decision-making process (*Paton v Trustees of the British Pregnancy Advisory Service* [1979] QB 276; *C v S* [1988] QB 135, but see Mason and Laurie, 2006, p. 163, who claim that 'morally speaking' fathers should ideally be entitled to a hearing).

7.7.2 Nurses and conscientious objection

Lord Denning famously said how nurses are expected to be mobile throughout the hospital system (in the 1981 *Royal College of Nursing* case, above). To the extent that this is still an expectation (and in the light of increasing use of more modern non-surgical methods of termination), the scope of the conscientious objection clause in the Abortion Act 1967 is an important one. This is particularly so if we accept Mason and Laurie's assertion that 'the sensibilities of nursing staff are inadequately recognized in the abortion debate … and there can be no doubts as to their *rights* to special consideration' (Mason and Laurie, 2006, p. 162; see further NMC, 2006).

Section 4 of the Abortion Act 1967 states that no person is legally obliged to *participate* in any treatment authorised by the Act to which they have a conscientious objection. In emergencies, however, i.e. when the life of the pregnant woman is at stake or she faces grave permanent injury, the exemption does not apply. Yet s.4 is limited by a proximity test, i.e. the word 'participate' only covers those involved in the therapeutic team. As such, it did not apply to a doctor's receptionist who refused to type a letter of referral, i.e. since she was not participating in treatment, she could not claim exemption under the Act (*Janaway v Salford AHA* [1989] AC 537).

> ## Key points
>
> - Competent minors under 18 have the legal right to consent to an abortion without their parents' knowledge (or consent).
> - Except in emergencies, nurses and other health professionals can refuse to take part in an abortion.
> - Fathers do not have the legal right to challenge or veto an abortion; nor do they have the legal right to be consulted.

7.8 Sterilisation

Few forms of treatment are as controversial as non-consensual sterilisation. That it raises fundamental issues of law, ethics and medical practice is irrefutable and was eloquently yet succinctly acknowledged in the case of *Re D* [1976] All ER 326 when Mrs Justice Heilbron said:

> Sterilization is an operation which involves the deprivation of a basic human right, namely the right to reproduce, and therefore it would, if performed on a woman for non-therapeutic reasons and without her consent be a violation of that right.

Where the procedure is carried out on children (*Re D* concerned an 11-year-old girl), it is perhaps even more contentious, which is why, as we see below, it may require the court's permission. But we begin by discussing the main ethical concerns raised by non-voluntary sterilisation.

7.8.1 Moral aspects

The most common moral concerns about non-consensual (or non-voluntary) sterilisation are the following.

Eugenics

Put simply, eugenic sterilisation is the belief that mental capacity and behaviour are genetically determined. This means that any 'disadvantages' can be eliminated by selective sterilisation (Mason, 1998, p. 69). Put more starkly, the aim is to make sure that the 'unfit' or 'defective' do not reproduce, or, as Justice Holms infamously asserted in *Buck v Bell* (1927) US 200, at 207:

> It is better for all the world, if instead of waiting to execute degenerate offspring for crime, or to let them starve for their imbecility, society can prevent those who are manifestly unfit from continuing their kind . . .

No judge would now make such remarks, but see Montgomery, who suggests that case law (e.g. *Re M* [1988] 2 FLR 497, *Re P* [1989] 1 FLR 182) demonstrates how eugenic arguments have been 'introduced through the back door' (Montgomery, 2003, p. 400). As Scott points out, that the term 'eugenics' is almost always taken to be a negative moral term (driven by a mixture of nationalist and racist concerns) is not surprising given its historical association with compulsory sterilisation programmes practised under the Nazi regime, but also in other countries such as Sweden, the US and the UK (see further Glover, 1998).

The right to reproduce

The importance of the concept of a right to reproduce in this context was first noted in the case of *Re D* (see above). The case prompted wide debate about the scope and meaning of such a right. But as Fortin points out, even though the concept may have emotional appeal, it lacks substance. Thus she argues that, rather than providing an absolute right to reproduce, a more widely accepted interpretation of the concept – which is in line with international human rights documents seeking to protect individuals from eugenic practices – is that it instead refers to a right to choose whether or not to reproduce (Fortin, 2003, p. 335). Interpreted this way, which, according to Mason, is essentially no more than a specific expression of the right of control over one's own body, if patients are unable to give consent, the issue of non-voluntary sterilisation is arguably less morally contentious. As such, it is not difficult to justify a court's authorisation on the grounds of an individual's inability to make a choice (Mason, 1998, p. 85).

But, as we see below, the court's authorisation is not always necessary. Furthermore, there is alternative interpretation of the right to reproduce, namely, that it refers to the right to retain the capacity to reproduce. Cleary, if the right to reproduce is understood in this way, non-consensual sterilisation, even if sanctioned by a court, is harder to justify.

Best interests

Moral objections to non-voluntary sterilisation tend to focus on the uncertainty and subjective nature of the concept of 'best interests'. In particular, there is criticism of the so-called social reasons that are typically given to justify sterilisations of learning disabled women that are carried out for so-called social reasons; e.g.:

- They cannot cope with the complexities of contraception.
- Despite being sexually active, they have no understanding of the relationship between sex and pregnancy.
- The pain and emotional trauma of childbirth (or abortion) would be too great a burden.
- Lacking maternal instincts and unable to understand the responsibilities of parenthood, it is unlikely that such women could even care for a child, yet they would be traumatised if their babies were taken away from them (Hendrick, 2004, p. 180).

Key points

- The term 'eugenics' refers to the belief that mental capacity and behaviour can be genetically determined (and so can be eliminated by selective sterilisation).
- The concept of a 'right to reproduce' is not an absolute right but refers instead to the idea of a right to choose whether or not to reproduce.

7.8.2 Legal aspects

Over the last 30 years, a number of cases have reached the courts concerning the non-consensual sterilisation of women, children (and most recently, men). Although decisions such as these have inevitably been made on a case-by-case basis, a common set of principles have emerged about the factors that all involved in the decision-making process are expected to consider. These will be summarised below, but first it is worth considering why the issue of non-consensual sterilisation of adolescents – which was so controversial in the 1980s – now seems to generate so little case law. Fortin offers several explanations. First, that contraception and methods of menstrual management have become more effective – so there is less need for radical surgery. Second, that the Human Rights Act 1998 has forced parents and health professionals to be more considerate of the human rights of incompetent adolescents. The third, more worrying explanation, is that because most sterilisations of minors are being carried out for therapeutic reasons, the court need not be involved.

7.8.3 Court involvement – therapeutic versus non-therapeutic sterilisation

Before a person can be sterilised without their consent, a court declaration must normally be sought that the procedure is lawful (*Practice Note: Medical and Welfare Decisions for Adults who Lack Capacity* [2001] 2 FLR 158; Mental Capacity Act Code of Practice; DCA, 2007, para 8.18). However, this rule now only applies to 'non-therapeutic' sterilisations. This means that a therapeutic sterilisation can be performed without any judicial scrutiny (provided it is the least intrusive form of treatment). What then is the distinction? Briefly, treatment is therapeutic when it is medically necessary, i.e. a hysterectomy performed to alleviate 'menstrual disorder'. If, on the other hand, sterilisation is proposed for contraceptive purposes – because it is the only effective means of preventing pregnancy – then sterilisation is non-therapeutic.

In practice, however, the boundary line between therapeutic and non-therapeutic is difficult to draw; i.e. some operations do not fit clearly in either category. In such cases the court's authorisation should be sought (*Re S, Adult Patient: Sterilization* [2000] 2 FLR 389). Note that it has also been suggested that it may be wise to seek the court's authorisation in non-urgent cases even if sterilisation is therapeutic (Brazier and Cave, 2007, p. 289).

Activity

Critically consider *Practice Note: Medical and Welfare Decisions for adults who lack capacity* [2001] 2 FLR 158. Do you think it can adequately protect the interests of adolescents?

7.8.4 Factors the court will consider – the 'best interests' test

The factors the courts will consider in applying the 'best interests' test are contained in the Mental Capacity Act 2005 (for 16- and 17-year-olds), the Children Act 1989 and common law.

MCA principles (section 4)
In brief, the Act requires decision-makers to focus on the individual patient and take proper account of her views. The dignity of the patient (including those who have never had capacity) is also expected to be respected (Brazier and Cave, 2007, p. 137). In particular, the Act requires a decision-maker to consider:

- The person's past and present wishes and feelings,
- The beliefs and values that would be likely to influence her decision if she had capacity, and
- The other factors she would be likely to consider if she were able to do so.

The decision-maker must also consult, for example:

- Anyone caring for the person or interested in his welfare, and
- Any deputy appointed by the courts.

A particularly important fundamental principle is that 'best interests' should be interpreted in the way that least restricts the person's rights and freedoms (MCA s.1(6)). Note also that the MCA Code (para 8.22) makes it clear that the courts are expected to interpret a patient's 'best interests' according to common law principles developed in earlier case law.

Common law principles

In brief, the main principles derived from case law (e.g. *Re B* [1988] AC 199; *Re H.G.* [1993] 1 FLR 587; *Re F* [1990] 2 AC 1; *Re S* [2000] 2 FLR 389) are as follows:

- The best interests test is not the same as the *Bolam* test. In other words, acting in a person's best interests amounts to more than not treating them negligently.
- Medical factors must be considered in addition to broader ethical, social, moral and welfare considerations.
- Sterilisation must be a 'last resort' (i.e. it must be impossible for the patient to use a less invasive alternative).
- The operation is needed because there is a real risk of pregnancy (i.e. there must be a real likelihood of sexual contact; see further Jackson, 2001, pp. 55–69).

The court's approach in practice

Notwithstanding the benefits of sterilisation, notably, that it gives adolescents more freedom and thus the ability to live more fulfilled lives (including the 'right' to sexuality that is free from the risk of pregnancy) and the fact that judges now seem to be more willing to question the need for sterilisation, criticisms of the courts' approach include the following:

- In some cases judges have been clearly influenced by eugenic considerations (see, e.g. *Re M* [1988] 2 FLR 497).
- Because it is more difficult to claim that sterilising men is in their best interests, it could be argued that the law is gender biased (see, e.g. *Re A* [2000] 1 FLR 549).
- The courts may be too ready to decide that a patient is incompetent. They may also fail to recognise that an individual's competence fluctuates (Jackson, 2001, p. 55, and see *Re P* [1989] 1 FLR 182). In addition, the courts seem to accept (wrongly) that mental age is a static concept.
- The lack of clarity over the distinction between therapeutic and non-therapeutic sterilisations has been exploited; i.e. so-called menstrual management may too readily be invoked to justify the claim that the sterilisation is therapeutic (and therefore there is no need to get the court's permission).
- Sterilisation does not protect women from sexual abuse or sexually transmitted disease (Brazier and Cave, 2007, p. 285; see further Mason and Laurie, 2006, pp. 131–141; McHale and Fox, 2007, pp. 926–948).

Key points

- The court's prior approval will be required for non-therapeutic sterilisation of patients who lack capacity.
- The guiding principle in non-consensual sterilisation is the patient's 'best interests'.

7.9 Family Planning and the Law

In this section, we look at those aspects of family planning that are most relevant to young people, namely, provision and access to contraception, consent, confidentiality, the effect of the Sexual Offences Act 2003 and finally the legality of various forms of contraception.

7.9.1 Provision and access to contraception

Contraception has been available on NHS prescription since 1967. In 1974, the NHS assumed responsibility for family planning clinics. This ensured that a much broader range of services became available than general practitioners (GPs) were able to provide. The duty to provide contraceptive services is now contained in the NHS Act 2006. However, the duty is qualified in two ways. Firstly, services are not absolute; i.e. they must be provided to 'meet all reasonable requirements'. Secondly, doctors can (but do not have to) undertake to provide them. Nevertheless, the provision of contraceptive advice and treatment by GPs has significantly increased in the last few decades (McHale and Fox, 2007, p. 861). Yet whilst access to contraception is in theory straightforward, teenage girls do not always find it easy to attend GPs' surgeries or family planning clinics (Jackson, 2001, p. 281).

That access is, in practice, self-evidently problematic (but vital given that one-third of young people have sex before they are 16; TPIAG, 2008) may explain why teenage pregnancy rates in the UK have typically been the highest in Europe (Fortin, 2003, p. 186; SEU, 1999). Research suggests that the main factors deterring young people from accessing contraception are the following:

- *Ignorance*: Young people may be unaware that one of the commonest forms of contraception, notably the female contraceptive pill, is available for free from GPs; they may also be fearful that they will be reported for having underage sex (under the Sexual Offences Act 2003, see below).
- *Confidentiality*: Anxiety about confidentiality has been identified as the major deterrent to asking for contraceptive advice (DoH, 2004).
- *Limited access*: Research suggests that young people find the opening hours of GP surgeries and clinics restrictive (Herring, 2008, p. 244).

But difficulty in accessing contraceptive services is only one of the causes for high teenage pregnancy rates. Other factors include poverty, having been in care, educational problems, not being involved in education, training or work post 16, experience of abuse and mental health problems (DCSF, 2004). Inadequate sex education, particularly in schools, is also a significant cause (Fortin, 2003, pp 186–191; see further Teenage Pregnancy Independent Advisory Group, 2008, http://www.gov.uk).

7.9.2 Consent

In so far as the various family planning methods described below constitute medical treatment, one area which particularly concerns health professionals is whether they can provide advice and treatment to young people without involving or consulting parents. To answer this question, we need to distinguish between young people of 16 and 17 and those under 16.

The 16- and 17-year-olds

According to s.8 of the Family Law Reform Act 1969, young people of 16 and 17 are treated like adults for the purposes of consent. So, providing they are competent, they can give consent to any surgical, medical or dental treatment (which includes contraceptive advice and treatment, advice on sexually transmitted infections, STIs, and abortion; see Chapter 4).

Under 16-year-olds

Case law and DoH guidance on 'best practice' (notably the *Gillick* case [1986] and *R (Axon) v Secretary of State for Health* [2006] EWHC 37; DoH, 2004) have established that practitioners (working in a wide variety of settings) can provide young people under 16 with contraceptive, abortion and STI advice and treatment without parental knowledge or consent provided that:

- They have sufficient maturity to understand all aspects of the advice (i.e. understand all the implications of what is involved);
- The practitioner cannot persuade the young person to inform his or her parents or to allow the practitioner to do so;
- In relation to contraception and STIs, the young person is very likely to begin or continue to have sex with or without treatment;
- Their physical or mental health or both are likely to suffer unless they receive such advice and treatment;
- It is in the best interests of the young person to receive the advice and treatment on sexual matters without parental consent or notification.

Note that the above criteria are usually referred to as the Fraser guidelines and are expected to be 'strictly observed' (per Silber J in the *Axon* case; for further guidance, see GMC, 2007; RCN, 2008).

7.9.3 Confidentiality

The legal position in relation to confidentiality is clear (for both the under 16-year-olds and those of 16 and 17) and can be briefly stated; i.e. young people receiving advice and treatment about contraception, sexual and reproductive health have a right to confidentiality (RCN, 2008, p. 9). However, the duty of confidentiality is not absolute (see Chapter 5). This means that when a practitioner believes that there is a risk to the health, safety or welfare of a young person (e.g. they are being sexually abused) or others which is so serious as to outweigh the young person's right to privacy, they can breach confidentiality (GMC, 2007).

7.9.4 Criminal liability

Nurses' concern that they may face criminal charges (for facilitating a child sex offence) if they provide contraceptive advice and treatment is understandable in the light of the plethora of new offences created by the Sexual Offences Act 2003 (relating to unlawful sexual relations with people under 16). However, the Act does not affect the ability of health professionals (likewise anyone who acts to protect a child, e.g. teachers) from providing contraceptive advice or treatment, abortions or any health care relating to an under 16-year-old's sexual health. This is because, according to section 73, a person is not guilty of aiding, abetting or counselling a sexual offence against a child if they are acting to:

- Protect a child from pregnancy (or STI),
- Protect the physical safety of the child, and
- Promote a child's emotional well-being by giving the advice.

Key points

- Under 18-year-olds can give consent to 'contraceptive' treatment (e.g. in relation to birth control, sexual and reproductive health) if they are competent.
- Young people under 18 receiving contraceptive treatment are owed a duty of confidentiality.
- Parents of competent under 18-year-olds have no legal right to be informed that their children are receiving such treatment.
- Health professionals who provide contraceptive advice and treatment will not face criminal charges under the Sexual Offences Act 2003 (s.73)

7.9.5 Legality of family planning methods

In this section, the legal implications of various forms of contraception are briefly discussed.

Contraception

There is no legal definition of contraception, but it is nevertheless assumed for legal purposes that it includes any birth control method which prevents fertilisation. It therefore includes barrier methods, for example, the male condom, the female condom and the diaphragm or cap, as well as oral and injectable contraceptives. Other than ensuring that under 16-year-olds can give valid consent, none of these methods present any legal difficulty although defective contraceptive drugs may give rise to claims either under the law of negligence or the Consumer Protection Act 1987 (Brazier and Cave, 2007, p. 274, and see further McHale and Fox, 2007, pp. 203–209). Similarly, health professionals who prescribe oral or injectable contraceptives without taking a full medical history or conducting appropriate tests or examinations could face liability in negligence. In addition, for consent to be valid, side effects, risks and so forth have to be explained.

Post-coital methods

Post-coital birth control, namely, the so-called (but misnamed) emergency hormonal 'morning after' pill (misnamed because it can be taken within 72 hours of intercourse), and the intrauterine device (IUD) are designed to act after fertilisation but before implantation. As such, they prevent gestation and so can be described as 'interceptive' (Mason, 2007, p. 35). Since 2000, a version of the post-coital pill has been available over the counter without prescription. This controversial decision prompted the Pro-Life Alliance to take legal action on the basis that the pill was an abortifacient. As such, it contravened the Offences Against the Person Act 1861 – because it procured a miscarriage by prevented implantation. The court disagreed. It held that the word 'miscarriage' should be understood in its ordinary sense of terminating an established pregnancy. Before implantation there is no pregnancy. Therefore, there can be no miscarriage (R, *on the application of Smeaton v Secretary of State for Health* [2002] 2 FCR 193).

The IUD also aims to prevent implantation and if fitted before intercourse presents no special legal problem. However, if one is fitted post-coitally it can have the effect of dislodging an implanted embryo. As Mason (2007, p. 37) explains, timing of its use is therefore critical in respect of the law. That this is so is apparent from *R v Dinghra* (*Daily Telegraph*, 25 January 1991) in which a doctor was charged under the 1861 Act after fitting a woman with an IUD 11 days after he had had sexual intercourse with her. He was acquitted because the judge held 'that it was highly unlikely that any ovum became implanted and only at completion of implantation does an embryo become a foetus'.

Case study

Cody is almost 15 but looks much younger. For several months she has been going out with Tony, who is 17. She wants to go on the pill, but has been told that because she is under 16 her GP will not prescribe it. She is also reluctant to go to her GP because her mother has told her that she has a right to be notified should Cody approach a health professional for advice/treatment. She also insists that, as Cody's mother, her daughter could only be prescribed contraception if she agreed.

Is Cody owed a duty of confidentiality and can she be prescribed the pill without her mother's knowledge?

Cody's right to confidentiality

The legal and moral position with regard to a minor's right to confidentiality is clear: once an obligation to maintain confidentiality has arisen, it is owed as much to children and young people under 18 as it is to any other person, providing they are sufficiently mature to form a relationship of trust. What this means is that irrespective of a young person's competence, she is nonetheless owed a moral and legal duty of confidence if she understands what it means to trust someone with secret information (subject, of course, to any relevant exception; see Chapter 5). As none of the exceptions apply to Cody (i.e. there is no evidence that she is being sexually abused), there is no doubt that she is owed a duty of confidentiality; i.e. her mother has no right to be informed that she has sought contraceptive advice and treatment.

Cody's consent to contraception

As Cody is 15, the issue of consent is governed by the *Gillick* test. The question is therefore, is she sufficiently mature to understand the GP's advice and its implications in respect of sexual activity; cannot be persuaded to inform her mother; is likely to begin (or continue) having intercourse etc. (see further DoH, 2004), and then; if yes, she can make her own family planning decisions without her mother's consent or knowledge. In acknowledging a mature under 16-year-old's right to consent to treatment, the law is therefore clearly recognising autonomous decision-making by young people (see further Chapter 4). The fact that Cody looks young for her age is irrelevant since her ability to understand the nature and implications of treatment etc. depends on her maturity, not on her looks. It is also now clear that just as Cody's mother has no right to veto her mature daughter's independent legal right to consent to treatment, she also has no legal right to be informed of her approach to the GP (*R (Axon) v Secretary of State for Health* [2006] EWHC 37).

7.10 The Relationship between Law and Ethics

7.10.1 Abortion

- The Abortion Act 1967 recognises the legal and moral status of the fetus by, for example, limiting 'late' abortions.
- The Act attempts to balance the legal and moral status of the fetus and the pregnant woman.
- The 'conscience' clause in the Act acknowledges the moral and legal rights of third parties to refuse to participate in abortions.

7.10.2 Non-consensual sterilisation

- The idea that there is a 'right to reproduce' is recognised in both law and ethics, but neither is regarded as an absolute right.
- In deciding whether to sterilise an adolescent without his/her consent, law and ethics adopt the same guiding principle – the 'best interests' test.

7.10.3 Family planning

- Both law and ethics recognise the concept of children's autonomy in relation to family planning.
- Mature minors have the right to consent to, for example, contraception and abortion, irrespective of their parents' knowledge or wishes.

References

Beauchamp, T.L. and Childress, J.F. (2009) *Principles of Biomedical Ethics*. Oxford: Oxford University Press.

Bennett, R. and Harris, J. (2007) Reproductive choice. In Rhodes, R., Francis, L.P. and Silvers, A. (eds) *The Blackwell Guide to Medical Ethics*. Oxford: Blackwell.

BMA (2007) *The Law and Ethics of Abortion: BMA Views*. London: BMA.

Brazier, M. and Cave, E. (2007) *Medicine, Patients and the Law*. London: Penguin.

DCA (2007) *Mental Capacity Act 2005: Code of Practice*. London: DCA.

DCSF (2005) *Teenage Parenthood and Social Exclusion: Summary Report of Findings*. London: Social Science Research Council.

DES (2004) *Every Child Matters: Change for Children*. London: DES.

Dimond, B. (2008) *Legal Aspects of Nursing*, 5th edn. Harlow: Pearson Education.

DoH (2004) *Best Practice Guidance for Doctors and Other Health Professionals on the Provision of Advice and Treatment to Young People under 16 on Contraception, Sexual and Reproductive Health*. London: DoH.

Dworkin, R. (2001) What is sacred? In Harris, J. (ed.) *Bioethics*. Oxford: Oxford University Press.

Fortin, J. (2003) *Children's Rights and the Developing Law*, 2nd edn. London: Butterworths.

Fox, M. (1998) A woman's right to choose? A feminist critique. In Harris, J. and Holm, S. (eds) *The Future of Human Reproduction: Ethics, Choice and Regulation*. Oxford: Oxford University Press.

Glover, J. (1998) Eugenics: some lessons from the Nazi experiments. In Harris, J. and Holm, S. (eds) *The Future of Human Reproduction*. Oxford: Oxford University Press.

GMC (2007) *0–18 Guidance for All Doctors*. London: GMC.

Hare, R. (1975) Abortion and the golden rule. *Philosophy and Public Affairs* 4:201.

Harris, J. (1985) *The Value of Life*. London: Routledge and Keegan Paul.

Harris, J. and Holm, S. (2005) Abortion. In LaFollette, H. (ed.) *The Oxford Handbook of Practical Ethics*. Oxford: Oxford University Press.

Hendrick, J. (2004) *Law and Ethics: Foundations in Nursing and Health Care*. Cheltenham: Nelson Thornes.

Herring, J. (2008) *Medical Law and Ethics*, 2nd edn. Oxford: Oxford University Press.

Jackson, E. (2001) *Regulating Reproduction: Law, Technology and Autonomy*. Oxford: Hart.

Jackson, E. (2006) *Medical Law: Text, Cases and Materials*. Oxford: Oxford University Press.

Marquis, D. (2006) Abortion and the beginning and end of human life. *Journal of Law, Medicine and Ethics* 34(1):16.

Mason, J.K. (1998) *Medico-Legal Aspects of Reproduction and Parenthood*, 2nd edn. Aldershot: Dartmouth.

Mason, J.K. (2007) *The Troubled Pregnancy*. Cambridge: Cambridge University Press.

Mason, J.K. and Laurie, G.T. (2006) *Mason and McCall Smith's Medical Law and Ethics*, 7th edn. Oxford: Oxford University Press.

McDonagh, E.L. (1999) My body, my consent: securing the constitutional right to abortion funding. *Albany Law Review* 62:1057.

McHale, J. and Fox, M. (2007) *Health Care Law*, 2nd edn. London: Sweet & Maxwell.

Montgomery, J. (2003) *Health Care Law*, 2nd edn. Oxford: Oxford University Press.

NMC (2008) *Advice Sheet on Conscientious Objection*. London: NMC.

Pattinson, S.D. (2006) *Medical Law and Ethics*. London: Sweet & Maxwell.

Quinn, W. (1984) Abortion, identity and loss. *Philosophy and Public Affairs* 13:24.

RCN (2008) *Abortion Care: RCN Guidance for Nurses, Midwives and Specialist Community Public Health Nurses*. London: RCN.

RCOG (2001) *Further Issues Relating to Late Abortion, Fetal Viability and Registration of Birth*. London: RCOG.

Scott, R. (2007) *Choosing Possible Lives: Law and Ethics of Prenatal and Preimplantation Diagnosis*. Oxford: Hart.

SEU (1999) *Teenage Pregnancy*. London: SEU

Sheldon, S. (1997) *Beyond Control: Medical Power and Abortion Law*. London: Pluto Press.

Singer, P. (1993) *Practical Ethics*. Cambridge: Cambridge University Press.

Teenage Pregnancy Independent Advisory Group (2008) *Review of Sex and Relationship Education Delivery*. London: DCSF.

Thomson, J.J. (1971) A defence of abortion. *Philosophy and Public Affairs* 1:47.

Tooley, M. (1983) *Abortion and Infanticide*. Oxford: Clarendon Press.

Warren, M.A. (1973) On the moral and legal status of the abortion. *Monist* 57(1):43.

Warren, M.A. (1993) Abortion. In Singer, P. (ed.) *A Companion Guide to Ethics*. Oxford: Blackwell.

Warren, M.A. (1997) *Moral Status: Obligations to Persons and Other Living Things*. Oxford: Oxford University Press.

Whyte, A. (1997) Fertile ground. *Nursing Times* 93(14):16.

Wicks, E., Wyldes, M. and Kilby, M. (2004) Late termination of pregnancy for foetal abnormality: medical and legal perspectives. *Medical Law Review* 12(3):285.

CHAPTER 8

Birth and its Regulation

Learning outcomes

By the end of this chapter you should be able to:

- Discuss the legal and ethical implications of assisted reproduction and surrogacy;
- Consider the scope of a pregnant adolescent's autonomy;
- Evaluate the role of the law in regulating pregnancy;
- Understand how the law regulates parentage.

Introduction

The birth of Louise Brown, the world's first 'test tube baby', in 1978 through in vitro fertilisation (IVF) is a landmark date in the development of assisted reproduction. It attracted enormous publicity and captured the public's imagination. Since then, of course, assisted reproduction has come a long way. Yet just because IVF is now widely regarded as routine treatment for infertility, it should not be assumed that reproductive technologies (particularly those that have begun to converge with developments in genetic technology) have ceased to be controversial. Thus, for example, the technologies that make it possible to predict whether an embryo or fetus has a particular disease (and thus enable a couple to avoid having a particular kind of child) raise profound ethical questions about the impact of disease and disability on individuals and society.

Because of limited space, however, the legal and philosophical dimensions of these technologies (and others such as cloning, so-called 'designer babies', saviour siblings and sex selection) are not discussed in this chapter (see further Harris, 1998, pp. 5–37; Wachbroit and Wasserman, 2005, pp. 137–160). Rather, the focus here is primarily on those aspects of assisted reproduction, pregnancy and birth that are most likely to affect the lives of children and young people (or potential children). It therefore considers, firstly, the moral objections to assisted reproduction that are concerned with children's welfare and the legal framework governing treatment; secondly, how the law ascribes parentage (in particular, children's right to information about who are their 'real' parents); thirdly, ethical aspects of surrogacy and the legal position of children born under surrogacy arrangements; fourthly, how the law regulates pregnancy and finally, legal remedies arising from prenatal injuries.

8.1 Assisted Reproduction

It is estimated that about one in seven couples will experience some difficulty in conceiving and each year about 30 000 couples receive treatment in the UK (Herring, 2008,

p. 315). There is no objective definition of infertility, but the standard medical definition is the failure to conceive after 12 months of unprotected sexual intercourse, or
the occurrence of three or more miscarriages or stillbirths (Jackson, 2001, p. 252). Several different reproductive techniques are now available. These range from the relatively
simple to the more sophisticated and include, for example, artificial insemination by hus-
band/partner (AIH/AIP), donor insemination (DI), in vitro fertilisation (IVF), natural cy-
cle IVF, gamete intra-fallopian transfer (GIFT), intra-cytoplasmic sperm injection (ICSI),
intrauterine insemination (IUI) and in vitro maturation (see further Herring, 2008).

8.1.1 Moral objections to assisted reproduction

Although this section focuses on child welfare concerns, it is worth noting that for some
critics the main reason why reproductive technologies are morally 'wrong' is that they
are 'unnatural'; i.e. they interfere with the sacred process of life (which is up to God)
and sever the link between sex and procreation (see further Liu, 1991; Tighe et al.,
1999; Warnock, 2002). Other critics – who can be broadly described as 'feminist' –
believe that reproductive technologies harm women's physical or mental well-being by,
for example, reinforcing the idea that child-rearing is a woman's natural destiny and
proper role (without which they cannot be completely fulfilled) or by taking power over
the reproductive process away from women and putting it in the hands of (largely male)
medical professionals (see further Jackson, 2001, p. 178, and for a summary of other
'feminist' responses, Herring, 2008, pp. 323–324).

8.1.2 Harm to children

The range of 'harms' critics of assisted reproduction claim that children will suffer if they
are born as a result of assisted reproduction include the medical dangers associated with
multiple births (a known risk for IVF babies) as well as the psychological trauma caused
by discovering the unusual circumstances of their birth. In addition, so it is claimed, such
children will have no clear family identity or sense of kinship. But as Herring (2008,
p. 321–322) notes, there is little evidence that children born using assisted reproductive
techniques suffer psychologically (or physically; see further MRC, 2004). Furthermore,
critics seem to assume that the circumstances of the birth of such children will be kept
secret and that they will therefore never know for certain (but may nevertheless suspect)
the truth about their origins. Thus, the argument that this deception will blemish, if
not destroy the trust that ideally exists within the family is unsustainable (Cohen, 2005;
Overall, 2002, pp. 305–321; see further Radin, 2005).

8.1.3 Threats to 'the family'

If we accept that the 'dominant ideology of the family' is that of a heterosexual, married
couple, with children, all living under the same roof, i.e. the traditional nuclear family
unit (see Diduck and Kaganas, 2006; Gittins, 1993; McGlynn, 2006), it is perhaps
not surprising that fertility treatments that offer increased reproductive choices to non-
conventional families are perceived by some as a threat to traditional family values.
As Deech explains, 'assisted reproduction affects assumptions which we bring to the
understanding of family life and also to the very understanding of family life itself; it
goes to the heart of our beliefs about the family, marriage and humanity' (Deech, 2003).
The family structures that have provoked most concern are the following.

Single women
Concerns about solo mothers (i.e. those with no current partner who intend to raise their
child alone) being offered assisted reproduction centre on the effects of growing up in
fatherless families, i.e. the fear that such children will suffer in terms of their cognitive,

social and emotional development. Such claims are, however, difficult to substantiate. Thus, although there is evidence that children raised in single parent households do less well according to a variety of indicators, these negative outcomes may be explained by economic factors and other social deprivations suffered by lone parents. In other words, these outcomes cannot necessarily be generalised to children born to solo mothers following assisted reproduction. Indeed, there is ample evidence that what is more damaging to children is the effect of experiencing parental conflict (Brinsden, 2005, p. 37).

Lesbian couples

Legislative changes (notably the Adoption and Children Act 2002 which permits same-sex couples to adopt a child and the Civil Partnership Act 2004 which recognises same-sex relationships) may have made the possibility of a lesbian couple conceiving children through assisted reproduction less controversial than it once was. Yet some thinkers – particularly those of the 'New Right' (e.g. Dennis and Erdos, 2000) – have two main concerns about lesbian motherhood. These are, firstly, that children will be bullied and ostracised by their peers, causing psychological problems, and, secondly, that they would show atypical gender development; i.e. boys would be less masculine in their identity and behaviour, and girls less feminine, than boys and girls from heterosexual families. Yet research involving families where the children have grown up without a father right from the start shows that such children do not differ from their peers in two-parent, heterosexual families in terms of either their emotional well-being or gender development. The only clear difference to emerge is that co-mothers in two-parent lesbian families are more involved in parenting than are fathers from two-parent homes (see further Golombok, 1999, 2002).

Activity

Read Hope et al. (1999, pp. 116–123), 'An ethical debate: should older women be offered IVF' in *Bioethics: An Anthology*. Do you agree with their conclusion that it is not right to withhold fertility treatment from post-menopausal women? If not, why not?

8.2 Legal Regulation of Assisted Reproduction

8.2.1 Overview of the Human Fertilisation and Embryology Act 1990 (as amended by the Human Fertilisation and Embryology Act 2008)

The 1990 Act adopts a threefold approach to regulating assisted reproduction. This consists of the establishment of the Human Fertilisation and Embryology Authority (HFEA), a licensing system and detailed consent requirements. Although the 1990 Act was amended by the 2008 Act, it left the existing model of regulation intact.

Briefly, the HFEA's main statutory functions are to:

- License and regulate UK fertility clinics that carry out IVF and other conception procedures and centres that undertake research on human embryos;
- License and monitor the storage of gametes and embryos;
- Publish a code of practice giving guidance to clinics on how they should carry out their licensed activities;
- Maintain a formal register of information about donors, fertility treatments and children born as a result of those treatments;
- Provide relevant advice and information to patients, donors and clinics.

Licensing system

One of the main ways in which the Act regulates infertility treatment and embryo research is to prohibit certain activities altogether (e.g. placing a non-human embryo in a woman). Other activities are only permitted under licence (see further sections 3 and 4 of the 1990 Act). Note that some activities do not require any licence (e.g. so-called DIY, i.e. 'do it yourself' insemination).

Consent requirements

As regards the law of consent, assisted reproduction is no different from other medical treatment that involves touching patients (see Chapter 4). Note, however, the detailed consent requirements imposed by Schedule 3 of the Act and the Code of Practice (2009) which include the requirement that consent must be in writing. The issue of consent – or rather its absence – was central in *R v HFEA ex parte Blood* [1997] 2 All ER 687. The case received huge publicity, much sympathy for Mrs Blood's predicament and outrage at the HFEA's intransigence. The case involved sperm being removed from Mrs Blood's comatose husband (at her request) after he had contracted meningitis. Because Mr Blood had not consented to the removal of his sperm, the HFEA refused to allow its posthumous use – even though Mrs Blood claimed he would have wanted his sperm to be removed had he known of the circumstances. Eventually, Mrs Blood was allowed to take the sperm out of the UK so that she could receive treatment abroad. Following the birth of her two children, she then successfully campaigned to have her deceased husband registered as the father (see further Human Fertilisation and Embryology (Deceased Fathers) Act 2003; see also *Evans v Amicus Healthcare Ltd and others* [2004] 3 All ER 1025).

Activity

Read the *Evans* case. Do you agree with the court's decision? Give your reasons.

8.2.2 Access to treatment – the child's welfare

Following changes made by the 2008 Act, access to treatment is now governed by an amended child welfare provision, namely, section 13(5) which states that 'a woman shall not be provided with treatment services unless account has been taken of the welfare of any child who may be born as a result of treatment (including the need of that child for supportive parenting), and of any other child who may be affected by the birth'. The amended section is less contentious than the one it replaced (which referred to the child's need for a father) and has been welcomed in so far as it represents a change in attitudes towards what constitutes the 'ideal' family (Collier and Sheldon, 2008).

Yet concerns remain. Thus, even though on the face of it the provision merely requires any prospective child's welfare to be considered – and so falls well short of making its welfare paramount (which is what almost all other legislation concerned with children requires) – criticisms that were made of the original wording of s.13(5) remain valid. These are as follows:

- Section 13(5) was motivated by political rather than welfare considerations, i.e. to promote traditional family values and screen out socially 'undesirable' parents, such as lesbians whose parenting skills were assumed to be somehow worse than the average heterosexual couple (Douglas, 1993; Jackson, 2002).
- If it is important to assess the parental 'fitness' of infertile individuals then should not all prospective parents be similarly licensed, i.e. be permitted to procreate only if they can demonstrate their adequacy as parents (Bennet and Harris, 2007)?

- It is intrinsically difficult to apply the best interests principle to such an abstract question as the welfare of a child who is already in existence. To apply it to one who does not yet exist is thus even harder, if not impossible (Short-Harris and Miles, 2007, p. 700).
- It is impossible to police section 13(5) effectively (Jackson, 2006, p. 813; see further Daniels et al., 2005).

Guidance on how clinics should apply section 13(5) is contained in the Code of Practice (2009). It seeks to ensure that people are treated 'fairly' and so gives detailed advice about the factors that should be considered when assessing patients' suitability for treatment, i.e. how the child welfare principle should be interpreted in a non-discriminatory way.

Activity

Read the guidance note on the welfare of the child (http://www.hfea.gov.uk). Critically consider how it describes 'supportive parenting'.

Key points

- The regulation of assisted reproduction consists of three elements: the Human Fertilisation and Embryology Authority, a licensing system and rigorous consent requirements.
- Access to treatment is governed by the child welfare provision in s.13(5) of the Act, which refers to the child's need for 'supportive parenting'.

8.3 Parentage

Determining parentage was once a relatively straightforward process in that it could be assumed that a child's genetic parents, i.e. those whose sperm and eggs led to its birth, were also those who were his or her legal parents. But as we see below, once assisted reproduction became more widely available, this traditional way of allocating legal parenthood was no longer adequate. This led to new rules about legal parentage being introduced by the HFEA 1990. But first, it is important to briefly consider what makes someone a parent.

8.3.1 What makes someone a parent?

The question of what is the basis for granting parenthood has been the subject of much debate. There are several possible approaches including the following (see further Herring, 2009, pp. 370–374):

Genetic parents (also called biological parents) are those who provide the gametes or embryo resulting in a child's conception (which would mean that a sperm donor would be a child's father).

Social parents are those with no genetic link to the child but who perform the caring role either now as foster or adoptive parents, for example, or in the future when the child is born. According to this approach, the 'jobs of parenthood' are more important than abstract notions of genetic parenthood – which in some cases may reflect no more than a 'one-night stand'. It also recognises the importance of a child's emotional relationship with the person who cares for her/him on a daily basis.

8.3.2 The legal position

Legal parenthood does not necessarily determine with whom a child shall live. In other words, the law provides no guarantee that a child's legal parents can exercise all the legal rights and duties of parenthood which can be exercised only by those with 'parental responsibility' (see Chapter 4). Yet establishing legal parentage is nonetheless still important for the following reasons. Firstly, legislation (which may either create rights or impose duties) may refer to a child's 'parents' (as in the Child Support Acts 1991–1995). Secondly, it may be the first essential step to acquiring parental responsibility. The third reason for establishing legal parentage is that it might arise in disputes about inheritance rights and immigration status. Although, in most cases, legal parentage will coincide with genetic parentage in relation to children born as result of egg, sperm or embryo donation, the legal position is clearly potentially more complex.

8.3.3 The legal mother

Section 27 of the HFEA 1990 provides that the woman who carries and gives birth to a child is its legal mother. Thus, even though carrying mothers may not have provided any of the child's genetic make-up (some or all of which could have been provided by another couple), legal motherhood is accorded to the woman who has carried the child through pregnancy (i.e. the gestational mother). Section 27 appears deceptively simple and is almost comprehensive, yet it can produce the 'wrong result' in surrogacy arrangements. This is because it makes the surrogate the legal mother and so defeats the whole purpose of the arrangement. To overcome this problem, s.30 of the Act was enacted, giving the commissioning parents the right to seek a 'parental order' (see below). Note too, following amendments made by the HFEA 2008, the lesbian partner of a birth mother can now acquire agreed female parenthood – which essentially recognises her as a parent.

8.3.4 The legal father

Section 28, which determines legal fatherhood, is a much more complex section. Overall, it aims to ensure a constant supply of donors by providing that there should be no legal relationship between the sperm donor and the child. To explain how the rules operate, it is necessary to distinguish between the following categories:

a. *Husbands*: According to s.28(2), if a married woman gives birth following treatment (such as IVF), her husband is the child's legal father. The husband can only avoid legal fatherhood if he can show that he is not the genetic father and did not consent to treatment.

b. *Partners*: As regards unmarried couples, s.28(3) provides that where donated sperm is used for a woman in the course of treatment provided for her and a man together under the licensing procedure of the Act, the woman's partner is the child's legal father (see *Evans v Amicus Healthcare Ltd and others* [2004] 3 All ER 1025 and *Re D, A Child* [2005] UKHL 33). Note that this only applies if the 'agreed fatherhood conditions' set out s.37 of the HFEA 2008 have been complied with (see further Herring, 2009, pp. 329–336).

c. *Sperm donors*: Another related subsection, 28(6), makes it clear that a sperm donor who has given all the relevant consents to his sperm being used is *not* to be treated as the child's legal father (under Schedule 3 of the Act). This means that when an unmarried woman has a DIY insemination (i.e. she inseminates herself through 'self-help' methods outside treatment services) then the sperm donor will be under the Act the child's legal father (*U v W* [1998] 1 FCR 526).

d. *Fatherless children*: Some children, albeit rarely, may have no father in law at all. This occurs when a single woman receives infertility treatment alone at a licensed clinic. In such cases the sperm donor avoids legal fatherhood (by virtue of s.28(6)), but because she is not being treated together with her partner, there is no one to qualify as a legal father. A similar situation may arise if a man's sperm is used after his death (Herring, 2009, p. 335).

> **Activity**
>
> Read *Leeds Teaching Hospital v A* [2003] EWHC 259. Do you agree with the court's decision? Give your reasons.

> **Key points**
>
> - A child's legal mother is the woman who has carried the child through pregnancy.
> - A child's legal father is normally either the husband of a woman who has given birth or her partner.
> - Sperm donors who comply with the HFEA 1990 are not treated as the child's legal father.
> - In rare cases, a child will be legally fatherless.

8.4 Children's Right to Know their Genetic Parentage

Questions about their heritage and the identity of their genetic parents may trouble children born as a result of assisted reproduction just as much as they may concern adopted children. Yet the so-called discovery rights of the former group to trace their origins and find out the truth about their genetic ancestry were – certainly until reforms were introduced in 2005 – far more limited despite the fact that many of the arguments in favour of a more open process apply equally to children of the 'reproductive revolution' as they do to adoptees.

8.4.1 Arguments supporting a child's right to know

These include the following:

Medical reasons: A child's family history may be important in assessing the likelihood of a genetic disease being passed on or a predisposition to a particular medical condition such as heart disease (see further Eekelaar, 2006; Warnock, 2002).

Sense of self: There is now a growing body of evidence (from research carried out in adoption studies) that knowledge of one's genetic background is crucial if we are to develop a secure sense of identity or sense of self. The negative outcomes of being denied this information are said to include low self-esteem, loss of trust in others, inability to form intimate relationships, depression, anxiety and lack of parenting skills (Donovan, 2000, p. 75; see further Short-Harris and Miles, 2007, pp. 713–720).

8.4.2 Arguments against the right to know

These include the following:

Security and privacy: Anonymity was widely assumed to be important in so far as it could protect parents who use assisted reproduction from the possible social stigma attached to such processes. Some commentators have suggested, however, that the real motivation for the policy of donor anonymity was to protect the nuclear family

(Thompson et al., 2006). In other words, the concern is that if their children discover the truth about their genetic origins, family relationships may be undermined; i.e. a child may no longer treat her father as her 'real father'.

Reduced 'donations': The assumption here is that unless donors remain anonymous, they will not come forward for fear of being sought out by their 'offspring' – who may, for example, make financial claims on them or disrupt their lives. Whilst evidence from Sweden (where donor anonymity was removed in 1985) has shown such fears to be misplaced, the removal of donor anonymity in the UK (in 2005) appears to have led to a significant drop in supply (Short-Harris and Miles, 2007, p. 719).

8.4.3 The legal framework

Whatever the arguments for and against disclosure of information, the solution initially adopted by the HFEA was somewhere between the 'extremes'; i.e. it did not endorse full disclosure but nor did it allow the process to be kept secret. Because of the reforms which came into force in July 2004, it is now necessary to distinguish between children conceived before 1 April 2005 and after that date.

Children conceived before 1 April 2005

Such children are entitled (once they reach 18) to ask the HFEA whether they were born following fertility treatment, and if they are related to a prospective spouse. They are also now entitled to non-identifying information (such as the donor's ethnic origin, occupation, religion and family medical history).

Children conceived after 1 April 2005

Additional information is now available to children born as a result of donations after the 1 April 2005. Particularly important is their right (once they reach 18) to identifying information as to the donor's surname, date of birth (and the town or district of birth), the appearance of the donor and his last known postal address (see further HFEA Regulations 2004, S1.2004/1511).

While the 2005 reforms certainly give children rights to more information about their genetic background, they still face a major obstacle: that is, they still have no legal right to be told they were born as a result of assisted reproduction. In other words, unless they know (or suspect) that they were conceived using donated gametes, they will be unaware that they can access such information. Given the strong evidence that the majority of parents do not tell their children the truth about their genetic origins, the reforms introduced in 2005 are thus unlikely to have much of an impact (Jackson, 2006, p. 828).

Activity

Critically consider the arguments for and against donor anonymity. Which do you think are the most persuasive?

8.5 Surrogacy

Although surrogacy has an ancient history going back to biblical times, it is only relatively recently that the practice has caused so much controversy. As we see below, much of the hostility provoked by surrogacy centres around child welfare concerns – i.e. that children born as result of a surrogacy arrangement will suffer a variety of different harms. But first we need to define what surrogacy is.

8.5.1 Definition of surrogacy

Essentially, surrogacy covers any situation in which a woman (the surrogate) agrees to bear a child for another. The intention behind all surrogacy arrangements is that the child should be handed over at birth to the 'commissioning couple' but they can take several forms. In 'partial' surrogacy, the surrogate mother is the child's genetic (and gestational) mother. But if the surrogacy is a 'full' or 'total' one, the commissioning couple provide the gametes, which are fertilised in vitro and implanted in the surrogate. This method produces a child genetically related to the commissioning couple (for other less common variants of total surrogacy, see Hendrick, 1997).

The incidence of surrogacy is almost impossible to gauge as there is no requirement that accurate records be kept. Nonetheless, there is evidence that surrogacy has not 'withered on the vine' (as was predicted when it first attracted media interest in the mid-1980s). Indeed, it seems that numbers are rising and are likely to continue to do so (Brazier, 1998, p. 28; see further http://www.surrogacy.org.uk).

8.5.2 Moral aspects – does surrogacy harm children?

Before we look at the objections to surrogacy, it is worth briefly noting that there are compelling arguments in support of the practice. It might, for example, be the only way some forms of infertility can be alleviated. Another persuasive moral argument is based on the concept of autonomy. According to this view, a woman's right of self-determination includes the right to use her body to have a baby for another. Surrogacy, in other words, is a legitimate reproductive choice or as it is sometimes called, an expression of her 'reproductive autonomy' (for the distinction between this concept and 'reproductive liberty', see Bennet and Harris, 2007, pp. 201–220; Herring, 2008, pp. 317–320).

Turning now to the potential risk to the welfare of children born as a result of a surrogacy arrangement, the main concerns are the following.

Commodification/baby selling

For Freeman, the most substantial argument against surrogacy is its detrimental effect on children. He contends that whether a child is born as a result of altruism (whereby a fertile sister 'gives' her infertile one a child) or the child's birth follows a commercial arrangement, a potential consequence is that children may come to be seen as commodities. In other words, the danger is that surrogacy degrades children by encouraging the perception that children 'complete a family like any other consumer durable' such as a TV or fridge (Freeman, 1989, p. 175). Radin similarly warns against the dangers of a 'capitalist baby industry' which she claims will not only turn the baby into a commodity but will also commodify all of its personal attributes – sex, eye colour, predicted IQ, height and so on (Radin, 1987, pp. 1925–1926).

The idea that surrogacy may turn babies into a market commodity, purchasable if the price is right, may seem a little far fetched – even Freeman conceded the argument was a little exaggerated and had something of a 'slippery slope' about it. Furthermore, as Mason and Laurie (2006, p. 115) note, the fear that children may become objects for barter is valid only so long as surrogacy itself is regarded as objectionable. Nevertheless, it can be plausibly argued that in so far as surrogacy treats children as property rather than persons, it may pose a threat to our notion of childhood and to an ideal of children for which the children's rights movement strives (Freeman, 1989, p. 176).

Psychological harm

Much has also been made of the psychological and emotional problems surrogate children may experience when they find out about their true identity, i.e. that the parents who have brought them up are not their 'real' mother or father. The threat to their sense of security has also been identified as a potential problem. As Brazier explains, this may arise particularly in cases where children have a poor relationship with the commissioning couple when the knowledge that they had been brought into the world as a result of a commercial arrangement may not only further damage family relationships but also interfere with a child's development and positive self-esteem. A related concern is how well a child will cope with the knowledge that she has been created for the purpose of being given away (Brazier, 1998, pp. 31–32). What too of the surrogate's own children? How will they cope with seeing their mother give up a sibling? Will they fear that they too may be given up in the future?

In the absence of any clear empirical data on the long-term psychological consequences of surrogacy, it is, of course, only possible to make predictions about its impact on children and families. In the meantime, we should perhaps avoid 'pessimistic speculation' and deal instead with the practice in an honest and common sense way (Purdy, 1999, p. 108). Or to put it another way, even though surrogacy may be problematic, it is not necessarily more so than other types of unconventional families (Mason and Laurie, 2006, p. 116). Nor are the dangers either inevitable or insurmountable. We should therefore focus on how the practice can be better regulated, i.e. as to whether current legislation is adequate.

Activity

Read Purdy (1999, pp. 103–113), 'Surrogate mothering: exploitation or empowerment', in *Bioethics: An Anthology*. Do you accept her views about the impact of surrogacy on children? If not, why not?

8.6 The Legal Regulation of Surrogacy

8.6.1 The Surrogacy Arrangements Act 1985 (as amended by the Human Fertilisation and Embryology Act 2008)

Almost all surrogacy arrangements come within the Surrogacy Arrangements Act 1985. The Act was passed within a few months of the famous 'baby Cotton' case (*Re C* [1985] FLR 846) which concerned an American couple who arranged a surrogacy in England through an American commercial agency. The agency was paid approximately £10 000, half of which went to the surrogate. Not surprisingly, the case was hyped up by the media into a sordid tale of baby selling and profit making.

The Act does not make surrogacy in the UK illegal or unlawful, but instead tries to discourage it. Firstly, it makes surrogacy arrangements legally unenforceable. The effect of this is that the surrogate cannot be forced to give the baby up if she changes her mind and a court thinks it is in the baby's best interests to stay with her (see, e.g. *W v H (Child Abduction: Surrogacy) (No 2)* [2002] 2 FLR 252; *Re S (Surrogacy: Residence)* December [2007] Family Law 1135; *Re N (a child)* [2007] EWCA Civ 1053). Secondly, it criminalises the commercial exploitation of surrogacy. However, s.59 of the HFEA 2008 allows bodies that operate on a not-for-profit basis to receive payment for providing some surrogacy services. It will remain the case, however, that not-for-profit bodies will not be permitted to receive payment for offering to negotiate a surrogacy arrangement. Note finally that payments made to the surrogate for, e.g. loss of earnings or reasonable expenses, are also lawful.

8.6.2 Legal parentage and surrogacy

A child's legal parentage in a surrogacy arrangement can be problematic. This is because, firstly, the surrogate is the legal mother (regardless of the child's genetic make-up). Secondly, if the surrogate is married, her husband will be the legal father (assuming he consented to the procedure) even if the commissioning father's sperm was used. How, therefore, can a commissioning couple acquire legal parentage or at least the ability to exercise the rights and responsibilities of parenthood? One option is for them to adopt the child. But this is a lengthy process. Another is to seek a residence order under the Children Act 1989. Arguably, the most appropriate option is to apply for a 'parental order', i.e. an order that the child will be treated in law as a child of the parties (s.30 of the HFEA 1990).

But a section 30 order will not suit all commissioning couples as a number of stringent conditions have to be satisfied (although some of these were relaxed by the HFEA 2008); e.g.:

- Only married couples (likewise civil partners or those in an 'enduring family relationship').
- There must be a partial genetic link, i.e. either the commissioning mother or father must have provided gametes.
- The surrogate must have been impregnated by artificial means.
- The surrogate must freely consent to the order being made (at least 6 weeks after the birth, see further s.30).

Once the court is satisfied that all the conditions have been met, it can then decide whether to grant the order.

Key points

- A surrogacy arrangement can be 'full' or 'partial'.
- Surrogacy is regulated by the Surrogacy Arrangements Act 1985.
- Commissioning couples can be granted a 'parental order', which gives them legal parenthood.

8.7 Pregnancy and Childbirth

This section begins by examining whether pregnant adolescents should be free to adopt whatever lifestyle they want during pregnancy – in other words, whether there is any moral justification for regulating behaviour which puts the fetus at risk. It also discusses the law's role in regulating pregnancy, in particular what legal rights unborn children have and what legal duties are owed to them for any prenatal injuries they suffer.

8.7.1 Moral aspects – what moral obligations are owed to a fetus?

Although there is now a growing body of evidence of the ways in which a fetus can be harmed, i.e. what will most detract from its health and development, it is quite another matter to say that as a consequence a pregnant adolescent (or indeed any pregnant woman) has a moral duty to provide such an environment. Yet if pregnant adolescents either neglect their own health (e.g. by abusing drugs, smoking or drinking excessively) or take other risks that may compromise their child's future health, then in so far as these risks are unnecessary and unreasonable, it is at least arguable that taking them is morally wrong (Steinbock, 1992, p. 128). In so far, too, as pregnant adolescents are now the legitimate targets of health promotion campaigns (see, e.g. DoH 2004), it is evidently also apparent that it is widely accepted that the decision to have a baby brings with it certain moral obligations to the child who will be born.

But although the idea may seem relatively uncontroversial, i.e. that all pregnant women (including adolescents) have moral obligations to their fetuses, there is likely to be far less agreement about the precise scope of these moral obligations, in particular what sacrifices women must undergo 'for the sake of the baby'. Should they, for example, stop drinking and eat only 'healthy' foods as soon as they know they are pregnant. As we see below, even though many may agree that pregnant women have a moral duty to at least consider the impact of their behaviour on the developing fetus, to assert that as a consequence they have a moral responsibility to lead a healthy prenatal lifestyle is a step too far.

The main arguments for limiting the moral responsibility of pregnant women are the following.

Autonomy

Constraining a pregnant adolescent would infringe her autonomy – or rather one particular aspect of the principle, namely, the right to bodily integrity, i.e. that one's body should not be invaded or even touched without consent. That this is a persuasive argument in this context is self-evident since constraining a pregnant woman's behaviour would inevitably involve infringing that right (Hope et al., 2008, p. 145).

Yet the autonomy argument is more complex in this context that it might first seem, especially in 'problematic pregnancies' (i.e. when there are concerns about the effects of the pregnant woman's lifestyle on the fetus). Thus, as Blake argues, at the very least, such pregnancies challenge our ordinary understanding of autonomy because they beg the following question: is the autonomous decision to give birth to a healthy, viable child, or is it to satisfy the craving resulting from addiction? In other words, decisions made during pregnancy by women who abuse drugs or drink may not be autonomous at all (even less so if they are adolescents acting on an uninformed basis). As a consequence, the value of autonomy is not engaged (Blake, 2000, p. 285).

For Norrie too, the autonomy principle is at best an incomplete answer to attempts to prevent pregnant women from acting as they wish. His argument is this: even if we concede that a woman's right to self-determination is necessarily stronger than the fetus's contingent rights, it does not necessarily follow that a pregnant woman is entirely free to deliberately (or even negligently) harm the fetus. As he concludes, 'while every human person has rights and freedoms, so too does he or she have responsibilities and duties, and so long as these responsibilities and duties serve a legitimate purpose then they are not generally regarded by society as an infringement of autonomy' (Norrie, 2000, pp. 228–230).

Variable standard of behaviour

The burgeoning literature and information – some of which is contradictory – and the uncertainty as to what is 'safe' during pregnancy, together with the wide variations in the quality of antenatal care (and access to it), make it unlikely that an appropriate standard of behaviour could be agreed. Note too that despite research into the effects of maternal behaviour on the fetus, medical prognosis remains far from certain. Thus, the connection between smoking and low birth weight may be well known, but the effect of other factors, such as a stressful working environment, is less clear (Blake, 2000, p. 284). Furthermore, the idea that inappropriate drug or alcohol use automatically results in harm to the fetus is simplistic – not least because research has shown, for example, that fetal alcohol syndrome affects a significantly higher number of poorer women than wealthier ones (Herring, 2008 p. 306). To expect the same standard of behaviour of all pregnant women irrespective of the differences in their lives is thus not just unrealistic but also 'unfair'.

Individual versus collective responsibility

The argument here is that the health promotion advice and preventive health programmes concerned with fetal health typically target pregnant women with advice about the steps they should take to ensure the birth of a healthy baby. As a consequence, other factors such as, for example, poverty, inadequate social care and environmental pollution (which can potentially have just as much, if not a more significant impact on fetal development) are neglected. In other words, society's collective responsibility for fetal health (i.e. the social causes of disease) is unfairly shifted to pregnant women themselves (Jackson, 2001, p. 159).

A related argument is the way in which gender has shaped much of the debate about the effect of lifestyle on the developing fetus. Thus, as Daniels and Golden point out, research on 'male-mediated' harm (i.e. the effect on reproductive health of men's drug and alcohol use etc.) has been neglected for much of the twentieth century. They also question why the research that has been carried out is far less judgemental (Daniels and Golden, 2000, p. 375). As they conclude, 'there has been no movement to post signs or print labels warning men of the risk of testicular atrophy, increased rates of miscarriage, and the possibility of genetic damage that can arise from their consumption of alcohol' (Daniels and Golden, 2000, p. 376).

Activity

Which of the above arguments do you find the most persuasive in relation to pregnant adolescents? Explain why.

8.8 Legal Aspects of Pregnancy

8.8.1 The role of law in controlling behaviour during pregnancy

In considering the role of the law in regulating pregnant women, we are really asking whether any moral duties that pregnant women may have towards their fetus can be translated into legal duties. In other words, can pregnant women be legally restrained (or punished) from acting in a way that may harm the fetus. Currently, in the UK, such legal intervention is unlawful. The main reasons usually given for the law's 'hands-off' approach are as follows.

Counterproductive

If pregnant women fear prosecution (or some other legal consequence), there is the very real possibility that they would not seek medical help at all – which might endanger the fetus even more. Moreover, the idea of using the criminal law to change behaviour is based on misplaced faith in its deterrent effect. Yet as most commentators agree, there is little empirical evidence that deterrence 'works' (i.e. that it stops or reduces abusing behaviour) not least because of the lack of control over their lives that characterises most addicts (Norrie, 2000, p. 241).

Pragmatic reasons

Consider first the enormous practical difficulties of enforcing legal restrictions. Would it really be feasible to keep pregnant women under constant surveillance until they gave birth? Who would undertake such a task? And what legal sanction would ensue if the 'illegal' behaviour was discovered – an injunction or a custodial sentence? In a liberal society, of course, none of these measures are acceptable. Nor for reasons mentioned above would they necessarily be effective even if they were thought appropriate.

Secondly, the trust that is essential to the health professional–patient relationship would be destroyed if – as would be required for the law to be effectively enforced – health professionals would be turned into police informers (Mason and Laurie, 2006, p. 205).

8.8.2 The legal status of the fetus

The legal status of the fetus was clearly established in *Re F* [1988] 2 All ER 193. The case involved a local authority that tried to make a fetus a ward of court so that it could be protected from its mother – a 36-year-old woman with long-standing mental health problems who was abusing drugs. If successful, these proceedings would have required the mother to live in a specified place and attend hospital. The court rejected the local authority's application and decided that until it was born (and had a separate existence from its mother) a fetus was not a legal person (nor is it possible to bring proceedings in the name of the fetus; *Paton v Trustees of the BPAS* [1979] QB 276).

The effect of *Re F* does not mean the fetus has no legal protection at all. Thus, for example:

- If it is harmed in utero as a result of a criminal act committed against its mother then, provided it is born alive, the perpetrator can face criminal charges (*Attorney General's Reference (No. 3 of 1994)* [1998] AC 245).
- Under the Congenital Disabilities (Civil Liability) Act 1976, a fetus can sue for certain prenatal injuries (see below).
- Various other legal provisions also go some way towards protecting the future interests of the fetus, e.g. care proceedings taken after birth (see Chapter 11).

Key points

- The fetus has no legal rights of its own until birth.
- The fetus has legal protection whilst in utero (i.e. it can sue for prenatal injuries once born).

8.9 Prenatal Injuries

Few drug tragedies attracted more national concern than Thalidomide, a tranquillizer prescribed during pregnancy which caused deformities, some of them very severe, in 8000 children worldwide born between 1959 and 1962. The claim against the drug company dragged on for years (and out-of-court settlement was only reached because of a media campaign). The tragedy drew attention to the vulnerability of the fetus, and the deficiencies in the common law led ultimately to the Congenital Disabilities (Civil Liability) Act 1976. But although the deformities suffered by the Thalidomide babies shocked the world, disabilities and childhood death can be caused by several other factors unrelated to drugs. Furthermore, now that genetic screening and prenatal diagnosis have become increasingly available, the more likely it is that 'something will go wrong'.

What then are the legal consequences of negligent genetic screening and prenatal testing? Supposing parents are wrongly advised about the risks of passing on a genetic disorder? Do they (or their disabled child) have any legal remedy? Before addressing these questions, the various types of injuries that a fetus can suffer must be described.

8.9.1 Types of injuries

Pre-conception injuries
Damage to either parent's reproductive capacity before conception can affect their ability to have a healthy child – e.g. failure to offer the mother immunisation against rubella (Pattinson, 2006, p. 283). Pre-conception exposure to chemicals, excessive radiation or other toxic substances could also damage sperm and cause gene mutation. A child's disability can also be caused by negligent fertility treatment (i.e. before implantation) due to the negligent selection or storage of an embryo (Jackson, 2006, p. 641).

Injuries during pregnancy
This category covers cases where the fetus is damaged in utero. Drugs taken during pregnancy are perhaps the most typical example. Less common are those injuries which arise from an operation which goes wrong when the mother is pregnant (see, e.g. *Burton v Islington HA; de Martell v Merton and Sutton HA* [1992] 3 All ER 833).

Injuries during birth
Negligent delivery procedures are the main cause of injuries in this category, such as occurred in *Whitehouse v Jordan* [1981] 1 All ER 267, where it was alleged that brain damage was caused because the doctor pulled too hard and too long with forceps as a result of which the baby was severely disabled.

8.9.2 Types of claims – by or on behalf of the child

Generally, all these types of injuries give rise to a claim by the child that it has been harmed as the result of someone's negligent conduct. Such claims will usually be brought under the Congenital Disabilities (Civil Liability) Act 1976 (see also Consumer Protection Act 1987).

Congenital Disabilities (Civil Liability) Act 1976
Section 1 of the Act establishes the right of disabled children to obtain compensation for injuries sustained before birth. Despite the Act's good intentions, however, it is a notoriously complex piece of legislation. Its major flaw is undoubtedly that it retains the fault principle. Compensation therefore depends on proving breach of duty (to a parent) and, in addition, causation. As was noted in Chapter 3, these are very difficult, if not significant, hurdles to overcome in any negligence claim (whether the NHS Redress Act 2006 will be more useful to potential claimants is, as yet, unclear).

Briefly, for a detailed analysis, see Grubb and Laing (2004, pp. 789–851): the main aspects of the Act are that a child can sue:

- If it was born alive after 21 July 1976 (it must survive for 48 hours);
- For a disability (defined as 'any deformity, disease or abnormality, including predisposition to physical or mental defect in the future');
- For an 'occurrence' (i.e. the various types of injuries outlined above) which must have made the defendant liable in tort to a parent.

Other points to note are as follows:

- Liability generally does not arise if the parents knew of the risk of the child's being born disabled.
- Where a parent is partly to blame for the child's disabilities, compensation can be reduced to take account of his/her share of the responsibility.
- The mother is not liable to the child (unless the injuries to the fetus were caused while she was driving).

Wrongful life actions

Claims under the 1976 Act are essentially claims that the defendant was responsible for the child's disabilities, i.e. the defendant's actions caused the damage. A different kind of claim, albeit one that is also caused by a negligent act or omission, is one that asserts that, although the defendant's behaviour did not directly damage the fetus, it nevertheless resulted in the birth of a disabled child who would never otherwise have been conceived or, having been conceived, would not have been born alive. This kind of claim – in which the child is basically claiming that it would have been better off not to have been born at all – is called the 'wrongful life' action.

A wrongful life action is likely to arise out of negligent genetic counselling or prenatal testing, and less frequently, negligent infertility treatment. To date, the courts have not allowed these claims (although it remains unclear whether such a claim could be made under the 1976 Act for injuries caused by negligent selection of embryos). The main reasons for the courts' approach were set out in *McKay v Essex AHA* [1982] 2 All ER 771, notably:

- To recognise wrongful life claims would, in effect, impose on doctors a duty to persuade pregnant women to abort.
- Such a duty would compromise the value of human life by implicitly suggesting that a disabled child has the 'right' to be born whole or not at all.
- It would be impossible to assess the amount of damages because this would involve assessing the difference between the value of life with disabilities, and non-existence (see further Mason and Laurie, 2006, pp. 189–198).

These reasons have been criticised on a number of grounds, for example, that they are excessively legalistic (Lee, 1989, p. 188; see also Mason, 2007, pp. 188–240). There is also evidence that courts in other jurisdictions are more willing than in the past to consider such wrongful life actions. Whether UK courts will follow suit is, of course, uncertain (Mason, 2007, p. 237). That said, in practice, it may not matter since the facts which give rise to such an action are generally indistinguishable from those which can give rise to a 'wrongful birth' action (Jackson, 2006, p. 688; see further Harris, 2005; Heyd, 2005; Murray, 2005).

8.9.3 Types of claims – by parents

Wrongful conception

These actions arise from, for example, a negligently performed sterilisation (or failed abortion) as a result of which a woman becomes or remains pregnant. Case law in this area is complex, but in summary it is now clear that the mother can recover damages for the pain of pregnancy and childbirth and any directly attributable financial losses. Damages can also be awarded for the additional costs of bringing up a disabled child, but not a healthy one (*McFarlane v Tayside Health Board* [2000] 2 AC 59, and see Pattinson, 2006, pp. 300–309).

Wrongful birth

Wrongful birth is a claim that the defendant breached a legal duty owed to the parent to give information or to perform a medical procedure, resulting in the birth of a child. It arises out of the same circumstances as the wrongful life claim and will thus be concerned with the following: whether appropriate screening or testing (or both) was offered; whether the results were accurately interpreted; and whether the results were effectively communicated (Scott, 2007, p. 167). As Jackson (2006, p. 687) explains, the negligence might arise in several different contexts, for example, before conception or during fertility treatment (e.g. where a couple is undergoing preimplantation diagnosis or screening).

Wrongful birth actions, although rare, have been recognised in the English courts, but can only succeed if the principles of breach of duty and causation are established. So, for example, in a claim based on negligent genetic counselling, a woman must prove that she would not have become pregnant if she had been properly advised. And if the negligence was a failure to detect fetal abnormalities, success will depend on proving first, that an abortion was available (i.e. The Abortion Act 1967 applied), and second, that she would have had one (*Rand v East Dorset HA* (2000) 56 BMLR 39; *Enright v Kwun* [2003] EWHC 1000, and see further Scott, 2007, pp. 160–178).

Activity

Do you agree that it is unjust to compensate parents for the birth of a healthy child? If not, why not?

Key points

- Negligent sterilisations may give rise to wrongful conception claims.
- Wrongful birth actions may be available: (a) for failure to detect fetal abnormality, (b) giving a pregnant woman inaccurate information about the results of a prenatal test and (c) negligent fertility treatment.

Case study

Sarah is 34 weeks pregnant and will be a few weeks short of 18 when the baby is due. On her last antenatal visit, she was advised that a caesarean section was almost certainly going to be necessary. Sarah is very unhappy about this advice – she has always wanted a natural birth. Several hours ago Sarah was rushed into hospital, as her labour was well underway. As anticipated, however, it soon becomes clear that without a caesarean Sarah's life and that of her baby are at risk. Nevertheless, Sarah – who fully understands all the risks (both to her life and that of her baby) – is adamant. She will not have a caesarean.

Can Sarah be forced to have a caesarean against her wishes?

8.9.4 Moral issues

The central moral dilemma raised by forced caesareans is that, on the one hand, a situation in which health professionals allow a mature fetus to rupture its mother's womb (when this can be prevented) does serious damage to the concept of the sanctity of life. On the other hand, the thought that health professionals could carry out invasive and potentially risky treatment on unwilling patients is deeply troubling to the concept of individual autonomy – another cherished concept in liberal society and one which all ethical guidelines for health professionals endorse. In other words, the principle of respect for autonomy has priority in cases of maternal–fetal conflicts at birth (at least in relation to adults).

There is a complicating factor in this scenario, however, namely, that Sarah is not yet 18? Does this mean that respecting her autonomy is not a moral priority? But what if Sarah's ability to act autonomously is not in doubt – as seems to be the case here? As we saw in Chapter 4, overriding the autonomous choices of mature adolescents is far more ethically controversial than making decisions for younger incompetent children. Accordingly, forcing Sarah to have a caesarean could only be justified if a liberal paternalistic approach is taken. Briefly, this asserts that even though adolescents should increasingly be entitled to make their own decisions they should be protected from making those that are self-destructive. As it is not only Sarah's life that is at risk but also her baby's, this approach is likely to be the most widely supported one. Whether it is morally 'right' is, of course, another matter.

8.9.5 Legal considerations

A spate of high-profile cases in the 1990s (e.g. *Re MB* [1997] 2 FLR 426) established beyond doubt that, providing a pregnant woman is competent (and an adult, i.e. 18) she has the absolute legal right to refuse treatment – even if that means she and/or the fetus will die or be seriously harmed. Furthermore, this legal right exists 'even if her thinking process was unusual, bizarre, irrational and contrary to the overwhelming majority of the community at large' (*St George's Healthcare NHS Trust v S* [1998] 3 All ER 673), but see Herring (2000, pp. 269–282), who suggests that rather than conceiving the problem of caesareans as a conflict between the mother and fetus (which the courts resolve by making the mother's autonomy paramount), the law should focus on the unique relationship between the fetus and the pregnant woman. This approach, he claims, is less likely to result in a conflict at the moment of the operation because the wishes of the pregnant woman would have been heard throughout the pregnancy.

But Sarah is not yet 18. This means that even if she is competent, her informed refusal to have a caesarean can be overridden both by those with parental responsibility and by a court (see Chapter 4). Notwithstanding the legality of forcing Sarah to have a caesarean, health professionals may, of course, be understandably reluctant to carry it out given the practical implications of such a course of action.

8.10 The Relationship between Law and Ethics

8.10.1 Similarities between law and ethics

- The legal and moral framework regulating pregnancy and surrogacy and assisted conception seeks to reconcile potentially conflicting interests, i.e. those of society as a whole, the fetus, would-be parents and individual families.
- The legal principles governing how parentage is allocated in law are underpinned by moral concerns about the welfare of the family and the social role of parents (rather than genetic identity).

- Law and morality attempt to answer common questions in relation to surrogacy, namely, under what circumstances surrogacy might be allowed, whether anyone should be permitted to profit from it and what criteria must be satisfied before a 'commissioning couple' can be given the rights and responsibilities of parenthood.
- Even though the law does not recognise the fetus as a legal person in its own right, its moral status is recognised in law by the legal protection it is given before birth.

8.10.2 Differences between law and ethics

- In regulating access to assisted conception, the law places the interest of the 'future' child at centre stage (see, e.g. section 13(5) HFEA 1990).
- In recognising the right of competent pregnant women of 18 and over to refuse medical treatment, the law clearly places the autonomy of the woman above any moral interests of the fetus.
- In exempting mothers from liability for injuries caused to the fetus, the law fails to protect any moral claims it may have as a result of harm suffered as a consequence of her behaviour during pregnancy.
- Although the moral claims of the fetus are widely recognised, the law does not restrict women's behaviour during pregnancy.

References

Bennet, R. and Harris, J. (2007) Reproductive choice. In Rhodes, R., Francis, L. and Silvers, A. (eds) *Blackwell Guide to Medical Ethics*. Oxford: Blackwell.

Blake, M. (2000) Policing pregnancy: rights and wrongs. In Freeman, M. and Lewis, A. (eds) *Law and Medicine: Current Legal Issues*. Oxford: Oxford University Press.

Brazier, M. (1998) *Surrogacy: Review for the Health Minister of Current Arrangements for Payments and Regulations*. London: DoH.

Brinsden, P. (2005) *Textbook of In Vitro Fertilisation and Assisted Reproduction*, 3rd edn. Abingdon: Taylor & Francis.

Cohen, C.B. (2005) Give me children or I shall die: new reproductive technologies and harm to children. In Freeman, M. (ed.) *Children, Medicine and the Law*. Farnham: Ashgate.

Collier, R. and Sheldon, S. (2008) *Fragmenting Fatherhood: A Socio-Legal Study*. Oxford: Hart.

Daniels, C. and Golden, J. (2000) The politics of paternity: foetal risks and reproductive harm. In Freeman, M. and Lewis, A. (eds) *Law and Medicine: Current Legal Issues*. Oxford: Oxford University Press.

Daniels, R., Blyth, E., Hall, D. and Hanson, M. (2005) The best interests of the child in assisted human reproduction: the interplay between state, professionals and parents. In Freeman, M. (ed.) *Children, Medicine and the Law*. Farnham: Ashgate.

Deech, R. (2003) The HFEA – 10 years on. In Gunning, J. and Szoke, H. (eds) *The Regulation of Assisted Reproductive Technology*. Aldershot: Ashgate.

Dennis, N. and Erdos, G. (2000) *Families without Fathers*, 3rd edn. London: Institute for the Study of Civil Society.

DoH (2004) NSF for Children, Young People and Maternity Services. London: DoH.

Diduck, A. and Kaganas, F. (2006) *Family Law, Gender and the State*. Oxford: Hart.

Donovan, K. (2000) Interpretations of children's identity rights. In Fottrell, D. (ed.) *Revisiting Children's Rights*. The Hague: Kluwer.

Douglas, G. (1993) Assisted reproduction and the welfare of the child. *Current Legal Problems* 46(2):53.

Eekelaar, J. (2006) *Family Law and Personal Life*. Oxford: Oxford University Press.

Freeman, M. (1989) Is surrogacy exploitative? In McLean, S. (ed.) *Legal Issues in Human Reproduction*. Aldershot: Dartmouth.

Gittins, D. (1993) *The Family in Question: Changing Households and Familiar Ideologies*, 2nd edn. Basingstoke: Macmillan.

Golombok, S. (1999) Lesbian mother families. In Bainham, A., Day-Sclater, S. and Richards, M. (eds) *What is a Parent? A Socio-Legal Analysis*. Oxford: Hart.

Golombok, S. (2002) Adoption by lesbian couples: is it in the best interests of the child? *British Medical Journal* 324:1407.

Grubb, A. and Laing, J. (eds) (2004) *Principles of Medical Law*, 2nd edn. Oxford: Oxford University Press.

Harris, J. (1998) Rights and reproductive choice. In Harris, J. and Holm, S. (eds) *The Future of Human Reproduction*. Oxford: Oxford University Press.

Harris, J. (2005) The wrong of wrongful life. In Freeman, M. (ed.) *Children, Medicine and the Law*. Farnham: Ashgate.

Hendrick, J. (1997) *Legal Aspects of Child Health Care*. London: Chapman & Hall.

Herring, J. (2000) The caesarean section cases and the supremacy of autonomy. In Freeman, M. and Lewis, A. (eds) *Law and Medicine: Current Legal Issues*. Oxford: Oxford University Press.

Herring, J. (2008) *Medical Law and Ethics*, 2nd edn. Oxford: Oxford University Press.

Herring, J. (2009) *Family Law*, 4th edn. Harlow: Pearson Education.

Heyd, D. (2005) Prenatal diagnosis: whose right? In Freeman, M. (ed.) *Children, Medicine and the Law*. Farnham: Ashgate.

Hope, T., Lockwood, G.D., Jackson, J. and Bewley, S. (1999) Should older women be offered in vitro fertilisation? In Kuhse, H. and Singer, P. (eds) *Bioethics: An Anthology*. Oxford: Blackwell.

Hope, T., Savulescu, J. and Hendrick, J. (2008) *Medical Ethics and Law*, 2nd edn. Edinburgh: Elsevier.

Jackson, E. (2001) *Regulating Reproduction*. Oxford: Hart.

Jackson, E. (2002) Conception and the irrelevance of the welfare principle. *Modern Law Review* 65:176.

Jackson, E. (2006) *Medical Law: Text, Cases and Materials*. Oxford: Oxford University Press.

Lee, R. (1989) To be or not to be: is that the question? The claim of wrongful life. In Lee, R. and Morgan, D. (eds) *Birthrights: Law and Ethics at the Beginnings of Life*. London: Routledge.

Liu, A. (1991) *Artificial Reproduction and Reproductive Rights*. Aldershot: Dartmouth.

Mason, J.K. (2007) *The Troubled Pregnancy*. Cambridge: Cambridge University Press.

Mason, J.K. and Laurie, G.T. (2006) *Mason and McCall Smith's Medical Law and Ethics*, 7th edn. Oxford: Oxford University Press.

McGlynn, C. (2006) *Families and the European Union: Law, Politics and Pluralism*. Cambridge: Cambridge University Press.

MRC (2004) *Assisted Reproduction: A Safe and Sound Future*. London: MRC.

Murray, T.H. (2005) Wrongful life and death: moral obligations to the not-yet-born: the fetus as patient. In Freeman, M. (ed.) *Children, Medicine and the Law*. Farnham: Ashgate.

Norrie, K. (2000) Protecting the unborn child from its drug or alcohol abusing mother. In Freeman, M. and Lewis, A. (eds) *Law and Medicine: Current Legal Issues*. Oxford: Oxford University Press.

Overall, G. (2002) Do new reproductive technologies benefit or harm children? In Dickenson, D.L. (ed.) *Ethical Issues in Maternal Foetal Medicine*. Cambridge: Cambridge University Press.

Pattinson, S. (2006) *Medical Law and Ethics*. London: Sweet & Maxwell.

Purdy, L (1999) Surrogate mothering: exploitation or empowerment? In Kuhse, H. and Singer, P (eds) *Bioethics: An Anthology*. Oxford: Blackwell.

Radin, J.M. (1987) Market inalienablity. *Harvard Law Review* 100:1849.

Radin, J. (2005) Assisted reproduction: its implications for children: market inalienability. In Freeman, M. (ed.) *Children, Medicine and the Law*. Farnham: Ashgate.

Scott, R. (2007) *Choosing between Possible Lives: Law and Ethics in Prenatal and Pre-Implantation Genetic Diagnosis*. Oxford: Hart.

Short-Harris, S. and Miles, J. (2007) *Family Law: Text, Cases and Materials*. Oxford: Oxford University Press.

Steinbock, B. (1992) *Life before Birth*. Oxford: Oxford University Press.

Thompson, I.E., Melia, K., Boyd, K.M. and Horsburgh, D. (2006) *Nursing Ethics*. Edinburgh: Elsevier.

Tighe, M., Tonti-Filippini, N., Rowland, R. and Singer, P. (1999) IVF: a debate. In Kuhse, H. and Singer, P. (eds) *Bioethics: An Anthology*. Oxford: Blackwell.

Wachbroit, R. and Wasserman, D. (2005) Reproductive technology. In LaFollette, H. (ed.) *The Oxford Handbook of Practical Ethics*. Oxford: Oxford University Press.

Warnock, M. (2002) *Making Babies: Is there a Right to Have Children?* Oxford: Oxford University Press.

CHAPTER 9

Research, Organ Donation and Tissue Transplantation

Learning outcomes

By the end of this chapter you should be able to:

- Describe the ethical principles relevant to ethical research;
- Understand the key moral concerns in carrying out research with children;
- Discuss the role of law in regulating research;
- Explain the implications of the Human Tissue Act 2004.

Introduction

Research with children has a long history. The most well-known experiments were those carried out in the late 1700s by Edward Jenner to test smallpox vaccines (Lederer and Grodin, 1994). Although these experiments involved deliberately injecting the children with smallpox, they raised few of the concerns – for example about consent or best interests – which are so central to current debates about research with children.

Since then, of course, our understandings of children and childhood have been transformed (likewise our understanding of children's competence). Few would therefore now accept the idea that children can be 'used' as research subjects with no safeguards in place to protect their welfare or without taking their wishes into account. Yet, even though it is now widely accepted that children's active participation in research should be sought and maintained, the need to protect them from harm and exploitation is also acknowledged (Farrell, 2005, p. 167). It is thus perhaps inevitable that the tension between these two agendas, i.e. protecting children from unnecessary risk and harm on the one hand, and respecting their independent rights to contribute to research knowledge on the other, permeates current ethical guidelines and the legal framework regulating research.

There are similar tensions in the legal framework governing blood, bone marrow and organ donation. While these are not the only areas regulated by the Human Tissue Act 2004, they are nevertheless the most ethically troublesome – not least because they raise fundamental questions about the concept of a child's best interests. It is therefore these aspects of the Act that this chapter addresses.

9.1 Research

9.1.1 Types of research

Surprisingly, perhaps, the term 'research' is not easy to define precisely. This is because it is commonly used interchangeably with a variety of other terms (such as service evaluations, clinical trials, innovative treatment and experimentation) to describe processes by which information is collected and analysed. The Department of Health (DoH, 2005) defines research as the attempt to derive generalisable new knowledge by addressing clearly defined questions with systematic and rigorous methods (this includes studies that aim to generate hypotheses as well as studies that aim to test them). Research involving humans can be divided into the following:

- *Biomedical research*: A general term covering medicine, genetics, physiology or biochemistry.
- *Clinical research*: A subdivision of the above typically concerned with the development of a drug, medical device or new surgical technique.
- *Clinical trial*: A specific type of clinical research in which new medicines are tested on humans to assess their efficacy, safety and quality (POST, 2005).

Traditionally, a further distinction has also been made, namely:

- *Therapeutic research* – which aims to benefit patients by, for example, using new methods or a new procedure that is more likely to cure their disease or improve their condition. As such, it combines research with the care and treatment of patients.
- *Non-therapeutic research* – which aims principally to gain scientific knowledge in general. In short, it is carried out solely to obtain information of use to others, i.e. not to treat any illness or condition participants may have.

Although much of the literature continues to distinguish between therapeutic and non-therapeutic, this categorisation – which suggests that the terms are mutually exclusive – has been increasingly challenged in recent years. It is claimed, for example, that although the distinction is clear at a conceptual level, in practice it is blurred because many research projects contain elements of therapy and non-therapy (Elliston, 2007; Spriggs, 2004). In other words, the distinction is misleading since it hides the fact that therapeutic research may include aspects that are designed solely for their scientific value, and may even expose the patient to additional risks (Weijer, 2000).

Other key terms used in research contexts are the following:

Innovative treatment: Refers to medical procedures that are part of a patient's treatment but (unlike research) are not designed to test a hypothesis or to develop new knowledge – although they may lead to its development.

Experimentation: Like research, it involves departing from standard practice, but also involves a more speculative, ad hoc approach (rather than a predetermined protocol). As such, the experiment may be modified (in contrast to research which continues until its ineffectiveness is satisfactorily demonstrated; Mason and Laurie, 2006, p. 651). The distinction between research and experimentation is significant because research is governed by the regulatory procedures described below, whereas experimental treatment must comply with the *Bolam* standard (see Chapter 3 and *Simms v Simms* [2003] 1 *All ER* 669, for the courts' approach to experimentation).

Key points

- Research is defined as the attempt to obtain new knowledge by addressing clearly defined questions with systematic and rigorous methods.
- Research can be therapeutic or non-therapeutic.

9.1.2 The importance of research with children

There are three main reasons why research with, and for, children is essential:

1. Children are not small adults. In other words, certain diseases are childhood diseases. This means that the process of diseases and their reaction to treatment can only be understood in the context of children's development and growth (MRC, 2004).
2. Given the metabolic differences between children and adults, extrapolating pharmacological data from adults to children is problematic. This explains why European Commission (EC) Regulations (EC Reg No 1901/2006) now require all drugs to be tested on and developed for children, as part of a paediatric investigation plan.
3. To make sure that treatments given to children are appropriate, research must be carried out to reveal what is normal development, i.e. conditions can only be identified as abnormal in relation to what is considered normal (Royal College of Paediatrics and Child Health (RCPCH), 2000).

9.2 Ethical Considerations and Principles

Research is morally problematic because in generating new scientific knowledge, i.e. improving the diagnosis, treatment and prevention of disease, it inevitably exposes participants to risks (Buchanon and Miller, 2007, p. 381). Ethical safeguards must therefore be put in place to protect participants from exploitative and unfair practices. There is a broad agreement amongst ethicists as to ethical standards and principles that must underpin research. These include the requirement that the research has social or scientific value, i.e. is designed to answer specific scientific questions; has scientific validity, i.e. must be well-designed and based on sound knowledge and proper scientific methods (see further Beauchamp and Childress, 2009, pp. 317–324; Buchanon and Miller, 2007, pp. 373–392). But here we focus on the ethical considerations that are most relevant to children. We begin, however, by clarifying their ethical status.

9.2.1 Ethical status of children

According to Morrow and Richards (1996), the 'biggest ethical challenge for researchers working with children is the disparities in power and status between adults and children'. Or to put it another way, their claim is that the way researchers view children – i.e. their particular perceptions and constructions of childhood – can profoundly influence not just the planning and design of research projects but also the way research reports are interpreted. It is thus crucial to clearly identify the various possible levels of child involvement – in short, to clarify their ethical status.

Briefly, in research situations, children are typically perceived in the following ways:

As objects: Refers to children who are seen as dependent, incompetent and unable to cope with information. Hence, they are not asked for their consent and may even be unaware that they are involved in research.

As subjects: Refers to children who occupy a more central place in the research process, but their involvement is nevertheless subject to adult perceptions of their maturity and cognitive ability.

As autonomous/active participants: Refers to children who are treated as autonomous individuals in their own right (i.e. they are entitled to adult ethical standards) and those who are genuinely active participants in the sense that they are not only informed, involved and consulted but are also increasingly seen as co-researchers (see further Alderson, 2004, pp. 97–112; Glantz, 2005; Robinson and Kellett, 2004, pp. 81–96).

9.2.2 Respect for autonomy

As was noted in Chapter 4, respecting children and young people's autonomy means not just acknowledging the rights of competent older children and adolescents to act autonomously but also enhancing younger children's autonomy (by facilitating their participation in decision-making). Basically, this requires their participation to be based on the principle of consent, i.e. that it is voluntary (free from coercion) and fully informed.

9.2.3 Voluntary and free – consent/assent

Consent

It is now generally accepted that children should give positive consent to any participation in research; in other words, not simply fail to register assent (Hill, 2005). There is also a consensus that consent is an active, ongoing process, which involves checking throughout a project that children are willing to continue participating (Alderson, 2004, p. 107). A child's consent is only valid, however, if she is competent, i.e. has sufficient understanding and intelligence of what is proposed, in particular the capacity to choose between alternative courses of action (RCN, 2005). In practice, this means determining the child's understanding of a range of issues including:

- What the research is about?
- Who is carrying out the research?
- What is expected of participants?
- What will happen to the information provided?
- What benefits might the study have for participants and the wider community?
- Whether there are any potential harmful side effects (see further Gibson and Twycross, 2007; NRES, 2007)?

Assent

If a child is not considered competent to consent to research then consent should be obtained from those with parental responsibility. Yet even if a parent agrees, the child still has the right to refuse to take part (Twycross et al., 2008). In other words, informed consent in the context of research with young children is best described as a combination of parental permission and (when appropriate) the assent of the child (Kodish, 2003; see further NCB, 2003). Assent can be defined as a child's permission or affirmative agreement to participate (Broome and Richards, 1998). It requires the child to have an understanding of the research process and, most importantly, to have had an opportunity to express his/her opinions and concerns (see further Piercy and Hargate, 2004, and for strategies for 'opening the research conversation' with children, Danby and Farrell, 2005; Twycross et al., 2008).

9.2.4 Fully informed

To make free and rational choices, participants need adequate information. They have the right, in short, to be fully informed about:

- The purpose of the research,
- Any possible risks,
- How great or small the risks might be,
- What they will have to do if they participate in the study, and
- Who the researchers are.

In addition, if the research involves new or different treatment, the following information should be provided:

- What the standard treatment would be, and
- Any possible alternatives (see DoH, 2001a, for further information).

When providing the information outlined above, there is now an expectation that it should be delivered in a cognitively and psychologically appropriate way (Ungar, 2006). This may require the use of information leaflets that are specifically designed for different age ranges – NRES (2007), for example, recommends that information sheets be produced for 5 years and under, 6–10 years and 11–15 years (see further Alderson and Morrow, 2004).

Key points

- Consent to participate in research requires participants to be fully informed, i.e. free from coercion.
- Assent refers to the right that incompetent children have to have their say, i.e. give their permission to participate.

Activity

Critically assess the NRES advice on information sheets for children (http://www.nres.npsa.nhs.uk).

9.2.5 Confidentiality

Another aspect of respecting autonomy requires researchers to protect participants' identities. This means ensuring that sensitive personal information such as their biographical details, medical history and particulars about relationships – all of which may be essential to the project in question – is only used to facilitate data collection and analysis (Long, 2007, pp. 56–57). According to guidance from the RCN (2007), it is thus wise for the confidentiality and anonymity of participants to be preserved by coding data (or by using pseudonyms). It is also important to stress that protecting confidentiality means making sure that information is not divulged or made available to anyone other than those involved in the research process without consent. However, as Masson notes, there are two areas where a child's entitlement to confidentiality in research may differ from an adult's, namely, where a child discloses abuse or neglect and where a researcher identifies a condition which her parents need to know about (Masson, 2004, p. 52; see also RCN, 2007, pp. 4–5). In such circumstances, she claims, failure to reveal the relevant confidential information would be ethically questionable.

9.2.6 Balancing risks and benefits

The purpose of balancing risks and benefits is to make sure that participants are only involved in research when the benefits clearly outweigh the possible risks (or the potential for harm). In other words, the risks must be proportionate to the anticipated benefits. Risk is defined as the potential harm or potential consequence of an action. It may be physical or social and may be immediate or delayed. Risk assessment requires researchers to evaluate and estimate several factors – e.g. the potential harm associated with particular types of interventions as well as their magnitude, probability and how long they are likely to last (Buchanon and Miller, 2007).

Types of harm

Information about the harms associated with particular interventions are, of course, key concerns for all research participants – not only because there is an element of risk in most procedures but also because the possible harms may range widely – from, for example, significant physical injury to less serious side effects such as discomfort, fatigue, boredom and, emotional stress, as well as lack of privacy (Long, 2007, p. 47). But for children such information is even more urgent because their reactions to, and perceptions of procedures, particularly invasive ones, can differ considerably from adults. They may, for example, be far more affected by the immediate discomfort or pain of some procedures than adults. In short, what adults consider a low risk may be distressing and burdensome to children (El-liston, 2007, pp. 221–223). It for these reasons that researchers should assess the psychological harm posed by the discomfort or the invasiveness of a procedure separately from the risk of physical injuries – even if these may be less likely to occur (Weisstub et al., 1998, pp. 392–393). But if we accept there are risks in all interventions, a further question needs to be addressed, namely, what is an acceptable level of risk?

Levels of risk

Although risk levels can be categorised in several different ways, the most commonly recognised are as follows:

- *Minimal risk*: Includes questioning and observing children and taking bodily fluids without invasive procedures; a risk is minimal if it involves risk of injury or death that is no greater than that faced in everyday life.
- *Low risk*: Includes procedures that cause brief pain or tenderness, and small bruises or scars, injections and venepuncture.
- *High risk*: Refers to procedures such as lung or liver biopsy, arterial or lumbar puncture (see further Mason and Laurie, 2006, pp. 686–693; RCPCH, 2000).

The main reason for distinguishing between these various categories is briefly this: the less likely the research is to benefit participants (i.e. it can be described as non-therapeutic), the less risk they should be exposed to.

9.2.7 Justice

Put very simply, we can say that justice is about fairness. In research situations, justice means the fair selection of participants – especially those who are 'vulnerable', i.e. have characteristics or are in situations that inhibit their ability to make autonomous decisions (Buchanon and Miller, 2007, pp. 382–384). Vulnerable groups include not just incompetent children but also older ones who are disadvantaged in some way (for example, they may be institutionalised). Other factors that should be considered in ensuring 'fair selection' of children include the following:

- *Selection process*: Participants should be selected on the basis of research needs rather than because they are disadvantaged, i.e. because they are easily available and so more convenient to use.
- *Distribution of risks and benefits*: The distribution of risks and benefits must be as fair as possible; i.e. no one group of children should benefit overwhelmingly or be unjustly excluded – e.g. because of age, gender, ability (including learning and speech), ethnicity, social backgrounds or language (Alderson, 2005, p. 32).

Key points

The main ethical principles and considerations in research are the following:

- Respect for autonomy,
- Justice,
- Confidentiality, and
- Risk/benefit analysis.

9.3 Regulation of Research

Research is regulated in several ways – by ethical codes, National Health Service (NHS) research governance, research ethics committees (RECs), European regulations, various statutes and the law of consent. The combined effect of these various overlapping mechanisms is to provide a comprehensive, albeit complex, framework for the conduct of research.

9.3.1 Ethical codes and professional guidelines

The Nuremberg Code (1949) – undoubtedly the most famous international code and the first to provide guidance on the ethical principles that should govern research – has been hugely influential. Published as a direct response to the atrocities committed by doctors under the Nazi regime, the Code was later supplemented by the Declaration of Helsinki, first drawn up in 1964 but subsequently revised several times (most recently in 2008). Since then, the Declaration has been supplemented by a huge range of international, national and professional ethical codes and guidelines. These include the Royal College of Paediatrics and Child Health (RCPCH) (2000), Medical Research Council (MRC) (2004), British Medical Association (BMA) (2004), Department of Health (DoH) 2005, Council for International Organizations of Medical Sciences (CIOMS) (2002) and Royal College of Physicians (2007).

Although these codes and guidelines do not have legal force, they are nevertheless very influential – largely because of the uncertainty of some aspects of the law (Elliston, 2007, p. 200). It is worth noting too that even though they vary in length, focus and detail, several key principles are consistently emphasised (Hope et al., 2008, p. 219). Below we summarise, firstly, those that apply to all participants and, secondly, those that focus on children.

General ethical principles
- The research must be scientifically sound.
- It must satisfy the proportionality test, i.e. benefits must clearly outweigh risks.
- No coercion must be brought to bear on potential participants.
- Ideally, those involved should be competent.
- Participants should be fully informed.
- Payments may be made only to offset reasonable costs and must not be used to induce people to take part (see further Hope et al., 2008, p. 219).

Additional ethical safeguards for children
- Research involving children is important for the benefit of all children and should be supported, encouraged and conducted in an ethical manner.
- Children are not small adults, but they have an additional, unique set of interests.
- Research should only be carried out on children if comparable research on adults could not answer the same question.
- In general, it is preferable to recruit older children rather than younger ones (since more understanding is likely). Nevertheless, it must be remembered that younger children may react very differently to both illness and treatment compared with older children.
- All proposals involving medical research on children should be submitted to an REC.
- Legal valid consent should be obtained from the child, parent or guardian as appropriate. When parental consent is obtained, the agreement of school-aged children who take part should also be requested.

- An articulated refusal of a child to participate or continue in research should always be respected. Evidence of significant upset should be accepted as a valid refusal.
- Research in which incompetent children are submitted to more than minimal risks with only slight, uncertain or no benefit to themselves deserves serious ethical consideration.

Activity

Critically consider the current Helsinki Declaration guidance on research with children (http:// www.wma.net).

9.3.2 Research ethics committees

RECs have evolved in a haphazard and incremental way over several decades. First set up on a voluntary basis in the late 1960s, they are now overseen by the UK Ethics Committee Authority (UKECA, which is part of the National Patient Safety Authority). All RECs operating within the NHS are now subject to standard operating procedures. The current version (2008) applies to all NHS research reviewed by NHS RECs (for a detailed account of how RECs have evolved, see Fallon and Long, 2007, pp. 139–156).

9.3.3 Role of RECs

No research study within the NHS involving individuals, their organs, tissue or data may begin until it has a favourable opinion from an REC (DoH, 2005, 3.12.1). The main objectives of RECs are to maintain ethical standards of practice in research, to protect participants from harm and to preserve their rights, safety, dignity and well-being.

The remit of RECs is fully described in DoH guidance, Governance Arrangements for RECs (DoH, 2005, see below). In summary, this states that to ensure that a research proposal is ethical, a committee must be reassured about, for example:

- *The scientific design and conduct of the study*: i.e. is it statistically sound and are the risks outweighed by the benefits?
- *Recruitment*: Is there an adequate range of participants in term of gender, age, etc.?
- *Care and protection*: This focuses on, for example, the safety of any intervention and support of participants during and after the research.
- *Informed consent process*: This requires scrutiny of the process of obtaining consent and the adequacy and understandability of written and oral information.
- *Community considerations*: These include the impact/relevance of the research to local and concerned communities (see further DoH, 2001b, section 9)
- *Confidentiality*: i.e. are participants' rights to confidentiality adequately protected?

After considering an application, an REC has three options: it can give a favourable opinion, a provisional decision (in which the study is approved subject to clarifications or improvements) or an unfavourable opinion (which can be appealed).

Provisional approval is the most common outcome. If approval is withheld, the two major reasons are when the committee is not convinced of the robustness and scientific background of a proposed study or that the safety of participants has been compromised (i.e. their well-being has not been fully considered; see further Haigh, 2007, pp. 123–137).

Criticisms of RECs

There is no doubt that RECs have had a positive impact on the conduct of research – especially through their insistence on the provision of full and clear information (Fox, 2007). Yet they have all also been criticised. The most common criticisms are as follows:

- Inconsistencies between different RECs and the time and effort it takes to get through the process, which is unnecessarily complex (POST, 2005).
- Lack of continuous monitoring of the research, i.e. there is little supervision once the research has started (DoH, 2004).
- RECs need to maintain independence from political, institutional, professional or market influences. But their heavy workload, combined with lack of expertise of some committee members, has raised concerns about professional domination and failure to reflect the ethnic mix of society.
- Lack of accountability and transparency: most RECs meet in private. As they are not required to make minutes publicly available, there is little accountability, other than judicial review, which is unlikely to succeed (Herring, 2008; POST, 2005).

More recent concerns have questioned the whole process of ethical review itself. Thus, for example, Fallon and Long (2007, p. 154) claim that current overemphasis on ethics *approval* (rather than review) has disguised the lack of recognition of the more important activity of ongoing decision-making. A related concern is that various developments (e.g. the Medicines for Human Use (Clinical Trials) Regulations 2004, discussed below) have led to RECs adopting a regulatory rather than advisory role. As such, in addition to their original purpose (which was to address ethical concerns (i.e. to protect participants), they are now also expected to perform other functions (such as promoting 'best practice' and creating standards for research). This inevitably raises concerns about whether these 'new' functions can be incorporated into a process originally concerned with ethical deliberation (see further McGuiness, 2008, pp. 697–700).

9.3.4 Research governance framework

The research governance framework was first introduced in 2001. Revised in 2005, the framework applies to all research undertaken by the DoH or the NHS, as well as, for example, by industry and universities. In establishing a set of principles and standards, the framework aims to improve research and safeguard the public by enhancing ethical and scientific quality, promoting good practice, reducing adverse incidents and ensuring lessons are learned, preventing poor performance.

In recognising that research is multilayered, the framework is divided into five domains: ethics; science; information; health, safety and employment; and finance and intellectual property. In other sections, the responsibilities and accountabilities of the main people and organisations involved in health and social research are clarified (section 3), and the key attributes of a quality research culture are identified (section 2.7). Not surprisingly, there has been criticism of the research governance framework, i.e. that it is bureaucratic and unwieldy, is a potential deterrent to novice researchers, and has become a paper exercise rather than a robust monitoring system (see further Howarth and Kneafsey, 2007, pp. 103–121).

Activity

Do you think the NHS research governance framework adequately considers child participants? See http://www.dh.gov.uk.

> **Key points**
>
> - The main function of an REC is to advise health bodies on the ethical acceptability of research.
> - RECs are responsible for acting primarily in the interests of potential research participants.

9.4 Legal Regulation of Research

The law regulating research with children is now a complex mix of common law, statutes (Family Law Act 1969, Mental Capacity Act 2005) and Medicines for Human Use (Clinical Trials) Regulations 2004. For convenience, children and young people need to be divided into various age groups. Distinctions also need to be made between research which involves medicines and all other research.

9.4.1 Research involving medicinal products

Competent 16- and 17-year-olds
Clinical trials involving 16- and 17-year-olds are governed by the Medicines for Human Use (Clinical Trials) Regulations 2004. Key provisions include the following:

- Adults are defined as those aged 16 and over.
- A legal requirement that REC ethics approval is obtained before a trial can be undertaken.
- A requirement that trials comply with 'good clinical practice' (i.e. ethical principles set out in various national and international codes) as well as 15 principles (Schedule 1, Part 2).
- The Medicines and Healthcare Products Regulatory Agency can suspend or end the trial and/or issue infringement notices.
- A range of criminal offences such as providing false or misleading information.

Consent provisions in the Regulations specify that consent must be informed, i.e. given freely after the person is informed of the nature, significance, implications and risks of the trial. Consent must be evidenced in writing and the participant must have had an interview with the researcher during which he must have been given 'the opportunity to understand the objectives, risks, and inconveniences of the trial and the conditions under which it is to be conducted' (see further Sch 1, Pts 1 and 2).

Incompetent 16- and 17-year-olds
A range of provisions apply to 'incapacitated adults', i.e. persons (of 16 and over) who are unable by virtue of physical or mental incapacity to give informed consent. These are as follows:

- The trial has been designed to minimise pain, discomfort, fear and any other foreseeable risk.
- The risk threshold and the degree of risk have to be specially defined and constantly monitored.
- The participant has received information according to his capacity to understand.
- Allow the person to be entered into a trial providing consent has been given by, for example, a 'personal legal representative' (i.e. a close friend or relative such as a parent) or a 'professional legal representative').
- The clinical trial relates directly to a life-threatening or debilitating clinical condition from which the subject suffers.
- If the participant objects to being involved, her objections must be considered, but she can still be entered (for further, see Sch 1, Pts 3 and 4).

Under 16-year-olds

The Regulations (Sch 1, Pt 4) refer to this age group as minors. In addition to the first three bullet points (which apply to incompetent 16- and 17-year-olds), there are several other conditions, e.g.:

- A person with parental responsibility (or legal representative) must have given informed consent.
- The clinical trial relates directly to a clinical condition from which the minor suffers or is of such a nature that it can only be carried out on minors.
- Some direct benefit for the group of patients involved in the clinical trial is to be obtained from that trial.
- The clinical trial is necessary to validate data obtained in other clinical trials involving the person able to give informed consent, or by other research methods.
- A minor can be involved in a trial even if he objects (but his objections must nevertheless be considered).

Several points worth noting about these provisions are the following: no restriction is placed on the seriousness of the condition that the child is suffering from; direct benefit to the research group, rather than the individual child, is sufficient; a minor cannot give sole consent even if she is '*Gillick*' competent (i.e. children's involvement is limited to receiving age-appropriate information regarding the trial, its risks and benefits and to having their refusal of consent simply considered). Other concerns have been raised in relation to research involving children in emergency medicine (see further Elliston, 2007, pp. 234–241). Note finally that the Regulations have been supplemented by EU regulations that require all drugs to be tested on, and developed for children, as part of a paediatric investigation plan (EC 1901/2006 and EC 1902/2006).

Activities

Read current European guidance on the ethical considerations for clinical trials on medicinal products with the paediatric population. Do you think it properly balances the needs of young children with the emerging autonomy of young people?

Key points

- Clinical trials are regulated by the Medicines for Human Use (Clinical Trials) Regulations 2004.
- Consent must be obtained from competent 16- and 17-year-olds.
- In relation to under 16-year-olds, consent must be obtained from a proxy, i.e. a person with parental responsibility (even if the child is competent).

9.4.2 Research not involving medicines

In research not involving medicines, e.g. the testing of a new surgical or diagnostic procedure that does not involve the use of medicinal products, the position is more complicated. As before, children need to be divided into different age groups.

Competent 16- and 17-year-olds

Although the Family Law Reform Act 1969 (s.8) allows competent 16- and 17-year-olds to consent to treatment (likewise diagnostic procedures and possibly also innovative treatment), it is widely presumed that the Act does not extend to research. Instead, researchers must rely on common law principles of consent. Essentially, this means that consent to research is governed by the *Gillick* case and the best interests test. But what does the concept of best interests mean in research situations? We need to know the answer to this question because, even if young people are competent to give consent, their wishes can be overridden by the courts, on the basis that their decisions are not in their best interests (see Chapter 4).

In the absence of any clear legal authority on this question, it is only possible to speculate on how the courts would interpret the concept. That said, given that they have in the past accepted that a child's best interests can encompass his broader relationships within the community (rather than just his medical interests), it is certainly possible that they would apply a similar broad approach to best interests in research situations. However, if the research were non-therapeutic, the level of risk would have to be low and the young person sufficiently mature to understand the nature of altruism, and so be able to benefit from participating (Mason and Laurie, 2006, p. 689; McCall Smith, 1989, p. 496).

An alternative approach is that the best interests could be stretched to accommodate a young person's making decisions that were 'not against his interests' (Elliston, 2007, p. 232). The 'not against the interests of the child approach' is less restrictive and less protective of the child. However, providing the risks are minimal, it is one that is supported in DoH guidance (DoH, 2001a) and international and national guidelines (Elliston, 2007, p. 217). That said, given the absence of clear legal authority on this point, researchers would be wise to also obtain consent from a person with parental responsibility.

As regards therapeutic research, again it would be wise for researchers to obtain consent from those with parental responsibility (in addition to the competent young person). This is because, even though the question of a child's best interests is less problematic, it is sometimes difficult in practice to distinguish between non-therapeutic and therapeutic research (see above).

Incompetent 16- and 17-year-olds

If a 16- or 17-year-old lacks capacity to consent, the provisions of the Mental Capacity Act 2005 (sections 30–34) apply. The Mental Capacity Act applies to adults (those aged 16 and over). It allows both therapeutic and non-therapeutic research that is 'intrusive' (i.e. of a kind that would be unlawful if it were carried out on a person who had capacity to consent to it, but without his consent) under certain conditions, including the following:

- The research must be connected with an 'impairing condition' affecting the participant, or its treatment.
- The research must be approved by an REC.
- There must be reasonable grounds for believing that research of comparable effectiveness cannot be carried out if the project has to be confined to, or relate only to, persons who have capacity.
- If the research is non-therapeutic, the risks must be negligible and not interfere significantly with the participant's freedom or privacy, or be unduly invasive or restrictive.
- If the research is therapeutic, the research must have the potential to benefit the participant and not impose a burden that is disproportionate to the benefit.
- The research cannot be carried out if the participant appears to object.

It is also worth noting that there is an overlap between the Mental Capacity Act and the common law in relation to incompetent 16- and -17-year-olds. It is thus possible for researchers to use the common law principles that apply to incompetent under 16-year-olds (see below).

Competent under 16-year-olds

The legal position is much the same as in relation to competent 16- and 17-year-olds. Thus, in the absence of clear legal authority, if the child is *Gillick* competent, researchers should nevertheless obtain consent from both the child and a person with parental responsibility. This would certainly be the best course of action both for non-therapeutic research (because of doubts about how the 'best interests' should be interpreted) and for therapeutic research (given that the borderline between the two may be difficult to draw).

Incompetent under 16-year-olds

As to children under 16 who are not *Gillick* competent, consent must be obtained from a proxy, i.e. a person with parental responsibility. If the research is therapeutic, then according to guidance from the DoH, this would mean that a parent could consent 'where there is evidence that the trial therapy may be at least as beneficial to the patient as the standard therapy, i.e. ensuring, for example, that the benefits always outweighed the risks' (DoH, 2001a). That said, if a child has a serious illness it might be reasonable for the proxy to consent to research even if the risks are significant (Montgomery, 2003, p. 364).

A proxy's consent to non-therapeutic research is more problematic. As was noted above, the difficulty arises because of the uncertainty about the scope of the best interests test. In other words, only if the broader, less restrictive 'not against the child's interests' approach was adopted would a proxy's consent be lawful. Such an approach would certainly give parents wider discretion to volunteer their children for non-therapeutic research. Whether it would withstand a test of acceptability in term of what a 'reasonable' parent would do is perhaps another matter (see Mason, 1998, p. 324).

Key points

- In relation to under 16-year-olds, research not involving medicines is governed by the law of consent.
- In relation to incompetent 16- and 17-year-olds, research not involving medicines is governed by the common law and/or the Mental Capacity Act 2005.

9.5 Donation, Storage and Use of Organs and Tissue

The Human Tissue Act 2004 is a long and complex Act which regulates a wide range of activities. Although this section focuses on the most ethically and legally contentious aspects in relation to children, i.e. storage and use of the body parts from deceased children and blood, bone marrow and organ donation from the living, it begins with an outline of the Act.

9.6 Human Tissue Act 2004

Revelations in the later 1990s that medical schools and hospitals routinely retained human material without obtaining consent caused huge public outrage. But the major trigger for the Act was widespread revulsion over the retention of organs and body parts of deceased babies and children (without parental knowledge, let alone consent) at Alder Hey Children's Hospital and Bristol Royal Infirmary. In response to inquiries into the events (Kennedy, 2001; Redfern, 2001), the government radically reformed the law and introduced a comprehensive new legal framework for the storage and use of 'human material', i.e. tissue, cells, and organs of human beings. The Act also set up a new body, the Human Tissue Authority (HTA), to advise and oversee compliance with the Act. This includes operating a licensing system and issuing Codes of Practice (new versions of which are expected in 2010), which are designed to give practical guidance to those carrying out the Act's activities (for an overview of the Act, see Price, 2005).

According to guidance from the DoH, the purpose of the Act is 'to achieve a balance between the rights and expectations of individuals and families, and broader considerations, such as the importance of research, education, training, pathology and public health surveillance to the population as a whole' (DoH, 2004). That said, the Act nevertheless makes consent the fundamental principle underlying the storage and use of human bodies, body parts, organs and tissue and the removal of material from the bodies of deceased persons. However, consent requirements differ depending on whether tissue is taken from the living or the deceased.

9.6.1 Living donors

Activities requiring consent

It is important to note that the consent requirements of the Act do not apply to the *removal* of material from the living (which is governed by the common law), but 'appropriate consent', as it is referred to in the Act, is needed for the *storage* and *use* of tissue for the following purposes:

- Obtaining scientific or medical information that may be relevant to any other person (now or in the future);
- Research in connection with disorders, or the functioning, of the human body (but see below);
- Public display;
- Transplantation.

Activities that do not require consent

Consent is not needed for storage and use of tissue for the following 'purposes' (although it is nevertheless considered good practice to obtain it whenever possible):

- Clinical audit;
- Education or training relating to human health;
- Performance assessment – e.g. testing medical devices;
- Public health monitoring; and
- Quality assurance (Sch 1, Pt 2).

Controversially, too, no consent is needed if material from living bodies is stored for the purpose of research in connection with disorders or the functioning of the human body, providing (a) the research is ethically approved (i.e. by an REC), and, (b) the tissue is anonymised (see further Code 9, 2008).

9.6.2 Competent children and consent

Under the Act a child is defined as being under 18 years old. Children may consent to the storage and use of their tissue if they are competent to do so. Their capacity is assessed according to the *Gillick* case; i.e. they are competent to give valid consent to a proposed intervention if they have sufficient intelligence and understanding to enable them to fully understand what is involved. In addition, several other conditions must also be met for a donation to be lawful (these vary according to the nature of the donation).

Peripheral blood stem cells and allogeneic bone marrow donation

Conditions that must be met include the following:

- The person obtaining consent must complete a donor consent form that includes a statement by the donor that she/he has received and understood sufficient information to give informed consent.
- Donors should be informed:
  1. About the donation procedure and the long- and short-term risks;
  2. Of the potential advantages for the recipient and the fact that a positive outcome cannot be guaranteed;
  3. If there is adverse outcome that it is not their fault;
  4. The donation is voluntary and they have a right not to be coerced or pressured;
  5. Blood or marrow is always tested and the implications of positive results;
  6. They can withdraw consent at any time (and the consequences of the withdrawal);
  7. They can discuss any worries with other members of the transplant team (see further Code 6, para 37).

Although not a legal requirement, it is recommended 'as best practice' that written consent to the donation be obtained (Code 6, para 30). The Code also recommends that even if a child is competent, it is good practice to consult a person with parental responsibility (Code 6, para 28). Note that such a person can also give consent should a competent child choose not to make a decision (Code 6, para 26).

In conclusion, it seems clear that *Gillick* competent children under 18 can give valid consent to blood and bone marrow donations (which their parents cannot veto). Whether the Act provides sufficient safeguards to ensure that a child has consented voluntarily (i.e. has not been unduly pressured to donate by her family) is another matter (Elliston, for example, doubts that this is the case; see further Elliston, 2007, pp. 262–265).

Organ donation

The removal of an organ is governed by the common law. Given the uncertainty as to whether the removal of a solid organ is lawful (i.e. in the donor's best interests), prior court approval should be sought. Furthermore, although the Act authorises donations by competent young people (providing various conditions are satisfied and approval from a panel of the HTA is sought), it is noted that in practice children will be living donors only in extremely rare circumstances (Code 2, para 30).

Key points

- Competent under 18-year-olds can give valid consent to donations of blood and bone marrow.
- Competent under 18-year-olds can give valid consent to organ donation, but in practice they are only very rarely likely to be considered as suitable donors.

9.6.3 Incompetent children

The core concept governing storage and use of tissue and organs from incompetent children is the best interests test. How this concept is interpreted varies according to the nature of the material that is to be used. But in all cases consent must be sought from a person with parental responsibility (Code 6, para 26).

Peripheral blood stem cells and bone marrow

Note the following guidance (in Code 6):

- The best interests test should not be limited to medical interests, and should take account of emotional, psychological and social benefits as well as the risks (para 25).

- The senior clinician involved must assess the child's best interests by discussing the matter with the child and ascertaining his views (para 48).
- The HTA and accredited assessor must be satisfied about several issues. These include:
  1. That the child's best interests have been considered;
  2. The child and person with parental responsibility have been interviewed;
  3. The child has received all necessary information;
  4. The person with parental responsibility understands the nature of the medical procedure in question, including the risks and possible side effects;
  5. Consent was not obtained by duress;
  6. There is no evidence of an offer of reward (see further paras 48–52).

In the light of the criteria for approval outlined, it would seem that review by the HTA and assessor should ensure that the interests of incompetent children are safeguarded. In any event, court approval can always be sought should the parties involved disagree about a proposed course of action.

Organ donation

The Act allows a person with parental responsibility to consent to the storage and use of transplantable material providing the donation is in the child's best interests. That said, it is only very rarely that children will be considered as donors (Code 2, para 30). Most commentators agree with this position (see, e.g. Herring, 2008; Mason and Laurie, 2006; but see Elliston, 2007, pp. 265–272, for a contrasting view).

Activity

Do you think Code 6 includes sufficient safeguards to protect children's best interests? (http://www.hta.gov.uk).

Key points

- Consent to bone marrow and blood donations from an incompetent under 18-year-old must be obtained from a person with parental responsibility.
- Donations are lawful only if they are in the child's best interests and the HTA and accredited assessor approve.
- Consent to organ donation from an incompetent under 18-year-old must be obtained from a person with parental responsibility; the donation must be in the child's best interests but is only very rarely (if ever) likely to take place.

9.7 Organ Transplants from the Dead

The Human Tissue Act 2004 regulates a wide range of activities relating to the bodies of the deceased (which are summarised below). Here, we focus on organ transplantation – a process that has undoubtedly been clarified and simplified by the Act. Other issues discussed here are the role of parents and some of the ethical considerations raised by organ donation.

9.7.1 Activities regulated by the Act

Consent is the fundamental principle regulating the removal, storage and use of tissues from the deceased (although it is not always required).

Activities requiring consent
Consent is needed for the following:

- Anatomical examination;
- Determining the cause of death;
- Establishing the efficacy of any drug or other treatment;
- Obtaining scientific or medical information, which may be relevant to any other person;
- Research in connection with disorders of the functioning of the human body;
- Transplantation;
- Clinical audit;
- Education and training (see further Sch 1, Pt 1);
- Public display.

Activities not requiring consent
Consent is not needed for the following:

- Carrying out an investigation into the cause of death (under a coroner's authority);
- Keeping material after a post-mortem (under a coroner's authority);
- Keeping material in connection with a criminal investigation.

The HTA clearly authorises a wide range of activities in relation to the deceased. While these may be uncontroversial in relation to adults, they are clearly more so in relation to young children and babies – as is evident from the scandals at Alder Hey and Bristol Royal Infirmary noted above. But the question we consider briefly below is this: how important are the views of parents about what should happen to their children's bodies?

9.7.2 The role of parents

As Herring explains, one of the most important themes to emerge from the scandals at Alder Hey and Bristol Royal Infirmary was how important it was to parents that they were involved in decisions about what should happen to the bodies of their deceased children. But as he asks, is this any more than sentiment (Herring, 2008, p. 389)? For Brazier, the answer is clear. Thus, although she concedes that a child has no enduring interests after death, she nonetheless strongly argues that her parents do, in particular they have interests in controlling their child's body. She identifies the following overlapping parental interests:

- The child is still 'theirs' and belongs to them; i.e. they are still parents, albeit bereaved parents.
- They are guardians of the family's values, whether they are religious, cultural imperatives or personal convictions.
- Regaining control may enable them to come to terms with their loss of the joys of parenthood.
- Their mental health and emotional well-being are at stake (see further Brazier, 2003, pp. 30–33; 2002, p. 550).

Other commentators, however, have taken a different approach. Broadly, their concern is that deference to the sensitivities of bereaved and grieving parents may hamper scientific advances, i.e. favour individuals over the collective (Herring, 2008, p. 390). Whether the Act achieves a fair balance between individuals and the public is, of course, a matter for debate. But first we need to set the discussion and consider some of the ethical issues that arise in organ donation.

9.7.3 Ethical issues in organ donation

The main issues are the following:

'Opting in' or 'opting out'
Organs for donation are scarce. In the UK, supply is regulated by an 'opt in' system (where individuals are able to volunteer to become organ donors). An alternative approach is the 'opt out' system. Under this system (which operates in several countries such as Belgium and Spain), consent is presumed (but people who object can 'opt out' by registering their objection). Unsurprisingly, the advantages and disadvantages of each system have been widely debated (for a summary of the arguments, see Jackson, 2006, pp. 720–724; BMA 2004).

Relatives' wishes
What power of veto should relatives have over the deceased wishes? And should they be involved at all or only when the deceased's wishes are unknown?

Conditional donations
Should donors be allowed to donate conditionally? In other words, is it ethically acceptable for a donor to select the recipient of her organs? If so, on what basis? Are criteria based on age, religion and gender unacceptable (see further Hope et al., 2008, pp. 198–200)?

9.7.4 Organ donation by children

As we have seen above, the Act permits the removal, storage and use of human material from the deceased for a wide range of activities (some but not all requiring consent). Here we focus only on organ transplantation (for which consent is needed). Two questions need to be addressed: firstly, has the deceased child made a decision? Secondly, if not, can someone else make the decision for them?

Competent under 18-year-olds
The Act makes it clear that children and young people (i.e. those under 18) who, when alive were *Gillick* competent to reach a decision, can control what happens to their organs after death. This means that they can either give valid consent to the lawful removal, storage or use of organs or tissues or they can refuse to do so. Either way their wishes must be respected; i.e. their parents have no legal right of veto. Nevertheless, even though a competent child's consent is sufficient, the Code recommends that the views of the child's family should be considered before any decision is made about how to proceed. It also suggests that it may be advisable to discuss with a person with parental responsibility whether the child was indeed competent to make the decision in question (Code 1, para 62).

In cases where a deceased child's wishes are not known, then every effort is expected to be made to ascertain the wishes of a person with parental responsibility, or if there is no such person then the consent of a person who is in the highest ranked 'qualifying relationship' with the child, i.e. spouse, parent, brother or sister, grandparent (see further HTA 2004 s.27(4)). Finally, it is important to note that gaining appropriate consent (whether from the competent child herself or another person) makes the activity lawful if it goes ahead, but does not make it obligatory.

Incompetent under 18-year-olds

If a child under 18 is not competent to make a decision then the legal position is relatively straightforward, i.e. consent must be obtained from a person with parental responsibility, and if there is no such person, then consent should be sought from a person ranked highest in a qualifying relationship. In such situations it is also recommended that the issue should be fully discussed with relatives and that careful thought should be given as to whether to proceed if a disagreement arises between parents or other family members (Code 1, para 64). Any previously stated wishes of the deceased child are also expected to be considered (taking into account their age and understanding).

Key points

- The consent to donate an organ by a competent under 18-year-old cannot be vetoed by a person with parental responsibility.
- Consent to organ donation in relation to an incompetent child under 18 must be obtained from a person with parental responsibility.

Case study

Linden, who is 15 ½, has leukaemia. He has been in and out of hospital for several years, but recently has had a relapse and does not seem to be responding to treatment. His mother, Daisha, is distraught and desperate for Linden to try out any new treatment. Linden's consultant, Connie, wants to include him in a research project, testing the effect of a new drug. She raises the issue with them and gives them some information about the nature of the research and how she hopes it will benefit Linden. She also explains that some of the procedures may cause him pain and considerable discomfort. But she does not provide any information about other potentially more serious consequences (nor the vomiting and nausea that Linden is likely to experience). On leaving, Connie hands Daisha a consent form, which she says she will collect in a few days' time.

The next day Connie bumps into Daisha and asks if she and Linden have decided what to do. Daisha explains that Linden is reluctant to be involved in the research and wants more information. Connie says she is too busy to explain at the moment but wants Daisha to give her the signed consent form so that 'things can get moving'. Daisha gives her the form, expecting to meet with Connie later that day. No meeting takes place.

A few days later Daisha finds Linden in great distress. He has been given the new drug and has felt continually nauseous as well as some pain and discomfort. He is very upset that he was not told that the research had started (as is Daisha).

What ethical issues does this scenario raise?
Is Linden's consent required?
If not, is Daisha's consent valid?
What difference would it make if Linden were 17?

9.7.5 Ethical issues

Even if we assume that the research project has received ethical approval from an REC, there is little doubt that by only providing partial information – to both Daisha and Linden – Connie has failed to respect their autonomy. Furthermore, by rushing them into a decision, Daisha's consent is arguably not voluntary, i.e. free from undue pressure. Connie has also clearly failed to comply with national and professional guidelines, all of which insist that no coercion be brought to bear on potential participants (or their proxies), and that their consent must be fully informed (see, e.g. CIOMS, 2002; EC, 2008; RCPCH, 2000).

9.7.6 Legal considerations

Since the research project involves a clinical trial, it is governed by the 2004 Clinical Trials Regulations. As Linden is 15, his consent is not a legal requirement. Instead, consent must be obtained from a person with parental responsibility (i.e. Daisha). That said, the Regulations do provide for Linden's objections to be considered. Whether researchers should proceed in the light of a child participant's objection is certainly questionable, however – not least because most codes and professional guidelines recommend that the participant's assent or agreement be sought (in addition to parental consent).

9.7.7 Daisha's consent

As a person with parental responsibility for Linden, Daisha's consent is required by the Regulations. However, the Regulations impose several information requirements, in particular that information about the nature, significance, implications and risks of the trial must be protected. In addition, the Regulations require researchers to comply with 'good practice' (i.e. ethical guidelines set out in codes and professional guidelines). Connie's failure to give Daisha full information, especially about the potentially serious consequences of the research, means that her consent is unlikely to comply with the Regulations.

9.7.8 If Linden were 17

As a 17-year-old Linden is an adult according to the 2004 Regulations. Assuming he is competent to give consent, Daisha's consent would not be required. However, since he has received very limited information, it is doubtful that his consent would be legally valid.

9.8 The Relationship between Law and Ethics

9.8.1 Similarities between law and ethics

- **Abuse and mistreatment:** The legal and ethical concerns raised by research focus on the same issues: how abuse and mistreatment can be prevented and how to achieve proper balance between protecting the rights of the individual and the advancement of science.
- **Independent review:** Both law and ethics recognise the need for independent review of the design and conduct of research to ensure that ethical and legal standards are met.
- **Fundamental rights:** The legal and ethical frameworks regulating research seek to safeguard the same basic rights of participants, namely, autonomy, confidentiality and fair treatment.
- **Additional safeguards:** Ethical guidelines, legislation and regulations impose conditions and requirements that are designed to enhance the emerging autonomy of young people and protect younger children from exploitative practices.

9.8.2 Differences between law and ethics

- **Codes/professional guidelines:** In comparison with the numerous codes and professional guidelines regulating research, the law's approach rests largely on the common law and Medicine for Human Use (Clinical Trial) Regulations 2004; ethical guidance is generally much more detailed than the law.
- **Standard of disclosure:** The ethical standard of disclosure (as reflected in codes and professional guidelines) is generally higher than the legal standard; i.e. the law seems to require less information to be disclosed to participants than is expected to be disclosed in ethical guidance (which typically insists that participants should be fully informed).

References

Alderson, P. (2004) Ethics. In Fraser, S., Lewis, V., Ding, S., Kellett, M. and Robinson, C. (eds) *Doing Social Research with Children*. London: Sage.

Alderson, P. (2005) Designing ethical research with children. In Farrell, A. (ed.) *Ethical Research with Children*. Buckingham: Open University Press.

Alderson, P. and Morrow, V. (2004) *Ethics, Social Research and Consulting with Children and Young People*. Barkingside: Barnardos.

Beauchamp, T.L. and Childress, J.F. (2009) *Principles of Medical Ethics*, 6th edn. Oxford: Oxford University Press.

BMA (2004) *Medical Ethics Today: The BMA's Handbook of Ethics and Law*. London: BMA.

Brazier, M. (2002) Retained organs: ethics and humanity. *Legal Studies* 22:550.

Brazier, M. (2003) Organ retention and return: problems of consent. *Journal of Medical Ethics* 29:30.

Broome, M. and Richards, D. (1998) Involving children in research. *Journal of Child and Family Nursing* 1(1):3–7.

Buchanon, D.R. and Miller, F.G. (2007) Justice in research on human subjects. In Rhodes, R., Francis, L. and Silvers, A. (eds) *Blackwell's Guide to Medical Ethics*. Oxford: Blackwell.

CIOMS (2002) *International Guidelines for Biomedical Research Involving Human Subjects*. Geneva: CIOMS.

Danby, S. and Farrell, A. (2005) Opening the research conversation. In Farrell, A. (ed.) *Ethical Research with Children*. Buckingham: Open University Press.

DoH (2001a) *Seeking Consent: Working with Children*. London: DoH.

DoH (2001b) *Governance Arrangements for NHS Research Ethics Committees* London: DoH.

DoH (2004) *Research Governance Framework for Health and Social Care*. London: DoH.

DoH (2005) *Research Governance Framework for Health and Social Care*, 2nd edn. London: DoH.

EC (2008) *Ethical Considerations for Clinical Trials on Medicinal Products Conducted with the Paediatric Population*. Brussels: EC.

Elliston, S. (2007) *The Best Interests of the Child in Healthcare*. London: Routledge-Cavendish.

Fallon, D. and Long, T. (2007) Ethics approval, ethical research and delusion of efficacy. In Long, T. and Johnson, M. (eds) *Medical Research in the Real World: Issues and Solutions*. Edinburgh: Churchill Livingstone/Elsevier.

Farrell, A. (ed.) (2005) New times in ethical research with children. In Farrell, A. (ed.) *Ethical Research with Children*. Buckingham: Open University Press.

Fox, M. (2007) Clinical research and patients: the legal perspective. In Tingle, J. and Cribb, A. (eds) *Nursing Law and Ethics*, 3rd edn. Oxford: Blackwell.

Gibson, F. and Twycross, A. (2007) Children's participation in research. *Paediatric Nursing* 19(4):14.

Glantz, L.H. (2005) Children as subjects of research. In Freeman, M. (ed.) *Children, Medicine and the Law*. Farnham: Ashgate.

Haigh, C. (2007) Getting ethics approval. In Long, T. and Johnson, M. (eds) *Research Ethics in the Real World: Issues and Solutions for Health and Social Care*. Edinburgh: Churchill Livingstone/Elsevier.

Herring, J. (2008) *Medical Law and Ethics*, 2nd edn. Oxford: Oxford University Press.

Hill, M. (2005) Ethical consideration in researching children's experiences. In Green, S. and Hogan, D. (eds) *Researching Children's Experience: Approaches and Methods*. London: Sage.

Hope, T., Savulescu, J. and Hendrick, J. (2008) *Medical Ethics and Law: The Core Curriculum*, 2nd edn. Edinburgh: Elsevier.

Howarth, M. and Kneafsey, R. (2007) Research governance: an international perspective. In Long, T. and Johnson, M. (eds) *Research Ethics in the Real World: Issues and Solutions for Health and Social Care*. Edinburgh: Churchill Livingstone/Elsevier.

Jackson, E. (2006) *Medical Law: Text, Cases and Materials*. Oxford: Oxford University Press.

Kennedy, I. (2001) *The Report of the Public Inquiry into Children's Heart Surgery at the Bristol Royal Infirmary 1984–1995: Learning from Bristol*. CM 5207(1). London: DoH.

Kodish, E. (2003) Informed consent for paediatric research: is it really possible? *Journal of Paediatrics* 142(2):89.

Lederer, S. and Grodin, M.A. (1994) Historical overview: paediatric experimentation. In Grodin, M.A. and Glantz, L. (eds) *Children as Research Subjects*. New York: Oxford University Press.

Long, T. (2007) What are the ethical issues in research? In Long, T. and Johnson, M. (eds) *Research Ethics in the Real World: Issues and Solutions for Health and Social Care*. Edinburgh: Churchill Livingstone/Elsevier.

Mason, J.K. (1998) *Medico-Legal Aspects of Reproduction and Parenthood*, 2nd edn. Aldershot: Dartmouth.

Mason, J.K. and Laurie, G. (2006) *Mason and McCall Smith's Law and Medical Ethics*, 7th edn. Oxford: Oxford University Press.

Masson, J. (2004) The legal context. In Fraser, S., Lewis, V., Ding, S., Kellett, M. and Robinson, C. (eds) *Doing Social Research with Children*. London: Sage.

McCall Smith, A. (1989) Research and experimentation involving children. In Mason, J.K. (ed.) *Paediatric Forensic Medicine and Pathology*. London: Chapman & Hall.

McGuiness, S. (2008) Research ethics committees: the role of ethics committees in a regulatory authority. *Journal of Medical Ethics* 34:695.

Montgomery, J. (2003) *Health Care Law*, 2nd edn. Oxford: Oxford University Press.

Morrow, V. and Richards, M.P. (1996) The ethics of social research with children: an overview. *Children and Society* 10:90.

MRC (2004) *Medical Research Involving Children*. London: MRC.

NCB (2003) *Guidelines for Research*. London: NCB.

NRES (2007) *Information Sheets and Consent Forms for Researchers*. London: NRES.

Piercy, H. and Hargate, M. (2004) Social research on the under 16s: a consideration of the issues from a UK perspective. *Journal of Child Health Care* 8(4):253.

POST (2005) *Ethical Scrutiny of Research*. London: POST.

Price, D. (2005) The Human Tissue Act 2004. *Modern Law Review* 68:798.

RCN (2005) *Informed Consent in Health and Social Care Research*. London: RCN.

RCN (2007) *Research Ethics: Guide for Nurses*. London: RCN.

Redfern, M. (2001) *The Royal Liverpool Children's Inquiry Report*. London: TSO.

Robinson, G. and Kellett, M. (2004) *Power*. In Fraser, S., Lewis, V., Ding, S., Kellett, M. and Robinson, C. (eds) *Doing Social Research with Children*. London: Sage.

Royal College of Paediatrics and Child Health (2000) Guidelines for the ethical conduct of medical research involving children. *Archives of Diseases of Childhood* 86(2):177.

Royal College of Physicians (2007) *Guidelines on the Practice of Ethics Committees in Medical Research*. London: RCP.

Spriggs, M. (2004) Canaries in the mines: children, risk, non-therapeutic research and justice. *Journal of Medical Ethics* 30:176.

Twycross, A., Gibson, F. and Coad, J. (2008) Guidance on seeking agreement to participate in research from children. *Paediatric Nursing* 20(6):14.

Ungar, D. (2006) Children are not small adults: documentation of assent for research involving children. *Journal of Paediatrics* 149:531.

Weijer, C. (2000) Ethical analysis of risk. *Journal of Law and Medicine* 28:344.

Weisstub, D.N., Verdun-Jones, S.N. and Walker, J. (1998) Biomedical experimentation with children: balancing the need for protective measures with the need to respect children's developing ability to make significant life decisions for themselves. In Weisstub (ed.) *Research on Human Subjects: Ethics, Law and Social Policy*. Kidlington: Elsevier Science.

CHAPTER 10

Mental Health

Learning outcomes

By the end of this chapter you should be able to:

- Understand how health care decisions are made for those who are informal patients in hospital;
- Discuss the legal and moral implications of compulsory detention and treatment;
- Outline the key provisions of the Mental Health Act 1983.

Introduction

Many different labels are used to describe children and young people whose behaviour is considered 'problematic', such as mentally ill or disordered, aggressive, emotionally disturbed, antisocial or beyond control. More often than not the 'labels' have no legal significance – not least because they are often used interchangeably. But in some cases they are very important as they identify in which of the four different systems children with similar behaviour patterns are (or could be) placed.

Briefly, in the four systems, the first is the criminal (or youth) justice system. In England and Wales, the age of criminal responsibility is 10 years (which is low by European standards where ages of responsibility range from 14 to 18). If convicted, 'young offenders' can be subjected to a wide range of sentences, some of which may be custodial. The second system is the childcare system. Children in this system are 'looked after' by a local authority (see Chapter 11). The third system is the education one, under which children are assessed for special needs. Once identified as having a learning difficulty, special educational provision may be made available. The fourth system is the psychiatric system. A child or young person entering this system is likely to be referred to as having mental health problems. Each of the four systems has its own distinct philosophy, legal framework and terminology. As a consequence, the way children are treated can vary significantly, as can their legal status.

This chapter discusses children and young people in the fourth system, i.e. those whose care and treatment is governed largely by the Mental Health Act 1983 (MHA 1983). It focuses on those aspects which have been substantially reformed by recent legislation, notably the admission and treatment provisions (likewise Chapter 36 of the Code of Practice which provides guidance on particular issues arising in relation to children and young people under 18). Other topics examined in this chapter include a discussion of the impact of being diagnosed with mental disorder and the moral justification for compulsory detention and treatment. But we begin by defining what we mean by the term 'mental disorder'.

10.1 Defining 'Mental Disorder'

In government publications and literature about children's mental health, the term 'mental disorder' refers to a clinically recognisable set of symptoms or behaviour associated in most cases with considerable distress and substantial interference with personal functions (Office for National Statistics, ONS, 2008, p. 11). The term has become widely adopted following publication of the influential 1995 Health Advisory Committee Report into child and adolescent mental health services. The committee was concerned about the lack of clarity in the terminology used to describe children's mental health problems which it felt led to confusion and uncertainty about the suffering involved and how treatable problems and disorders were.

The four main groups of disorders covered by the term 'mental disorder' are as follows:

1. Emotional disorders such as anxiety, depression and obsessions;
2. Conduct disorders characterised by awkward, troublesome, aggressive and antisocial behaviours;
3. Hyperactivity disorders involving inattention and overactivity;
4. Less common disorders such as autistic spectrum disorders, vocal and motor tics and eating disorders (ONS, 2008; see further National Association for Mental Health; MIND, 2008).

Note that the term 'mental disorder' (as distinct from psychiatric disorder or mental health problems) is not intended to indicate that the problem is entirely within the child. Rather it aims to acknowledge that disorders arise for a variety of reasons, often interacting. It also acknowledges that in certain circumstances a mental disorder (which describes a constellation or syndrome of features) may 'indicate the reactions of a young person to external circumstances, which, if changed, could largely resolve the problem' (ONS, 2008, p. 10).

Notwithstanding widespread use of the term 'mental disorder', the following points are worth noting:

- There is no universally agreed cut-off point between 'normal' behaviour and that described as 'mental disorder'. What is considered abnormal behaviour or an abnormal reaction to circumstances differs between cultures and generations as well as between social groups within the same culture. In other words, society's understanding of mental illness is very flexible. Or as Herring succinctly puts it: 'Today's mental illness may be tomorrow's normality' (Herring, 2008, p. 541).
- In general, people from minority ethnic groups are overrepresented in the mental health system; i.e. they are more likely to be diagnosed with a mental health problem, be admitted to hospital, to experience a poor outcome from treatment, and be more likely to disengage from mainstream mental health services (MIND, 2008). These differences may be explained by a number of factors including racism, social deprivation and exclusion (Bartlett and Sandland, 2007, pp. 140–145). But whatever the explanation, there is little doubt that young people who experience racism or discrimination on account of their race, colour or religion are at an increased risk of developing mental health problems (MIND, 2008).
- While attention has focused on children's mental health problems in recent years, there has been relatively little discussion about the factors that contribute to 'good' mental health. As the Mental Health Foundation explains, 'good' mental health is not just about the absence of mental health problems; it is about allowing 'children and young people to develop the resilience to cope with whatever life throws at them and grow into well-rounded, healthy adults' (MHF, 2008). Things that can help keep children and young people mentally well include, for example, being in good physical health, having time and freedom to play, being part of a family that gets along most of the time,

and going to a school that looks after the well-being of all its pupils (see further MHF, 2008; ONS, 2008, Chapter 6, which discusses the protective factors that contribute to children's well-being).

- The so-called antipsychiatry movement (prominent in the 1960s), whose leading proponent Thomas Szasz (1960) famously said that 'mental illness is a myth and is no more real than witchcraft', question whether mental illness and insanity exist at all. According to Szasz, psychiatric disorders such as schizophrenia, depression and mania are not illnesses but 'states of being' that are basically forms of deviant behaviour that people who are powerful (and so can influence debate and policy) find morally objectionable. Szasz's views are less popular than in the past, but even though few would now accept that mental illness is a myth, it is nevertheless difficult to deny that ascriptions of mental illness do rest, at least in part, on value judgements – about what are desirable and undesirable attitudes and conduct (see further Szasz, 2002, 2005).

10.2 Incidence of Mental Disorders in Young People

A major survey carried out by the ONS (2004) found that:

- Ten per cent of 5–16-year-olds had a clinically diagnosed mental disorder.
- Four per cent had an emotional disorder.
- Six per cent had a conduct disorder.
- Two per cent had a hyperkinetic disorder.
- One per cent had a less common disorder (such as an eating disorder or autism).
- About two per cent had more than one disorder.

Note that although the 2004 survey found no difference in prevalence in overall proportions of children with mental disorder between 1999 (its previous survey) and 2004, a follow-up survey carried out between 2004 and 2007 found that 3% of children who did not have an emotional or conduct disorder in 2004 had developed one by 2007 (see further ONS, 2008).

Activity

Consider the implications of the socio-demographic variations (e.g. poverty and social background) in the incidence of mental disorders in children and young people identified in the ONS (2004) survey (and the ONS, 2008 follow-up survey; http://www.statistics.gov.uk).

10.3 Guidance Governing Children's Mental Health

Although this chapter focuses mainly on the MHA 1983, it is important to understand that several other statutes and government initiatives play a key role in promoting children's mental health and well-being. The most important are the following:

1. *Every Child Matters: Change for Children 2004*: It sets out a vision of integrated and universal children's services to promote children's well-being from birth to 19. It aims to ensure five key outcomes for children: being healthy, staying safe, enjoying and achieving, making a positive contribution and achieving economic well-being (see further Chapter 6 and http://www.everychildmatters.gov.uk).
2. *Children Act 2004*: It provides the legislative framework for developing more effective and accessible services. It emphasises the importance of multidisciplinary working, avoidance of duplication of services and increased accountability (see further

Chapter 11 and Children and Young Persons Act 2008, in particular s.7 which imposes a general duty on the Secretary of State to promote the well-being of children).

3. *The National Service Framework for Children*: Standard 9 states that all children and young people up to 18 who are affected by mental health problems should have access to 'timely, integrated, high quality, multidisciplinary mental health services to ensure effective assessment, treatment and support, for them and their families' (see further Interim Report on the Implementation of Standard 9, DoH, 2006, http://www.dh.gov.uk).

4. *Child and adolescent mental health services (CAMHS)*: Broadly, the term 'CAMHS' refers to all those services that contribute to the mental health care of children and young people (whether provided by health, education, social services or other agencies). It therefore includes universal services (such as GPs and schools, i.e. Tier 1 of the 'Four Tier Strategic Framework') as well as specialist services. But, more narrowly, the term is also used to refer only to specialist child and adolescent mental health services. In practice, this means those services operating in Tiers 2 (e.g. specialist working in community and primary settings), 3 (e.g. community mental health clinics or child psychiatry outpatients' service) and 4 (e.g. secure forensic adolescent units, eating disorder units).

Other relevant guidance covering the educational context of mental health includes the National Healthy School Status Programme, 2005 (NHSS – http://www.gov.nhss); Social and Emotional Aspects of Learning (SEAL, 2007 – http://www.healthyschools.gov.uk); the Targeted Mental Health in Schools Project, 2007 (http://www.dscf.seal), and guidance from NICE (2008) on promoting the social and emotional well-being of primary school-aged children (http://www.dcsf.gov.uk).

Activity

Critically consider the current review of CAMHS by the Department for Children, Schools and Families (http://www.dcsf.camhs).

10.4 The Impact of a Diagnosis of Mental Disorder

There is strong evidence that mental health problems in children are associated with educational failure, family disruption, disability, offending and antisocial behaviour. Furthermore, if left untreated they may not only create distress for the children (and their families and carers) but may continue into adult life (DoH, 2004, Standard 9, p. 6). However, one of the most significant consequences of mental disorder is the stigma that is associated with the diagnosis.

10.4.1 Stigma

Although society no longer treats mental illness as it did in Victorian times, widespread (but mistaken) beliefs and misconceptions mean that the label continues to attract considerable stigma (Bartlett, 2003). Stigma marks the individual out as being different from others in society, i.e. it sets them aside from 'people like us' (Hendrick, 2004, p. 189). Stigma not only has a negative impact on a person's self-worth (i.e. internalised stigma), but it can also have life-long repercussions. It is, for example, well documented that many people with mental disorders are systematically disadvantaged in most areas of their lives with forms of social exclusion and inequality occurring at home, in the workplace, in education and in health care (MHF, 2006).

10.6 Informal Admission and Treatment

10.6.1 Admission

A total of 971 young people under 18 years old (of which 503 were females and 468 males) were admitted to hospital on an informal basis in 2007–2008 (Health and Social Care Information Centre, 2009). This so-called voluntary admission is governed by s.131 of the Act. The section was substantially reformed by the Mental Health Act 2007 – overall, the intention being to establish a range of safeguards to protect the independent rights of young people to make their own decisions when possible. These provisions are complex and only a summary is provided here. More detailed analysis can be obtained from a wide range of guidance (e.g. Chapter 36 of the MH Code; National Institute for Mental Health in England, NIMHE, 2009) and leaflets published by the Department of Health explaining the Act's main provisions (http://www.gov.uk).

Different provisions apply depending on whether the young person is under or over 16.

10.6.2 Competent 16- and 17-year-olds

Consent to admission

According to s.131 of the MHA 1983, 16- and 17-year-olds who are competent – as defined by the Mental Capacity Act (MCA) 2005 (see Chapter 4) – can independently consent to being admitted to hospital. Note that their consent cannot be overridden by a person with parental responsibility.

Refusal of consent

Competent 16- and 17-year-olds who refuse to consent to admission can only be admitted to hospital if (1) the relevant criteria in the MHA 1983 for compulsory admission apply (see below); or (2) if these criteria do not apply, the court's permission must be sought, unless (3) a life-threatening emergency exists; i.e. admission is required because failure to admit and treat the young person is likely to lead to the young person's death or severe permanent injury (and it is not possible to obtain a court order first, see further Chapter 36.51 of the Code).

10.6.3 Incompetent 16- and 17-year-olds

Admission under s.131 does not apply to incompetent 16- and 17-year-olds (incompetence being defined according to the MCA 2005), i.e. they cannot understand the information about the decision to be made, retain the information in their mind, use and weigh it up as part of the decision-making process, or communicate their decision (s.3 MCA 2005). But several other options can be relied on. These are the following:

1. *Admission under the MCA 2005*: Admission under the MCA 2005 is lawful provided the principles and provisions of the MCA 2005 are complied with, i.e. it is in their best interests (s.4 MCA 2005). Importantly, however, the MCA 2005 cannot be used if admission will have the effect of depriving the young person of their liberty. Factors that are likely to be relevant in deciding whether a person has been deprived of their liberty include whether restraint is used (including sedation) and the extent to which staff have control over the person's movements (for other reasons why reliance on the MCA 2005 may not be possible, see NIMHE, 2009, pp. 38–39, and Chapter 4.20—21 of the Code).

2. *Admission under common law principles – consent of a person with parental responsibility*: If the MCA 2005 cannot be used to admit incompetent 16- and 17-year-olds,

common law principles can be relied on. This means that consent for admission can be obtained from a person with parental responsibility. But such consent is only lawful if the decision to admit is within the so-called zone of parental control. According to the Code (Chapter 36.9–15), assessing whether a particular decision falls within the zone of parental control involves asking two key questions: firstly, is the decision one that a parent would be expected to make bearing in mind what society would consider 'normal' parental practice? And secondly, are there any indications that the parent might not be acting in the young person's best interests (see further NIMHE, 2009, pp. 26–31)? But notwithstanding that admission is within the zone of parental control, it may not be possible to rely on parental consent (e.g. because the young person is unable to consent to admission for reasons falling outside the MCA 2005; Dimond, 2008).

3. *Mental Health Act 1983*: If the decision to admit is outside the zone of parental control, admission could be authorised under the compulsory provisions of the MHA 1983 (see below).
4. *Court authorisation*: If the MHA criteria for admission cannot be met, it may be necessary to seek the court's permission.
5. *Life-threatening emergency*: In cases where failure to provide treatment is likely to lead to the young person's death or severe permanent injury (and it is not possible to obtain the court's permission in time), then they can be admitted to hospital and treated without consent.

Key points

- Competent 16- and 17-year-olds can admit themselves voluntarily to hospital (under s.131) as informal patients.
- The consent of competent 16- and 17-year-olds to be admitted as an informal patient cannot be overridden by a person with parental responsibility.
- Competent 16- and 17-year-olds who refuse to be admitted voluntarily can be admitted under the compulsory provisions of the MHA 1983, the court's authorisation, or in an emergency.
- Incompetent 16- and 17-year-olds can be admitted under the MCA 2005, common law principles, MHA 1983, the court's authorisation, or in an emergency.

10.6.4 Competent under 16-year-olds

Consent to admission

Under s.131 of the MHA 1983, *Gillick* competent under 16-year-olds (see Chapter 4 on the assessment of *Gillick* competence) can independently consent to be informally admitted to hospital.

Refusal of consent

As guidance makes clear, given the recent trend to respect the autonomy of young people, the refusal of *Gillick* competent under 16-year-olds is a very important consideration in deciding whether their admission should nevertheless be authorised. Accordingly, it is unwise to rely on the consent of a person with parental responsibility. This means *Gillick* competent under 16-year-olds who refuse consent to admission can only be admitted to hospital if (1) they meet the criteria for compulsory admission under the MHA 1983 (see below), (2) court authorisation is obtained, or (3) a life-threatening emergency exists (see above).

10.6.5 Incompetent under 16-year-olds

The options available to admit under 16-year-olds who are not *Gillick* competent are these:

1. *Admission under common law principles – consent of a person with parental responsibility*: As with incompetent 16- and 17-year-olds, consent of those with parental responsibility can only be relied on if admission is within the zone of parental control (see above). However, as the Code makes clear, the young person's views should be taken into account even if they are not *Gillick* competent (Chapter 36.47–49 of the MH Code).
2. *Mental Health Act 1983*: If the matter is outside the zone of parental control (or the consent of a person with parental responsibility is not given), the young person cannot be treated informally. In such cases, the criteria for admission under the compulsory provisions of the MHA 1983 may apply (see below).
3. *Court authorisation*: If the criteria for compulsory admission under the MHA cannot be met, authorisation from the court may be sought.
4. *Life-threatening emergency*: Admission without consent is lawful to safeguard a child's life (or avoid severe permanent injury).

Key points

- *Gillick* competent under 16-year-olds can voluntarily admit themselves to hospital as informal patients under s.131.
- *Gillick* competent under 16-year-olds who refuse to be admitted voluntarily can be admitted under the MHA 1983, the court's authorisation, or in an emergency.
- Incompetent under 16-year-olds can be admitted under common law principles, the MHA 1983, the court's authorisation, or without consent if a life-threatening emergency exists.

10.6.6 Informal treatment

This section considers the main considerations that are relevant to the treatment of mental disorder of children and young people. Almost all the powers – which consist of several overlapping powers – mirror those discussed above in relation to informal admission.

10.6.7 Competent 16- and 17-year-olds

Consent to treatment
Consent to treatment of young people in this age group is governed by s.8 of the Family Law Reform Act 1989 (see Chapter 4). In brief, this section states that 16- and 17-year-olds are presumed to be capable of consenting to their own medical treatment (and to any ancillary procedures involved in that treatment). Although it is not legally necessary to obtain consent from a person with parental responsibility, the Code suggests it is good practice to involve the young person's family (Chapter 36.32 of the MH Code).

Refusal of consent
Competent 16- and 17-year-olds who refuse to consent to treatment can be treated without their consent in the following circumstances: if (1) the criteria for detention under the MHA apply (see below), (2) authorisation is obtained from the court, or (3) the young person is facing a life-threatening emergency.

10.6.8 Incompetent 16- and 17-year-olds

The 16- and 17-year-olds who are unable to consent to the proposed treatment for their mental disorder may be treated without their consent in the following circumstances:

1. *Treatment relying on the MCA 2005*: As with informal admission, treatment under the MCA 2005 only applies if treatment is in the young person's best interests and they will not be deprived of their liberty (see above).
2. *Treatment on the basis of parental consent*: Whether or not the MCA 2005 applies, a person with parental responsibility can consent but only if treatment is within the zone of parental control (see above).
3. *Mental Health Act 1983*: If the MCA 2005 does not apply (e.g. because treatment involves a deprivation of liberty) or it is outside the zone of parental control, the MHA may be applicable (see below).
4. *Court authorisation*: If the MHA is not applicable, the court's permission may be necessary.
5. *Life-threatening emergency*: If failure to treat is likely to lead to the young person's death or severe permanent injury, they may be admitted and treated without consent. However, such treatment must be no more than necessary to meet the emergency.

Key points

- Competent 16- and 17-year-olds can consent to treatment for their mental disorder.
- The refusal of competent 16- and 17-year-olds to treatment cannot be overridden by a person with parental responsibility.
- Competent 16- and 17-year-olds may be treated without their consent if the compulsory provisions of the MHA 1983 apply, the court's permission is sought or a life-threatening emergency exists.
- Incompetent 16- and 17-year-olds can be treated on the basis of the MCA 2005, the consent of a person with parental responsibility, the MHA 1983, the court's authorisation or without consent if a life-threatening emergency exists.

10.6.9 Competent under 16-year-olds

Consent to treatment
The consent of under 16-year-olds who are *Gillick* competent is sufficient authority for treatment for their mental disorder to be carried out without the need for consent from a person with parental responsibility.

Refusal of consent
As with admission, if a *Gillick* competent child refuses treatment, guidance suggests it would not be wise to rely on the consent of a person with parental responsibility in order to treat the child (NIMHE, 2009, p. 62). Instead, the following options are available: (1) treatment under the MHA 1983 (if the criteria for detention are met, see below); (2) application to court; and (3) if a life-threatening emergency exists, the child can be admitted to hospital and treated without consent.

10.6.10 Incompetent under 16-year-olds

The powers that can be relied on to treat mental disorders of children who are not *Gillick* competent are the following:

1. *Consent of person with parental responsibility*: Under common law, a person with parental responsibility can give consent to the proposed treatment provided it is

within the zone of parental control. If the child has expressed an unwillingness to accept the proposed treatment, it may nevertheless not be appropriate for the parent to consent (NIMHE, 2009, p. 62).

2. *Mental Health Act 1983*: If consent of a person with parental responsibility cannot be relied on, the detention provisions of the MHA may be possible (see below).
3. *Court authorisation*: If the criteria under the MHA cannot be met, the court's permission should be sought.
4. *Life-threatening emergency*: As was noted above, incompetent young people can be admitted and treated without consent if such action is necessary to prevent their death or severe permanent injury.

Key points

- *Gillick* competent under 16-year-olds can consent to treatment for their mental disorder.
- *Gillick* competent under 16-year-olds who refuse treatment can be treated under the MHA 1983, the court's authorisation, or when a life-threatening emergency exists.
- Incompetent under 16-year-olds can be treated on the basis of the consent of a person with parental responsibility, the MHA 1983, the court's authorisation or without consent when a life-threatening emergency exists.

10.7 Compulsory Admission – Detaining Young People against their Will

The main sections under which patients can be admitted and detained against their will are described below. Only a small minority of under 18-year-olds are admitted compulsorily each year (439 in 2007–2008, NHS Information Centre for Health and Social Care, 2009). However, as we see, such admission may lead to very intrusive medical treatment – some of it compulsory. It is therefore important to outline how the MHA 1983 regulates admission and treatment.

10.7.1 Admission for assessment (s.2)

This order allows compulsory admission and detention for up to 28 days. It is a short-term measure that can be made if the patient is:

a. Suffering from a mental disorder of a nature or degree which warrants detention in hospital for assessment; and
b. Ought to be detained in the interests of his/her own health or safety or that of others.

Detention is only lawful if several conditions are met, including (among other things) two medical recommendations and a requirement that the applicant – the 'nearest relative' (NR) or an approved mental health professional (AMHP) – must have seen the patient within the period of 14 days ending with the date of the application.

10.7.2 Admission for treatment (s.3)

Admission for treatment is a long-term provision, which can initially last for 6 months and, on first renewal, for a further 6 months and at yearly intervals thereafter. The grounds for admission are that the patient:

a. Is suffering from a mental disorder of a nature or degree which makes it appropriate to receive medical treatment in hospital; and

b. It is necessary for the health and safety of the patient or that of others that he should receive such treatment, which cannot be provided unless he is detained; and

c. Appropriate medical treatment is available.

Overall, admission for treatment is intended for patients whose condition is believed to require a period of treatment as an inpatient. Again, several conditions must be complied with (e.g. two medical recommendations and a requirement that if the applicant is AMHP, he must consult the NR before making the application). The term 'appropriate' means medical treatment which is appropriate to the patient's care, taking into account the nature and degree of the patient's mental disorder (whether this could result in a patient being detained even though he is 'untreatable' is as yet unclear (Herring, 2008, pp. 520–21, see further Chapter 6 of the Code)).

10.7.3 Emergency admission (s.4)

Emergency admissions – which can last up to 72 hours – are designed for 'genuine emergencies' and not as an administrative convenience (Code 5.5). Section 4 admission can be applied for by an AMHP or NR but only requires one medical recommendation. Grounds for the order are the following:

a. The criteria for detention under s.2 are met.

b. The patient's detention is required as a matter of urgent necessity.

c. Obtaining a second medical recommendation would cause undesirable delay.

According to the Code, an emergency arises 'where the patient's mental state or behaviour presents problems which those involved cannot reasonably be expected to manage while waiting for a second opinion'. Evidence of an emergency includes 'an immediate and significant risk of mental or physical harm to the patient or to others; danger of serious harm to property; or a need for physical restraint' (Code 5.5–6; see also DoH, 2008b, Chapter 2.46–54).

Activity

Read Chapter 4 of the Code. Critically consider its guidance about how to choose whether to admit a patient under s.2 or s.3.

10.7.4 Voluntary patients – holding powers (s.5(2))

This power lasts up to 72 hours during which time the patient can be assessed. It can be used when the doctor or approved clinician (a role that can now be fulfilled by practitioners from professions such as nursing, occupational therapy and social work) in charge of the treatment of a hospital inpatient decides that an application for detention should be made. Essentially, therefore, this order can be used to detain informal patients who decide they are going to leave. It can be exercised only after the doctor or approved clinician has personally examined the patient.

10.7.5 Voluntary patients – nurses' holding powers (s.5(4))

Prescribed nurses (i.e. those qualified in either mental health nursing or disability learning) have 'holding' powers that can last up to 6 hours. This allows them to detain informal patients (who want to leave hospital) for a short time. The power can be used where the nurse considers that:

a. The patient is suffering from mental disorder to such a degree that it is necessary for the patient to be immediately prevented from leaving the hospital either for his health or safety or that of others; and
b. It is not practicable to secure the immediate attendance of a doctor or approved clinician who can submit a report under s.5(2).

A nurse's decision to invoke the power is a personal one, i.e. she cannot be instructed to exercise the power by anyone else. However, detailed guidance about the factors that should be considered before invoking the power is provided in the Code (Chapter 12; see also DoH, 2008a; see also Chapter 2.71–85 DoH, 2008b).

Points to note:

- Those who qualify as a patient's 'nearest relative' have extensive powers under the MHA 1983 (e.g. to apply for admission, to be consulted and object to s.3 admission for treatment, to discharge the patient). The definition in s.26 is complex. It includes spouse, parents, brothers and sisters.
- Other routes into compulsory detention include various police powers under sections 135 and 136 of the MHA 1983.
- Children who are wards of court cannot be admitted to hospital without a court order (s.33 MHA 1983).
- Special provisions (in sections 27 and 116 MHA 1983) apply to children and young people who are in local authority care.

> **Key points**
>
> - Under the MHA, patients can be detained without their consent under sections 2 or 3 or 4 (in an emergency).
> - Holding powers (under s.5(2) and (4)) authorise short-term detention of informal patients who want to leave hospital.

10.8 Treatments Regulated by Part 4 of the MHA 1983

Part 4 of the MHA 1983 contains several provisions regulating treatment for mental disorder (e.g. those detained under sections 2 and 3). The provisions that authorise treatment without the patient's consent are usually referred to as the compulsory treatment provisions. But first two important preliminary points must be noted:

1. The compulsory treatment provisions do not apply to those detained under s.4 (emergency admission), the holding powers (in s.5(2) and (4)), s.35 (remands in hospital for reports) and sections 135 and 136.
2. Some provisions in Part 4 apply to patients whether or not they are detained or are informal patients (e.g. neurosurgery (s.57); electroconvulsive treatment, ECT, s.58A, see below).

10.8.1 Neurosurgery and surgical implants (s.57)

Treatments regulated by s.57 involve brain surgery or hormonal implants. They can only be given with the patient's consent, and if certain conditions are met – e.g. that a second opinion appointed doctor (SOAD) certifies that it is appropriate treatment. Section 57 applies to informal patients.

10.8.2 Medication (after an initial 3-month period) except medication administered as part of ECT (s.58)

Drugs given to patients for longer than 3 months from the time the patient was first given them are only lawful in the following circumstances (drugs given before then are regulated by s.63, see below):

a. The patient consents and the approved clinician in charge of the treatment / SOAD certifies that the patient is capable of understanding the nature, purpose and likely effects of the treatment and that the patient has consented to it; or

b. An SOAD certifies in writing either that the patient is not capable of understanding the nature, purpose and likely effects of the treatment or the patient is capable and has not consented to it, but it is appropriate for the treatment to be given.

Section 58 applies only to patients who are subject to the compulsory treatment provisions of Part 4 (for guidance to nurses on the various legal requirements that must be met, see Care Quality Commission, 2008).

10.8.3 ECT and medication administered as part of ECT (s.58A)

Section 58A (inserted by the Mental Health Act 2007) provides new safeguards for patients under 18.

Detained patients under 18

In relation to detained under 18-year-olds who are subject to the compulsory treatment provisions in Part 4, the legal position is as follows: those who are capable of consenting to ECT can be given the treatment providing: (a) an SOAD has certified in writing that they are capable of understanding the nature, purpose and likely effects of ECT; and (b) it is appropriate treatment. If they are not capable of consenting to the ECT, it can only be given (a) if the SOAD certifies that they are incapable; (b) it is appropriate for the treatment to be given; and (c) the ECT does not conflict with a court order. Note that unlike medication for mental disorder, there is no initial 3-month period during which an SOAD certificate is not needed.

Informal patients under 18

Children and young people under 18 who are in hospital as informal patients can be given ECT in the following circumstances: (1) they are capable of consenting to the treatment (either under s.8 of the Family Law Reform Act 1969 or they are *Gillick* competent); (2) under the MCA 2005 (if they are incompetent 16- and 17-year-olds) unless the treatment amounts to a deprivation of liberty; or (3) with the court's authorisation. Although there is nothing in the Act itself to prevent a person with parental responsibility consenting to ECT on behalf of an informal child patient who lacks capacity, the Code states that it is not advisable to rely on such consent (36.60 and 4.34).

Note finally that s.58 does not apply if the treatment is immediately necessary to save the patient's life or to prevent serious deterioration in their condition. Furthermore, all children and young people (whether or not they are detained) for whom ECT is proposed should have access to an independent mental health advocate.

10.8.4 Urgent treatment (s.62)

Sections 57, 58 and 58A do not apply when urgent treatment is necessary. Urgent treatment is defined as that which is immediately necessary to save the patient's life, prevent serious deterioration in their condition, alleviate serious suffering or prevent patients behaving violently or being a danger to themselves or others (Chapter 24.32–37 of the Code).

10.8.5 All other forms of medical treatment for mental disorder (s.63)

Section 63 covers all forms of medical treatment for the mental disorder the patient is suffering (that are not covered by sections 57, 58 or 58A). It therefore includes medication given during the first 3 months of detention. Treatment under this section can be given only to patients who are subject to the compulsory treatment provisions of Part 4. It can be given without their consent if it is given by or under the direction of the approved clinician in charge of the treatment in question. Because the courts have (albeit controversially) interpreted s.63 very widely, it seems that treatment can be given without consent in a wide range of circumstances. As Lord Justice Hoffman said (at p. 298) in *B v Croydon HA* [1995] 2 WLR 294, if treatment is capable of being ancillary to core treatment – that is, it is nursing care 'concurrent with the core treatment or as a necessary prerequisite to such treatment or to prevent the patient from causing harm to himself or to alleviate the consequences of the disorder'– it will be upheld as lawful under s.63 (see further *Reid v Secretary of State for Scotland* [1991] 2 AC 512; *R v Ashworth Hospital, ex parte B* [2005] 2 AC 278).

Points to note:

- Throughout the MHA 1983, the term 'medical treatment' includes nursing, psychological intervention and specialist mental health habilitation, rehabilitation and care, as well as medication and other forms of treatment, which might more normally be regarded as being 'medical' (s.145). Furthermore, when the Act talks about 'medical treatment for mental disorder', it means medical treatment for the purpose of alleviating or preventing a worsening of a mental disorder or one or more of its symptoms. This includes treatment of physical health problems only to the extent that such treatment is part of, or ancillary to, treatment for mental disorder (see further DoH Reference *Guide*, DoH, 2008b, 1.16–1.20; Chapter 23.2–4 of the Code).
- Section 131A of the MHA 1983 (inserted by the MHA 2007) requires age-appropriate services to be available for children and young people by April 2010. This means that children and young people admitted to hospital for the treatment of mental disorder should be accommodated in an environment that is suitable for their age (subject to their needs, see further Chapter 36.67–74 of the Code).
- The MHA 1983 includes a new power to create supervised community treatment orders (together with various medical treatment provisions). However, as very few children and young people likely to be subject to these orders, they are not discussed here (see Chapters 25 and 36.64–5 of the Code).

Key points

- Under Part 4 of the MHA 1983, patients who are detained under long-term detention provisions can in certain circumstances be given compulsory treatment.
- The provisions regulating neurosurgery and surgical implants apply to informal patients.
- All young people for whom ECT is proposed should have access to an Independent Mental Capacity Advocate.

10.9 Ethical Issues

As we have seen above, a diagnosis of mental disorder can have very serious repercussions – leading in some cases to compulsory admission and treatment under the MHA 1983. So how can these draconian powers be justified? Or to put it another way, what moral justification is there for restricting the liberty of people with mental disorders and taking away a fundamental human right, namely to consent to medical treatment? One is to protect the public and the other is to protect the mentally disordered from themselves.

10.9.1 The protection of others

Justifying compulsory intervention on the basis that society needs protection strongly suggests that some people with mental disorders are a threat to the community. In some cases this may be true – because they have committed a serious crime, for example. However, in the vast majority of cases it is because of the fear that they may do so unless they are detained in hospital and/or compulsorily treated. Yet there is strong evidence that most psychiatric difficulties are only very occasionally associated with criminality (Prins, 1990; Thornicroft, 2006). Indeed, recent large-scale research found no evidence, for example, that schizophrenia was a risk factor for violence (Monahan et al., 2001); see also Peay (2007), who suggests that mental disorders account for only a tiny proportion of violence.

Yet fear (on its own) can only be a sufficiently strong moral ground to deprive someone of their liberty and force them to have treatment if we have a very clear idea of what that person might do. In other words, compulsory intervention in the lives of those who are mentally disordered can only be justified if they are really 'dangerous', i.e. likely to harm other people. The problem here is, of course, as was noted above, that terms like 'dangerous' (and 'harm') are value-laden social constructs. Thus as the line between 'normality' and abnormality' is blurred, it is inevitably very difficult to define these terms objectively (Ainsworth, 2000).

Not surprisingly, it is thus also often very difficult to accurately predict who might become dangerous. As Bartlett and Sandland report, studies generally find that between a half and three-quarters of those identified as dangerous by psychiatric professionals do not in the end turn out to be violent (Bartlett and Sandland, 2007, p. 147; see also Bartlett, 2003). Prediction of dangerousness is therefore not an exact science. But even if it were – and we all agreed that society had the right to protect itself from the dangerously mentally ill – we would still face the dilemma of deciding where, how and by whom they should be detained for the purpose of prevention (Herring, 2008, pp. 544–545).

10.9.2 The protection of self

The other justification for compulsory detention of the mentally disordered is that it is in their best interests. In other words, without paternalistic intervention they will harm themselves in some way. Three versions of paternalism are usually distinguished in this context, notably physical paternalism, which aims to safeguard an individual's own physical health and safety; psychological paternalism, which is concerned with preventing psychological harm (i.e. to his or her mental health); and moral paternalism, which is aimed at the individual's moral welfare, the concern being to make the individual a morally better person and ensure she/he does not come to moral harm (Cadavino, 1989). The extent to which these three different kinds of paternalism can ever justify compulsory detention and treatment is, of course, debatable.

Yet notwithstanding this debate, even if it were possible to agree on which version of paternalism was appropriate, it would still be necessary to provide a convincing argument as to why the mentally disordered should be subject to compulsory action for their own good when we let other people – e.g. smokers and heavy drinkers – to act as they please, irrespective of the potential danger to their health. The usual response is that the crucial moral distinction lies in the inability of the mentally disordered to make 'rational' choices. Thus, even though there may be little consensus on what it means to make a rational decision, most of us accept that it is appropriate to intervene in some circumstances, notably when someone, for example, makes a decision based on delusional beliefs or a deep disturbance in the functioning of memory or perception. Furthermore, when this happens, and when, in addition, it is likely that their consequent actions (or failure to act) will cause themselves harm, then even a lay person will be able to identify that they are behaving differently from those who are just 'stupid, or wicked, or both' (Lesser, 2007, p. 209). As Lindley explains, a man who thinks he is superman (and so can fly) can justifiably be stopped from jumping off a cliff. On the other hand, it is far harder to justify preventing people from smoking or drinking once they have been informed about and understand the risks they are exposing themselves to (Lindley, 1978, p. 42).

Key points

- The moral justification for compulsory intervention is twofold: (a) to protect the public and (b) to protect the mentally ill themselves.
- The concept of 'dangerousness' is a value-laden concept that can be interpreted in a number of ways.

Activity

Read the chapter on 'Ethical problems in mental health and psychiatric care' in *Ethics in Clinical Practice*, Hawley (ed.). Do you agree with his conclusions?

Case study

Shirley is 17 and suffers from a psychotic illness. Following a fatal car accident in which her father was killed, she is also suffering from post-traumatic stress disorder. Recently, Shirley has become very depressed and has cut herself deliberately several times. She has therefore been detained under s.2 of the MHA 1983 in an adolescent intensive care unit. Although Shirley is no longer harming herself, she has refused to eat and has also rejected all forms of treatment.

Caroline, the approved clinician in charge of Shirley's treatment, wants to know what treatment options are available.

Shirley's treatment is regulated under Part 4 of the MHA 1983. According to s.63, Shirley can be given medication (by or under the direction of the approved clinician in charge of the treatment in question) for an initial period of 3 months (starting from the day when she was first given the medication following her detention under s.2). Although treatment can be given to Shirley without her consent under s.63, the Code (23.37) advises practitioners to obtain consent wherever possible. It also reminds them that when authorising treatment without consent they are subject to the provisions of the Human Rights Act 1998. As such, they must not act in a way which is incompatible with a patient's rights as set out in the European Convention on Human Rights (23.37–41). Other relevant guidance in the Code stresses the importance of treatment plans (23.42–51).

After Shirley has been given medication for 3 months, s.58 applies. This provision includes several safeguards. These vary according to whether Shirley consents to the treatment (see above).

As regards other treatment that might be considered necessary, it seems that s.63 (which has been interpreted expansively by the courts) can be used to authorise a wide range of treatments (even force feeding; see, e.g. *Re KB (Adult) Mental Patient: Medical Treatment* (1994) 19 BLMR 144; see further Bartlett and Sandland, 2007, pp. 299–318, which includes several case studies to demonstrate treatment options for under 18-year-olds). Note that s.63 cannot be used to force any other sort of treatment on a detained patient, i.e. to treat a physical condition that is not connected to her mental disorder.

10.10 Relationship between the Law and Ethics

10.10.1 Similarities between law and ethics

- The legal and ethical principles justifying compulsory treatment are broadly similar – protecting society and protecting patients from self-harm (i.e. from themselves).
- Compulsory detention and treatment is legally and ethically justified providing it properly balances the needs of the community with the rights of patients.
- There is a legal and ethical presumption that compulsion should be avoided if at all possible.
- The legal and ethical justification for treating incompetent patients is the 'best interests' principle.

10.10.2 Differences between law and ethics

- The MHA 1983 imposes strict conditions before patients can be compulsorily detained and treated: in contrast, the ethical principles underpinning paternalistic intervention are less clearly expressed.
- The ethical and legal approach to the treatment of mental disorder may be based on the same principles, but reforms introduced by the MHA 1983 (and the revised Code) now arguably give decision-makers less discretion to make value judgements.

References

Ainsworth, P.B. (2000) *Psychology and Crime: Myths and Reality*. Harlow: Longman.

Bartlett, P. (2003) The test of compulsion in mental health law: capacity, therapeutic benefit and dangerousness as possible criteria. *Medical Law Review* 11:326.

Bartlett, P. and Sandland, R. (2007) *Mental Health Law: Policy and Practice*, 3rd edn. Oxford: Oxford University Press.

Cadavino, M. (1989) *Mental Health Law in Context*. Aldershot: Dartmouth.

Care Quality Commission (2008) *Nurses, the Administration of Medicine for Mental Disorder and the Mental Health Act 1983*. London: CQC.

DES (2004) *Every Child Matters: Change for Children*. London: DES.

Dimond, B. (2008) *Legal Aspects of Mental Capacity*. Oxford: Blackwell.

DoH (2004) *NSF for Children, Young People and Maternity Services: The Mental Health and Psychological Well-Being of Children and Young People*. London: DoH.

DoH (2006) *Interim Report on the Implementation of Standard 9*. London: DoH.

DoH (2008a) *Mental Health Act 1983 Code of Practice*. London: TSO.

DoH (2008b) *Reference Guide to the Mental Health Act 1983*. London: DoH.

Hawley, G. (2007) *Ethics in Clinical Practice: An Interprofessional Approach*. Harlow: Pearson Education.

Health and Social Care Information Centre (2009) Statistical bulletin 2007/8.

Hendrick, J. (2004) *Law and Ethics: Foundations in Nursing and Health Care*. Cheltenham: Stanley Thornes.

Herring, J. (2008) *Medical Law and Ethics*. 2nd edn. Oxford: Oxford University Press.

Lesser, H. (2007) An ethical perspective – compulsion and autonomy. In Tingle, J. and Cribb, A. (eds) *Nursing Law and Ethics*, 3rd edn. Oxford: Blackwell.

Lindley, R. (1978) Social philosophy. In Lindley R., Fellows R. and Macdonald G (eds), *What Philosophy Does*. London: Open Books.

Mental Health Foundation (MHF) (2006) *Ignorance, Prejudice and Stigma*. London: MHF.

Mental Health Foundation (MHF) (2008) *Children and Young People*. London: MHF.

Monahan, J., Steadman, H., Silver, E. et al. (2001) *Rethinking Risk Assessment: The MacArthur Study of Mental Disorder and Violence*. Oxford: Oxford University Press.

National Association for Mental Health (MIND) (2008) *Children, Young People and Mental Health*. London: MIND.

NHS Information Centre for Health and Social Care (2009) *Mental Health Minimum Dataset*. London: NHS.

National Institute for Mental Health in England (2009) *The Legal Aspects of the Care and Treatment of Children and Young People with Mental Disorder: A Guide for Professionals*.

Office of National Statistics (2004) *Mental Health of Children and Young People in Great Britain*. London: TSO.

Office for National Statistics (2008) *Three Years on: Survey of the Development and Emotional Well-Being of Children and Young People*. London: TSO.

Peay, J. (2007) Mentally disordered offenders, mental health and crime. In Maguire, M., Morgan, R. and Reiner, R. (eds) *The Oxford Handbook of Criminology*, 4th edn. Oxford: Oxford University Press.

Prins, H. (1990) Dangerousness: a review. In Bluglass, R. and Bowden, R. (eds) *Principle and Practice of Forensic Psychiatry*. Edinburgh: Churchill Livingstone.

Szasz, T. (1960) The myth of mental illness. *American Psychologist* 15:113.

Szasz, T. (2002) *Liberation by Oppression: A Comparative Study of Slavery and Psychiatry*. New Brunswick, NJ: Transaction.

Szasz, T. (2005) Idiots, infants, and the insane: mental illness and legal incompetence. *Journal of Medical Ethics* 31:78.

Thornicroft, G. (2006) *Shunned: Discrimination against People with Mental Illness*. Oxford: Oxford University Press.

CHAPTER 11
Child Protection

Learning outcomes

By the end of this chapter you should be able to:

- Understand how child welfare policies have evolved;
- Identify children 'in need' and describe the services they can access;
- Distinguish between short- and long-term methods of child protection;
- Assess the implications of interagency cooperation in safeguarding children.

Introduction

When the Children Act 1989 (the Act) came into force in 1991, it was described as the most comprehensive reform in living memory, which would bring about a new beginning to the philosophy and practices of the childcare system. Yet despite this description and the Act's claim to strike a 'new' balance between the role of the state, the rights of children and the responsibilities of parents, the whole Act built upon principles that had been long established in previous legislation. This will be evident from the brief outline of the development of child welfare services with which this chapter begins. But for health professionals the Act's main impact is in relation to child protection work and the various orders, both short- and long-term, in which they may play a significant role. This chapter therefore focuses mainly on these aspects of the Act. However, it also describes the contribution health professionals may make to the provision of services for 'children in need'.

11.1 Development of Children's Welfare Policies

To understand the Act fully, it must be put into context. In other words, we need to trace how changing perceptions of the state's role in protecting children have shaped childcare policies in the last century. For reasons of space, only a sketch is provided here (for a more detailed historical survey, see Cretney, 2003).

11.1.1 Children Act 1948

The first major statute concerned with children's welfare – the Prevention of Cruelty to and Protection of Children Act 1889 – was enacted 100 years before the Children Act 1989. But a comprehensive childcare service was only fully established by the Children Act 1948. The 1948 Act was a landmark statute. Until then, concern for children's welfare had oscillated between prevention and protection (i.e. between working with families and 'saving' children from them (Diduck and Kaganas, 2006, p. 341). However, the new principles of childcare set out in the 1948 Act 'to help children whose homes had failed them; lessen or prevent the trauma of separation … or grossly inadequate parenting' were firmly focused on prevention and rehabilitation rather than rescue (Hendrick, 1994, pp. 152–153). Perhaps even more importantly, the Act heralded a new approach to parent–child relations, which encouraged the newly established Children's Departments 'to view children as individual human beings with both shared and individualised needs, rather than an indistinct mass' (Hendrick, 2005).

11.1.2　Children and Young Person's Act 1969

The new duties imposed on local authorities by the 1948 Act (in particular to receive deprived children into care) led to childcare services working more closely with families. With this new focus came a growing awareness of the link between social and economic factors and 'problem families'. Equally 'new' was the belief that juvenile delinquency – about which there had been increasing concern in the late 1950s and 1960s – was caused by 'deprivation' rather than 'depravity'. Thus while preventive work was still family oriented (i.e. coercive intervention was the last resort), the emerging social welfare model of intervention treated 'offending' children in virtually the same way as non-offenders (Parton, 1991). It was therefore not surprising that the resulting legislation, the Children and Young Person's Act 1969, targeted both groups of children (providing 'treatment' for the 'delinquent' child) with the overall aim of preventing either coming before the courts (Lowe and Douglas, 2007, p. 694).

11.1.3　Children Act 1975

By the 1970s a new problem had been 'discovered': child abuse. As Hendrick (1997, p. 58) explains, until then child physical abuse was regarded as essentially a medical problem caused by individual pathology, i.e. the character or personality of the abusing parent. But that perception began to change as theorists such as Parton (1985) suggested that this medical model was inadequate – largely because it ignored the economic and social position of the family, especially the effect of pollution, poor health services and bad housing. This approach led to increasing interest in child abuse in the press (and among professionals). Indeed, some would say it generated a 'moral panic' (in which child abuse was seen as a threat to societal values and interests). Following the huge public interest prompted by the inquiry into the death of Maria Colwell, aged 7, caused by her stepfather (she was returned from foster care to her natural family even though she strongly opposed the move), it was therefore almost inevitable that child abuse became established as a major social problem. The inquiry report strongly criticised the childcare system for failing to protect Maria, blaming in particular the emphasis placed by social workers on maintaining the 'natural' or 'birth' family, thereby downplaying focus on the child (a fundamental premise of the 1948 Act). The resulting legislation, the Children Act 1975, accordingly placed much more emphasis on substitute care (including adoption) and on protecting children *from* their families (Hendrick, 1997, p. 60). The 1975 Act was also significant in recognising children as individuals in their own right – hence the requirement to give 'first consideration' to their welfare.

11.1.4　Children Act 1989

The concerns of the 1980s shifted to the harm suffered by children in care. As research emerged (see, e.g. Millham, 1986) of the detrimental effect of local authority care on family links, so social workers, who had reacted by doing everything possible to prevent children entering into the care system, were criticised for denying care to those who needed it (Masson et al., 2008, p. 714). On the other hand, they were also blamed for relying too heavily on coercive measures – with the Cleveland crisis in the mid-1980s (concerned with a sudden huge increase of the removal of children from their homes because of alleged sexual abuse) being almost universally condemned as an overreaction by zealous social workers who had become too powerful at the expense of family autonomy (Freeman, 1992; Lowe and Douglas, 2007, p. 695).

There was thus widespread agreement that the primary aim of the Act should be to strike a new balance between family autonomy and local authority powers to protect children, i.e. one that provided sufficient protection to vulnerable children but also respected the integrity of the family (Bainham, 2005, p. 470). The Act attempted to achieve this balance in several ways, e.g. by enhancing children's legal status, redefining parental power in terms of parental responsibility and reorganising the court system (for an overview of the Act, see Freeman, 1992). But at its heart were two fundamental principles:

- *Prevention rather than intervention – the primacy of the family*: One of the Act's most pervasive themes is the belief that children are best cared for by their families. It is most forcibly expressed in the 'non-intervention' principle (s.1(5)) which effectively creates a presumption against court action unless it is absolutely necessary and will positively improve the child's welfare. Local authorities are thus expected to use their powers and duties to keep children at home so that, even when children are at risk, compulsory intervention and their removal from home can be avoided. In addition, where children are living away from home, there are provisions aimed at maintaining their links with their families and promoting reunification and rehabilitation (Lowe and Douglas, 2007, p. 698; Masson et al., 2008, pp. 713–715).
- *Partnership and cooperation*: Although the word 'partnership' does not appear anywhere in the Act, the idea is given statutory force to the extent that children and families are given greater rights than in the past to be consulted, kept fully informed and to challenge decisions which affect them. It is also reflected in the local authorities' duty to promote the upbringing of children within their families and to provide support for children 'in need' (see below). The essential principles supporting partnership are spelt out in detail in Department of Health guidance (see 1991 vol. 3, Family Placements, paras 2.10–11). In practice, of course, the concept of partnership is problematic – not least because the local authority will always have the 'upper hand'. In other words, the partnership is far from equal.

Activity

Read the discussion of the partnership principle in the chapter 'Child abuse – a public or private matter' in Diduck. A. and Kaganas, F., *Family Law, Gender and the State*. Do you agree with their analysis?

11.1.5 Children Act 2004

The Act was passed following the death of Victoria Climbie, who suffered horrendous abuse at the hands of a great aunt and her cohabitant. The inquiry into her death (Laming, 2003) laid much of the blame on the professionals involved for failing to follow good practice, for poor investigative standards and poor communication. It led to the enactment of the Children Act 2004, which incorporated many of the recommendations made by Laming, in particular those that aimed to improve cooperation, partnership and the sharing of information between agencies. The inquiry also led to the formulation of the Every Child Matters initiative (2004; see Chapter 6).

Key points

- Two key principles underpinning the Children Act 1989 are (a) children are best cared for by their families, and (b) local authorities and families should work in partnership to safeguard children.
- The Children Act 2004 requires local authorities and other agencies (e.g. health, housing and the police) to cooperate to improve children's well-being.

11.2 Models of State Intervention

If state intervention into family life is to be justified, two key questions need to be asked: firstly, what fundamental principles should govern the state's initial intervention; and, secondly, what long-term goals should guide decision-making once it has been decided that intervention is necessary (Short-Harris and Miles, 2007, p. 900)? According to Fox-Harding (1996), whose analysis of historical and contemporary childcare policies has been widely accepted, the answers lie in establishing which of the basic approaches the law could take in cases of suspected child abuse and neglect. In brief, these are as follows:

1. *Laissez faire and patriarchy*: Prominent in the late nineteenth century, this approach is based on minimal state intervention – the aim being to respect family privacy and autonomy except in extreme circumstances.
2. *State paternalism and child protection*: This approach – which emphasises the vulnerability and dependence of children – justifies authoritarian state intervention whenever it is necessary to 'protect' them. As such, parents' rights and the integrity of the original birth family are given a low priority.
3. *The defence of the birth family and parents' rights*: This approach seeks (whenever possible) to maintain the bonds between children and their parents. The state's role is thus neither paternalist nor laissez faire, but supportive, i.e. providing services to enable the family to stay together. In recognising the effect of poverty and deprivation on family life, this approach sees coercive intervention as disproportionately targeting deprived families.
4. *Children's rights and child liberation*: The child's viewpoint is central to this approach. Broadly, it emphasises children's autonomy and competence rather than their vulnerability, but different positions can be taken. One is to claim that the state should intervene only at a child's request. A less extreme position is to give children greater rights to participate in decisions that affect them.

These four different approaches are reflected (to a greater or lesser extent) in childcare policies throughout the last century. But in relation to family support and prevention, the third approach is the most prevalent – in Part III of the Children Act 1989.

11.3 Welfare Services – Family Support and Prevention

Part III of the Act covers the responsibilities of local authorities towards children and their families. It gives them a wide range of duties and powers aimed at supporting the family and ensuring that children can be brought up at home. In so doing it builds upon many of the provisions in previous legislation which recognised the link between protecting children at risk and supporting families who cannot care for their children without help. These services are either 'preventive' (i.e. preventing neglect or abuse and reducing the need for admission to care) or 'supportive' (i.e. aimed at supporting children at home). They can be given not just to children but also to their families. Note that most of the duties and powers in Part III are targeted on a special group of children who are considered especially vulnerable, i.e. 'children in need'.

11.3.1 'Children in need'

The concept of 'children in need' is a crucial one since it operates as a threshold to a wide range of statutory services offered by local authorities.
A child is in need if:

- He is unlikely to achieve or maintain a reasonable standard of health or development without the provision of services.
- His health or development is likely to be significantly impaired unless services are provided.
- He is disabled (see further s.17(10) and (11)).

The definition of 'in need' is deliberately wide – the intention being to target not just children who are already in need but those who might be in the future unless services are provided. Detailed guidance about the process of assessment of children in need is provided in the Framework for the Assessment of Children in Need and their Families (hereinafter Assessment Framework; DoH et al., 2000). It aims to provide a systematic basis for collecting and analysing information about a child's developmental needs, the capacity of parents or caregivers to respond appropriately to those needs and the impact of the wider family and environmental factors on the parents and child (see also Working Together to Safeguard Children, hereinafter Working Together, DoH et al., 2006b, and the Common Assessment Framework for Children and Young People: A Guide for Practitioners, DoH et al., 2006a). But notwithstanding the emphasis on preventive support, research into policy and practice since the Act's implementation has shown how lack of resources has resulted in services being concentrated on children who are considered at risk. In short, the emphasis has been on crisis-led child protection work rather than prevention and support (Short-Harris and Miles, 2007, p. 919).

11.3.2 Role of health professionals

The role of health professionals will, of course, depend on the particular setting in which they work (see further DoH et al., 2000, paras 5.17–39). In brief, however, there is an expectation that, generally, health professionals are likely to be a key source of referral to social services of children who are, or may be, in need. As they are likely to know these children and their families, they will also have a key role to play in helping social services carry out their assessments of children in need (DoH et al., 2000, para 1.22). In brief, knowledge of the Assessment Framework means that practitioners working with children and their families should be able to:

- Identify the risk factors and recognise children in need of support and/or safeguarding;
- Understand the range of different and complex developmental needs which must be met during different stages of childhood;
- Assess the capacity of parents/carers to meet their children's needs;
- Carry out specific examinations (e.g. development checks);
- Recognise the needs of parents who may need extra help in bringing up their children;
- Liaise closely with other agencies (including other health professionals) in the assessment process;

- Contribute to formulating any necessary plan for a child in need;
- Ensure that record keeping is factual, accurate, accessible and comprehensive.

Activity

Read the Referral Chart (Appendix C) of the Assessment Framework (DoH et al., 2000) (http://www.open.gov.uk/doh/quality). Did you find it useful? If not, why not?

There are a wide range of services that can be provided to children in need and their families under Part III. These include accommodation, day care, foster care, family centres (see further Children Act 1989, Schedule 2 and Assessment Framework, 2000, Chapter 5). In exceptional circumstances, 'services' can also include assistance in cash. Note finally that if at any stage of assessing a child's need there are suspicions that she/he may be or is likely to suffer significant harm, health professionals should follow procedures set out in the guidance Working Together (DoH et al., 2006b) (see further, s.47 enquiries, below).

Key points

- Part III of the Act covers the responsibilities of local authorities towards children and their families.
- Almost all the duties in Part III are targeted on children in need.

Activity

What does the current Care Quality Commission report reveal about the role of health professionals in protecting children from abuse and neglect (http://www.cqc.org.uk/)?

11.4 Investigation of Child Abuse and Neglect

Because there is no mandatory reporting law in the UK (unlike many states in the USA), neither local authorities nor anyone else is legally obliged to report suspected cases of child abuse. Nevertheless, s.47 of the Children Act 1989 imposes a statutory duty on local authorities to investigate a child's welfare in a number of circumstances.

11.4.1 Purpose of s.47 enquiries

The purpose of a s.47 investigation is to determine whether action is needed to safeguard a child's welfare. It is a complex section which centres on the concept of 'significant harm' – a term that is the basis for all compulsory action under the Act (for a detailed analysis of the term, see the section on care orders below). Briefly, s.47 imposes a legal duty on local authorities to initiate investigations when a child is subject to an emergency protection order (see below); is in police protection; has contravened a curfew order; or where there is reasonable cause to suspect that a child is suffering or is likely to suffer 'significant harm'. Basically, therefore, s.47 comprises four main tasks: to establish the facts, decide if there are grounds for concern, identify sources and levels of risk and decide protective or other action.

11.4.2 Role of health professionals

As was noted above, although there is no statutory duty on health professionals to report abuse, they are legally required to assist local authorities with their enquires (in particular by providing relevant information and advice) if called upon to do so, unless to do so would be unreasonable in all the circumstance of the case (s.47(9)–(11) Children Act 1989, see also ss.10 and 11 Children Act 2004). This 'assistance' can take several forms but is likely to involve taking part in the 'core assessment' of a child (i.e. an in-depth assessment which addresses the central or most important aspects of the needs of the child; Assessment Framework, 2000, 3.11). According to Working Together (DoH et al., 2006b), para 5.60, a core assessment is the means by which a s.47 investigation is carried out. Note, however, it may also have been carried out during the process of assessing whether the child is 'in need' (and thus eligible for Part III services, see above). Other key roles that health professionals may play in safeguarding children include the following.

Referral

As Working Together explains, everybody who works with or has contact with children needs to know how to act on evidence that a child's health or development is being, or may be, impaired (DoH et al., 2006b, paras 5.5–14). This means that everyone working with children should be familiar with and follow their organisation's procedures and protocols when referring a child to social services. In brief, this involves:

- Including any information that is relevant to the child's developmental needs;
- Seeing the child to ascertain his wishes and feelings;
- Communicating with the child in an age-appropriate way;
- Recording in writing all concerns, discussion about the child, decisions (see further What to Do If You're Worried a Child Is Being Abused, 2006, paras 10.1–10.11).

Exchange information

Effective child protection depends on sharing and exchanging information. However, as Working Together explains, health professionals will need to consider their legal obligations, including whether they have a duty of confidentiality (DoH et al., 2006a, 5.21). This, of course, involves making a judgement on the facts of each case. Note in particular the 'seven golden rules' for information sharing, e.g. ensuring the disclosure is necessary, proportionate, relevant, accurate, timely and secure; being honest and open and most importantly remembering that the Data Protection Act 1998 is not a barrier to sharing information (see further Information Sharing: Guidance for Practitioners and Managers, DCSF, 2008b; core guidance on information sharing; What to Do if You're Worried a Child is Being Abused, DfES, 2006, Appendix 3).

Activity

Forms for the 'core' assessment of a child reflect different age bands. Compare and contrast the differences they highlight (forms can be downloaded from DoH website at http://www.open.gov.uk/doh/quality).

11.4.3 Actions following s.47 investigation

Following enquiries made as part of the s.47 investigation, the local authority must decide what action to take. If, for example, concerns about the child's welfare are substantiated (but the child is not judged to be at continuing risk), a plan for ensuring the child's safety will need to be formulated. On the other hand, if a child is judged to be at continuing risk of significant harm, an initial child protection conference must be convened (see further DoH et al., 2006b, paras 5.79–5.136).

Key points

- Section 47 imposes a duty on local authorities to investigate a child's welfare in certain circumstances.
- Health professionals (among others) are legally required to assist local authorities in their investigations.

11.5 Protection of Children in Emergencies

We now consider the two short-term orders under Part V of the Children Act 1989. As the guidance explains, the local authority is expected to make all reasonable efforts to persuade parents to cooperate with s.47 enquiries before deciding to apply for either of these orders (Children Act 1989: Guidance and Regulations, Volume 1: Court Orders, 2008, para 4.73).

11.5.1 Child assessment order (s.43)

The child assessment order (CAO) provides an opportunity to assess a child whose health, development or treatment is causing real concern but who is not thought to be in any immediate danger. According to guidance, the CAO is usually more appropriate where the harm appears to be longer term and cumulative rather than sudden and severe – e.g. there is persistent concern about a child who is failing to thrive (DCSF, 2008a, para 4.12). Best described as an evidence-seeking order, which is needed to establish basic facts about a child's condition, the court may make the order if it is satisfied that there is reasonable cause to suspect that a child is suffering, or is likely to suffer, significant harm, but this cannot be established without a court order. A CAO lasts for 7 days. Usually, the child will stay at home during the assessment, but in exceptional circumstances he or she can be kept away from home (e.g. if an overnight stay in hospital is required). Note that in practice orders are rare (Masson et al., 2008, p. 775).

11.5.2 Role of health professionals

Key roles for health professionals include the following:

- *Communicating with parents*: A CAO is unlikely to be granted unless the court is satisfied that reasonable efforts have been made to persuade the child's parents (or other carers) to cooperate with voluntary assessment. A familiar and trusted health professional may be the most appropriate person to talk to a child's carer.
- *Court directions – health assessments*: The court has wide powers to include directions about the nature and objective of the assessment. Directions could, for example, specify that the assessment be limited to a medical examination or cover other aspects of the child's health or development. It could direct where and by whom it should be carried out. Note that if the assessment is to involve an intrusive examination, such as a biopsy or genital examination, specific directions should be given.
- *Communicating with children*: Before carrying out any examination of a child, health professionals must ascertain who has the right to consent – bearing in mind that court directions do not normally override the rights of mature children to refuse to submit to any examination or assessment (s.43(8)).

Action after a CAO will clearly depend on what it reveals about the child's health and development. In some cases, voluntary arrangements may be appropriate, while in others compulsory measures such as an interim care order or emergency protection order will be necessary.

> **Key points**
>
> - A CAO is a short-term order, which provides an opportunity to assess a child who is not thought to be in immediate danger.
> - A CAO can last up to 7 days.
> - A CAO may include directions about the medical or other assessment of a child.

11.5.3 Emergency protection order (s.44)

Designed for genuine emergencies where immediate short-term protection is necessary, the emergency protection order (EPO) is one of the Act's most draconian compulsory powers. An EPO is expected to be used only if there is compelling evidence that the situation is sufficiently serious to justify such interference with family life; in other words, not as an automatic response to suspected child abuse or as a routine first step to initiating care proceedings (DSCF, 2008b, para 4.27, see further *Re X: Emergency Protection Orders* [2006] EWHC 510).

There are basically two types of situations where an EPO is appropriate (both of which require the court to consider the welfare and non-intervention principles). The first allows any person to cope with an urgent crisis. The court will grant the order if it is satisfied that there is reasonable cause to believe that significant harm is likely if the child is not removed to, or kept in, a safe place. The second type of order can only be granted to social workers or the National Society for the Prevention of Cruelty to Children (NSPCC) (in the case of the NSPCC slightly different criteria apply) and allows them to continue their investigations when there are urgent concerns about a child to whom access is being 'unreasonably refused'. It can be granted on a lesser standard of proof than the first order – one based on 'suspicion' of significant harm rather than on a belief that such harm is likely to occur.

The effects of an EPO include the following:

- It can last initially up to 8 days, but it can be extended (once only) for a further 7 days.
- Any person who is in a position to do so must comply with the order and produce the child; the court can also authorise the applicant to enter and search premises.
- It can authorise the child's removal or prevent his removal from current accommodation, such as a hospital.
- It can add an exclusion requirement: such an order requires the person named to leave the child's home or a defined area (see further s.44A).
- Whoever obtains an EPO also acquires limited parental responsibility. It only lasts while the order is in force and only permits short-term decisions, i.e. those that are reasonably required to safeguard and promote the child's welfare.

11.5.4 Role of health professionals

Key roles for health professionals include the following:

- *Medical assistance*: To provide immediate medical aid or determine whether a child needs to be moved, it may be necessary for a health professional to be present when an EPO is exercised. Accordingly, an order can direct that a doctor, nurse or midwife accompanies social workers exercising any of their powers under the order (s.45(12)).

- *Court directions: medical and psychiatric examination or other assessment*: The court has wide powers to give directions it considers appropriate (if any) with respect to the examination or assessment of the child. These can be given either when the order is made, or subsequently, and can be varied at any time. They can also be very detailed and could, for example, prohibit any type of examination, or direct that the child's general practitioner observe or participate in the examination. Directions do not, however, override the right of mature children and young people to refuse to submit to them (but see *South Glamorgan County Council v W and B* [1993] 1 FLR 574).

An EPO will either be followed by further compulsory measures, such as an interim care or supervision order, or it may result in the child's returning home (with or without the provision of Part III services).

Key points

- An EPO is designed for genuine emergencies rather than as an automatic response to suspected child abuse.
- An EPO can last up to 8 days (but can be extended once for a further 7 days).
- An EPO can include directions about the medical and psychiatric examination or other assessment of a child.

Activity

Find out how many children are subject to a child protection plan in your area.

11.5.5 Police powers (s.46)

Included in this section, despite not requiring a court's permission, are the powers the police have under s.46 to prevent children being removed from a safe place or to remove them to suitable accommodation if they have reasonable cause to believe that the children would otherwise be likely to suffer significant harm. These protective powers only last 72 hours and do not involve any transfer of parental responsibility. Section 46 does not include any rights of entry and search. Should entry be refused, an EPO can be sought (together with a warrant). Alternatively, the police could rely on the Criminal Evidence Act 1984, which authorises them to enter and search premises without a warrant in dire emergencies.

11.6 Long-Term Orders – Care and Supervision

This section describes the two long-term orders available under the Act, namely, care and supervision orders. It focuses on the grounds upon which the orders can be made but begins by noting the distinction between them (for other aspects, e.g. how the orders can be discharged, contact with children in care, and duties of local authority towards children who have left care, see Lowe and Douglas, 2007, Chapter 14; Masson et al., 2008, Chapter 21). As we see, although the effects of the two orders are very different, the trigger for action is the same (i.e. significant harm); both only apply to children under

17 and can only be made following a court order. Briefly, the distinction is as follows (for other differences, see further Short-Harris and Miles, 2007, pp. 953–965).

11.6.1 Care orders

A care order gives the local authority parental responsibility (s.33(6)) which they share with those who already have it (usually the child's parents). The authority thus has considerable control over children's lives (and a positive duty to promote their welfare, see ss.22–24). It can, for example, limit (or sometimes even refuse) contact between the child and her parents. Nevertheless, it does not have the power to make certain major decisions, e.g. agree to a child's adoption or cause the child to be brought up in a different religion. Normally, a care order involves the child leaving home. However, in some cases the child may remain at home or perhaps return home on a 'trial' basis before the care order ends. A child may also be placed with relatives while subject to a care order. A care order ceases to have effect once the child reaches 18 (unless it is discharged before then).

11.6.2 Supervision orders

Made less often than care orders, supervision orders are designed to help and assist a child whilst leaving parental responsibility intact. They are normally made so that a child can be supported and monitored at home. The impact of a supervision order is thus far less drastic than a care order (see s.35 and Parts I and II of Schedule 3). Unless discharged earlier, a supervision order can last initially for 1 year (although it can be extended up to a maximum of 3 years).

11.6.3 Interim care and supervision orders

Interim care and supervision orders are short, temporary holding measures made when proceedings are adjourned – because, for example, important evidence remains outstanding or unresolved. For health professionals, the main significance of interim orders is that they may be involved in carrying out medical examinations and assessments that may be attached to such orders (see below).

Activity

Find out how many children are the subject of care and supervision orders in your area. Have the numbers remained fairly constant in the last 2 years? If not, can you explain the change?

Key points

- A care order gives the local authority parental responsibility.
- A supervision order does not vest parental responsibility in the local authority.

11.6.4 Grounds for care and supervision orders – the 'threshold' criteria

The grounds for a care or supervision order are set out in s.31(2), i.e.:

a. That the child concerned is suffering, or is likely to suffer significant harm; and
b. The harm or likelihood of harm is attributable to:

i. The care given to the child or likely to be given to him if the order were not made, not being what it would be reasonable to expect a parent to give him; or
ii. The child is beyond parental control.

Some of the terms used in the Act are defined by the Act (or require further explanation), for example, the following.

Harm (s.31(9))

'Harm' means ill-treatment or the impairment of health or development including, for example, impairment suffered from seeing or hearing the ill-treatment of another; 'development' means physical, intellectual, emotional, social or behavioural development.

'Health' means physical or mental health.
'Ill-treatment' includes sexual abuse and forms of ill-treatment which are not physical.

Note in particular that:

- There is no specific reference to physical and emotional abuse or neglect (but these are included by implication), nor is sexual abuse defined (see DoH et al., 2006b, paras 1.29–1.33, which provides more detail about the different forms of abuse and neglect).
- The definition of 'harm' is thus wide enough to cover any case of neglect, e.g. poor nutrition, low standards of hygiene, poor emotional care or failure to seek treatment for an illness or condition; it can also cover 'moral danger' (Lowe and Douglas, 2007, p. 738).

Significant (s.31(10))

In contrast to the expansive definition of 'harm', the word 'significant' is not defined. The only statutory guidance is contained in s.31(10). This provides that where the facts relate to health or development (as opposed to ill-treatment), the child's health and development must be compared with that which could be reasonably expected of a similar child. Points to note here are as follows:

- There is no absolute criteria on which to judge what constitutes significant harm; essentially it is matter for the court to decide on the particular facts of the case.
- Consideration of the severity of ill-treatment may include the degree and the extent of physical harm, the duration and frequency of abuse and neglect, and the extent of premeditation, degree of threat and coercion, sadism, and bizarre or usual elements in child sexual abuse.
- In relation to ill-treatment it has been held that 'significant' means 'the exceptional rather than the commonplace' (*Re L (Care: Threshold Criteria)* [2007] 1 FLR 2064).
- Sometimes a single traumatic event may constitute significant harm, e.g. a violent assault; more often it is a compilation of significant events which interrupt, change or damage the child's development.
- Comparison with a hypothetical 'similar' child (only necessary in cases of impairment of health and development) involves a comparison with a child of the same age and with similar characteristics.
- To understand and establish significant harm, it is necessary to consider a range of factors, e.g. the nature of the harm, the impact on the child's health and development, the family context, and any special needs, such as a medical condition, that may affect the child's development (see further DoH et al., 2006b, paras 1.26–1.29).

'Is suffering' or 'is likely to suffer'

Care and supervision proceedings can be based on either actual (current) or likely (future) harm. The word 'likely' is not defined in the Act. But it has recently been held that the risk of future harm is to be judged on the basis of the civil standard of proof, namely, the balance of probabilities (i.e. that harm was more probable than not, *Re B (Children)* [2008] UKHL 35, see also *Re H (Minors) (Sexual Abuse: Standard of Proof)* [1996] AC563 and Maclean and Hall, 2008). Note that the time when the threshold criteria must be met is immediately before the local authority started proceedings, not the time of the final hearing.

'Attributable to the care given to the child'

If the issue is adequacy of parenting, there must be a direct connection between the harm suffered (or likely to be suffered) by the child and the care given by the parent. Harm caused solely by a third party is irrelevant (unless the parent could have been expected to intervene to prevent it and, unreasonably, did not do so). The word 'care' is not defined in the Act but is expected to be interpreted as including responsibility for making proper provision for the child's health and welfare (including promoting his physical, intellectual, emotional, social and behavioural development) and not just meeting basic survival needs (DCSF, 2008a, para 3.40).

'Beyond control'

This term covers cases where whatever the standard of care available, the child is not benefiting from it because of lack of parental control. In such cases, the court will expect the local authority to demonstrate how the child's situation will improve if the court makes an order.

Note finally that even though a court is satisfied that the threshold criteria have been established it must still apply the general principles under s.1 of the Act. This means it must apply the welfare test, using the checklist (s.1(3)) and the non-intervention principle (s.1(5)). Another important consideration is that of human rights, namely, that the level of intervention must be proportionate to the nature and gravity of the harm established or feared. In relation to care orders, the court must also consider the local authority's care plan for the child (s.31A).

Key points

- A court can only make a care or supervision order if the threshold conditions in s.31 are satisfied.
- The central concept in the threshold criteria is 'significant harm'.

11.6.5 Court directions – medical and psychiatric examinations and assessments

The court has wide powers to give such directions (if any) as it considers appropriate about medical, psychiatric and other assessments. Directions can be included in interim care and supervision orders and full supervision orders. Directions can be given either when an order is made or subsequently, and they can be varied at any time. In some cases the court may prohibit examinations or assessments altogether, or it can require that they take place subject to its specific approval (s.38(7)). Court directions about examination and treatment do not, however, override the right of children under 16 who have sufficient understanding to make informed decisions to refuse to submit to an examination or assessment (16-year-olds are presumed to be capable of giving or withholding consent unless there is evidence of incapacity; see further s.38(6); DCSF, 2008a, para 3.52).

As regards final supervision orders (but not final care orders), the court can make directions not just about medical examinations and assessments but also about treatment (Schedule 3, paras 2–5). Note that again children who have the capacity to make informed decisions can refuse to submit to them.

> **Activity**
>
> Do you think that children who are abused or neglected always benefit from being removed from their families? If not, why not?

11.6.6 The Children Act in practice

In the light of the topics covered in this chapter, it is more appropriate to conclude with two hypothetical case studies (rather than a comparison between law and ethics). Note that these studies are necessarily very brief (for a more detailed discussion of the roles of health professionals, see Powell, 2007, especially Chapter 4).

> **Case study 1**
>
> Bob is nearly 20 months old and his sister Cara is 3 ¹/₂ years old. They live with their mother Diana. Bob was a premature baby and now suffers from repeated chest infections. He is also failing to thrive. Diana does the best she can, but she is finding it increasingly difficult to cope, especially as she lives in very cramped and damp accommodation. With winter only a few weeks away, Diana is getting more and more depressed as she wonders how the children's health will be affected by the cold and damp. Cara seems to be developing normally, but as Diana has no money to spare, Cara has few toys nor anything else to keep her occupied. She rarely plays with children of her own age.
>
> Diana's next door neighbour, Cathy, has a daughter, Meryll, aged 3, who has Down's syndrome and has recently been diagnosed as having hearing problems. There is also some concern about her development, which is well below average.
>
> Are Bob, Cara and Meryll children 'in need'? If so, which services could be provided and what would be the likely involvement of health professionals?

Local authorities owe a general duty to safeguard and promote the welfare of children in need within their area. Bob is almost certainly such a child in that he is 'unlikely to achieve or maintain or have the opportunity of maintaining, a reasonable standard of health or development without service provision' (s.17(10)). Arguably, too, his 'health is likely to be significantly impaired, or further impaired without such services'. Less certain is whether Cara can be classified as a child in need. But even if she is not, she could still benefit from those services which local authorities can give the family. Meryll, on the other hand, is undoubtedly a child in need as she is disabled, which according to the Act means 'blind, deaf or dumb or suffers from a mental disorder of any kind or is substantially or permanently handicapped by illness, injury or congenital deformity or such other disability as may be prescribed' (s.17(11)).

As to the services that the family could be offered, it is likely that Bob might benefit from some form of day care support. Other appropriate services could include advice and counselling. Temporary accommodation (or even rehousing) might also be useful if the family's housing problems are the main cause of his failure to thrive (see further Assessment Framework, DoH et al., 2000, Chapter 5). Discretionary services for Cara could also include day care provision. As a disabled child, Meryll could benefit from a wide range of services, some of which could be specifically designed to minimise the effects of her disability (see further Council for Disabled Children at http://www.ncb.org.uk/cdc).

Health professionals are most likely to be involved in identifying and assessing the children's health needs, in particular, by contributing to the initial and core assessment of their needs (in accordance with the Assessment Framework 2000 and the Common Assessment Framework 2006a).

> ## Case study 2
>
> Peter is just over 1 year old. His mother, Lucy, is 19 and has recently split up from Peter's father. She is finding it difficult to cope on her own as Peter is a sickly child. The health visitor, Oprah, is concerned about Peter as the last time she saw him he had what looked like an old cigarette burn on his arm. When she asked Lucy what had happened, she said she thought he had caught his arm on the cooker but was not sure. Oprah is also worried about Peter's eyesight and wants him to have a check-up. Lucy does not think anything is wrong and has repeatedly refused to arrange an appointment.
>
> 1. Is Oprah under any legal obligation to report her concerns?
> 2. Can she examine Peter without Lucy's consent?
> 3. If she is denied access to Peter what action should she take?

1. Oprah does not have to report her suspicions as there is no mandatory reporting law in the UK. Nor does she have a legal duty to initiate investigations into Peter's well-being under s.47 of the Children Act 1989. But if Oprah believes that Peter is at risk of harm, she should follow local procedures and protocols and refer her concerns to children's social care or the police. Furthermore, Oprah does, however, have a statutory obligation under s.47 to cooperate with the local authority (among other agencies) when they are carrying out their investigations. This means that she will not only be involved in assessing whether Peter is at risk but also contributing to any action that is proposed following the s.47 investigations.

2. Because Peter is too young to give consent, Oprah cannot examine Peter without the consent of a person with parental responsibility (i.e. Lucy).

3. If access to Peter is not an emergency because there are no urgent fears for his safety but nonetheless attempts to arrange a voluntary assessment have failed, a child assessment order could be sought (under s.43). Note that Oprah cannot apply for one herself as it can only be granted to the local authority (or the NSPCC). If, on the other hand, the attempts by the local authority to carry out its s.47 investigations to establish whether Peter is at risk of significant harm are being frustrated by denial of access then an Emergency Protection Order should be sought (under s.44).

References

Bainham, A. (2005) *Children: The Modern Law*, 3rd edn. Bristol: Jordan Publishing.

Cretney, S. (2003) *Family Law in the Twentieth Century*. Oxford: Oxford University Press.

CWDC (2007) *Common Assessment Framework*. Leeds: CWDC.

DCSF (2008a) *Children Act 1989 Guidance and Regulations, Vol. 1: Court Orders*. London: DCSF.

DCSF (2008b) *Information Sharing: Guidance for Practitioners and Managers*. London: DCSF.

DfES (2006) *Core Guidance on Information Sharing: What to Do if You're Worried a Child is Being Abused*. London: DfES.

Diduck, A. and Kaganas, F. (2006) *Family Law, Gender and the State*. Oxford: Hart.

DoH et al. (2000) *Framework for the Assessment of Children in Need and their Families*. London: DoH.

DoH et al. (2006a) *Common Assessment Framework for Children and Young People: A Guide for Practitioners*. London: DoH.

DoH et al. (2006b) *Working Together to Safeguard Children: A Guide to Inter-Agency Working to Safeguard and Promote the Welfare of Children*. London: DoH.

Fox-Harding, L.M. (1996) *Family, State and Social Policy*. Basingstoke: Macmillan.

Freeman, M. (1992) *Children, their Families and the Law*. Basingstoke: Macmillan.

Hendrick, H. (1994) *Child Welfare: England 1872–1989*. London: Routledge.

Hendrick, H. (1997) *Children, Childhood and English Society, 1880–1990*. Cambridge: Cambridge University Press.

Hendrick, H. (2005) *Child Welfare and Social Policy: An Essential Reader*. Bristol: Policy Press.

Laming, Lord (2003) *Victoria Climbie Inquiry Report*. London: TSO.

Lowe, N.V. and Douglas, G. (2007) *Bromley's Family Law*, 10th edn. Oxford: Oxford University Press.

Maclean, K. and Hall, E. (2008) The standard of proof in children's cases. *Family Law* 38:737.

Masson, J., Bailey-Harris, R. and Probert, R. (2008) *Cretney Principles of Family Law*. London: Sweet & Maxwell.

Millham, S. (1986) *Lost in Care: The Problem of Maintaining Links between Children in Care and their Families*. Aldershot: Gower.

Parton, N. (1985) *The Politics of Child Abuse*. Basingstoke: Macmillan.

Parton, N. (1991) *Governing the Family: Childcare, Child Protection and the State*. Basingstoke: Macmillan.

Powell, C. (2007) *Safeguarding Children and Young People: A Guide for Nurses and Midwives*. Milton Keynes: Open University Press.

Short-Harris, S. and Miles, J. (2007) *Family Law: Cases and Materials*. Oxford: Oxford University Press.

CHAPTER 12

Death, Dying and the Incurably Ill Child

Learning outcomes

By the end of this chapter you should be able to:

- Understand the moral and legal principles that guide decision-making at the end of life;
- Describe the legal and ethical duties owed to the dying and incurably ill;
- Critically assess the role of parents in the decision-making process.

Introduction

Deciding how to treat a dying or incurably ill infant clearly raises issues of consent, in particular the right that parents and others have to give (or withhold) consent on behalf of minors who lack capacity. Different but nonetheless consent-related issues are also raised when older children and adolescents are terminally or incurably ill. But irrespective of who is the decision-maker, there are several other profoundly important issues that have to be addressed in this context, for example, whether there is an absolute obligation to prolong life; in what circumstances life-saving treatment can be withdrawn or withheld; whether there a distinction between killing and letting die and between foreseeing and intending death.

End-of-life decision-making has, of course, long been ethically and legally controversial. Yet the dilemmas it raises are arguably more urgent than they once were, especially in relation to treatment of the newborn. Thus, while advances in fetal and neonatal medicine have enabled children who would have previously died to survive and lead healthy and fulfilling lives, some will live no longer than a few weeks or months and others will have major abnormalities and chronic illness. With the number of babies born extremely prematurely rising, it therefore becomes even more important than ever to consider whether it is always unquestionably beneficial to prolong the lives of *all* very ill babies, especially those with no (or very little) hope of recovery or improvement or those who will live only as 'passive prisoners of medical technology'.

In discussing the legal and ethical principles that underpin end-of-life decisions, this chapter focuses on those that are most relevant to the care and treatment of infants, children and young people. It will thus not provide an exhaustive account of all the major themes in the 'euthanasia' debate, in particular debates about the rights and wrongs of euthanasia (e.g. so-called slippery slope arguments) and assisted suicide (on which, see Huxtable, 2007, Chapters 1, 3 and 6). Nor will it debate the moral status of the fetus, which has been discussed elsewhere (see Chapter 7).

12.1 Definitions

Many of the issues examined in this chapter involve, directly or indirectly, the following key terms: euthanasia, death and medical treatment. But as we see below, these terms (among others) mean different things to different people.

12.1.1 Euthanasia

The word 'euthanasia', translated literally from Greek, means a 'good death'. However, because the term is now more often used to describe the deliberate ending of life, contemporary definitions are much more varied. Thus advocates of euthanasia describe it as 'mercy killing' and regard the 'right to die', i.e. to decide the time and manner of one's death as a legitimate right to self-determination (see e.g. Coggon, 2006; Dworkin et al., 1998; Pedain, 2003). In contrast, opponents of euthanasia see it as immoral and tantamount to murder. But despite conflicting interpretations, the following categorisation is typically found in the literature (for a detailed discussion of the term, see Huxtable, 2007, pp. 1–9).

- *Voluntary euthanasia*: A competent person makes an informed and free decision to end his/her life.
- *Non-voluntary euthanasia*: A decision is taken to end a person's life; it is non-voluntary because the person cannot take an active part in decision-making (due to immaturity or incapacity).
- *Involuntary euthanasia*: Ending someone's life without regard to their wishes, when they are competent to give them, or against their expressed wishes.
- *Active euthanasia*: A positive action is taken to end life, e.g. administering a lethal injection.
- *Passive euthanasia*: Involves allowing a patient to die by omitting to act, e.g. by withholding (or withdrawing) life-saving treatment (Hawley, 2007, pp. 204–206).

12.1.2 Death

There is no statutory definition of death, but in two key cases – *Re A* [1992] 3 MLR 303 and *Airedale NHS Trust v Bland* [1993] AC 789 – the courts accepted that the clinical criterion for brain-stem death was the legal definition of death (see further *Code of Practice for the Diagnosis of Brain Stem Death*, DoH, 1998, which sets out diagnostic tests confirming brain-stem death). As Herring notes, although this definition has been widely adopted, it is controversial and alternative definitions have been proposed. These include the end of breathing, the end of the organism, death of every cell and death as a process (Herring, 2008, pp. 434–439).

12.1.3 Medical treatment

Following the *Bland* case it is clear that life-sustaining treatment and medical support measures, such as artificial nutrition and hydration, through the use of nasogastric tubes, percutaneous endoscopic gastrostomy and intravenous lines, are forms of medical treatment. As such, they are no different from other forms of treatment (and so can be withheld and withdrawn in certain circumstances, see below).

> **Activity**
>
> Read Hendrick (2000, pp. 220–224), *Law and Ethics in Nursing and Healthcare*. Having considered the major arguments for and against euthanasia, identify their limitations and inconsistencies.

12.2 Is there an Ethical Obligation to Prolong Life?

In examining whether there is an ethical obligation to prolong life, this section focuses on the two contrasting approaches that are commonly taken.

12.2.1 Sanctity of life

The doctrine explained

The sanctity of life doctrine has a long history in Western thought. Traditionally the roots of the doctrine lie in the Judaeo-Christian, and particularly Roman Catholic, belief that the intentional ending of human life is morally wrong – the most common theological explanation being that as life is a gift from God, only He has the right to take it away (see Kuhse, 1987, for an analysis of how the concept became so central in Western thought). The belief that life is sacred and thus inviolable in a religious sense is, of course, less tenable in a secular society (see, e.g. Dworkin, 1993; Sommerville, 2001). But there is still universal acceptance of the principle that all lives are of equal value and that it is therefore wrong to kill. That this principle is defended by secularists on the basis of the inviolability of human life (i.e. that it has intrinsic dignity or value irrespective of theist connotations) makes it no less convincing.

But despite widespread support for the sanctity of life doctrine (which is now enshrined in Article 2 of the Human Rights Act 1998), it is nevertheless important to note that there are several different versions (Price, 2007, p. 550). Thus, its most extreme form, namely, vitalism, holds that human life is an absolute value (i.e. is an absolute good) and must be preserved whatever the cost. A more commonly accepted version, on the other hand, asserts that the core of the doctrine is the principle prohibiting intentionally killing. In short, it is that principle that is absolute (rather than that life must always be prolonged whatever the cost). Keown, who is most famously associated with the sanctity-of-life position, explains, 'The sanctity of life principle holds that there can be no moral obligation to administer or undergo a treatment which is not worthwhile' (Keown, 1997, p. 485). This is a position which does not require treatment which is 'futile' (see below). But Keown insists that in taking this position, he is making a judgement only about the worthwhileness of a proposed treatment, not the worthwhileness or value of a patient's life (see further Keown, 2002, Chapter 4).

Criticisms

Keown's approach is controversial and has been criticised on a number of grounds. Price, for example, claims that it wrongly conflates assessments of the value of individuals' lives to them and the consequent value we attach to such persons (Price, 2007, p. 563). Other critics contend that his focus on the worthwhileness of treatment might appear to emphasise medical outcomes (i.e. whether treatment is medically indicated) and thus be morally neutral. But as Ramsey (1978) explains, accurate medical diagnosis and prognosis may be indispensable, but a judgement about whether to use life-prolonging measures rests unavoidably on the anticipated quality of life of the patient, not merely on the standard of what is medically indicated. Quality-of-life considerations are similarly central for Harris (1985) and Freeman (2001) who both argue that treatment is worthwhile only if the life is worthwhile. Accordingly, we need to consider the experiences, relationships and activities which give meaning and purpose to human life, e.g. being aware of his/her surroundings or other people (Herring, 2008, p. 471; see also Bridgeman, 2007, pp. 175–177). What is being suggested here, therefore, is that in some circumstances factors other than the preservation of life should be taken into account in deciding whether to prolong a person's life. Inevitably, therefore, one of the most ethically controversial questions in health care has to be addressed, namely, what makes a life instrumentally valuable? Or to put it more simply, when is a life worth living?

> **Key points**
>
> - The sanctity of life doctrine refers to the belief that human life is valuable for its own sake; it is therefore morally wrong to deliberately end it.
> - There are several versions of the doctrine.

12.2.2 Quality of life

The doctrine explained

Discussions about what makes a life worth living (or 'quality-of-life' debates, which is how they are usually referred to) typically make reference to a person's emotional, social and physical well-being as well as their intellectual capability and ability to perform the ordinary tasks of life (Nuffield, 2007, Chapter 9). Such debates are inevitably contentious because assessing these characteristics not only involves making value judgements about what gives life meaning but also implies that some patients may be better off dead (Huxtable, 2007, p. 15). Thus, unsurprisingly, there is no widely accepted view on how the notion of quality of life should be measured, defined or applied. In other words, different people have different attitudes to various characteristics that are usually regarded as constituting a 'quality of life', i.e. degree of pain and suffering, what it means to be healthy, ill, happy, to function effectively, to be valued and respected, and so forth. Self-evident too is the fact that things that once made a person valuable may change over time, becoming less or more significant as they age.

Criticisms

One of the main criticisms of the quality-of-life approach is that it is inherently subjective. In other words, while few may disagree that a person's capacity to function socially, physically and emotionally and to derive satisfaction from so doing are important, there is less consensus on how able they must be in performing those functions, how rational, autonomous and self-aware (Hendrick, 2000, p. 226). For some writers, however (such as Doyal, 2006; Harris, 1985; Singer, 1993), much of the controversy surrounding quality-of-life debates can be limited if it is accepted that judgements made about a person's quality of life are essentially relative; i.e. the person's quality of life is or will be very poor, relative to their previous 'good' health, or to the 'good' health of others. Yet as Huxtable (2007, p. 26) explains, even if such an approach is a useful moral guide, it still leaves us with the problem of deciding what moral imperatives flow from a patient's belief that their life has no value.

   Nevertheless, if we accept that quality-of-life considerations are relevant – assuming some agreement can be reached on individual cases – then it becomes possible to make decisions about whether particular treatments ought to be withheld or withdrawn. But this does not automatically lead to the conclusion that it is morally justifiable to take *active* steps to end a person's life. In other words, there is no moral difference between killing and letting die (for further discussion of sanctity of life / quality of life, see Singer, 1995).

> **Key points**
>
> - The quality-of-life approach to the end(ing) of life refers to the belief that a life is worth living only if it is 'worthwhile'.
> - The approach requires assessments to be made of what makes a life 'worthwhile'.

12.3 Is there a Moral Distinction between Killing and Letting Die?

12.3.1 The distinction explained

The distinction between killing and letting die (also known as the acts/omissions doctrine) is a critical one in health care for several reasons. Firstly, it has long been relied on to separate acceptable medical practice from the condemnable (Beauchamp and Childress, 2009, p. 172). Secondly, as we see below, the distinction has been recognised by the courts, and thirdly, it informs current debates about whether the law should be reformed (e.g. to allow physician-assisted suicide). Put simply, the acts and omissions doctrine maintains that an action that results in some undesirable consequence is morally worse than a failure to act. Or to put it another way, it is morally worse to kill a patient (active euthanasia) than it is to allow a patient to die, i.e. not to intervene in that course of events (passive euthanasia).

The acts/omissions doctrine is a comforting one (in the sense that it lets us off the 'moral hook') for several reasons:

- Most of us intuitively feel less responsible for our omissions than we do for our actions, even if the same consequences occur.
- It reflects our assumption (albeit a false one) that letting die is invariably a peaceful process, chosen because it best serves the demands of beneficence and non-maleficence.
- The phrase 'letting die' strongly suggests that the patient is already trying to die, so all that we need to do is not stand in their way.

But is there really a moral distinction between giving a lethal injection to a patient who is dying and in great pain and withdrawing or withholding life-saving treatment? After all, in all these three situations the patient will eventually die, albeit sooner following a lethal injection. In short, the outcome for the patient is the same. And in all cases the behaviour of any health care professional involved will be intentional and deliberate (i.e. their state of mind is the same). So where does the moral distinction lie?

One way of justifying the distinction between acts/omissions and distinguishing between killing and letting die is to say that by giving a patient a lethal injection something is made to happen, i.e. death is caused. In contrast, when treatment is withheld or withdrawn, it can be said that nature is being allowed to take its course. Thus, death is not being made to happen; instead, the omission consists of merely letting something happen, i.e. letting a patient die from the normal progress of his/her disease. Another justification is the claim that if we do not believe that there is moral distinction between acts and omissions we must be either very guilty about all the good we fail to do or much less judgemental about those who carry out 'evil' acts (Hope et al., 2008, p. 188).

12.3.2 Criticisms

To many writers, however, these justifications are at best unconvincing or at worst, illogical. Firstly, the distinction masks the fact that some so-called omissions can actually make something happen (and so are more like positive actions). As such, they are not cases of 'letting something' happen and thus can be just as morally wrong as an action that causes death (Beauchamp and Childress, 2009, p. 175). Put another way, we can say that the distinction is conceptually unclear because it is not always easy to categorise behaviour – i.e. switching off a life-support machine could be defined as an act or an omission, i.e. as omitting to continue treatment or as removing treatment, i.e. in the language of omission or commission (Pattinson, 2006, p. 517). Secondly, according to Harris, the distinction is indefensible because he maintains that we should hold a person morally responsible for anything that he voluntarily and knowingly brings about, regardless of whether the outcome was 'caused' by an act or an omission (Harris, 1985,

1995a, and see Glover, 1977, Chapter 7, for detailed analysis of the acts/omissions distinction).

The difficulties of designating different kinds of behaviour as actions or omissions have prompted alternative attempts to assess the morality of euthanasia. One of the most popular is the principle of 'double effect'.

Key points

- The acts/omissions doctrine is the belief that it is morally worse to actively kill someone than it is to allow them to die by failing to act (to save or preserve their life).
- The doctrine assumes that 'acts' can be unequivocally distinguished from 'omissions'.

12.4 Is there a Moral Distinction between Intending and Foreseeing a Consequence?

12.4.1 The distinction explained

This distinction (which is usually referred to as the principle of double effect) evolved from the sanctity of life position. It was developed by mediaeval Catholic theologians to determine in what circumstances an action that has both good and bad consequences is morally acceptable. However, the doctrine now attracts a much wider audience. Essentially, it attempts to answer the following question: when is it permissible to do something that is intended to produce a good result but will also have a harmful effect?

In the treatment of terminally ill patients, the principle is used to justify medical treatment, typically pain relief that may shorten a patient's life. Justification lies in the fact that, although the patient's death is foreseen, it is an indirect result of the treatment and unintended. Although it can be described in different ways (and its exact meaning is contested), classic formulations of the principle usually require four conditions to be met. Briefly, these are as follows:

1. The act itself must be good (or at least morally neutral).
2. The agent intends only the good effect; i.e. the bad outcome (e.g. death of the patient) must not be directly intended (even if it is foreseen).
3. The bad effect must not be a means to the good effect.
4. The good outcome must outweigh the bad (for a detailed analysis of the principle of double effect, see Keown, 2002).

12.4.2 Criticisms

Although all the conditions are contentious, it is the core claim (i.e. the second condition), namely, that there is a moral distinction between foreseeing a result and intending a result, that has attracted the most criticism. Warnock (2001), for example, describes the distinction as 'absurdly pedantic'. Other criticisms are the following.

It is morally dishonest

Is it really possible to deny that you have 'intended' a consequence that you can foresee is certain, or at least very probable? In other words, foreseeing a bad consequence is no different from intending it because, despite knowing that a bad consequence is pending, the agent deliberately refrains from preventing it.

Difficulty of determining intention

As Pattinson notes, it can be difficult to determine whether a particular consequence was intended. In short, the concern here is that it is not always possible to establish exactly what someone intended – because the individual concerned might not be sure what he intends (or does not intend). Consequently, it is almost inevitable that no one else will 'know' his intention either (Pattinson, 2006, p. 514; see further Wilkinson, 2000).

The distinction has no moral significance

For Harris, one of the main reasons to reject the principle is again his claim that a person is responsible for the 'world' which he or she creates, including through unintentional but voluntary action (Harris, 1995b, pp. 36–45). The following example explains his position: a person who drinks can intend an outcome (e.g. to get drunk). At the same time he may foresee the consequence (i.e. the hangover) even though he does not intend to have it. Nevertheless, the 'drunk' is still responsible for the hangover (and so we can justly blame him if he unable to work the following day). Applied to the treatment of the terminally ill, this means that a person is morally responsible for a patient's death if she/he knowingly and voluntarily brought it about (irrespective of whether this outcome was intended).

Key point

The double-effect principle emphasises the moral difference between what we intend (e.g. to relieve pain) and what happens (death is hastened) when a patient is given pain relief.

Activity

Read Hope et al. (2008, pp. 185–187), *Medical Law and Ethics*. Critically consider the case of the trapped lorry driver.

12.5 What Legal Duties are Owed at the End of Life?

In the last few decades, a spate of very high-profile end-of-life cases has reached the courts. As we see below, several of these have been very controversial. Indeed, as Herring notes, some critics claim that in cases involving adults who are severely disabled (but not in persistent vegetative state (PVS)) the courts appear to be becoming increasingly willing to accept that it is in a patient's best interests to die, even where a patient is not in particular pain (Herring, 2008, p. 457). Yet none of these cases has resolved all the legal issues that arise at the end of life. This is perhaps unsurprising as the law has developed in a piecemeal way. Nevertheless, some legal principles have emerged about the legal duties that are owed to the terminally and incurably ill.

12.5.1 Duty of care

One of the most fundamental duties that the law imposes is a duty of care. But what does this mean when patients are dying or incurably ill? This question raises two issues: first, what standard of care must be reached, and, second, what actual treatment (or non-treatment) options are recognised by the law.

As regards the first issue, the Court of Appeal has made it clear (in *R (Burke) v GMC* [2005] EWCA Civ 1003) that once a patient is accepted into hospital, the medical staff come under a positive duty at common law to care for the patient (para 32, see also paras 82–87 *R (On the Application of Burke) v GMC* [2004] EWHC 1879). This means that although the *Bolam* test is no longer determinative of best interests, it is a threshold that must be reached before any treatment can potentially meet the individualised test of best interests. Yet, even though the *Bolam* test has been modified by the *Bolitho* approach, it is likely that the legal standard of care will normally continue to be set by professional practice, i.e. one that is recognised as proper by a responsible body of medical opinion. In short, despite *Bolitho*, the courts are unlikely to challenge professional opinion very often (if at all, in this context, see further Chapter 3). As Lord Goff stated in *Airedale NHS Trust v Bland* [1993] AC 789, 'the truth is that in their work, doctors frequently have to make decisions which may affect the continued survival of the their patients, and are in reality far more experienced in matters of this kind than are the judges'.

As to the treatment the law requires, this is arguably a more difficult and controversial issue. Nonetheless, bearing in mind that the objectives of medical treatment in this context are preventing or retarding a deterioration in the patient's condition and the relief of pain and suffering, it is clear that a wide range of options are lawful. These include the following:

1. Withholding life-saving treatment,
2. Withdrawing life-saving treatment, and
3. Giving pain-killing drugs that may hasten death.

Activity

Read paras 82–87 *R (On the Application of Burke) v GMC* [2004] EWHC 1879. Consider the practical implications of a duty of care for your practice.

12.5.2 To act in the patient's best interests

Almost all the cases that have reached the courts in this area have involved either newborns and infants, patients in PVS (or near PVS), or those who despite being sensate are very severely impaired. As a consequence, the 'best interests' concept has been invoked to determine what medical treatment they should receive. But the test has also been applied when competent older children or adolescents want to refuse life-saving treatment (albeit raising different issues). We deal with each separately.

Treatment of infants and the newborn

Although the legal issues raised in relation to the newborn and infants are essentially no different from those that apply to terminally ill children or adolescents, most legal texts treat the subject separately for several reasons:

1. Infants cannot speak for themselves and unlike older children have never had the opportunity to express their views or imply their preferences. In short, their wishes cannot be established nor can they be consulted.
2. Very sick infants know of no other existence. Consequently their expectations and experiences are almost certainly going to be different from (and not comparable to) those children who have been well but who are now dying or incurably ill.
3. Neonaticide (the term 'neonate' usually refers to infants up to 4 weeks old) and some aspects of abortion are closely linked in that it is at least arguable that the legal distinction between terminating a late pregnancy on the grounds of substantial risk of serious handicap (which is lawful) and the deliberate killing of a seriously disabled neonate (which is not) is inconsistent.

4. The potentially long life expectancy of a surviving newborn, 'burdened with disability', renders the stakes of decision-making particularly high (Cuttini et al., 2004).

How the concept of best interests should be interpreted in this context has been the central issue in several poignant cases, which first reached the courts in the 1980s and early 1990s (e.g. *Re B* [1981] 1 WLR 1421; *Re C* [1989] 2 WLR 240; *Re J* [1990] 2 WLR 140) and more recently (*Re C* [1998] 1 FLR 384; *Re J* [1998] 1 FCR 1; *Re T* [1997] 1 WLR 242; *An NHS Trust v D* [2000] 2 FLR 677; *Re A* [2001] 2 WLR 480; *Re Wyatt* [2005] EWHC 2293 and [2006] EWHC 319; *Re L* [2004] EWHC 2713; *Re MB* [2006] EWHC 507; *NHS Trust v A* [2008] 1 FLR 70).

The guidelines that emerge from these cases are as follows:

- A court can never sanction positive steps to end life.
- There is a strong presumption in favour of a course of action that will prolong life.
- Best interests should be determined broadly, i.e. to include not just medical factors but also social, emotional, sensory (pleasure, pain and suffering) and instinctive considerations.
- Best interests has to be decided from the assumed perspective of the infant concerned.
- The determination of best interests necessarily depends on the facts of each individual case. Accordingly, no list of specific criteria should be provided (which could limit how subsequent cases are decided).
- Being alive is not an overriding benefit.
- In deciding whether treatment should be provided, a balancing exercise should be carried out in which the relative benefits and burdens of treatment are assessed in the light of the child's prognosis.
- Although the touchstone of best interests is not that the infant's life is 'intolerable', intolerability is not a criterion to be utterly dismissed, i.e. it remains a valuable guide.
- The matter must be decided by the application of an objective approach or test.

These guidelines have been criticised on a number of grounds, e.g. for their vagueness and indeterminate nature, overreliance on medical factors and failure to take into account other relevant factors, in particular the views of nurses who are actually providing the day-to-day care; the history of practices of caring (which would differ, for example, if the child's condition means that they have left hospital or if they have been cared for at home) and the different roles of parents and other professionals arising out of their relationship with the child (see further Brazier, 2005; Elliston, 2007). Overall, these criticisms (and others) are summarised by Bridgeman who writes 'the determination of best interests of the child necessitates a more grounded analysis of the needs of the specific child, the parental and professional roles, the wider social, political, cultural or religious context and the support provided to parents in caring for the child' (Bridgeman, 2007, p. 126).

Finally, we should note here comprehensive guidelines issued by the Nuffield Council on Bioethics. In 2007 it published a lengthy report on critical care decision-making in fetal and neonatal medicine (see also Royal College of Paediatrics and Child Health guidance on withholding and withdrawing life-sustaining treatment, 2004). Very briefly (the report is very wide ranging, encompassing both legal and ethical principles), it suggests that the following questions should be considered in determining what treatment is in a baby's best interests, i.e.:

- What degree of pain, suffering and mental distress the treatment will inflict?
- What benefits will the future child get from the treatment, e.g. will the child be able to survive independently of life support, be capable of establishing relationships with other people, and be able to experience pleasure of any kind?
- What kind of support is likely to be available to provide the optimum care for the child?

- What are the views and feelings of the parents as to the interests of the baby?
- For how much longer is it likely that the baby will survive if life-sustaining treatment is continued?

Although the report has generally been welcomed – not least for its valuable contribution to the discussion of decision-making – it has also been widely criticised (see, e.g. April and Parker, 2007; Brazier and Archard, 2007).

Activity

Compare the criticisms of April and Parker (2007), 'End of life decision-making in neonatal care', *Journal of Medical Ethics* 33:126, with Brazier and Archard (2007), 'Letting babies die', *Journal of Medical Ethics* 33: 125.

Terminally and incurably ill children and young people

The legal duties noted above that have been established in the 'infant' cases apply equally to all incompetent terminally and incurably ill minors. Given the overlap between the common law and the Mental Capacity Act (MCA) 2005, the best interests of incompetent 16- and 17-year-olds may now be decided according to the MCA. But even if they are, the outcome is likely to be the same; i.e. the MCA 2005 is unlikely to change the law in relation to this age group (Pattinson, 2006, p. 508). Note too that advance directives (refusing life-saving treatment) are only effective if the patient is over 18 (they are therefore not discussed further).

But what about older children and adolescents who are competent? Does the law allow them to make what can, in practice, be life or death decisions? Clearly, this question raises fundamental questions about the law of consent – in particular whether the law should respect the autonomous decisions of mature under 18-year-olds. As we saw in Chapter 4, the courts have overridden the wishes of competent teenagers who had refused life-saving treatment if they consider doing so is in their best interests (e.g. *Re W* [1992] 4 All ER 627; *Re E* [1993] 1 FLR 386; *Re L* [1998] 2 FLR 810; *Re P* [2004] 2 FLR 1117). It may well be, however, that the limitations on teenage autonomy imposed in the past by the courts may have to be reconsidered in the light of (a) changing perceptions of the competence of young people to make medical decisions (Alderson, 2005; Weir and Peters, 2005); (b) the Human Rights Act (HRA) 1998; and (c) the Convention on Human Rights and Biomedicine 1997 (Article 6(2)), which states that the 'opinion of a minor shall be taken into consideration as an increasing determining factor in proportion to his or her age and degree of maturity'. At the very least their combined effect should signal a new respect for a young person's point of view and right to participate in decision-making (Delaney, 2007, p. 227; for further discussion of the impact of the HRA, see Elliston, 2007, pp. 169–173).

Whether the young person's wishes should be determinative is, of course, another matter. But if a competent minor were dying (or incurably ill with no chance of getting better), would the courts be quite so willing to override his or her rejection of treatment? In some circumstances, it may at least be arguable that such treatment would not be in the minor's best interests given the minor's disabilities, pain and suffering, chances of improvement, risks of treatment, and so forth.

12.5.3 Suicide Act 1961

Although the Suicide Act 1961 decriminalised suicide and attempted suicide, it remains a criminal offence to 'aid, abet, counsel or procure the suicide of another or an attempt by another to commit suicide'. An example of aiding and abetting would include providing drugs or equipment or advice that would help someone commit suicide. It is an especially controversial issue in relation to patients who have sought confirmation from the courts that a family member would not be prosecuted if he or she assisted in the patient's suicide. To date these have been unsuccessful (see, e.g. *Pretty v UK* [2002] 2 FCR 97). Furthermore, since they have all involved adults (i.e. over 18-year-olds), they are not discussed further (but see Huxtable, 2007, Chapter 3, for a detailed analysis of the law and proposals for reform). Instead, we consider whether there is a legal obligation to prolong life.

Key points

- Terminally and incurably ill patients are owed a legal duty of care.
- Health professionals must act in a patient's best interests when deciding what treatment to provide.
- Case law has provided guidelines about the factors that should be considered in determining what treatment is in a patient's best interests.

12.6 Is there a Legal Obligation to Prolong Life?

This question raises a debate discussed earlier in this chapter – the relationship between the sanctity of life doctrine and the quality-of-life approach. How far, in short, does the law allow quality-of-life considerations to compromise a patient's right to life?

The principle of the sanctity of life is recognised in the HRA 1998 (Article 2). It has also long been respected by the courts, who have repeatedly confirmed that there is a strong legal presumption in favour of a course of action that prolongs life (see, e.g. *Bland* [1993]). But the principle is not an absolute one. Thus even though, as we see below, the law prohibits taking active steps to end life, it does not require every patient to be resuscitated or put (or kept) on life support. To put it simply, health professionals do not have to preserve life at all costs as there is no absolute legal right to life. The courts' acceptance that simply being alive is not of itself an overriding benefit was first made explicit by Lord Donaldson in *Re J* [1990] 2 WLR 140 when he stated that 'in the end there will be cases in which the answer must be that it is not in the interests of the child to subject it to treatment which will cause increased suffering and produce no benefit, giving the fullest possible weight to the child's, and mankind's desire to survive' (at p. 150).

In effect, then, the law clearly recognises a 'qualified' sanctity of life principle. Essentially this is a compromise position, i.e. one that acknowledges that there is something special about human life but at the same time takes a 'more relaxed view about allowing qualified of life considerations to determine when third parties need not act to prolong life' (Stauch et al., 2006, pp. 634–635). More recent cases in which this compromise position has been explicitly endorsed include *Re A (Children) (Conjoined Twins: Surgical Separation)* [2001] 2 WLR 480 and the *Charlotte Wyatt Litigation* [2005] EWCA 1181.

It is clear, therefore, that there is no legal obligation to prolong life. This general principle, however, tells us little about the nature of medical treatment itself, in particular, whether withholding and withdrawing such treatment is categorised in law as an omission. Definitional clarity is crucial in this context because the courts have repeatedly stated that until such time as Parliament legislates otherwise they will never sanction active measure to shorten life. In essence, therefore, what we need to address is whether the law 'accepts' the acts/omissions distinction outlined above.

Key point

There is no legal duty to prolong life whatever the costs and whatever the circumstances.

12.7 Is it Lawful to Withhold and Withdraw Life-Saving Treatment from Children?

Despite the uncertainty as to whether there is a moral distinction between an act and an omission, the law accepts the distinction unequivocally. In short, there is now no doubt that in law there is a fundamental difference between giving a patient a lethal injection (an active step which is an unlawful criminal act) and withdrawing or withholding treatment (an omission which is lawful). Much of the law in this area derives from the famous 1993 *Bland* case, which concerned a patient in PVS. However, the legal principles it established can be applied to other terminally and incurably ill patients, in particular those for whom treatment is considered 'futile' (see below).

12.7.1 PVS patients

The leading case on this issue is *Bland*. Antony Bland, 21 when the case came to court, had been crushed in the Hillsborough football stadium disaster 3 years earlier. Since then, he had been in PVS but his brain was still functioning. In law, therefore, Antony was still alive. He was able to breathe and to digest food (but not swallow it), but he could not see, hear, communicate, taste or smell. His bowels were evacuated by enema, and a catheter drained his bladder. He was fed through a nasogastric tube and lay in bed with his eyes open and his limbs crooked and taut. He had repeated infections and had also been operated on for various genitourinary problems. With constant care he could be kept alive for many years but would never regain consciousness.

The House of Lords decided that discontinuing treatment, including ventilation, nutrition and hydration, was an omission. In other words, stopping life support was simply allowing nature to take its course. As a consequence health professionals were not legally responsible for Anthony's death. The effect of *Bland* (which essentially legalised passive euthanasia) is therefore that:

- Artificial feeding and hydration is medical treatment.
- Withholding and/or withdrawing life-sustaining treatment is an omission.
- Passive euthanasia is lawful.
- Court permission is normally required to withdraw treatment from PVS patients.

As one of the most important decisions in medical law, it is not surprising that the principles established in *Bland* have been incorporated in professional guidance (see, e.g. Royal College of Paediatrics and Child Health guidance on withholding and withdrawing life-sustaining treatment in children, RCPCH 2004; also BMA, 2007). That said, it has not been universally welcomed. Pattinson, for example, argues that describing the withdrawal of treatment as an omission is little more than a 'legal fiction', which prompts the question why a quick death is unlawful in circumstances where it is lawful to bring about a slow death following non-treatment or even dehydration and starvation (Pattinson, 2006, p. 518). On the other hand, since the removal of treatment led to Antony's death, other critics condemn the decision because it violates the sanctity of life (Finnis, 1993; Keown, 1997). Even one of the Law Lords in the case conceded that the effect of the decision was to leave the law 'morally and intellectually misshapen' (Lord Mustill p. 887).

Despite the inconsistencies that *Bland* gave rise to (for a detailed analysis, see Huxtable, 2007, Chapter 5), it has withstood numerous challenges and thus remains the law (see, e.g. *A Hospital v SW* [2007] EWHC 425; *An NHS Trust v J* [2006] EWHC 3152). However, it should be noted that judicial approval should normally be sought for withdrawal of treatment in PVS cases, even though the failure to do so does not render the subsequent action unlawful (Lewis, 2007). The legality of non-treatment decision in respect of patients in PVS (or near-PVS) is therefore clear. But what about other patients, i.e. those who are not in PVS but who are, for example, irreversibly brain damaged? Treatment decisions for such patients (and others whose conditions are comparable) do not normally require prior judicial approval. Withholding or withdrawing treatment will thus depend on whether treatment is considered 'futile'.

Key points

- Case law has established that artificial feeding and hydration is a form of medical treatment.
- In law there is no difference between withholding and withdrawing treatment.
- Withholding and withdrawing treatment is categorised as an omission in law.
- Passive euthanasia is lawful.

12.7.2 The concept of futility

All discussions of futility invariably begin by noting the many different ways the concept can be understood, i.e. as treatment which is useless or ineffective; likely to be more burdensome than beneficial; does not offer a reasonable chance of survival; fails to offer a minimum quality of life (see, e.g. Jecker and Pearlman, 1992; Veatch and Spicer, 1996). Evidently, as Beauchamp and Childress explain (2009, p. 167), the term can therefore cover many situations 'of predictable improbable outcomes, improbable success, and unacceptable benefit–burden ratios'. But despite the concept's inherent ambiguity, use of the term 'futility' does at least draw attention to a fundamentally important distinction, namely, between the effect of treatment (e.g. whether antibiotics can cure an infection) and its benefit (to the patient's overall welfare). In other words, a distinction is being made between *physiological* and *normative* futility.

As we noted above, the concept of futility is controversial because it implies a quality-of-life judgement, i.e. whether it is worthwhile to keep the patient alive (Pattinson, 2006, p. 504). But leaving aside these concerns, there is no doubt that the UK courts have applied the broader, more normative, meaning of futility (even if they do not expressly use the term, see, e.g. *A NHS Trust v D* [2005] EWHC 2439; Elliston, 2007, p. 167). Or to put it another way, they have adopted a quality-of-life approach. In *Bland*, for example, futility was defined by the House of Lords as that which has no therapeutic benefit of any kind. In other cases the courts have authorised the withdrawal or withholding of treatment when its burdens have outweighed any overall benefit to the patient (see, e.g. *Re C* [1998] 1 FCR 1; *Re K* [2006] EWCA 1007).

Limited space prevents a detailed account of how the concept of futility has been applied in individual cases. But according to Mason and Laurie, court decisions in recent years reflect a subtle change of emphasis. Thus, while in the past judges 'would opt for the salvaging of life', the writers now detect 'the supremacy of quality of life as the basis of assessment' (Mason and Laurie, 2006, p. 555). They also claim that there has been a relatively steady extension of the conditions which render non-treatment unlawful (see further Bridgeman, 2007, Chapter 5). It should be noted finally that although virtually all the cases in which treatment has been withheld or withdrawn on the basis of futility have concerned newborns and infants, the legal principles they establish apply to all patients (i.e. older children and adults).

Although futility remains a contested concept, it continues to be used in professional guidance (see, e.g. GMC, 2002; see also BMA, 2007). But now we turn to a related, equally controversial issue, namely, the doctrine of double effect. As we see below, this doctrine raises the question whether it is ever lawful to deliberately kill a patient.

Activity

Identify (and then consider) the moral values in BMA (2007) guidance on withholding and withdrawing life-prolonging treatment.

Key points

- There is no legal obligation to provide futile treatment.
- Treatment is futile if it confers no medical benefit or when its burdens outweigh the benefits.

12.8 Can a Child be Deliberately Killed?

It is very rare for a health professional to be convicted for an offence in connection with euthanasia. Nevertheless, it is beyond question that it is unlawful to terminate life deliberately. Killing a patient (of whatever age) is murder and any practitioner who takes steps which are solely intended to accelerate death is likely to face a murder charge, even though juries have traditionally been reluctant to convict those who carry out what they regard as 'mercy killings'.

One of the few cases to reach the courts on this issue was *R v Cox* [1992] 12 BLMR 38. Dr Cox was convicted of attempted murder after his elderly terminally ill patient – who was in acute pain and had repeatedly asked him to kill her – died within minutes of being injected with potassium chloride (Cox was charged with attempted murder because her body was cremated making it impossible to prove that the injection killed her). But the verdict in the case would have been different, indeed, Dr Cox would never have been charged, had he used morphine (or some other pain-relieving drug) because then his primary intention would have been to relieve pain. As such, his actions would have been lawful – under the doctrine of double effect – even if his patient's life had been shortened by the effect of the drug. Such practice, it seems, is not uncommon. Indeed, a study of doctors working in neonatal intensive care found that 70% of those surveyed in the UK reported administering sedatives or analgesics to suppress pain, despite the risk of death (Cuttini et al., 2000).

Although the doctrine of double effect has been accepted as an established legal rule by the House of Lords (in *Bland*) and two Lords Select Committees (reporting in 1994 and 2005), its legal basis remains unclear (likewise its precise status in law). Despite this uncertainty, Ward J has stated (in *Re A* [2001] 1 FLR 1) that he could 'readily see' how the doctrine would work in cases where pain killers are administered to deal with acute pain (see also *R v Woolin* [1999] 1 AC 82 and Huxtable, 2007, Chapter 4).

Activity

Read *Re A (Children) (Conjoined Twins: Surgical Separation)* [2000] 4 All ER 961. Do you think the outcome was legally and morally defensible (for a discussion of the case see, e.g. Michalowski, 2001)?

Key points

It is lawful to administer drugs that hasten death if:

- The patient is dying.
- It is the 'right' treatment.
- The intention is to relieve suffering.

12.9 What Rights do Parents have to Determine Treatment?

12.9.1 Incompetent children

Put simply, there is no doubt that although parents (or others with parental responsibility) have a central role in decision-making their wishes are not conclusive and can be overridden by a court. This means they do not have the legal right to insist that treatment is withdrawn or withheld nor that treatment is initiated. Nevertheless, as an incompetent child's or infant's proxy, their views are very important and thus a significant factor in determining his or her best interests. Clearly, therefore, they must be given appropriate information, such as the treatment options and their likely outcomes, benefits and risks as well as the infant's prognosis (with and without treatment). The importance of providing truthful and accurate information (and delivering it sensitively) has been confirmed by research that shows how withholding information on a poor prognosis – on the basis that it might distress parents – may have the opposite effect, i.e. be seen as disempowering and cruel rather than kind (McHaffie, 2001; McHaffie et al., 2001; see further BMA, 2007; Nuffield, 2007; RCPCH, 2004, and most recently, guidance from the GMC which calls on doctors to display greater sensitivity to parents facing agonising decisions; GMC, 2009).

The views of parents have been a central issue in most of the high-profile cases that have reached the courts. Many, but by no means all, such cases have involved parents with strong religious beliefs (e.g. *Re S* [1993] 1 FLR 376; *Re O* [1993] 2 FLR 149; *Re B* [2009] 1 FLR 1264). However, irrespective of the nature of the disagreement between parents and health professionals, it has been suggested that the courts appear to place greater weight on parents' views where professionals accept them as 'reasonable' ones, even if they are not shared by doctors (Pedain, 2005). But irrespective of the reasonableness of the parents' views (on which see Elliston, 2007, Chapters 1 and 4), the European Court of Human Rights has emphasised (in *Glass v UK* [2004] 39 EHRR 15) that parents have the right to be involved in significant decisions about their children's treatment and that a failure to do so may constitute a breach of a child's Article 8 right to respect for private and family life.

The *Glass* decision does not make parents' wishes determinative. It may, however, influence how courts resolve disputes in future, in particular it may force the courts to 'properly examine' the parents' role in decision-making. For Bridgeman, this is crucial if the courts are to make decisions that are truly in the child's best interests. Thus, although she does not recommend a simple shift of power away from doctors to parents, she nevertheless provides several compelling reasons for taking the views of parents more seriously. These include the following:

- Parents who have been caring for their child will be in a better position to provide insights into the quality of their child's life; i.e. they will have more opportunities to assess his overall quality of life, and in particular how they can contribute to his care.
- The parental relationship with a child is different from that between professional and child, i.e. parental attachment contrasts with professional detachment.

- A proper examination of parental views (including their intuitive feelings) would reveal whether they are 'overly optimistic' about the improvements their child has made and/whether 'their hopes have blinded them to reality' (Bridgeman, 2007, p. 186, see further Chapters 4 and 5).

Activity

Read *Glass v UK* [2004] 39 ECHR 15. Has the decision changed the way parents are involved in treatment decisions in your practice? If so, how?

12.9.2 Competent children and young people

The role of parents in the decision-making process may be thought less important in relation to competent children. Yet as we saw in Chapter 4, case law has established that health professionals can rely on the consent of a person with parental responsibility should a competent young person refuse treatment. Why this approach is now more likely to be challenged than in the past was also discussed. That said, when the proposed treatment is life saving, it may remain the case that parental wishes will continue to be an important factor in determining the child's best interests, in particular whether treatment should proceed.

Activity

Read the guidelines published by the Resuscitation Council on Do Not Attempt Resuscitation Orders (http://www.resus.org.uk). Do you agree with their recommendations in relation to the wishes of competent young people? If not, why not?

Key points

- Parents' views are a significant factor in the determination of a child's best interests.
- Parents' wishes are not determinative; i.e. they do not have a legal right to insist that treatment be provided, withdrawn or withheld.
- Except in emergencies, health professionals wishing to treat, withhold or withdraw treatment from a child without parental consent should apply to court.

12.10 The Court's Role

Court intervention in treatment decisions involving children is rare (despite the media attention that such cases usually attract, which suggests otherwise). However, as was first made clear in *Re B* [1981] 1 WLR 421, it is the courts (rather than parents or health professionals) who have ultimate responsibility for making decisions. It is important to note, however, that the purpose of an application to court for a declaration giving consent to the provision, withdrawal or withholding of treatment from a child is to provide an independent assessment of the conflicting conclusions as to the best interests of the child. This means that courts do not order doctors to treat, rather they make a declaration as to the lawfulness of proposed treatment (Brazier and Cave, 2007, p. 288).

12.10.1 Types of dispute

These can be broadly categorised into two groups.

Disputes between parents and health professionals

Typically, such disputes will arise because doctors wish to withdraw or withhold treatment which parents want to initiate or continue (as in the *Wyatt* litigation and *An NHS Trust v D* [2000] 2 FLR 677). Alternatively, albeit very rarely, parents are opposed to continuing treatment which doctors consider should be provided. This was the central issue in the much criticised case of *Re T* [1997] 1 WLR 242. T was a 4-year-old child with a life-threatening liver defect. Medical opinion was unanimous that a liver transplant would be successful but T's mother refused consent. The Court of Appeal controversially held that the transplant was not in T's best interests.

Also included in this category are cases where a young person refuses life-saving treatment (as do his/her parents), but medical opinion is that it should be given. Examples include *Re E* [1993] 1 FLR 386 and *Re S* [1994] 2 FLR 1065. Note that in both cases the court declared treatment to be lawful in spite of evidence that both minors would refuse treatment when they became adults (i.e. 18).

Disputes between parents and children

If a competent young person refuses life-saving treatment but consent has been provided by a person with parental responsibility, the dispute should be referred to the court (except in an emergency when treatment can be provided on the basis of necessity).

12.10.2 The court's decision

The role of the courts was clarified in *Glass*. In summary, Lord Woolf stated that:

- The courts would not interfere with clinical judgement where this can be avoided.
- The refusal of the court to dictate treatment to clinicians was subject to their power to decide what course of action is in the child's best interests.
- The purpose of an application to court giving consent to withdrawing or withholding treatment must be to provide an independent assessment of the conflicting conclusions as to the best interests of the child.
- A court order is permissive; i.e. the parties can return to court should circumstances alter or if there is new evidence (see also *Re MB* [2006] EWHC 507).

It should be evident by now that the court (whether making decisions under the common law or under the Mental Capacity Act 2005 in respect of incompetent 16- and 17-year-olds) has a wide discretion to determine what is an infant's or young person's best interests. As such, it can overrule parents, competent children (and young people) and health professionals. As most writers conclude, however, the courts will usually follow the doctor's opinion (especially in cases involving severely disabled infants). Indeed, there is only one reported case where the courts have supported the parents' views against those of health professionals (*Re T* [1997] 1 WLR 242 above and see further Bridgeman, 2007, pp. 190–195; Elliston, 2007, p. 178; Herring, 2008, p. 459).

Activity

Do you think the informed refusal of life-saving treatment by competent children should be respected by the courts? Justify your answer (with particular reference to the Human Rights Act 1998).

Key points

- The courts are the ultimate arbiters of what course of action is in a child's best interests.
- The courts can overrule parents, competent children and health professionals.
- The courts will not require health professionals to provide treatment against their clinical judgement.

Case study

Myrtle is now 15 months old and suffers from the fatal disease, spinal muscular atrophy. She is very severely disabled. She is in intensive care and on ventilation. Medical opinion is unanimous, namely, that she should not be resuscitated in the event of a respiratory arrest but should be given palliative care only. Myrtle's parents refuse their consent to the proposed withdrawal of treatment.

Is the withdrawal of treatment in Myrtle's best interests?

Ethical approach

The issues raised by this case study focus on respect for sanctity of life and the relevance of quality-of-life considerations. Rights too are important, in particular to have access to the highest obtainable standard of health. These and other rights are acknowledged in guidelines issued by the Royal College of Paediatrics and Child Health (RCPCH, 2004). These guidelines aim to provide a framework for practice in five situations whenever withholding or withdrawal of medical treatment might be considered: the brain dead child, the PVS child, the 'no-chance' situation, the 'no-purpose' situation and the 'unbearable' situation.

Myrtle is terminally ill. She therefore arguably 'fits' the 'no-chance' situation (i.e. the child has such severe disease that life-sustaining treatment simply delays death without significant alleviation of suffering). Note that more recent guidelines from the Nuffield Council of Bioethics (2007) use the term 'intolerability' to describe Myrtle's situation (likewise the 'no-purpose' or unbearable suffering categories). In acknowledging the ambiguity of the concept, the Nuffield guidance nevertheless variously defines it as, for example, 'interventions' that are 'distressing and futile'; or those that are burdensome (i.e. for a baby whose life 'will be bereft of any of those features which give meaning and purpose to life', Nuffield Council of Bioethics, 2007, paras 2.9–2.16). The decision to withhold treatment from Myrtle should be based on several principles:

- **A duty of care and the partnership of care:** The duty of care is not an absolute duty to preserve life at all costs. There is therefore no obligation to provide treatment if (1) its use is inconsistent with the aims and objectives of an appropriate treatment plan and (2) the benefits of that treatment no longer outweigh the burden to the patient. There is nevertheless an absolute duty to comfort and cherish the child and to prevent pain and suffering.
- **Best interests:** In fulfilling the obligations imposed by the duty of care, the health care team and parents will enter into a partnership whose function is to serve the best interests of the child. This partnership approach is endorsed by the Nuffield guidance. Thus, it acknowledges, first, that parents have interests too, and secondly, that even though there may be real difficulties in knowing what is best for the patient (not least because health care professionals, parents and lawyers have relationships with him/her), 'seeking agreement between parents and professionals as to the best interests of the baby is, in principle, appropriate' (Nuffield Council of Bioethics, 2007, para 9.31).

Applying these principles to Myrtle would mean that it would ultimately be appropriate to withdraw treatment. However, given the disagreement between the parents and health professionals – which the Nuffield guidance suggests could perhaps be resolved through either the involvement of a clinical ethics committee or mediation – court intervention may be necessary.

Legal issues

In legal terms, the central issue is whether it is in Myrtle's best interests to withdraw treatment, bearing in mind that essentially what is being measured is the quality of the process of dying rather than the quality of living. Given Myrtle's suffering, the very poor prognosis and cases like *Re J* [1990] 3 All ER 930, *Re C* [1989] 2 All ER 782 and *Re C* [1996] 2 FLR 43 (in which the court authorised the withdrawal of treatment from a very severely disabled 3-month-old boy with at most 2 years to live), it is therefore almost certain that withdrawing treatment from Myrtle would be lawful.

Following the *Glass* case, however, and given Myrtle's parents' refusal of consent, an application to the court should be made. Once the court has determined what is in her best interests, the matter is then decided, i.e. the treatment is provided, withdrawn or the circumstances prompting the application occur and treatment is withheld.

12.11 The Relationship between Law and Ethics

It is perhaps appropriate that this book should end with a chapter where law and ethics converge more obviously than in any other context. Perhaps this is to be expected given the impact of modern technology on the care and treatment of those who are terminally and critically ill and the progress that has been made in saving and improving patients' lives. In particular, it has meant that very difficult and sometimes tragic choices have to be made – about whether someone will live or die. Inevitably, these 'life-or-death' decisions have exposed the inadequacies of exiting ethical and legal frameworks. Not surprisingly, therefore – in the absence of any specific guidance on euthanasia – the courts have become increasingly involved in the decision-making process. That they have been tempted to use professional and ethical guidance to make their decisions is understandable, especially in the treatment of terminally ill newborns and infants.

But the interdependence between law and ethics is also reflected in the fact that the main concepts and concerns in the euthanasia debate underpin all decision-making in this context. In so doing they pose dilemmas for both the courts and ethicists. In the light of this convergence, we conclude with a summary of some key points.

12.11.1 Ethics

- There is no absolute ethical duty to prolong life at all costs and by all means.
- The principle of double effect maintains that there is a difference between intending and foreseeing death.
- The acts/omissions doctrine maintains that there is a moral distinction between killing and letting die.
- Ethical guidelines from professional bodies recognise that even though there is something special about human life, nevertheless quality-of-life considerations are relevant in making decisions about ending life.

12.11.2 Law

- The courts will never sanction positive steps to end life, i.e. active euthanasia (such as a lethal injection).

- In some circumstances, life-prolonging treatment can be withheld or withdrawn – thus legalising passive euthanasia.
- In law, there is no difference between withdrawing and withholding treatment; furthermore, both are regarded as omissions.
- There is no legal obligation to give treatment that is futile; the administration of pain-relieving drugs may be lawful even if they hasten death.

References

Alderson, P. (2005) Everyday and medical life choices: decision-making among 8–15 year old school children. In Freeman, M. (ed.) *Children, Medicine and the Law*. Farnham: Ashgate.

April, C. and Parker, M. (2007) End of life decision-making in neonatal care. *Journal of Medical Ethics* 33:126.

Beauchamp, T.L. and Childress, J.F. (2009) *Principles of Biomedical Ethics*. Oxford: Oxford University Press.

BMA (2007) *Withholding and Withdrawing Life Prolonging Treatment: Guidance for Decision-Making*. London: BMA.

Brazier, M. (2005) An intractable dispute: when parents and professionals disagree. *Medical Law Review* 13:412.

Brazier, M. and Archard, D. (2007) Letting babies die. *Journal of Medical Ethics* 33:125.

Brazier, M. and Cave, M. (2007) *Medicine, Patients and the Law*. London: Penguin.

Bridgeman, J. (2007) *Parental Responsibility, Young Children and Healthcare Law*. Cambridge: Cambridge University Press.

Coggon, J. (2006) Could the right to die with dignity represent a new right to die in English law? *Medical Law Review* 14:219.

Cuttini, M., Nadai, M., Kaminski, M., Hansen, G., de Leeuw, R., Lenoir, S., Persson, J., Rebagliato, M., Reid, M., de Vonderweid, U., Lenard, H.G., Orzalesi, M. and Saracci, R. (2000) End-of-life decisions in neonatal intensive care: physicians' self-reported practices in seven European countries. *Lancet* 355:2112.

Cuttini, M., Kaminski, M., Cassotto, V. et al. (2004) Should euthanasia be legal? An international survey of neonatal intensive care unit staff'. *Archives of Disease in Childhood: Fetal and Neonatal Edition* 89:F19.

Delaney, L. (2007) The critically ill patient: a legal perspective. In Tingle, J. and Cribb, A. (eds) *Nursing Law and Ethics*, 3rd edn. Oxford: Blackwell.

DoH (1998) *Code of Practice for the Diagnosis of Brainstem Death*. London: DoH.

Doyal, L. (2006) Dignity in dying should include the legislation of non-voluntary euthanasia. *Clinical Ethics* 1:65.

Dworkin, R. (1993) *Life's Dominion*. London: Harper Collins.

Dworkin, G., Frey, R. and Bok, S. (1998) *Euthanasia and Physician-Assisted Suicide*. Cambridge: Cambridge University Press.

Elliston, S. (2007) *The Best Interests of the Child in Healthcare*. Abingdon: Routledge-Cavendish.

Finnis, J. (1993) *Bland*: crossing the Rubicon. *Law Quarterly Review* 109:329.

Freeman, M.D. (2001) Whose life is it anyway? *Medical Law Review* 9(3):259.

Glover, J. (1977) *Causing Death and Saving Lives*. Harmondsworth: Penguin.

GMC (2002) *Withholding and Withdrawing Life Prolonging Treatment: Good Practice in Decision-Making*. London: GMC.

GMC (2009) *Tomorrow's Doctors*. London: GMC.

Harris, J. (1985) *The Value of Life: An Introduction to Medical Ethics*. London: Routledge and Keegan Paul.

Harris, J. (1995a) Euthanasia and the value of life. In Keown, J. (ed.) *Euthanasia Examined*. Cambridge: Cambridge University Press.

Harris, J. (1995b) The philosophical case against the philosophical case against euthanasia. In Keown, J. (ed.) *Euthanasia Examined*. Cambridge: Cambridge University Press.

Hawley, G. (2007) *Ethics in Clinical Practice: An Interprofessional Approach*. Harlow: Pearson Education.

Hendrick, J. (2000) *Law and Ethics in Nursing and Health Care*. Cheltenham: Stanley Thornes.

Herring, J. (2008) *Medical Law and Ethics*, 2nd edn. Oxford: Oxford University Press.

Hope, T., Savulescu, J. and Hendrick, J. (2008) *Medical Ethics and Law: The Core Curriculum*, 2nd edn. Edinburgh: Elsevier.

House of Lords Select Committee (1994) *Report of the Select Committee on Medical Ethics, Volume 1 (Session 1993–1994)*. London: HMSO.

House of Lords Select Committee (2005) *Assisted Dying for the Terminally Ill Bill, Volume 1: Report HL Paper 86*. London: HMSO.

Huxtable, R. (2007) *Euthanasia, Ethics and the Law: From Conflict to Compromise*. Abingdon: Routledge-Cavendish.

Jecker, N.S. and Pearlman, P.A. (1992) Medical futility: who decides? *Archives of Internal Medicine* 152:1140.

Keown, J. (1997) Restoring moral and intellectual shape to the law after *Bland*. *Law Quarterly Review* 113:482.

Keown, J. (2002) *Euthanasia, Ethics and Public Policy: An Argument against Euthanasia*. Cambridge: Cambridge University Press.

Kuhse, H. (1987) *The Sanctity of Life Doctrine in Medicine*. Oxford: Oxford University Press.

Lewis, P. (2007) Withdrawal of treatment from a patient in a PVS: judicial involvement and innovative treatment. *Medical Law Review* 15:392.

Mason, J.K. and Laurie, G.T. (2006) *Mason and McCall Smith's Law and Medical Ethics*, 7th edn. Oxford: Oxford University Press.

McHaffie, H.E. (2001) Withdrawing treatment from infants: key elements in the support of families. *Journal of Neonatal Nursing* 7(3):85.

McHaffie, H.E. (in association with Fowlie, P.W., Hume, R., Laing, I.A., Lloyd, D.J. and Lyon, A.J.) (2001) *Crucial Decisions at the Beginning of Life: Parents' Experiences of Treatment Withdrawal from Infants*. Oxford: Radcliffe Medical Press.

Michalowski, S. (2001) Reversal of fortune – *Re A* (conjoined twins) and beyond: who should make treatment decisions on behalf of young children? *Health Law Journal* 9:149.

Nuffield Council on Bioethics (2007) *Critical Care Decisions in Fetal and Neonatal Medicine: Ethical Issues*. London: Nuffield Council on Bioethics.

Pattinson, S.D. (2006) *Medical Law and Ethics*. London: Sweet & Maxwell.

Pedain, A. (2003) The human rights dimension of the *Diane Pretty* case. *Cambridge Law Journal* 118.

Pedain, A (2005) Doctors, parents and the courts: legitimising restrictions on the continued provision of life-span-maximising treatments for severely handicapped non-dying babies. *Child and Family Law Quarterly* 17:535.

Price, D. (2007) My view of the sanctity of life: a rebuttal of John Keown's critique. *Legal Studies* 27(4):549.

Ramsey, P. (1978) *Ethics at the Edge of Life*. London: Yale University Press.

RCPCH (2004) *Withholding and Withdrawing Life Sustaining Treatment in Children: A Framework for Practice*, 2nd edn. London: RCPCH.

Singer, P. (1993) *Practical Ethics*, 2nd edn. Cambridge: Cambridge University Press.

Singer, P. (1995) *Rethinking Life and Death*. Oxford: Oxford University Press.

Sommerville, M. (2001) *Death Talk: The Case against Physician-Assisted Suicide*. Montreal, Canada: McGill-Queen's University Press.

Stauch, M., Wheat, K. and Tingle, J. (2006) *Text, Cases and Materials on Medical Law*. Abingdon: Routledge-Cavendish.

Veatch, R.M. and Spicer, C.M. (1996) Futile care: physicians should not be allowed to refuse to treat. In Beauchamp, T. and Veatch, R.M. (eds) *Ethical Issues in Death and Dying*, 2nd edn. London: Prentice Hall.

Warnock, M. (2001) *An Intelligent Person's Guide to Ethics*. London: Duckworth.

Weir, F. and Peters, C. (2005) Adolescents and life or death decisions: affirming the decisions adolescents make about life and death. In Freeman, M. (ed.) *Children, Medicine and the Law*. Farnham: Ashgate.

Wilkinson, S. (2000) Palliative care and the doctrine of double effect. In Dickinson, D., Johnson, M. and Samson Katzm, J. (eds) *Death, Dying and Bereavement*. London: Sage.

Index